50% OFF
CBEST Test Prep Course!

By Mometrix University

Dear Customer,

We consider it an honor and a privilege that you chose our CBEST Study Guide. As a way of showing our appreciation and to help us better serve you, we are offering **50% off our online CBEST Prep Course.** Many CBEST courses are needlessly expensive and don't deliver enough value. With our course, you get access to the best CBEST prep material, and **you only pay half price.**

We have structured our online course to perfectly complement your printed study guide. The CBEST Test Prep Course contains **in-depth lessons** that cover all the most important topics, over **650 practice questions** to ensure you feel prepared, more than **600 flashcards** for studying on the go, and over **170 instructional videos**.

Online CBEST Prep Course

Topics Included:

- Reading
  - Literary Analysis
  - Main Idea and Supporting Details
  - Elements of a Text
- Writing
  - Foundations of Grammar and Punctuation
  - Style and Form
  - Outlining and Organizing Ideas
- Mathematics
  - Numbers and Operations
  - Advanced Equations
  - Statistical Analysis
- And More!

Course Features:

- CBEST Study Guide
  - Get access to content from the best reviewed study guide available.
- Track Your Progress
  - Our customized course allows you to check off content you have studied or feel confident with.
- 7 Full-Length Practice Tests
  - With 650+ practice questions and lesson reviews, you can test yourself again and again to build confidence.
- CBEST Flashcards
  - Our course includes a flashcard mode consisting of over 600 content cards to help you study.

To receive this discount, visit our website at mometrix.com/university/cbest/ or simply scan this QR code with your smartphone. At the checkout page, enter the discount code: **CBEST50OFF**

If you have any questions or concerns, please contact us at support@mometrix.com.

SCAN HERE

TEST PREPARATION

CBEST

Prep Book

Secrets Study Guide
for the California Basic
Educational Skills Test

Full-Length Practice Test

Step-by-Step
Video Tutorials

4th Edition

Written and edited by Matthew Bowling

Printed in the United States of America

This paper meets the requirements of ANSI/NISO Z39.48-1992 (Permanence of Paper).

Mometrix offers volume discount pricing to institutions. For more information or a price quote, please contact our sales department at sales@mometrix.com or 888-248-1219.

Paperback
ISBN 13: 978-1-5167-1994-5
ISBN 10: 1-5167-1994-8

DEAR FUTURE EXAM SUCCESS STORY

First of all, **THANK YOU** for purchasing Mometrix study materials!

Second, congratulations! You are one of the few determined test-takers who are committed to doing whatever it takes to excel on your exam. **You have come to the right place.** We developed these study materials with one goal in mind: to deliver you the information you need in a format that's concise and easy to use.

In addition to optimizing your guide for the content of the test, we've outlined our recommended steps for breaking down the preparation process into small, attainable goals so you can make sure you stay on track.

We've also analyzed the entire test-taking process, identifying the most common pitfalls and showing how you can overcome them and be ready for any curveball the test throws you.

Standardized testing is one of the biggest obstacles on your road to success, which only increases the importance of doing well in the high-pressure, high-stakes environment of test day. Your results on this test could have a significant impact on your future, and this guide provides the information and practical advice to help you achieve your full potential on test day.

Your success is our success

We would love to hear from you! If you would like to share the story of your exam success or if you have any questions or comments in regard to our products, please contact us at **800-673-8175** or **support@mometrix.com**.

Thanks again for your business and we wish you continued success!

Sincerely,
The Mometrix Test Preparation Team

Need more help? Check out our flashcards at:
http://mometrixflashcards.com/CBEST

TABLE OF CONTENTS

Introduction

Thank you for purchasing this resource! You have made the choice to prepare yourself for a test that could have a huge impact on your future, and this guide is designed to help you be fully ready for test day. Obviously, it's important to have a solid understanding of the test material, but you also need to be prepared for the unique environment and stressors of the test, so that you can perform to the best of your abilities.

For this purpose, the first section that appears in this guide is the **Secret Keys**. We've devoted countless hours to meticulously researching what works and what doesn't, and we've boiled down our findings to the five most impactful steps you can take to improve your performance on the test. We start at the beginning with study planning and move through the preparation process, all the way to the testing strategies that will help you get the most out of what you know when you're finally sitting in front of the test.

We recommend that you start preparing for your test as far in advance as possible. However, if you've bought this guide as a last-minute study resource and only have a few days before your test, we recommend that you skip over the first two Secret Keys since they address a long-term study plan.

If you struggle with **test anxiety**, we strongly encourage you to check out our recommendations for how you can overcome it. Test anxiety is a formidable foe, but it can be beaten, and we want to make sure you have the tools you need to defeat it.

Secret Key #1 – Plan Big, Study Small

There's a lot riding on your performance. If you want to ace this test, you're going to need to keep your skills sharp and the material fresh in your mind. You need a plan that lets you review everything you need to know while still fitting in your schedule. We'll break this strategy down into three categories.

Information Organization

Start with the information you already have: the official test outline. From this, you can make a complete list of all the concepts you need to cover before the test. Organize these concepts into groups that can be studied together, and create a list of any related vocabulary you need to learn so you can brush up on any difficult terms. You'll want to keep this vocabulary list handy once you actually start studying since you may need to add to it along the way.

Time Management

Once you have your set of study concepts, decide how to spread them out over the time you have left before the test. Break your study plan into small, clear goals so you have a manageable task for each day and know exactly what you're doing. Then just focus on one small step at a time. When you manage your time this way, you don't need to spend hours at a time studying. Studying a small block of content for a short period each day helps you retain information better and avoid stressing over how much you have left to do. You can relax knowing that you have a plan to cover everything in time. In order for this strategy to be effective though, you have to start studying early and stick to your schedule. Avoid the exhaustion and futility that comes from last-minute cramming!

Study Environment

The environment you study in has a big impact on your learning. Studying in a coffee shop, while probably more enjoyable, is not likely to be as fruitful as studying in a quiet room. It's important to keep distractions to a minimum. You're only planning to study for a short block of time, so make the most of it. Don't pause to check your phone or get up to find a snack. It's also important to **avoid multitasking**. Research has consistently shown that multitasking will make your studying dramatically less effective. Your study area should also be comfortable and well-lit so you don't have the distraction of straining your eyes or sitting on an uncomfortable chair.

 The time of day you study is also important. You want to be rested and alert. Don't wait until just before bedtime. Study when you'll be most likely to comprehend and remember. Even better, if you know what time of day your test will be, set that time aside for study. That way your brain will be used to working on that subject at that specific time and you'll have a better chance of recalling information.

Finally, it can be helpful to team up with others who are studying for the same test. Your actual studying should be done in as isolated an environment as possible, but the work of organizing the information and setting up the study plan can be divided up. In between study sessions, you can discuss with your teammates the concepts that you're all studying and quiz each other on the details. Just be sure that your teammates are as serious about the test as you are. If you find that your study time is being replaced with social time, you might need to find a new team.

Secret Key #2 – Make Your Studying Count

You're devoting a lot of time and effort to preparing for this test, so you want to be absolutely certain it will pay off. This means doing more than just reading the content and hoping you can remember it on test day. It's important to make every minute of study count. There are two main areas you can focus on to make your studying count.

Retention

It doesn't matter how much time you study if you can't remember the material. You need to make sure you are retaining the concepts. To check your retention of the information you're learning, try recalling it at later times with minimal prompting. Try carrying around flashcards and glance at one or two from time to time or ask a friend who's also studying for the test to quiz you.

To enhance your retention, look for ways to put the information into practice so that you can apply it rather than simply recalling it. If you're using the information in practical ways, it will be much easier to remember. Similarly, it helps to solidify a concept in your mind if you're not only reading it to yourself but also explaining it to someone else. Ask a friend to let you teach them about a concept you're a little shaky on (or speak aloud to an imaginary audience if necessary). As you try to summarize, define, give examples, and answer your friend's questions, you'll understand the concepts better and they will stay with you longer. Finally, step back for a big picture view and ask yourself how each piece of information fits with the whole subject. When you link the different concepts together and see them working together as a whole, it's easier to remember the individual components.

Finally, practice showing your work on any multi-step problems, even if you're just studying. Writing out each step you take to solve a problem will help solidify the process in your mind, and you'll be more likely to remember it during the test.

Modality

Modality simply refers to the means or method by which you study. Choosing a study modality that fits your own individual learning style is crucial. No two people learn best in exactly the same way, so it's important to know your strengths and use them to your advantage.

For example, if you learn best by visualization, focus on visualizing a concept in your mind and draw an image or a diagram. Try color-coding your notes, illustrating them, or creating symbols that will trigger your mind to recall a learned concept. If you learn best by hearing or discussing information, find a study partner who learns the same way or read aloud to yourself. Think about how to put the information in your own words. Imagine that you are giving a lecture on the topic and record yourself so you can listen to it later.

For any learning style, flashcards can be helpful. Organize the information so you can take advantage of spare moments to review. Underline key words or phrases. Use different colors for different categories. Mnemonic devices (such as creating a short list in which every item starts with the same letter) can also help with retention. Find what works best for you and use it to store the information in your mind most effectively and easily.

3

Secret Key #3 – Practice the Right Way

Your success on test day depends not only on how many hours you put into preparing, but also on whether you prepared the right way. It's good to check along the way to see if your studying is paying off. One of the most effective ways to do this is by taking practice tests to evaluate your progress. Practice tests are useful because they show exactly where you need to improve. Every time you take a practice test, pay special attention to these three groups of questions:

- The questions you got wrong
- The questions you had to guess on, even if you guessed right
- The questions you found difficult or slow to work through

This will show you exactly what your weak areas are, and where you need to devote more study time. Ask yourself why each of these questions gave you trouble. Was it because you didn't understand the material? Was it because you didn't remember the vocabulary? Do you need more repetitions on this type of question to build speed and confidence? Dig into those questions and figure out how you can strengthen your weak areas as you go back to review the material.

 Additionally, many practice tests have a section explaining the answer choices. It can be tempting to read the explanation and think that you now have a good understanding of the concept. However, an explanation likely only covers part of the question's broader context. Even if the explanation makes perfect sense, **go back and investigate** every concept related to the question until you're positive you have a thorough understanding.

As you go along, keep in mind that the practice test is just that: practice. Memorizing these questions and answers will not be very helpful on the actual test because it is unlikely to have any of the same exact questions. If you only know the right answers to the sample questions, you won't be prepared for the real thing. **Study the concepts** until you understand them fully, and then you'll be able to answer any question that shows up on the test.

It's important to wait on the practice tests until you're ready. If you take a test on your first day of study, you may be overwhelmed by the amount of material covered and how much you need to learn. Work up to it gradually.

On test day, you'll need to be prepared for answering questions, managing your time, and using the test-taking strategies you've learned. It's a lot to balance, like a mental marathon that will have a big impact on your future. Like training for a marathon, you'll need to start slowly and work your way up. When test day arrives, you'll be ready.

Start with the strategies you've read in the first two Secret Keys—plan your course and study in the way that works best for you. If you have time, consider using multiple study resources to get different approaches to the same concepts. It can be helpful to see difficult concepts from more than one angle. Then find a good source for practice tests. Many times, the test website will suggest potential study resources or provide sample tests.

Practice Test Strategy

If you're able to find at least three practice tests, we recommend this strategy:

UNTIMED AND OPEN-BOOK PRACTICE

Take the first test with no time constraints and with your notes and study guide handy. Take your time and focus on applying the strategies you've learned.

TIMED AND OPEN-BOOK PRACTICE

Take the second practice test open-book as well, but set a timer and practice pacing yourself to finish in time.

TIMED AND CLOSED-BOOK PRACTICE

Take any other practice tests as if it were test day. Set a timer and put away your study materials. Sit at a table or desk in a quiet room, imagine yourself at the testing center, and answer questions as quickly and accurately as possible.

Keep repeating timed and closed-book tests on a regular basis until you run out of practice tests or it's time for the actual test. Your mind will be ready for the schedule and stress of test day, and you'll be able to focus on recalling the material you've learned.

Secret Key #4 – Pace Yourself

Once you're fully prepared for the material on the test, your biggest challenge on test day will be managing your time. Just knowing that the clock is ticking can make you panic even if you have plenty of time left. Work on pacing yourself so you can build confidence against the time constraints of the exam. Pacing is a difficult skill to master, especially in a high-pressure environment, so **practice is vital**.

Set time expectations for your pace based on how much time is available. For example, if a section has 60 questions and the time limit is 30 minutes, you know you have to average 30 seconds or less per question in order to answer them all. Although 30 seconds is the hard limit, set 25 seconds per question as your goal, so you reserve extra time to spend on harder questions. When you budget extra time for the harder questions, you no longer have any reason to stress when those questions take longer to answer.

Don't let this time expectation distract you from working through the test at a calm, steady pace, but keep it in mind so you don't spend too much time on any one question. Recognize that taking extra time on one question you don't understand may keep you from answering two that you do understand later in the test. If your time limit for a question is up and you're still not sure of the answer, mark it and move on, and come back to it later if the time and the test format allow. If the testing format doesn't allow you to return to earlier questions, just make an educated guess; then put it out of your mind and move on.

On the easier questions, be careful not to rush. It may seem wise to hurry through them so you have more time for the challenging ones, but it's not worth missing one if you know the concept and just didn't take the time to read the question fully. Work efficiently but make sure you understand the question and have looked at all of the answer choices, since more than one may seem right at first.

Even if you're paying attention to the time, you may find yourself a little behind at some point. You should speed up to get back on track, but do so wisely. Don't panic; just take a few seconds less on each question until you're caught up. Don't guess without thinking, but do look through the answer choices and eliminate any you know are wrong. If you can get down to two choices, it is often worthwhile to guess from those. Once you've chosen an answer, move on and don't dwell on any that you skipped or had to hurry through. If a question was taking too long, chances are it was one of the harder ones, so you weren't as likely to get it right anyway.

On the other hand, if you find yourself getting ahead of schedule, it may be beneficial to slow down a little. The more quickly you work, the more likely you are to make a careless mistake that will affect your score. You've budgeted time for each question, so don't be afraid to spend that time. Practice an efficient but careful pace to get the most out of the time you have.

Secret Key #5 – Have a Plan for Guessing

When you're taking the test, you may find yourself stuck on a question. Some of the answer choices seem better than others, but you don't see the one answer choice that is obviously correct. What do you do?

The scenario described above is very common, yet most test takers have not effectively prepared for it. Developing and practicing a plan for guessing may be one of the single most effective uses of your time as you get ready for the exam.

In developing your plan for guessing, there are three questions to address:

- When should you start the guessing process?
- How should you narrow down the choices?
- Which answer should you choose?

When to Start the Guessing Process

Unless your plan for guessing is to select C every time (which, despite its merits, is not what we recommend), you need to leave yourself enough time to apply your answer elimination strategies. Since you have a limited amount of time for each question, that means that if you're going to give yourself the best shot at guessing correctly, you have to decide quickly whether or not you will guess.

Of course, the best-case scenario is that you don't have to guess at all, so first, see if you can answer the question based on your knowledge of the subject and basic reasoning skills. Focus on the key words in the question and try to jog your memory of related topics. Give yourself a chance to bring the knowledge to mind, but once you realize that you don't have (or you can't access) the knowledge you need to answer the question, it's time to start the guessing process.

It's almost always better to start the guessing process too early than too late. It only takes a few seconds to remember something and answer the question from knowledge. Carefully eliminating wrong answer choices takes longer. Plus, going through the process of eliminating answer choices can actually help jog your memory.

Summary: Start the guessing process as soon as you decide that you can't answer the question based on your knowledge.

7

How to Narrow Down the Choices

The next chapter in this book (**Test-Taking Strategies**) includes a wide range of strategies for how to approach questions and how to look for answer choices to eliminate. You will definitely want to read those carefully, practice them, and figure out which ones work best for you. Here though, we're going to address a mindset rather than a particular strategy.

Your odds of guessing an answer correctly depend on how many options you are choosing from.

Number of options left	5	4	3	2	1
Odds of guessing correctly	20%	25%	33%	50%	100%

You can see from this chart just how valuable it is to be able to eliminate incorrect answers and make an educated guess, but there are two things that many test takers do that cause them to miss out on the benefits of guessing:

- Accidentally eliminating the correct answer
- Selecting an answer based on an impression

We'll look at the first one here, and the second one in the next section.

To avoid accidentally eliminating the correct answer, we recommend a thought exercise called **the $5 challenge**. In this challenge, you only eliminate an answer choice from contention if you are willing to bet $5 on it being wrong. Why $5? Five dollars is a small but not insignificant amount of money. It's an amount you could afford to lose but wouldn't want to throw away. And while losing

$5 once might not hurt too much, doing it twenty times will set you back $100. In the same way, each small decision you make—eliminating a choice here, guessing on a question there—won't by itself impact your score very much, but when you put them all together, they can make a big difference. By holding each answer choice elimination decision to a higher standard, you can reduce the risk of accidentally eliminating the correct answer.

The $5 challenge can also be applied in a positive sense: If you are willing to bet $5 that an answer choice *is* correct, go ahead and mark it as correct.

Summary: Only eliminate an answer choice if you are willing to bet $5 that it is wrong.

8

Which Answer to Choose

You're taking the test. You've run into a hard question and decided you'll have to guess. You've eliminated all the answer choices you're willing to bet $5 on. Now you have to pick an answer. Why do we even need to talk about this? Why can't you just pick whichever one you feel like when the time comes?

The answer to these questions is that if you don't come into the test with a plan, you'll rely on your impression to select an answer choice, and if you do that, you risk falling into a trap. The test writers know that everyone who takes their test will be guessing on some of the questions, so they intentionally write wrong answer choices to seem plausible. You still have to pick an answer though, and if the wrong answer choices are designed to look right, how can you ever be sure that you're not falling for their trap? The best solution we've found to this dilemma is to take the decision out of your hands entirely. Here is the process we recommend:

Once you've eliminated any choices that you are confident (willing to bet $5) are wrong, select the first remaining choice as your answer.

Whether you choose to select the first remaining choice, the second, or the last, the important thing is that you use some preselected standard. Using this approach guarantees that you will not be enticed into selecting an answer choice that looks right, because you are not basing your decision on how the answer choices look.

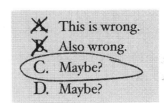

This is not meant to make you question your knowledge. Instead, it is to help you recognize the difference between your knowledge and your impressions. There's a huge difference between thinking an answer is right because of what you know, and thinking an answer is right because it looks or sounds like it should be right.

Summary: To ensure that your selection is appropriately random, make a predetermined selection from among all answer choices you have not eliminated.

Test-Taking Strategies

This section contains a list of test-taking strategies that you may find helpful as you work through the test. By taking what you know and applying logical thought, you can maximize your chances of answering any question correctly!

It is very important to realize that every question is different and every person is different: no single strategy will work on every question, and no single strategy will work for every person. That's why we've included all of them here, so you can try them out and determine which ones work best for different types of questions and which ones work best for you.

Question Strategies

☑ READ CAREFULLY

Read the question and the answer choices carefully. Don't miss the question because you misread the terms. You have plenty of time to read each question thoroughly and make sure you understand what is being asked. Yet a happy medium must be attained, so don't waste too much time. You must read carefully and efficiently.

☑ CONTEXTUAL CLUES

Look for contextual clues. If the question includes a word you are not familiar with, look at the immediate context for some indication of what the word might mean. Contextual clues can often give you all the information you need to decipher the meaning of an unfamiliar word. Even if you can't determine the meaning, you may be able to narrow down the possibilities enough to make a solid guess at the answer to the question.

☑ PREFIXES

If you're having trouble with a word in the question or answer choices, try dissecting it. Take advantage of every clue that the word might include. Prefixes and suffixes can be a huge help. Usually, they allow you to determine a basic meaning. *Pre-* means before, *post-* means after, *pro-* is positive, *de-* is negative. From prefixes and suffixes, you can get an idea of the general meaning of the word and try to put it into context.

☑ HEDGE WORDS

Watch out for critical hedge words, such as *likely, may, can, sometimes, often, almost, mostly, usually, generally, rarely,* and *sometimes.* Question writers insert these hedge phrases to cover every possibility. Often an answer choice will be wrong simply because it leaves no room for exception. Be on guard for answer choices that have definitive words such as *exactly* and *always.*

☑ SWITCHBACK WORDS

Stay alert for *switchbacks.* These are the words and phrases frequently used to alert you to shifts in thought. The most common switchback words are *but, although,* and *however.* Others include *nevertheless, on the other hand, even though, while, in spite of, despite,* and *regardless of.* Switchback words are important to catch because they can change the direction of the question or an answer choice.

10

⊘ Face Value

When in doubt, use common sense. Accept the situation in the problem at face value. Don't read too much into it. These problems will not require you to make wild assumptions. If you have to go beyond creativity and warp time or space in order to have an answer choice fit the question, then you should move on and consider the other answer choices. These are normal problems rooted in reality. The applicable relationship or explanation may not be readily apparent, but it is there for you to figure out. Use your common sense to interpret anything that isn't clear.

Answer Choice Strategies

⊘ Answer Selection

The most thorough way to pick an answer choice is to identify and eliminate wrong answers until only one is left, then confirm it is the correct answer. Sometimes an answer choice may immediately seem right, but be careful. The test writers will usually put more than one reasonable answer choice on each question, so take a second to read all of them and make sure that the other choices are not equally obvious. As long as you have time left, it is better to read every answer choice than to pick the first one that looks right without checking the others.

⊘ Answer Choice Families

An answer choice family consists of two (in rare cases, three) answer choices that are very similar in construction and cannot all be true at the same time. If you see two answer choices that are direct opposites or parallels, one of them is usually the correct answer. For instance, if one answer choice says that quantity x increases and another either says that quantity x decreases (opposite) or says that quantity y increases (parallel), then those answer choices would fall into the same family. An answer choice that doesn't match the construction of the answer choice family is more likely to be incorrect. Most questions will not have answer choice families, but when they do appear, you should be prepared to recognize them.

⊘ Eliminate Answers

Eliminate answer choices as soon as you realize they are wrong, but make sure you consider all possibilities. If you are eliminating answer choices and realize that the last one you are left with is also wrong, don't panic. Start over and consider each choice again. There may be something you missed the first time that you will realize on the second pass.

⊘ Avoid Fact Traps

Don't be distracted by an answer choice that is factually true but doesn't answer the question. You are looking for the choice that answers the question. Stay focused on what the question is asking for so you don't accidentally pick an answer that is true but incorrect. Always go back to the question and make sure the answer choice you've selected actually answers the question and is not merely a true statement.

⊘ Extreme Statements

In general, you should avoid answers that put forth extreme actions as standard practice or proclaim controversial ideas as established fact. An answer choice that states the "process should be used in certain situations, if..." is much more likely to be correct than one that states the "process should be discontinued completely." The first is a calm rational statement and doesn't even make a definitive, uncompromising stance, using a hedge word *if* to provide wiggle room, whereas the second choice is far more extreme.

☑ BENCHMARK

As you read through the answer choices and you come across one that seems to answer the question well, mentally select that answer choice. This is not your final answer, but it's the one that will help you evaluate the other answer choices. The one that you selected is your benchmark or standard for judging each of the other answer choices. Every other answer choice must be compared to your benchmark. That choice is correct until proven otherwise by another answer choice beating it. If you find a better answer, then that one becomes your new benchmark. Once you've decided that no other choice answers the question as well as your benchmark, you have your final answer.

☑ PREDICT THE ANSWER

Before you even start looking at the answer choices, it is often best to try to predict the answer. When you come up with the answer on your own, it is easier to avoid distractions and traps because you will know exactly what to look for. The right answer choice is unlikely to be word-for-word what you came up with, but it should be a close match. Even if you are confident that you have the right answer, you should still take the time to read each option before moving on.

General Strategies

☑ TOUGH QUESTIONS

If you are stumped on a problem or it appears too hard or too difficult, don't waste time. Move on! Remember though, if you can quickly check for obviously incorrect answer choices, your chances of guessing correctly are greatly improved. Before you completely give up, at least try to knock out a couple of possible answers. Eliminate what you can and then guess at the remaining answer choices before moving on.

☑ CHECK YOUR WORK

Since you will probably not know every term listed and the answer to every question, it is important that you get credit for the ones that you do know. Don't miss any questions through careless mistakes. If at all possible, try to take a second to look back over your answer selection and make sure you've selected the correct answer choice and haven't made a costly careless mistake (such as marking an answer choice that you didn't mean to mark). This quick double check should more than pay for itself in caught mistakes for the time it costs.

☑ PACE YOURSELF

It's easy to be overwhelmed when you're looking at a page full of questions; your mind is confused and full of random thoughts, and the clock is ticking down faster than you would like. Calm down and maintain the pace that you have set for yourself. Especially as you get down to the last few minutes of the test, don't let the small numbers on the clock make you panic. As long as you are on track by monitoring your pace, you are guaranteed to have time for each question.

☑ DON'T RUSH

It is very easy to make errors when you are in a hurry. Maintaining a fast pace in answering questions is pointless if it makes you miss questions that you would have gotten right otherwise. Test writers like to include distracting information and wrong answers that seem right. Taking a little extra time to avoid careless mistakes can make all the difference in your test score. Find a pace that allows you to be confident in the answers that you select.

⊘ Keep Moving

Panicking will not help you pass the test, so do your best to stay calm and keep moving. Taking deep breaths and going through the answer elimination steps you practiced can help to break through a stress barrier and keep your pace.

Final Notes

The combination of a solid foundation of content knowledge and the confidence that comes from practicing your plan for applying that knowledge is the key to maximizing your performance on test day. As your foundation of content knowledge is built up and strengthened, you'll find that the strategies included in this chapter become more and more effective in helping you quickly sift through the distractions and traps of the test to isolate the correct answer.

Now that you're preparing to move forward into the test content chapters of this book, be sure to keep your goal in mind. As you read, think about how you will be able to apply this information on the test. If you've already seen sample questions for the test and you have an idea of the question format and style, try to come up with questions of your own that you can answer based on what you're reading. This will give you valuable practice applying your knowledge in the same ways you can expect to on test day.

Good luck and good studying!

Reading

Prose

COMMON FORMS OF PROSE FICTION
HISTORICAL, PICARESQUE, GOTHIC, AND PSYCHOLOGICAL FICTION

Historical fiction is set in particular historical periods, including prehistoric and mythological. Examples include Walter Scott's *Rob Roy* and *Ivanhoe;* Leo Tolstoy's *War and Peace;* Robert Graves' *I, Claudius;* Mary Renault's *The King Must Die* and *The Bull from the Sea* (an historical novel using Greek mythology); Virginia Woolf's *Orlando* and *Between the Acts;* and John Dos Passos's *U.S.A* trilogy. **Picaresque** novels recount episodic adventures of a rogue protagonist or *pícaro,* like Miguel de Cervantes' *Don Quixote* or Henry Fielding's *Tom Jones.* **Gothic** novels originated as a reaction against 18th-century Enlightenment rationalism, featuring horror, mystery, superstition, madness, supernatural elements, and revenge. Early examples include Horace Walpole's *Castle of Otranto,* Matthew Gregory Lewis' *Monk,* Mary Shelley's *Frankenstein,* and Bram Stoker's *Dracula.* In America, Edgar Allan Poe wrote many Gothic works. Contemporary novelist Anne Rice has penned many Gothic novels under the pseudonym A. N. Roquelaure. **Psychological** novels, originating in 17th-century France, explore characters' motivations. Examples include Abbé Prévost's *Manon Lescaut;* George Eliot's novels; Fyodor Dostoyevsky's *Crime and Punishment;* Tolstoy's *Anna Karenina;* Gustave Flaubert's *Madame Bovary;* and the novels of Henry James, James Joyce, and Vladimir Nabokov.

NOVELS OF MANNERS

Novels of manners are fictional stories that observe, explore, and analyze the social behaviors of a specific time and place. While deep psychological themes are more universal across different historical periods and countries, the manners of a particular society are shorter-lived and more varied; the **novel of manners** captures these societal details. Novels of manners can also be regarded as symbolically representing, in artistic form, certain established and secure social orders. Characteristics of novels of manners include descriptions of a society with defined behavioral codes; language that uses standardized, impersonal formulas; and inhibition of emotional expression, as contrasted with the strong emotions expressed in romantic or sentimental novels. Jane Austen's detailed descriptions of English society and characters struggling with the definitions and restrictions placed on them by society are excellent models of the novel of manners. In the 20th century, Evelyn Waugh's *Handful of Dust* is a novel of social manners, and his *Sword of Honour* trilogy contains novels of military manners. Another 20th-century example is *The Unbearable Bassington* by Saki (the pen name of writer H. H. Munro), focusing on Edwardian society.

WESTERN-WORLD SENTIMENTAL NOVELS

Sentimental love novels originated in the movement of Romanticism. Eighteenth-century examples of novels that emphasize the emotional aspect of love include Samuel Richardson's *Pamela* (1740) and Jean-Jacques Rousseau's *Nouvelle Héloïse* (1761). Also in the 18th century, Laurence Sterne's novel *Tristram Shandy* (1760-1767) is an example of a novel with elements of sentimentality. The Victorian era's rejection of emotionalism caused the term "sentimental" to have undesirable connotations. However, even non-sentimental novelists such as William Makepeace Thackeray and Charles Dickens incorporated sentimental elements in their writing. A 19th-century author of genuinely sentimental novels was Mrs. Henry Wood (e.g., *East Lynne,* 1861). In the 20th century, Erich Segal's sentimental novel *Love Story* (1970) was a popular bestseller.

15

EPISTOLARY NOVELS

Epistolary novels are told in the form of letters written by their characters rather than in typical narrative form. Samuel Richardson, the best-known author of epistolary novels like *Pamela* (1740) and *Clarissa* (1748), widely influenced early Romantic epistolary novels throughout Europe that freely expressed emotions. Richardson, a printer, published technical manuals on letter-writing for young gentlewomen; his epistolary novels were fictional extensions of those nonfictional instructional books. Nineteenth-century English author Wilkie Collins' *The Moonstone* (1868) was a mystery written in epistolary form. By the 20th century, the format of well-composed written letters came to be regarded as artificial and outmoded. A 20th-century evolution of letters was tape-recording transcripts, such as in French playwright Samuel Beckett's drama *Krapp's Last Tape*. Though evoking modern alienation, Beckett still created a sense of fictional characters' direct communication without author intervention as Richardson had.

PASTORAL NOVELS

Pastoral novels lyrically idealize country life as idyllic and utopian, akin to the Garden of Eden. *Daphnis and Chloe*, written by Greek novelist Longus around the second or third century, influenced Elizabethan pastoral romances like Thomas Lodge's *Rosalynde* (1590), which inspired Shakespeare's *As You Like It*, and Philip Sidney's *Arcadia* (1590). Jacques-Henri Bernardin de St. Pierre's French work *Paul et Virginie* (1787) demonstrated the early Romantic view of the innocence and goodness of nature. Though the style lost popularity by the 20th century, pastoral elements can still be seen in novels like *The Rainbow* (1915) and *Lady Chatterley's Lover* (1928), both by D. H. Lawrence. Growing realism transformed pastoral writing into less ideal and more dystopian, distasteful and ironic depictions of country life in George Eliot's and Thomas Hardy's novels. Saul Bellow's novel *Herzog* (1964) may demonstrate how urban ills highlight an alternative pastoral ideal. The pastoral style is commonly thought to be overly idealized and outdated today, as seen in Stella Gibbons' pastoral satire, Cold Comfort Farm (1932).

BILDUNGSROMAN

Bildungsroman is German for "education novel." This term is also used in English to describe "apprenticeship" novels focusing on coming-of-age stories, including youth's struggles and searches for things such as identity, spiritual understanding, or the meaning in life. Johann Wolfgang von Goethe's *Wilhelm Meisters Lehrjahre* (1796) is credited as the origin of this genre. Two of Charles Dickens' novels, *David Copperfield* (1850) and *Great Expectations* (1861), also fit this form. H. G. Wells wrote *bildungsromans* about questing for apprenticeships to address the complications of modern life in *Joan and Peter* (1918) and from a Utopian perspective in *The Dream* (1924). School *bildungsromans* include Thomas Hughes' *Tom Brown's School Days* (1857) and Alain-Fournier's *Le Grand Meaulnes* (1913). Many Hermann Hesse novels, including *Demian, Steppenwolf, Siddhartha, Magister Ludi,* and *Beneath the Wheel* are *bildungsromans* about a struggling, searching youth. Samuel Butler's *The Way of All Flesh* (1903) and James Joyce's *A Portrait of the Artist as a Young Man* (1916) are two modern examples. Variations include J. D. Salinger's *The Catcher in the Rye* (1951), set both within and beyond school, and William Golding's *Lord of the Flies* (1955), a novel not set in a school but one that is a coming-of-age story nonetheless.

ROMAN À CLEF

Roman à clef, French for "novel with a key," refers to books that require a real-life frame of reference, or key, for full comprehension. In Geoffrey Chaucer's *Canterbury Tales,* the Nun's Priest's Tale contains details that confuse readers unaware of history about the Earl of Bolingbroke's involvement in an assassination plot. Other literary works fitting this form include John Dryden's political satirical poem "Absalom and Achitophel" (1681), Jonathan Swift's satire "A Tale of a Tub" (1704), and George Orwell's political allegory *Animal Farm* (1945), all of which cannot be understood completely without knowing their camouflaged historical contents. *Roman à clefs* disguise truths too dangerous for authors to state directly. Readers must know about the enemies of D. H. Lawrence and Aldous Huxley to appreciate their respective novels: *Aaron's Rod* (1922) and *Point Counter Point* (1928). Marcel Proust's *Remembrance of Things Past (À la recherché du temps perdu,* 1871-1922) is informed by his social context. James Joyce's *Finnegans Wake* is an enormous *roman à clef* containing multitudinous personal references.

> **Review Video: Major Forms of Prose**
> Visit mometrix.com/academy and enter code: 565543

OTHER COMMON TYPES OF PROSE

- A **narrative** is any composition that tells a story. Narratives have characters, settings, and a structure. Narratives may be fiction or nonfiction stories and may follow a linear or nonlinear structure. The purpose of a narrative is generally to entertain, but nonfiction narratives can be informative, as well. Narratives also appear in a variety of structures and formats.
- **Biographies** are books written about another person's life. Biographies can be valuable historical resources. Though they provide a narrow view of the relevant time period and culture, their specificity can also provide a unique context for that period or culture. Biographies, especially those whose subject was a well-known and influential figure, can provide a more complete picture of the figure's life or contributions. Biographies can also serve as a source of inspiration or communicate a moral because of their focus on one person over an extended period of time.
- **Myths**, or stories from mythology, exist in most ancient cultures and continue to influence modern cultures. Mythology is so influential that it has even inspired numerous pieces of modern literature and media in popular culture. While popular culture most clearly references mythology from the Ancient Greek and Roman cultures, literature has been influenced by mythologies from around the entire world. Since mythology is so prevalent in ancient literature, it makes sense that universal themes and morals often appear in mythology and even drive some myths. This suggests connections between cultures through the stories they pass down.
- **Fables** are short, didactic stories that typically feature imaginary creatures or talking animals. The famous story "The Tortoise and the Hare" is a fable. Fables are still told and used today because of their universally understandable morals and characters, making them suitable for children's literature and media.
- **Fairy tales** are stories that involve fictional creatures or realistic characters with fantastical traits and abilities. Fairy tales often end happily and depict the victory of good over evil. The plots and characters in fairy tales are often far-fetched and whimsical.
- **Folk Tales** are stories that have withstood time and are usually popular in a particular region or culture. Folk tales often depict the clever success of a common person, though the story may, alternatively, end poorly for the protagonist. Folk tales are easily confused with fairytales because fairytales can be a type of folk tale.
- **Legends** are stories that typically focus on one character and highlight their victory over a particular enemy or obstacle. Legends often feature some facts or are inspired by true events, but are still understood to be either exaggerated or partially fictional. Heroes are often the protagonists of legends as they often save or protect others as they conquer enemies and obstacles.

- A **short story** is a fictional narrative that is shorter than a novel. However, there is not a definite page or word count that defines the short story category. Short stories tend to focus on one or few elements of a story in order to efficiently tell the story. Though they are often brief, short stories may still contain a moral or impact their readers.

COMMON GENRES IN PROSE

- The **mystery** genre includes stories with plots that follow a protagonist as they work to solve an unexplained situation, such as a murder, disappearance, or robbery. Protagonists of mysteries may be hired professionals or amateurs who solve the mystery despite their lack of experience and resources. Mysteries allow the reader to solve the case along with the protagonist, and often grant the reader an advantageous perspective, creating dramatic irony. The *Sherlock Holmes* novels by Sir Arthur Conan Doyle are examples of mystery novels.

- **Science fiction** is a genre that is based on the manipulation and exaggeration of real scientific discoveries and processes. These works are speculative and frequently depict a world where scientific discoveries and society have progressed beyond the point reached at the time of the work's creation. Works of science fiction often take place in a distant location or time, allowing for the dramatic advancements and conveniences they often depict. *Dune*, written by Frank Herbert, is an example of a science-fiction novel.

- The **fantasy** genre includes stories that feature imaginary creatures and supernatural abilities, but often take place in settings that resemble real places and cultures in history. Fantasy novels usually follow a gifted protagonist from humble beginnings as they embark on a quest, journey, or adventure and encounter mystical beings and personally challenging obstacles. Common themes in the fantasy genre include personal growth, good versus evil, and the value of the journey. J.R.R. Tolkien's *The Lord of the Rings* trilogy belongs to the fantasy genre.

- **Realistic fiction** describes fictional narratives that include events and characters that do not exist, but could appear in reality. Within the narrative, these characters and events may be depicted in real places. For example, Pip, the protagonist of Charles Dickens's *Great Expectations*, was not a real person, but the novel shows him living in London, England for much of his young adulthood. Realistic fiction contains no far-fetched or impossible elements and presents situations that can or do occur in real life. A contemporary example of realistic fiction is *Wonder* by R.J. Palacio.

- **Historical fiction** includes works that take place in the past and model their setting after real historical cultures, societies, and time periods. These works may include real historical figures and events, but they also may not. Works of historical fiction must be fully informed by the period and location they are set in, meaning both the major and minor details of the work must be historically compatible with the work's setting. Examples of historical fiction include Kathryn Stockett's *The Help* and Markus Zusak's *The Book Thief*.

- The phrase **literary nonfiction** describes nonfiction narratives that present true facts and events in a way that entertains readers and displays creativity. Literary nonfiction, also called creative nonfiction, may resemble fiction in its style and flow, but the truth of the events it describes sets it apart from fictional literature. Different types of books may be considered literary nonfiction, such as biographies, if they appear to employ creativity in their writing. An example of literary nonfiction is *The Immortal Life of Henrietta Lacks* by Rebecca Skloot.

REALISM AND SATIRE

REALISM

Realism is a literary form with the goal of representing reality as faithfully as possible. Its genesis in Western literature was a reaction against the sentimentality and extreme emotionalism of the works written during the Romantic literary movement, which championed feelings and emotional expression. Realists focused in great detail on immediacy of time and place, on specific actions of their characters, and the justifiable consequences of those actions. Some techniques of **realism** include writing in vernacular (conversational language), using specific dialects, and placing an emphasis on character rather than plot. Realistic literature also often addresses ethical issues. Historically, realistic works have often concentrated on the middle classes of the authors' societies. Realists eschew treatments that are too dramatic or sensationalistic as exaggerations of the reality that they strive to portray as closely as they are able. Influenced by his own bleak past, Fyodor Dostoevsky wrote several novels, such as *Crime and Punishment* (1866) that shunned romantic ideals and sought to portray a stark reality. Henry James was a prominent writer of realism in novels such as *Daisy Miller* (1879). Samuel Clemens (Mark Twain) skillfully represented the language and culture of lower-class Mississippi in his novel *The Adventures of Huckleberry Finn* (1885).

SATIRE

Satire uses sarcasm, irony, and humor as social criticism to lampoon human folly. Unlike realism, which intends to depict reality as it exists without exaggeration, **satire** often involves creating situations or ideas that deliberately exaggerate reality to appear ridiculous to illuminate flawed behaviors. Ancient Roman satirists included Horace and Juvenal. Alexander Pope's poem "The Rape of the Lock" satirized the values of fashionable members of the 18th-century upper-middle class, which Pope found shallow and trivial. The theft of a lock of hair from a young woman is blown out of proportion: the poem's characters regard it as seriously as they would a rape. Irishman Jonathan Swift satirized British society, politics, and religion in works like "A Modest Proposal" and *Gulliver's Travels*. In "A Modest Proposal," Swift used essay form and mock-serious tone, satirically "proposing" cannibalism of babies and children as a solution to poverty and overpopulation. He satirized petty political disputes in *Gulliver's Travels*.

Poetry

POETRY TERMINOLOGY

Unlike prose, which traditionally (except in forms like stream of consciousness) consists of complete sentences connected into paragraphs, poetry is written in **verses**. These may form complete sentences, clauses, or phrases. Poetry may be written with or without rhyme. It can be metered, following a particular rhythmic pattern such as iambic, dactylic, spondaic, trochaic, or **anapestic**, or may be without regular meter. The terms **iamb** and **trochee**, among others, identify stressed and unstressed syllables in each verse. Meter is also described by the number of beats or stressed syllables per verse: **dimeter** (2), **trimeter** (3), **tetrameter** (4), **pentameter** (5), and so forth. Using the symbol ᴗ to denote unstressed and / to denote stressed syllables, **iambic** = ᴗ/; **trochaic** = /ᴗ; **spondaic** =//; **dactylic** =/ᴗᴗ; **anapestic** =ᴗᴗ/. **Rhyme schemes** identify which lines rhyme, such as ABAB, ABCA, AABA, and so on. Poetry with neither rhyme nor meter is called **free verse**. Poems may be in free verse, metered but unrhymed, rhymed but without meter, or using both rhyme and meter. In English, the most common meter is iambic pentameter. Unrhymed iambic pentameter is called **blank verse**.

MAJOR FORMS OF POETRY

From man's earliest days, he expressed himself with poetry. A large percentage of the surviving literature from ancient times is in **epic poetry**, utilized by Homer and other Greco-Roman poets. Epic poems typically recount heroic deeds and adventures, using stylized language and combining dramatic and lyrical conventions. **Epistolary poems**, poems that are written and read as letters, also developed in ancient times. In the fourteenth and fifteenth centuries, the **ballad** became a popular convention. Ballads often follow a rhyme scheme and meter and focus on subjects such as love, death, and religion. Many ballads tell stories, and several modern ballads are put to music. From these early conventions, numerous other poetic forms developed, such as **elegies**, **odes**, and **pastoral poems**. Elegies are mourning poems written in three parts: lament, praise of the deceased, and solace for loss. Odes evolved from songs to the typical poem of the Romantic time period, expressing strong feelings and contemplative thoughts. Pastoral poems idealize nature and country living. Poetry can also be used to make short, pithy statements. **Epigrams** (memorable rhymes with one or two lines) and **limericks** (two lines of iambic dimeter followed by two lines of iambic dimeter and another of iambic trimeter) are known for humor and wit.

HAIKU

Haiku was originally a Japanese poetry form. In the 13th century, haiku was the opening phrase of renga, a 100-stanza oral poem. By the 16th century, haiku diverged into a separate short poem. When Western writers discovered haiku, the form became popular in English, as well as other languages. A haiku has 17 syllables, traditionally distributed across three lines as 5/7/5, with a pause after the first or second line. Haiku are syllabic and unrhymed. Haiku philosophy and technique are that brevity's compression forces writers to express images concisely, depict a moment in time, and evoke illumination and enlightenment. An example is 17th-century haiku master Matsuo Basho's classic: "An old silent pond... / A frog jumps into the pond, / splash! Silence again." Modern American poet Ezra Pound revealed the influence of haiku in his two-line poem "In a Station of the Metro." In this poem, line 1 has 12 syllables (combining the syllable count of the first two lines of a haiku) and line 2 has 7, but it still preserves haiku's philosophy and imagistic technique: "The apparition of these faces in the crowd; / Petals on a wet, black bough."

SONNETS

The sonnet traditionally has 14 lines of iambic pentameter, tightly organized around a theme. The Petrarchan sonnet, named for 14th-century Italian poet Petrarch, has an eight-line stanza, the

20

octave, and a six-line stanza, the sestet. There is a change or turn, known as the volta, between the eighth and ninth verses, setting up the sestet's answer or summary. The rhyme scheme is ABBA/ABBA/CDECDE or CDCDCD. The English or Shakespearean sonnet has three quatrains and one couplet, with the rhyme scheme ABAB/CDCD/EFEF/GG. This format better suits English, which has fewer rhymes than Italian. The final couplet often contrasts sharply with the preceding quatrains, as in Shakespeare's sonnets—for example, Sonnet 130, "My mistress' eyes are nothing like the sun…And yet, by heaven, I think my love as rare / As any she belied with false compare." Variations on the sonnet form include Edmund Spenser's Spenserian sonnet in the 16th century, John Milton's Miltonic sonnet in the 17th century, and sonnet sequences. Sonnet sequences are seen in works such as John Donne's *La Corona* and Elizabeth Barrett Browning's *Sonnets from the Portuguese*.

> **Review Video: Structural Elements of Poetry**
> Visit mometrix.com/academy and enter code: 265216

Poetic Themes and Devices

CARPE DIEM TRADITION IN POETRY

Carpe diem is Latin for "seize the day." A long poetic tradition, it advocates making the most of time because it passes swiftly and life is short. It is found in multiple languages, including Latin, Torquato Tasso's Italian, Pierre de Ronsard's French, and Edmund Spenser's English, and is often used in seduction to argue for indulging in earthly pleasures. Roman poet Horace's Ode 1.11 tells a younger woman, Leuconoe, to enjoy the present, not worrying about inevitable aging. Two Renaissance Metaphysical Poets, Andrew Marvell and Robert Herrick, treated *carpe diem* more as a call to action. In "To His Coy Mistress," Marvell points out that time is fleeting, arguing for love, and concluding that because they cannot stop time, they may as well defy it, getting the most out of the short time they have. In "To the Virgins, to Make Much of Time," Herrick advises young women to take advantage of their good fortune in being young by getting married before they become too old to attract men and have babies.

"To His Coy Mistress" begins, "Had we but world enough, and time, / This coyness, lady, were no crime." Using imagery, Andrew Marvell describes leisure they could enjoy if time were unlimited. Arguing for seduction, he continues famously, "But at my back I always hear/Time's winged chariot hurrying near; / And yonder all before us lie / Deserts of vast eternity." He depicts time as turning beauty to death and decay. Contradictory images in "amorous birds of prey" and "tear our pleasures with rough strife / Through the iron gates of life" overshadow romance with impending death, linking present pleasure with mortality and spiritual values with moral considerations. Marvell's concluding couplet summarizes *carpe diem*: "Thus, though we cannot make our sun / Stand still, yet we will make him run." "To the Virgins, to Make Much of Time" begins with the famous "Gather ye rosebuds while ye may." Rather than seduction to live for the present, Robert Herrick's experienced persona advises young women's future planning: "Old time is still a-flying / And this same flower that smiles today, / Tomorrow will be dying."

EFFECT OF STRUCTURE ON MEANING IN POETRY

The way a poem is structured can affect its meaning. Different structural choices can change the way a reader understands a poem, so poets are careful to ensure that the form they use reflects the message they want to convey. The main structural elements in poetry include **lines** and **stanzas**. The number of lines within a stanza and the number of stanzas vary between different poems, but some poetic forms require a poem to have a certain number of lines and stanzas. Some of these forms also require each line to conform to a certain meter, or number and pattern of syllables. Many forms are associated with a certain topic or tone because of their meter. Poetic forms include sonnets, concrete poems, haiku, and villanelles. Another popular form of poetry is free verse, which is poetry that does not conform to a particular meter or rhyme scheme.

The arrangement of lines and stanzas determines the speed at which a poem is read. Long lines are generally read more quickly since the reader is often eager to reach the end of the line and does not have to stop to find the next word. Short lines cause the reader to briefly pause and look to the next line, so their reading is slowed. These effects often contribute to the meaning a reader gleans from a poem, so poets aim to make the line length compatible with the tone of their message.

For example, Edgar Allan Poe's poem "The Raven" is written with mostly long lines. The poem's speaker experiences troubling events and becomes paranoid throughout the poem, and he narrates his racing thoughts. Poe's use of long lines leads the reader to read each line quickly, allowing their reading experience to resemble the thoughts of the narrator:

> Deep into that darkness peering, long I stood there wondering, fearing,
> Doubting, dreaming dreams no mortal ever dared to dream before;
> But the silence was unbroken, and the stillness gave no token,
> And the only word there spoken was the whispered word, "Lenore?"
> This I whispered, and an echo murmured back the word, "Lenore!"—
> Merely this and nothing more.

The poem's meter also contributes to its tone, but consider the same stanza written using shorter lines:

> Deep into that darkness peering,
> long I stood there wondering, fearing,
> Doubting, dreaming dreams no mortal
> ever dared to dream before;
> But the silence was unbroken,
> and the stillness gave no token,
> And the only word there spoken
> was the whispered word, "Lenore?"
> This I whispered, and an echo
> murmured back the word, "Lenore!"—
> Merely this and nothing more.

Breaking the lines apart creates longer pauses and a slower, more suspenseful experience for the reader. While the tone of the poem is dark and suspense is appropriate, the longer lines allow Poe to emphasize and show the narrator's emotions. The narrator's emotions are more important to the poem's meaning than the creation of suspense, making longer lines more suitable in this case.

CONCRETE POETRY

A less common form of poetry is concrete poetry, also called shape poetry. **Concrete poems** are arranged so the full poem takes a shape that is relevant to the poem's message. For example, a concrete poem about the beach may be arranged to look like a palm tree. This contributes to a poem's meaning by influencing which aspect of the poem or message that the reader focuses on. In the beach poem example, the image of the palm tree leads the reader to focus on the poem's setting and visual imagery. The reader may also look for or anticipate the mention of a palm tree in the

poem. This technique allows the poet to direct the reader's attention and emphasize a certain element of their work.

FREE VERSE

Free verse is a very common form of poetry. Because **free verse** poetry does not always incorporate meter or rhyme, it relies more heavily on punctuation and structure to influence the reader's experience and create emphasis. Free verse poetry makes strategic use of the length and number of both lines and stanzas. While meter and rhyme direct the flow and tone of other types of poems, poets of free verse pieces use the characteristics of lines and stanzas to establish flow and tone, instead.

Free verse also uses punctuation in each line to create flow and tone. The punctuation in each line directs the reader to pause after certain words, allowing the poet to emphasize specific ideas or images to clearly communicate their message. Similar to the effects of line length, the presence of punctuation at the end of a line can create pauses that affect a reader's pace. **End-stopped** lines, or lines with a punctuation mark at the end, create a pause that can contribute to the poem's flow or create emphasis. **Enjambed** lines, or lines that do not end with a punctuation mark, carry a sentence to the next line and create an effect similar to long lines. The use of enjambment can speed up a poem's flow and reflect an idea within the poem or contribute to tone.

POETIC STRUCTURE TO ENHANCE MEANING

The opening stanza of Romantic English poet, artist and printmaker William Blake's famous poem "The Tyger" demonstrates how a poet can create tension by using line length and punctuation independently of one another: "Tyger! Tyger! burning bright / In the forests of the night, / What immortal hand or eye / Could frame thy fearful symmetry?" The first three lines of this stanza are **trochaic** (/ʊ), with "masculine" endings—that is, strongly stressed syllables at the ends of each of the lines. But Blake's punctuation contradicts this rhythmic regularity by not providing any divisions between the words "bright" and "In" or between "eye" and "Could." This irregular punctuation foreshadows how Blake disrupts the meter at the end of this first stanza by using a contrasting **dactyl** (/ʊʊ), with a "feminine" (unstressed) ending syllable in the last word, "symmetry." Thus, Blake uses structural contrasts to heighten the intrigue of his work.

In enjambment, one sentence or clause in a poem does not end at the end of its line or verse, but runs over into the next line or verse. Clause endings coinciding with line endings give readers a feeling of completion, but enjambment influences readers to hurry to the next line to finish and understand the sentence. In his blank-verse epic religious poem "Paradise Lost," John Milton wrote: "Anon out of the earth a fabric huge / Rose like an exhalation, with the sound / Of dulcet symphonies and voices sweet, / Built like a temple, where pilasters round / Were set, and Doric pillars overlaid / With golden architrave." Only the third line is end-stopped. Milton, describing the palace of Pandemonium bursting from Hell up through the ground, reinforced this idea through phrases and clauses bursting through the boundaries of the lines. A **caesura** is a pause in mid-verse. Milton's commas in the third and fourth lines signal caesuras. They interrupt flow, making the narration jerky to imply that Satan's glorious-seeming palace has a shaky and unsound foundation.

COUPLETS AND METER TO ENHANCE MEANING IN POETRY

When a poet uses a couplet—a stanza of two lines, rhymed or unrhymed—it can function as the answer to a question asked earlier in the poem, or the solution to a problem or riddle. Couplets can also enhance the establishment of a poem's mood, or clarify the development of a poem's theme. Another device to enhance thematic development is irony, which also communicates the poet's tone

23

and draws the reader's attention to a point the poet is making. The use of meter gives a poem a rhythmic context, contributes to the poem's flow, makes it more appealing to the reader, can represent natural speech rhythms, and produces specific effects. For example, in "The Song of Hiawatha," Henry Wadsworth Longfellow uses trochaic (/ ∪) tetrameter (four beats per line) to evoke for readers the rhythms of Native American chanting: "*By* the *shores* of *Gitche Gum*ee, / *By* the *shin*ing *Big*-Sea-*Wat*er / *Stood* the *wig*wam *of* No*kom*is." (Italicized syllables are stressed; non-italicized syllables are unstressed.)

REFLECTION OF CONTENT THROUGH STRUCTURE

Wallace Stevens' short yet profound poem "The Snow Man" is reductionist: the snow man is a figure without human biases or emotions. Stevens begins, "One must have a mind of winter," the criterion for realizing nature and life does not inherently possess subjective qualities; we only invest it with these. Things are not as we see them; they simply are. The entire poem is one long sentence of clauses connected by conjunctions and commas, and modified by relative clauses and phrases. The successive phrases lead readers continually to reconsider as they read. Stevens' construction of the poem mirrors the meaning he conveys. With a mind of winter, the snow man, Stevens concludes, "nothing himself, beholds nothing that is not there, and the nothing that is."

CONTRAST OF CONTENT AND STRUCTURE

Robert Frost's poem "Stopping by Woods on a Snowy Evening" (1923) is deceptively short and simple, with only four stanzas, each of only four lines, and short and simple words. Reinforcing this is Frost's use of regular rhyme and meter. The rhythm is iambic tetrameter throughout; the rhyme scheme is AABA in the first three stanzas and AAAA in the fourth. In an additional internal subtlety, B ending "here" in the first stanza is rhymed with A endings "queer," "near," and "year" of the second; B ending "lake" in the second is rhymed in A endings "shake," "mistake," and "flake" of the third. The final stanza's AAAA endings reinforce the ultimate darker theme. Though the first three stanzas seem to describe quietly watching snow fill the woods, the last stanza evokes the seductive pull of mysterious death: "The woods are lovely, dark and deep," countered by the obligations of living life: "But I have promises to keep, / And miles to go before I sleep, / And miles to go before I sleep." The last line's repetition strengthens Frost's message that despite death's temptation, life's course must precede it.

EFFECTS OF FIGURATIVE DEVICES ON MEANING IN POETRY

Through exaggeration, **hyperbole** communicates the strength of a poet's or persona's feelings and enhances the mood of the poem. **Imagery** appeals to the reader's senses, creating vivid mental pictures, evoking reader emotions and responses, and helping to develop themes. **Irony** also aids thematic development by drawing the reader's attention to the poet's point and communicating the poem's tone. Thematic development is additionally supported by the comparisons of **metaphors** and **similes**, which emphasize similarities, enhance imagery, and affect readers' perceptions. The use of **mood** communicates the atmosphere of a poem, builds a sense of tension, and evokes the reader's emotions. **Onomatopoeia** appeals to the reader's auditory sense and enhances sound imagery even when the poem is visual (read silently) rather than auditory (read aloud). **Rhyme** connects and unites verses, gives the rhyming words emphasis, and makes poems more fluent. **Symbolism** communicates themes, develops imagery, evokes readers' emotions, and elicits a response from the reader.

REPETITION TO ENHANCE MEANING

A **villanelle** is a nineteen-line poem composed of five tercets and one quatrain. The defining characteristic is the repetition: two lines appear repeatedly throughout the poem. In Theodore Roethke's "The Waking," the two repeated lines are "I wake to sleep, and take my waking slow," and

"I learn by going where I have to go." At first these sound paradoxical, but the meaning is gradually revealed through the poem. The repetition also fits with the theme of cycle: the paradoxes of waking to sleep, learning by going, and thinking by feeling represent a constant cycle through life. They also symbolize abandoning conscious rationalism to embrace spiritual vision. We wake from the vision to "Great Nature," and "take the lively air." "This shaking keeps me steady"—another paradox—juxtaposes and balances fear of mortality with ecstasy in embracing experience. The transcendent vision of all life's interrelationship demonstrates, "What falls away is always. And is near." Readers experience the poem holistically, like music, through Roethke's integration of theme, motion, and sound.

Sylvia Plath's villanelle "Mad Girl's Love Song" narrows the scope from universal to personal but keeps the theme of cycle. The two repeated lines, "I shut my eyes and all the world drops dead" and "(I think I made you up inside my head.)" reflect the existential viewpoint that nothing exists in any absolute reality outside of our own perceptions. In the first stanza, the middle line, "I lift my lids and all is born again," in its recreating the world, bridges between the repeated refrain statements—one of obliterating reality, the other of having constructed her lover's existence. Unlike other villanelles wherein key lines are subtly altered in their repetitions, Plath repeats these exactly each time. This reflects the young woman's love, constant throughout the poem as it neither fades nor progresses.

Drama

EARLY DEVELOPMENT

English **drama** originally developed from religious ritual. Early Christians established traditions of presenting pageants or mystery plays, traveling on wagons and carts through the streets to depict Biblical events. Medieval tradition assigned responsibility for performing specific plays to the different guilds. In Middle English, "mystery" referred to craft, or trade, and religious ritual and truth. Historically, mystery plays were to be reproduced exactly the same every time they were performed, like religious rituals. However, some performers introduced individual interpretations of roles and even improvised. Thus, drama was born. Narrative detail and nuanced acting were evident in mystery cycles by the Middle Ages. As individualized performance evolved, plays on other subjects also developed. Middle English mystery plays that still exist include the York Cycle, Coventry Cycle, Chester Mystery Plays, N-Town Plays, and Towneley/Wakefield Plays. In recent times, these plays began to draw interest again, and several modern actors, such as Dame Judi Dench, began their careers with mystery plays.

> **Review Video: Dramas**
> Visit mometrix.com/academy and enter code: 216060

DEFINING CHARACTERISTICS

In the Middle Ages, plays were commonly composed in **verse**. By the time of the Renaissance, Shakespeare and other dramatists wrote plays that mixed **prose**, **rhymed verse**, and **blank verse**. The traditions of costumes and masks were seen in ancient Greek drama, medieval mystery plays, and Renaissance drama. Conventions like **asides**, in which actors make comments directly to the audience unheard by other characters, and **soliloquies** were also common during Shakespeare's Elizabethan dramatic period. **Monologues** date back to ancient Greek drama. Elizabethan dialogue tended to use colloquial prose for lower-class characters' speech and stylized verse for upper-class characters. Another Elizabethan convention was the play-within-a-play, as in *Hamlet*. As drama moved toward realism, dialogue became less poetic and more conversational, as in most modern English-language plays. Contemporary drama, both onstage and onscreen, includes a convention of **breaking the fourth wall**, as actors directly face and address audiences.

COMEDY

Today, most people equate the idea of **comedy** with something funny, and of **tragedy** with something sad. However, the ancient Greeks defined these differently. Comedy needed not be humorous or amusing; it needed only a happy ending. The classical definition of comedy, as included in Aristotle's works, is any work that tells the story of a sympathetic main character's rise in fortune. According to Aristotle, protagonists need not be heroic or exemplary, nor evil or worthless, but ordinary people of unremarkable morality. Comic figures who were sympathetic were usually of humble origins, proving their "natural nobility" through their actions as they were tested. Characters born into nobility were often satirized as self-important or pompous.

SHAKESPEAREAN COMEDY

William Shakespeare lived in England from 1564-1616. He was a poet and playwright of the Renaissance period in Western culture. He is generally considered the foremost dramatist in world literature and the greatest author to write in the English language. He wrote many poems, particularly sonnets, of which 154 survive today, and approximately 38 plays. Though his sonnets are greater in number and are very famous, he is best known for his plays, including comedies, tragedies, tragicomedies and historical plays. His play titles include: *All's Well That Ends Well, As You Like It, The Comedy of Errors, Love's Labour's Lost, Measure for Measure, The Merchant of Venice,*

The Merry Wives of Windsor, A Midsummer Night's Dream, Much Ado About Nothing, The Taming of the Shrew, The Tempest, Twelfth Night, The Two Gentlemen of Verona, The Winter's Tale, King John, Richard II, Henry IV, Henry V, Richard III, Romeo and Juliet, Coriolanus, Titus Andronicus, Julius Caesar, Macbeth, Hamlet, Troilus and Cressida, King Lear, Othello, Antony and Cleopatra, and *Cymbeline.* Some scholars have suggested that Christopher Marlowe wrote several of Shakespeare's works. While most scholars reject this theory, Shakespeare did pay homage to Marlowe, alluding to several of his characters, themes, or verbiage, as well as borrowing themes from several of his plays (e.g., Marlowe's *Jew of Malta* influenced Shakespeare's *Merchant of Venice*).

When Shakespeare was writing, during the Elizabethan period of the Renaissance, Aristotle's version of comedies was popular. While some of Shakespeare's comedies were humorous and others were not, all had happy endings. *A Comedy of Errors* is a farce. Based and expanding on a Classical Roman comedy, it is lighthearted and includes slapstick humor and mistaken identity. *Much Ado About Nothing* is a romantic comedy. It incorporates some more serious themes, including social mores, perceived infidelity, marriage's duality as both trap and ideal, honor and its loss, public shame, and deception, but also much witty dialogue and a happy ending.

DRAMATIC COMEDY

Three types of dramas classified as comedy include the farce, the romantic comedy, and the satirical comedy.

FARCE

The **farce** is a zany, goofy type of comedy that includes pratfalls and other forms of slapstick humor. The characters in a farce tend to be ridiculous or fantastical in nature. The plot also tends to contain highly improbable events, featuring complications and twists that continue throughout, and incredible coincidences that would likely never occur in reality. Mistaken identity, deceptions, and disguises are common devices used in farcical comedies. Shakespeare's play *The Comedy of Errors,* with its cases of accidental mistaken identity and slapstick, is an example of farce. Contemporary examples of farce include the Marx Brothers' movies, the Three Stooges movies and TV episodes, and the *Pink Panther* movie series.

ROMANTIC COMEDY

Romantic comedies are probably the most popular of the types of comedy, in both live theater performances and movies. They include not only humor and a happy ending, but also love. In the typical plot of a **romantic comedy**, two people well suited to one another are either brought together for the first time, or reconciled after being separated. They are usually both sympathetic characters and seem destined to be together, yet they are separated by some intervening complication, such as ex-lovers, interfering parents or friends, or differences in social class. The happy ending is achieved through the lovers overcoming all these obstacles. William Shakespeare's *Much Ado About Nothing*, Walt Disney's version of *Cinderella* (1950), and Broadway musical *Guys and Dolls* (1955) are example of romantic comedies. Many live-action movies are also examples of romantic comedies, such as *The Princess Bride* (1987), *Sleepless in Seattle* (1993), *You've Got Mail* (1998), and *Forget Paris* (1995).

SATIRICAL COMEDY AND BLACK COMEDY

Satires generally mock and lampoon human foolishness and vices. **Satirical comedies** fit the classical definition of comedy by depicting a main character's rise in fortune, but they also fit the definition of satire by making that main character either a fool, morally corrupt, or cynical in attitude. All or most of the other characters in the satirical comedy display similar foibles. These include gullible types, such as cuckolded spouses and dupes, and deceptive types, such as tricksters, con artists, criminals, hypocrites, and fortune seekers, who prey on the gullible. Some classical examples of satirical comedies include *The Birds* by ancient Greek comedic playwright Aristophanes, and *Volpone* by 17th-century poet and playwright Ben Jonson, who made the comedy of humors popular. When satirical comedy is extended to extremes, it becomes **black comedy**, wherein the comedic occurrences are grotesque or terrible.

TRAGEDY

The opposite of comedy is tragedy, portraying a hero's fall in fortune. While by classical definitions, tragedies could be sad, Aristotle went further, requiring that they depict suffering and pain to cause "terror and pity" in audiences. Additionally, he decreed that tragic heroes be basically good, admirable, or noble, and that their downfalls result from personal action, choice, or error, not by bad luck or accident.

ARISTOTLE'S CRITERIA FOR TRAGEDY

In his *Poetics,* Aristotle defined five critical terms relative to tragedy:

- *Anagnorisis*: Meaning tragic insight or recognition, this is a moment of realization by a tragic hero or heroine that he or she has become enmeshed in a "web of fate."
- *Hamartia*: This is often called a "tragic flaw," but is better described as a tragic error. *Hamartia* is an archery term meaning a shot missing the bull's eye, used here as a metaphor for a mistake—often a simple one—which results in catastrophe.
- *Hubris*: While often called "pride," this is actually translated as "violent transgression," and signifies an arrogant overstepping of moral or cultural bounds—the sin of the tragic hero who over-presumes or over-aspires.
- *Nemesis*: translated as "retribution," this represents the cosmic punishment or payback that the tragic hero ultimately receives for committing hubristic acts.
- *Peripateia*: Literally "turning," this is a plot reversal consisting of a tragic hero's pivotal action, which changes his or her status from safe to endangered.

HEGEL'S THEORY OF TRAGEDY

Georg Wilhelm Friedrich Hegel (1770-1831) proposed a different theory of tragedy than Aristotle (384-322 BC), which was also very influential. Whereas Aristotle's criteria involved character and plot, Hegel defined tragedy as a dynamic conflict of opposite forces or rights. For example, if an individual believes in the moral philosophy of the conscientious objector (i.e., that fighting in wars is morally wrong) but is confronted with being drafted into military service, this conflict would fit Hegel's definition of a tragic plot premise. Hegel theorized that a tragedy must involve some circumstance in which two values, or two rights, are fatally at odds with one another and conflict directly. Hegel did not view this as good triumphing over evil, or evil winning out over good, but rather as one good fighting against another good unto death. He saw this conflict of two goods as truly tragic. In ancient Greek playwright Sophocles' tragedy *Antigone,* the main character experiences this tragic conflict between her public duties and her family and religious responsibilities.

REVENGE TRAGEDY

Along with Aristotelian definitions of comedy and tragedy, ancient Greece was the origin of the **revenge tragedy**. This genre became highly popular in Renaissance England, and is still popular today in contemporary movies. In a revenge tragedy, the protagonist has suffered a serious wrong, such as the murder of a family member. However, the wrongdoer has not been punished. In contemporary plots, this often occurs when some legal technicality has interfered with the miscreant's conviction and sentencing, or when authorities are unable to locate and apprehend the

28

criminal. The protagonist then faces the conflict of suffering this injustice, or exacting his or her own justice by seeking revenge. Greek revenge tragedies include *Agamemnon* and *Medea*. Playwright Thomas Kyd's *The Spanish Tragedy* (1582-1592) is credited with beginning the Elizabethan genre of revenge tragedies. Shakespearean revenge tragedies include *Hamlet* (1599-1602) and *Titus Andronicus* (1588-1593). A Jacobean example is Thomas Middleton's *The Revenger's Tragedy* (1606, 1607).

HAMLET'S "TRAGIC FLAW"

Despite virtually limitless interpretations, one way to view Hamlet's tragic error generally is as indecision. He suffers the classic revenge tragedy's conflict of whether to suffer with his knowledge of his mother's and uncle's assassination of his father, or to exact his own revenge and justice against Claudius, who has assumed the throne after his crime went unknown and unpunished. Hamlet's famous soliloquy, "To be or not to be" reflects this dilemma. Hamlet muses "Whether 'tis nobler in the mind to suffer the slings and arrows of outrageous fortune, / Or to take arms against a sea of troubles, / And by opposing end them?" Hamlet both longs for and fears death, as "the dread of something after death … makes us rather bear those ills we have / Than fly to others that we know not … Thus, conscience does make cowards of us all." For most of the play, Hamlet struggles with his responsibility to avenge his father, who was killed by Hamlet's uncle, Claudius. So, Hamlet's tragic error at first might be considered a lack of action. But he then makes several attempts at revenge, each of which end in worse tragedy, until his efforts are ended by the final tragedy— Hamlet's own death.

Informational Texts

TEXT FEATURES IN INFORMATIONAL TEXTS

The **title of a text** gives readers some idea of its content. The **table of contents** is a list near the beginning of a text, showing the book's sections and chapters and their coinciding page numbers. This gives readers an overview of the whole text and helps them find specific chapters easily. An **appendix**, at the back of the book or document, includes important information that is not present in the main text. Also at the back, an **index** lists the book's important topics alphabetically with their page numbers to help readers find them easily. **Glossaries**, usually found at the backs of books, list technical terms alphabetically with their definitions to aid vocabulary learning and comprehension. Boldface print is used to emphasize certain words, often identifying words included in the text's glossary where readers can look up their definitions. **Headings** separate sections of text and show the topic of each. **Subheadings** divide subject headings into smaller, more specific categories to help readers organize information. **Footnotes**, at the bottom of the page, give readers more information, such as citations or links. **Bullet points** list items separately, making facts and ideas easier to see and understand. A **sidebar** is a box of information to one side of the main text giving additional information, often on a more focused or in-depth example of a topic.

Illustrations and **photographs** are pictures that visually emphasize important points in text. The captions below the illustrations explain what those images show. Charts and tables are visual forms of information that make something easier to understand quickly. Diagrams are drawings that show relationships or explain a process. Graphs visually show the relationships among multiple sets of information plotted along vertical and horizontal axes. Maps show geographical information visually to help readers understand the relative locations of places covered in the text. Timelines are visual graphics that show historical events in chronological order to help readers see their sequence.

> **Review Video: Informative Text**
> Visit mometrix.com/academy and enter code: 924964

LANGUAGE USE

LITERAL AND FIGURATIVE LANGUAGE

As in fictional literature, informational text also uses both **literal language**, which means just what it says, and **figurative language**, which imparts more than literal meaning. For example, an informational text author might use a simile or direct comparison, such as writing that a racehorse "ran like the wind." Informational text authors also use metaphors or implied comparisons, such as "the cloud of the Great Depression." Imagery may also appear in informational texts to increase the reader's understanding of ideas and concepts discussed in the text.

> **Review Video: Figurative Language**
> Visit mometrix.com/academy and enter code: 584902

EXPLICIT AND IMPLICIT INFORMATION

When informational text states something explicitly, the reader is told by the author exactly what is meant, which can include the author's interpretation or perspective of events. For example, a professor writes, "I have seen students go into an absolute panic just because they weren't able to complete the exam in the time they were allotted." This explicitly tells the reader that the students were afraid, and by using the words "just because," the writer indicates their fear was exaggerated out of proportion relative to what happened. However, another professor writes, "I have had

students come to me, their faces drained of all color, saying 'We weren't able to finish the exam.'"
This is an example of implicit meaning: the second writer did not state explicitly that the students
were panicked. Instead, he wrote a description of their faces being "drained of all color." From this
description, the reader can infer that the students were so frightened that their faces paled.

> **Review Video: Explicit and Implicit Information**
> Visit mometrix.com/academy and enter code: 735771

TECHNICAL LANGUAGE

Technical language is more impersonal than literary and vernacular language. Passive voice makes
the tone impersonal. For example, instead of writing, "We found this a central component of protein
metabolism," scientists write, "This was found a central component of protein metabolism." While
science professors have traditionally instructed students to avoid active voice because it leads to
first-person ("I" and "we") usage, science editors today find passive voice dull and weak. Many
journal articles combine both. Tone in technical science writing should be detached, concise, and
professional. While one may normally write, "This chemical has to be available for proteins to be
digested," professionals write technically, "The presence of this chemical is required for the enzyme
to break the covalent bonds of proteins." The use of technical language appeals to both technical
and non-technical audiences by displaying the author or speaker's understanding of the subject and
suggesting their credibility regarding the message they are communicating.

TECHNICAL MATERIAL FOR NON-TECHNICAL READERS

Writing about **technical subjects** for **non-technical readers** differs from writing for colleagues
because authors place more importance on delivering a critical message than on imparting the
maximum technical content possible. Technical authors also must assume that non-technical
audiences do not have the expertise to comprehend extremely scientific or technical messages,
concepts, and terminology. They must resist the temptation to impress audiences with their
scientific knowledge and expertise and remember that their primary purpose is to communicate a
message that non-technical readers will understand, feel, and respond to. Non-technical and
technical styles include similarities. Both should formally cite any references or other authors' work
utilized in the text. Both must follow intellectual property and copyright regulations. This includes
the author's protecting his or her own rights, or a public domain statement, as he or she chooses.

NON-TECHNICAL AUDIENCES

Writers of technical or scientific material may need to write for many non-technical audiences.
Some readers have no technical or scientific background, and those who do may not be in the same
field as the authors. Government and corporate policymakers and budget managers need technical
information they can understand for decision-making. Citizens affected by technology or science
are a different audience. Non-governmental organizations can encompass many of the preceding
groups. Elementary and secondary school programs also need non-technical language for
presenting technical subject matter. Additionally, technical authors will need to use non-technical
language when collecting consumer responses to surveys, presenting scientific or para-scientific
material to the public, writing about the history of science, and writing about science and
technology in developing countries.

USE OF EVERYDAY LANGUAGE

Authors of technical information sometimes must write using non-technical language that readers
outside their disciplinary fields can comprehend. They should use not only non-technical terms, but
also normal, everyday language to accommodate readers whose native language is different than
the language the text is written in. For example, instead of writing that "eustatic changes like

thermal expansion are causing hazardous conditions in the littoral zone," an author would do better to write that "a rising sea level is threatening the coast." When technical terms cannot be avoided, authors should also define or explain them using non-technical language. Although authors must cite references and acknowledge their use of others' work, they should avoid the kinds of references or citations that they would use in scientific journals—unless they reinforce author messages. They should not use endnotes, footnotes, or any other complicated referential techniques because non-technical journal publishers usually do not accept them. Including high-resolution illustrations, photos, maps, or satellite images and incorporating multimedia into digital publications will enhance non-technical writing about technical subjects. Technical authors may publish using non-technical language in e-journals, trade journals, specialty newsletters, and daily newspapers.

MAKING INFERENCES ABOUT INFORMATIONAL TEXT

With informational text, reader comprehension depends not only on recalling important statements and details, but also on reader inferences based on examples and details. Readers add information from the text to what they already know to draw inferences about the text. These inferences help the readers to fill in the information that the text does not explicitly state, enabling them to understand the text better. When reading a nonfictional autobiography or biography, for example, the most appropriate inferences might concern the events in the book, the actions of the subject of the autobiography or biography, and the message the author means to convey. When reading a nonfictional expository (informational) text, the reader would best draw inferences about problems and their solutions, and causes and their effects. When reading a nonfictional persuasive text, the reader will want to infer ideas supporting the author's message and intent.

STRUCTURES OR ORGANIZATIONAL PATTERNS IN INFORMATIONAL TEXTS

Informational text can be **descriptive**, appealing to the five senses and answering the questions what, who, when, where, and why. Another method of structuring informational text is sequence and order. **Chronological** texts relate events in the sequence that they occurred, from start to finish, while how-to texts organize information into a series of instructions in the sequence in which the steps should be followed. **Comparison-contrast** structures of informational text describe various ideas to their readers by pointing out how things or ideas are similar and how they are different. **Cause and effect** structures of informational text describe events that occurred and identify the causes or reasons that those events occurred. **Problem and solution** structures of informational texts introduce and describe problems and offer one or more solutions for each problem described.

> **Review Video: Organizational Methods to Structure Text**
> Visit mometrix.com/academy and enter code: 606263

DETERMINING AN INFORMATIONAL AUTHOR'S PURPOSE

Informational authors' purposes are why they write texts. Readers must determine authors' motivations and goals. Readers gain greater insight into a text by considering the author's motivation. This develops critical reading skills. Readers perceive writing as a person's voice, not simply printed words. Uncovering author motivations and purposes empowers readers to know what to expect from the text, read for relevant details, evaluate authors and their work critically, and respond effectively to the motivations and persuasions of the text. The main idea of a text is what the reader is supposed to understand from reading it; the purpose of the text is why the author has written it and what the author wants readers to do with its information. Authors state some purposes clearly, while other purposes may be unstated but equally significant. When stated purposes contradict other parts of a text, the author may have a hidden agenda. Readers can better

32

evaluate a text's effectiveness, whether they agree or disagree with it, and why they agree or disagree through identifying unstated author purposes.

IDENTIFYING AUTHOR'S POINT OF VIEW OR PURPOSE

In some informational texts, readers find it easy to identify the author's point of view and purpose, such as when the author explicitly states his or her position and reason for writing. But other texts are more difficult, either because of the content or because the authors give neutral or balanced viewpoints. This is particularly true in scientific texts, in which authors may state the purpose of their research in the report, but never state their point of view except by interpreting evidence or data.

To analyze text and identify point of view or purpose, readers should ask themselves the following four questions:

1. With what main point or idea does this author want to persuade readers to agree?
2. How does this author's word choice affect the way that readers consider this subject?
3. How do this author's choices of examples and facts affect the way that readers consider this subject?
4. What is it that this author wants to accomplish by writing this text?

> **Review Video: Purpose**
> Visit mometrix.com/academy and enter code: 511819

EVALUATING ARGUMENTS MADE BY INFORMATIONAL TEXT WRITERS

When evaluating an informational text, the first step is to identify the argument's conclusion. Then identify the author's premises that support the conclusion. Try to paraphrase premises for clarification and make the conclusion and premises fit. List all premises first, sequentially numbered, then finish with the conclusion. Identify any premises or assumptions not stated by the author but required for the stated premises to support the conclusion. Read word assumptions sympathetically, as the author might. Evaluate whether premises reasonably support the conclusion. For inductive reasoning, the reader should ask if the premises are true, if they support the conclusion, and if so, how strongly. For deductive reasoning, the reader should ask if the argument is valid or invalid. If all premises are true, then the argument is valid unless the conclusion can be false. If it can, then the argument is invalid. An invalid argument can be made valid through alterations such as the addition of needed premises.

USE OF RHETORIC IN INFORMATIONAL TEXTS

There are many ways authors can support their claims, arguments, beliefs, ideas, and reasons for writing in informational texts. For example, authors can appeal to readers' sense of **logic** by communicating their reasoning through a carefully sequenced series of logical steps to help "prove" the points made. Authors can appeal to readers' **emotions** by using descriptions and words that evoke feelings of sympathy, sadness, anger, righteous indignation, hope, happiness, or any other emotion to reinforce what they express and share with their audience. Authors may appeal to the **moral** or **ethical values** of readers by using words and descriptions that can convince readers that something is right or wrong. By relating personal anecdotes, authors can supply readers with more accessible, realistic examples of points they make, as well as appealing to their emotions. They can provide supporting evidence by reporting case studies. They can also illustrate their points by making analogies to which readers can better relate.

33

Persuasive Techniques

PERSUASIVE TECHNIQUES

To **appeal using reason**, writers present logical arguments, such as using "If... then... because" statements. To **appeal to emotions**, authors may ask readers how they would feel about something or to put themselves in another's place, present their argument as one that will make the audience feel good, or tell readers how they should feel. To **appeal to character**, **morality**, or **ethics**, authors present their points to readers as the right or most moral choices. Authors cite expert opinions to show readers that someone very knowledgeable about the subject or viewpoint agrees with the author's claims. **Testimonials**, usually via anecdotes or quotations regarding the author's subject, help build the audience's trust in an author's message through positive support from ordinary people. **Bandwagon appeals** claim that everybody else agrees with the author's argument and persuade readers to conform and agree, also. Authors **appeal to greed** by presenting their choice as cheaper, free, or more valuable for less cost. They **appeal to laziness** by presenting their views as more convenient, easy, or relaxing. Authors also anticipate potential objections and argue against them before audiences think of them, thereby depicting those objections as weak.

Authors can use **comparisons** like analogies, similes, and metaphors to persuade audiences. For example, a writer might represent excessive expenses as "hemorrhaging" money, which the author's recommended solution will stop. Authors can use negative word connotations to make some choices unappealing to readers, and positive word connotations to make others more appealing. Using **humor** can relax readers and garner their agreement. However, writers must take care: ridiculing opponents can be a successful strategy for appealing to readers who already agree with the author, but can backfire by angering other readers. **Rhetorical questions** need no answer, but create effect that can force agreement, such as asking the question, "Wouldn't you rather be paid more than less?" **Generalizations** persuade readers by being impossible to disagree with. Writers can easily make generalizations that appear to support their viewpoints, like saying, "We all want peace, not war" regarding more specific political arguments. **Transfer** and **association** persuade by example: if advertisements show attractive actors enjoying their products, audiences imagine they will experience the same. **Repetition** can also sometimes effectively persuade audiences.

> **Review Video: Using Rhetorical Strategies for Persuasion**
> Visit mometrix.com/academy and enter code: 302658

CLASSICAL AUTHOR APPEALS

In his *On Rhetoric,* ancient Greek philosopher Aristotle defined three basic types of appeal used in writing, which he called *pathos, ethos,* and *logos.* **Pathos** means suffering or experience and refers to appeals to the emotions (the English word *pathetic* comes from this root). Writing that is meant to entertain audiences, by making them either happy, as with comedy, or sad, as with tragedy, uses *pathos.* Aristotle's *Poetics* states that evoking the emotions of terror and pity is one of the criteria for writing tragedy. **Ethos** means character and connotes ideology (the English word *ethics* comes from this root). Writing that appeals to credibility, based on academic, professional, or personal merit, uses *ethos.* **Logos** means "I say" and refers to a plea, opinion, expectation, word or speech, account, opinion, or reason (the English word *logic* comes from this root.) Aristotle used it to mean persuasion that appeals to the audience through reasoning and logic to influence their opinions.

CRITICAL EVALUATION OF EFFECTIVENESS OF PERSUASIVE METHODS

First, readers should identify the author's **thesis**—what he or she argues for or against. They should consider the argument's content and the author's reason for presenting it. Does the author offer **solutions** to problems raised? If so, are they realistic? Note all central ideas and evidence supporting the author's thesis. Research any unfamiliar subjects or vocabulary. Readers should then outline or summarize the work in their own words. Identify which types of appeals the author uses. Readers should evaluate how well the author communicated meaning from the reader's perspective: Did they respond to emotional appeals with anger, concern, happiness, etc.? If so, why? Decide if the author's reasoning sufficed for changing the reader's mind. Determine whether the content and presentation were accurate, cohesive, and clear. Readers should also ask themselves whether they found the author believable or not, and why or why not.

EVALUATING AN ARGUMENT

Argumentative and persuasive passages take a stand on a debatable issue, seek to explore all sides of the issue, and find the best possible solution. Argumentative and persuasive passages should not be combative or abusive. The word *argument* may remind you of two or more people shouting at each other and walking away in anger. However, an argumentative or persuasive passage should be a calm and reasonable presentation of an author's ideas for others to consider. When an author writes reasonable arguments, his or her goal is not to win or have the last word. Instead, authors want to reveal current understanding of the question at hand and suggest a solution to a problem. The purpose of argument and persuasion in a free society is to reach the best solution.

EVIDENCE

The term **text evidence** refers to information that supports a main point or minor points and can help lead the reader to a conclusion about the text's credibility. Information used as text evidence is precise, descriptive, and factual. A main point is often followed by supporting details that provide evidence to back up a claim. For example, a passage may include the claim that winter occurs during opposite months in the Northern and Southern hemispheres. Text evidence for this claim may include examples of countries where winter occurs in opposite months. Stating that the tilt of the Earth as it rotates around the sun causes winter to occur at different times in separate hemispheres is another example of text evidence. Text evidence can come from common knowledge, but it is also valuable to include text evidence from credible, relevant outside sources.

> **Review Video: Text Evidence**
> Visit mometrix.com/academy and enter code: 486236

Evidence that supports the thesis and additional arguments needs to be provided. Most arguments must be supported by facts or statistics. A fact is something that is known with certainty, has been verified by several independent individuals, and can be proven to be true. In addition to facts, examples and illustrations can support an argument by adding an emotional component. With this component, you persuade readers in ways that facts and statistics cannot. The emotional component is effective when used alongside objective information that can be confirmed.

CREDIBILITY

The text used to support an argument can be the argument's downfall if the text is not credible. A text is **credible**, or believable, when its author is knowledgeable and objective, or unbiased. The author's motivations for writing the text play a critical role in determining the credibility of the text and must be evaluated when assessing that credibility. Reports written about the ozone layer by an environmental scientist and a hairdresser will have a different level of credibility.

> **Review Video: Credible**
> Visit mometrix.com/academy and enter code: 827257

APPEAL TO EMOTION

Sometimes, authors will appeal to the reader's emotion in an attempt to persuade or to distract the reader from the weakness of the argument. For instance, the author may try to inspire the pity of the reader by delivering a heart-rending story. An author also might use the bandwagon approach, in which he suggests that his opinion is correct because it is held by the majority. Some authors resort to name-calling, in which insults and harsh words are delivered to the opponent in an attempt to distract. In advertising, a common appeal is the celebrity testimonial, in which a famous person endorses a product. Of course, the fact that a famous person likes something should not really mean anything to the reader. These and other emotional appeals are usually evidence of poor reasoning and a weak argument.

COUNTER ARGUMENTS

When authors give both sides to the argument, they build trust with their readers. As a reader, you should start with an undecided or neutral position. If an author presents only his or her side to the argument, then they are not exhibiting credibility and are weakening their argument.

Building common ground with readers can be effective for persuading neutral, skeptical, or opposed readers. Sharing values with undecided readers can allow people to switch positions without giving up what they feel is important. People who may oppose a position need to feel that they can change their minds without betraying who they are as a person. This appeal to having an open mind can be a powerful tool in arguing a position without antagonizing other views. Objections can be countered on a point-by-point basis or in a summary paragraph. Be mindful of how an author points out flaws in counter arguments. If they are unfair to the other side of the argument, then you should lose trust with the author.

RHETORICAL DEVICES

- An **anecdote** is a brief story authors may relate to their argument, which can illustrate their points in a more real and relatable way.
- **Aphorisms** concisely state common beliefs and may rhyme. For example, Benjamin Franklin's "Early to bed and early to rise / Makes a man healthy, wealthy, and wise" is an aphorism.
- **Allusions** refer to literary or historical figures to impart symbolism to a thing or person and to create reader resonance. In John Steinbeck's *Of Mice and Men*, protagonist George's last name is Milton. This alludes to John Milton, who wrote *Paradise Lost*, and symbolizes George's eventual loss of his dream.
- **Satire** exaggerates, ridicules, or pokes fun at human flaws or ideas, as in the works of Jonathan Swift and Mark Twain.
- A **parody** is a form of satire that imitates another work to ridicule its topic or style.
- A **paradox** is a statement that is true despite appearing contradictory.
- **Hyperbole** is overstatement using exaggerated language.
- An **oxymoron** combines seeming contradictions, such as "deafening silence."
- **Analogies** compare two things that share common elements.
- **Similes** (stated comparisons using the words *like* or *as*) and **metaphors** (stated comparisons that do not use *like* or *as*) are considered forms of analogy.
- When using logic to reason with audiences, **syllogism** refers either to deductive reasoning or a deceptive, very sophisticated, or subtle argument.
- **Deductive reasoning** moves from general to specific, **inductive reasoning** from specific to general.
- **Diction** is author word choice that establishes tone and effect.

36

- **Understatement** achieves effects like contrast or irony by downplaying or describing something more subtly than warranted.
- **Chiasmus** uses parallel clauses, the second reversing the order of the first. Examples include T. S. Eliot's "Has the Church failed mankind, or has mankind failed the Church?" and John F. Kennedy's "Ask not what your country can do for you; ask what you can do for your country."
- **Anaphora** regularly repeats a word or phrase at the beginnings of consecutive clauses or phrases to add emphasis to an idea. A classic example of anaphora was Winston Churchill's emphasis of determination: "[W]e shall fight on the beaches, we shall fight on the landing grounds, we shall fight in the fields and in the streets, we shall fight in the hills; we shall never surrender..."

Arguments and Logical Errors

AUTHOR'S ARGUMENT IN ARGUMENTATIVE WRITING

In argumentative writing, the argument is a belief, position, or opinion that the author wants to convince readers to believe as well. For the first step, readers should identify the **issue**. Some issues are controversial, meaning people disagree about them. Gun control, foreign policy, and the death penalty are all controversial issues. The next step is to determine the **author's position** on the issue. That position or viewpoint constitutes the author's argument. Readers should then identify the **author's assumptions**: things he or she accepts, believes, or takes for granted without needing proof. Inaccurate or illogical assumptions produce flawed arguments and can mislead readers. Readers should identify what kinds of **supporting evidence** the author offers, such as research results, personal observations or experiences, case studies, facts, examples, expert testimony and opinions, and comparisons. Readers should decide how relevant this support is to the argument.

> **Review Video: Argumentative Writing**
> Visit mometrix.com/academy and enter code: 561544

EVALUATING AN AUTHOR'S ARGUMENT

The first three reader steps to **evaluate an author's argument** are to identify the **author's assumptions**, identify the **supporting evidence**, and decide **whether the evidence is relevant**. For example, if an author is not an expert on a particular topic, then that author's personal experience or opinion might not be relevant. The fourth step is to assess the **author's objectivity**. For example, consider whether the author introduces clear, understandable supporting evidence and facts to support the argument. The fifth step is evaluating whether the author's **argument is complete**. When authors give sufficient support for their arguments and also anticipate and respond effectively to opposing arguments or objections to their points, their arguments are complete. However, some authors omit information that could detract from their arguments. If instead they stated this information and refuted it, it would strengthen their arguments. The sixth step in evaluating an author's argumentative writing is to assess whether the **argument is valid**. Providing clear, logical reasoning makes an author's argument valid. Readers should ask themselves whether the author's points follow a sequence that makes sense, and whether each point leads to the next. The seventh step is to determine whether the author's **argument is credible**, meaning that it is convincing and believable. Arguments that are not valid are not credible, so step seven depends on step six. Readers should be mindful of their own biases as they evaluate and should not expect authors to conclusively prove their arguments, but rather to provide effective support and reason.

EVALUATING AN AUTHOR'S METHOD OF APPEAL

To evaluate the effectiveness of an appeal, it is important to consider the author's purpose for writing. Any appeals an author uses in their argument must be relevant to the argument's goal. For example, a writer that argues for the reclassification of Pluto, but primarily uses appeals to emotion, will not have an effective argument. This writer should focus on using appeals to logic and support their argument with provable facts. While most arguments should include appeals to logic, emotion, and credibility, some arguments only call for one or two of these types of appeal. Evidence can support an appeal, but the evidence must be relevant to truly strengthen the appeal's effectiveness. If the writer arguing for Pluto's reclassification uses the reasons for Jupiter's classification as evidence, their argument would be weak. This information may seem relevant because it is related to the classification of planets. However, this classification is highly dependent on the size of the celestial object, and Jupiter is significantly bigger than Pluto. This use of evidence

38

is illogical and does not support the appeal. Even when appropriate evidence and appeals are used, appeals and arguments lose their effectiveness when they create logical fallacies.

OPINIONS, FACTS, AND FALLACIES

Critical thinking skills are mastered through understanding various types of writing and the different purposes of authors can have for writing different passages. Every author writes for a purpose. When you understand their purpose and how they accomplish their goal, you will be able to analyze their writing and determine whether or not you agree with their conclusions.

Readers must always be aware of the difference between fact and opinion. A **fact** can be subjected to analysis and proven to be true. An **opinion**, on the other hand, is the author's personal thoughts or feelings and may not be altered by research or evidence. If the author writes that the distance from New York City to Boston is about two hundred miles, then he or she is stating a fact. If the author writes that New York City is too crowded, then he or she is giving an opinion because there is no objective standard for overpopulation. Opinions are often supported by facts. For instance, an author might use a comparison between the population density of New York City and that of other major American cities as evidence of an overcrowded population. An opinion supported by facts tends to be more convincing. On the other hand, when authors support their opinions with other opinions, readers should employ critical thinking and approach the argument with skepticism.

> **Review Video: Fact or Opinion**
> Visit mometrix.com/academy and enter code: 870899

RELIABLE SOURCES

When you have an argumentative passage, you need to be sure that facts are presented to the reader from **reliable sources**. An opinion is what the author thinks about a given topic. An opinion is not common knowledge or proven by expert sources, instead the information is the personal beliefs and thoughts of the author. To distinguish between fact and opinion, a reader needs to consider the type of source that is presenting information, the information that backs-up a claim, and the author's motivation to have a certain point-of-view on a given topic. For example, if a panel of scientists has conducted multiple studies on the effectiveness of taking a certain vitamin, then the results are more likely to be factual than those of a company that is selling a vitamin and simply claims that taking the vitamin can produce positive effects. The company is motivated to sell their product, and the scientists are using the scientific method to prove a theory. Remember, if you find sentences that contain phrases such as "I think...", then the statement is an opinion.

BIASES

In their attempts to persuade, writers often make mistakes in their thought processes and writing choices. These processes and choices are important to understand so you can make an informed decision about the author's credibility. Every author has a point of view, but authors demonstrate a **bias** when they ignore reasonable counterarguments or distort opposing viewpoints. A bias is evident whenever the author's claims are presented in a way that is unfair or inaccurate. Bias can be intentional or unintentional, but readers should be skeptical of the author's argument in either case. Remember that a biased author may still be correct. However, the author will be correct in spite of, not because of, his or her bias.

A **stereotype** is a bias applied specifically to a group of people or a place. Stereotyping is considered to be particularly abhorrent because it promotes negative, misleading generalizations

about people. Readers should be very cautious of authors who use stereotypes in their writing. These faulty assumptions typically reveal the author's ignorance and lack of curiosity.

> **Review Video: Bias and Stereotype**
> Visit mometrix.com/academy and enter code: 644829

Literary Elements

LITERARY TERMINOLOGY

- In works of prose such as novels, a group of connected sentences covering one main topic is termed a **paragraph**.
- In works of poetry, a group of verses similarly connected is called a **stanza**.
- In drama, when early works used verse, these were also divided into stanzas or **couplets**.
- Drama evolved to use predominantly prose. Overall, whether prose or verse, the conversation in a play is called **dialogue**.
- Large sections of dialogue spoken by one actor are called **soliloquies** or **monologues**.
- Dialogue that informs audiences but is unheard by other characters is called an **aside**.
- Novels and plays share certain common elements, such as:
  - **Characters** - the people in the story.
  - **Plot** - the action of the story.
  - **Climax** - when action or dramatic tension reaches its highest point.
  - **Denouement** - the resolution following the climax.
- Sections dividing novels are called **chapters**, while sections of plays are called **acts**.
- Subsections of plays' acts are called **scenes**. Novel chapters usually do not have subsections. However, some novels do include groups of chapters that form different sections.

LITERARY ANALYSIS

The best literary analysis shows special insight into at least one important aspect of a text. When analyzing literary texts, it can be difficult to find a starting place. Many texts can be analyzed several different ways, often leaving an overwhelming number of options for writers to consider. However, narrowing the focus to a particular element of literature can be helpful when preparing to analyze a text. Symbolism, themes, and motifs are common starting points for literary analysis. These three methods of analysis can lead to a holistic analysis of a text, since they involve elements that are often distributed throughout the text. However, not all texts feature these elements in a way that facilitates a strong analysis, if they are present at all. It is also common to focus on character or plot development for analysis. These elements are compatible with theme, symbolism, and allusion. Setting and imagery, figurative language, and any external contexts can also contribute to analysis or complement one of these other elements. The application of a critical, or literary, theory to a text can also provide a thorough and strong analysis.

SETTING AND TIME FRAME

A literary text has both a setting and time frame. A **setting** is the place in which the story as a whole is set. The **time frame** is the period in which the story is set. This may refer to the historical period the story takes place in or if the story takes place over a single day. Both setting and time frame are relevant to a text's meaning because they help the reader place the story in time and space. An author uses setting and time frame to anchor a text, create a mood, and enhance its meaning. This helps a reader understand why a character acts the way he does, or why certain events in the story are important. The setting impacts the **plot** and character **motivations**, while the time frame helps place the story in **chronological context**.

EXAMPLE

Read the following excerpt from The Adventures of Huckleberry Finn by Mark Twain and analyze the relevance of setting to the text's meaning:

> We said there warn't no home like a raft, after all. Other places do seem so cramped up and smothery, but a raft don't. You feel mighty free and easy and comfortable on a raft.

This excerpt from *The Adventures of Huckleberry Finn* by Mark Twain reveals information about the **setting** of the book. By understanding that the main character, Huckleberry Finn, lives on a raft, the reader can place the story on a river, in this case, the Mississippi River in the South before the Civil War. The information about the setting also gives the reader clues about the **character** of Huck Finn: he clearly values independence and freedom, and he likes the outdoors. The information about the setting in the quote helps the reader to better understand the rest of the text.

THEME

The **theme** of a passage is what the reader learns from the text or the passage. It is the lesson or **moral** contained in the passage. It also is a unifying idea that is used throughout the text; it can take the form of a common setting, idea, symbol, design, or recurring event. A passage can have two or more themes that convey its overall idea. The theme or themes of a passage are often based on **universal themes**. They can frequently be expressed using well-known sayings about life, society, or human nature, such as "Hard work pays off" or "Good triumphs over evil." Themes are not usually stated **explicitly**. The reader must figure them out by carefully reading the passage. Themes are often the reason why passages are written; they give a passage unity and meaning. Themes are created through **plot development**. The events of a story help shape the themes of a passage.

EXAMPLE

Explain why "Take care of what you care about" accurately describes the theme of the following excerpt.

> Luca collected baseball cards, but he wasn't very careful with them. He left them around the house. His dog liked to chew. One day, Luca and his friend Bart were looking at his collection. Then they went outside. When Luca got home, he saw his dog chewing on his cards. They were ruined.

This excerpt tells the story of a boy who is careless with his baseball cards and leaves them lying around. His dog ends up chewing them and ruining them. The lesson is that if you care about something, you need to take care of it. This is the theme, or point, of the story. Some stories have more than one theme, but this is not really true of this excerpt. The reader needs to figure out the theme based on what happens in the story. Sometimes, as in the case of fables, the theme is stated directly in the text. However, this is not usually the case.

> **Review Video: Theme**
> Visit mometrix.com/academy and enter code: 732074

PLOT AND STORY STRUCTURE

The **plot** includes the events that happen in a story and the order in which they are told to the reader. There are several types of plot structures, as stories can be told in many ways. The most common plot structure is the chronological plot, which presents the events to the reader in the same order they occur for the characters in the story. Chronological plots usually have five main parts, the **exposition**, **rising action**, the **climax**, **falling action**, and the **resolution**. This type of plot structure guides the reader through the story's events as the characters experience them and is the easiest structure to understand and identify. While this is the most common plot structure, many stories are nonlinear, which means the plot does not sequence events in the same order the characters experience them. Such stories might include elements like flashbacks that cause the story to be nonlinear.

EXPOSITION

The **exposition** is at the beginning of the story and generally takes place before the rising action begins. The purpose of the exposition is to give the reader context for the story, which the author may do by introducing one or more characters, describing the setting or world, or explaining the events leading up to the point where the story begins. The exposition may still include events that contribute to the plot, but the **rising action** and main conflict of the story are not part of the exposition. Some narratives skip the exposition and begin the story with the beginning of the rising action, which causes the reader to learn the context as the story intensifies.

CONFLICT

A **conflict** is a problem to be solved. Literary plots typically include one conflict or more. Characters' attempts to resolve conflicts drive the narrative's forward movement. **Conflict resolution** is often the protagonist's primary occupation. Physical conflicts like exploring, wars, and escapes tend to make plots most suspenseful and exciting. Emotional, mental, or moral conflicts tend to make stories more personally gratifying or rewarding for many audiences. Conflicts can be external or internal. A major type of internal conflict is some inner personal battle, or **man versus self**. Major types of external conflicts include **man versus nature**, **man versus man**, and **man versus society**. Readers can identify conflicts in literary plots by identifying the protagonist and antagonist and asking why they conflict, what events develop the conflict, where the climax occurs, and how they identify with the characters.

Read the following paragraph and discuss the type of conflict present:

> Timothy was shocked out of sleep by the appearance of a bear just outside his tent. After panicking for a moment, he remembered some advice he had read in preparation for this trip: he should make noise so the bear would not be startled. As Timothy started to hum and sing, the bear wandered away.

There are three main types of conflict in literature: **man versus man**, **man versus nature**, and **man versus self**. This paragraph is an example of man versus nature. Timothy is in conflict with the bear. Even though no physical conflict like an attack exists, Timothy is pitted against the bear. Timothy uses his knowledge to "defeat" the bear and keep himself safe. The solution to the conflict is that Timothy makes noise, the bear wanders away, and Timothy is safe.

Review Video: **Conflict**
Visit mometrix.com/academy and enter code: 559550

RISING ACTION

The **rising action** is the part of the story where conflict **intensifies**. The rising action begins with an event that prompts the main conflict of the story. This may also be called the **inciting incident**. The main conflict generally occurs between the protagonist and an antagonist, but this is not the only type of conflict that may occur in a narrative. After this event, the protagonist works to resolve the main conflict by preparing for an altercation, pursuing a goal, fleeing an antagonist, or doing some other action that will end the conflict. The rising action is composed of several additional events that increase the story's tension. Most often, other developments will occur alongside the growth of the main conflict, such as character development or the development of minor conflicts. The rising action ends with the **climax**, which is the point of highest tension in the story.

CLIMAX

The **climax** is the event in the narrative that marks the height of the story's conflict or tension. The event that takes place at the story's climax will end the rising action and bring about the results of the main conflict. If the conflict was between a good protagonist and an evil antagonist, the climax may be a final battle between the two characters. If the conflict is an adventurer looking for heavily guarded treasure, the climax may be the adventurer's encounter with the final obstacle that protects the treasure. The climax may be made of multiple scenes, but can usually be summarized as one event. Once the conflict and climax are complete, the **falling action** begins.

FALLING ACTION

The **falling action** shows what happens in the story between the climax and the resolution. The falling action often composes a much smaller portion of the story than the rising action does. While the climax includes the end of the main conflict, the falling action may show the results of any minor conflicts in the story. For example, if the protagonist encountered a troll on the way to find some treasure, and the troll demanded the protagonist share the treasure after retrieving it, the falling action would include the protagonist returning to share the treasure with the troll. Similarly, any unexplained major events are usually made clear during the falling action. Once all significant elements of the story are resolved or addressed, the story's resolution will occur. The **resolution** is the end of the story, which shows the final result of the plot's events and shows what life is like for the main characters once they are no longer experiencing the story's conflicts.

RESOLUTION

The way the conflict is **resolved** depends on the type of conflict. The plot of any book starts with the lead up to the conflict, then the conflict itself, and finally the solution, or **resolution**, to the conflict. In **man versus man** conflicts, the conflict is often resolved by two parties coming to some sort of agreement or by one party triumphing over the other party. In **man versus nature** conflicts, the conflict is often resolved by man coming to some realization about some aspect of nature. In **man versus self** conflicts, the conflict is often resolved by the character growing or coming to an understanding about part of himself.

SYNTAX AND WORD CHOICE

Authors use words and **syntax**, or sentence structure, to make their texts unique, convey their own writing style, and sometimes to make a point or emphasis. They know that word choice and syntax contribute to the reader's understanding of the text as well as to the tone and mood of a text.

> **Review Video: Syntax**
> Visit mometrix.com/academy and enter code: 242280

ALLUSION

An allusion is an uncited but recognizable reference to something else. Authors use language to make allusions to places, events, artwork, and other books in order to make their own text richer. For example, an author may allude to a very important text in order to make his own text seem more important. Martin Luther King, Jr. started his "I Have a Dream" speech by saying "Five score years ago…" This is a clear allusion to President Abraham Lincoln's "Gettysburg Address" and served to remind people of the significance of the event. An author may allude to a place to ground

his text or make a cultural reference to make readers feel included. There are many reasons that authors make allusions.

COMIC RELIEF

Comic relief is the use of comedy by an author to break up a dramatic or tragic scene and infuse it with a bit of **lightheartedness**. In William Shakespeare's *Hamlet*, two gravediggers digging the grave for Ophelia share a joke while they work. The death and burial of Ophelia are tragic moments that directly follow each other. Shakespeare uses an instance of comedy to break up the tragedy and give his audience a bit of a break from the tragic drama. Authors sometimes use comic relief so that their work will be less depressing; other times they use it to create irony or contrast between the darkness of the situation and the lightness of the joke. Often, authors will use comedy to parallel what is happening in the tragic scenes.

MOOD AND TONE

Mood is a story's atmosphere, or the feelings the reader gets from reading it. The way authors set the mood in writing is comparable to the way filmmakers use music to set the mood in movies. Instead of music, though, writers judiciously select descriptive words to evoke certain **moods**. The mood of a work may convey joy, anger, bitterness, hope, gloom, fear, apprehension, or any other emotion the author wants the reader to feel. In addition to vocabulary choices, authors also use figurative expressions, particular sentence structures, and choices of diction that project and reinforce the moods they want to create. Whereas mood is the reader's emotions evoked by reading what is written, **tone** is the emotions and attitudes of the writer that she or he expresses in the writing. Authors use the same literary techniques to establish tone as they do to establish mood. An author may use a humorous tone, an angry or sad tone, a sentimental or unsentimental tone, or something else entirely.

MOOD AND TONE IN THE GREAT GATSBY

To understand the difference between mood and tone, look at this excerpt from F. Scott Fitzgerald's *The Great Gatsby*. In this passage, Nick Caraway, the novel's narrator, is describing his affordable house, which sits in a neighborhood full of expensive mansions.

> "I lived at West Egg, the—well the less fashionable of the two, though this is a most superficial tag to express the bizarre and not a little sinister contrast between them. My house was at the very tip of the egg, only fifty yard from the Sound, and squeezed between two huge places that rented for twelve or fifteen thousand a season … My own house was an eyesore, but it was a small eyesore, and it had been overlooked, so I had a view of the water, a partial view of my neighbor's lawn, and the consoling proximity of millionaires—all for eighty dollars a month."

In this description, the mood created for the reader does not match the tone created through the narrator. The mood in this passage is one of dissatisfaction and inferiority. Nick compares his home to his neighbors', saying he lives in the "less fashionable" neighborhood and that his house is "overlooked," an "eyesore," and "squeezed between two huge" mansions. He also adds that his placement allows him the "consoling proximity of millionaires." A literal reading of these details leads the reader to have negative feelings toward Nick's house and his economic inferiority to his neighbors, creating the mood.

However, Fitzgerald also conveys an opposing attitude, or tone, through Nick's description. Nick calls the distinction between the neighborhoods "superficial," showing a suspicion of the value suggested by the neighborhoods' titles, properties, and residents. Nick also undermines his critique of his own home by calling it "a small eyesore" and claiming it has "been overlooked." However, he follows these statements with a description of his surroundings, claiming that he has "a view of the water" and can see some of his wealthy neighbor's property from his home, and a comparison between the properties' rent. While the mental image created for the reader depicts a small house shoved between looming mansions, the tone suggests that Nick enjoys these qualities about his home, or at least finds it charming. He acknowledges its shortcomings, but includes the benefits of his home's unassuming appearance.

CHARACTER DEVELOPMENT

When depicting characters or figures in a written text, authors generally use actions, dialogue, and descriptions as characterization techniques. Characterization can occur in both fiction and nonfiction and is used to show a character or figure's personality, demeanor, and thoughts. This helps create a more engaging experience for the reader by providing a more concrete picture of a character or figure's tendencies and features. Characterizations also gives authors the opportunity to integrate elements such as dialects, activities, attire, and attitudes into their writing.

To understand the meaning of a story, it is vital to understand the characters as the author describes them. We can look for contradictions in what a character thinks, says, and does. We can notice whether the author's observations about a character differ from what other characters in the story say about that character. A character may be dynamic, meaning they change significantly during the story, or static, meaning they remain the same from beginning to end. Characters may be two-dimensional, not fully developed, or may be well developed with characteristics that stand out vividly. Characters may also symbolize universal properties. Additionally, readers can compare and contrast characters to analyze how each one developed.

A well-known example of character development can be found in Charles Dickens's *Great Expectations*. The novel's main character, Pip, is introduced as a young boy, and he is depicted as innocent, kind, and humble. However, as Pip grows up and is confronted with the social hierarchy of Victorian England, he becomes arrogant and rejects his loved ones in pursuit of his own social advancement. Once he achieves his social goals, he realizes the merits of his former lifestyle, and lives with the wisdom he gained in both environments and life stages. Dickens shows Pip's ever-changing character through his interactions with others and his inner thoughts, which evolve as his personal values and personality shift.

DIALOGUE

Effectively written dialogue serves at least one, but usually several, purposes. It advances the story and moves the plot, develops the characters, sheds light on the work's theme or meaning, and can, often subtly, account for the passage of time not otherwise indicated. It can alter the direction that the plot is taking, typically by introducing some new conflict or changing existing ones. **Dialogue** can establish a work's narrative voice and the characters' voices and set the tone of the story or of particular characters. When fictional characters display enlightenment or realization, dialogue can give readers an understanding of what those characters have discovered and how. Dialogue can illuminate the motivations and wishes of the story's characters. By using consistent thoughts and syntax, dialogue can support character development. Skillfully created, it can also represent real-life speech rhythms in written form. Via conflicts and ensuing action, dialogue also provides drama.

DIALOGUE IN FICTION

In fictional works, effectively written dialogue does more than just break up or interrupt sections of narrative. While **dialogue** may supply exposition for readers, it must nonetheless be believable. Dialogue should be dynamic, not static, and it should not resemble regular prose. Authors should not use dialogue to write clever similes or metaphors, or to inject their own opinions. Nor should they use dialogue at all when narrative would be better. Most importantly, dialogue should not slow the plot movement. Dialogue must seem natural, which means careful construction of phrases rather than actually duplicating natural speech, which does not necessarily translate well to the written word. Finally, all dialogue must be pertinent to the story, rather than just added conversation.

FORESHADOWING

Foreshadowing is a device authors use to give readers **hints** about events that will take place later in a story. Foreshadowing most often takes place through a character's dialogue or actions. Sometimes the character will know what is going to happen and will purposefully allude to future events. For example, consider a protagonist who is about to embark on a journey through the woods. Just before the protagonist begins the trip, another character says, "Be careful, you never know what could be out in those woods!" This alerts the reader that the woods may be dangerous and prompts the reader to expect something to attack the protagonist in the woods. This is an example of foreshadowing through warning. Alternatively, a character may unknowingly foreshadow later events. For example, consider a story where a brother and sister run through their house and knock over a vase and break it. The brother says, "Don't worry, we'll clean it up! Mom will never know!" However, the reader knows that their mother will most likely find out what they have done, so the reader expects the siblings to later get in trouble for running, breaking the vase, and hiding it from their mother.

SYMBOLISM

Symbolism describes an author's use of a **symbol**, an element of the story that **represents** something else. Symbols can impact stories in many ways, including deepening the meaning of a story or its elements, comparing a story to another work, or foreshadowing later events in a story. Symbols can be objects, characters, colors, numbers, or anything else the author establishes as a symbol. Symbols can be clearly established through direct comparison or repetition, but they can also be established subtly or gradually over a large portion of the story. Another form of symbolism is **allusion**, which is when something in a story is used to prompt the reader to think about another work. Many well-known works use **Biblical allusions**, which are allusions to events or details in the Bible that inform a work or an element within it.

POINT OF VIEW

Another element that impacts a text is the author's point of view. The **point of view** of a text is the perspective from which a passage is told. An author will always have a point of view about a story before he or she draws up a plot line. The author will know what events they want to take place, how they want the characters to interact, and how they want the story to resolve. An author will also have an opinion on the topic or series of events which is presented in the story that is based on their prior experience and beliefs.

The two main points of view that authors use, especially in a work of fiction, are first person and third person. If the narrator of the story is also the main character, or *protagonist*, the text is written in first-person point of view. In first person, the author writes from the perspective of *I*. Third-person point of view is probably the most common that authors use in their passages. Using third person, authors refer to each character by using *he* or *she*. In third-person omniscient, the narrator is not a character in the story and tells the story of all of the characters at the same time.

> **Review Video: Point of View**
> Visit mometrix.com/academy and enter code: 383336

FIRST-PERSON NARRATION

First-person narratives let narrators express inner feelings and thoughts, especially when the narrator is the protagonist as Lemuel Gulliver is in Jonathan Swift's *Gulliver's Travels*. The narrator may be a close friend of the protagonist, like Dr. Watson in Sir Arthur Conan Doyle's *Sherlock Holmes*. Or, the narrator can be less involved with the main characters and plot, like Nick Carraway in F. Scott Fitzgerald's *The Great Gatsby*. When a narrator reports others' narratives, she or he is a "**frame narrator**," like the nameless narrator of Joseph Conrad's *Heart of Darkness* or Mr. Lockwood in Emily Brontë's *Wuthering Heights*. **First-person plural** is unusual but can be effective. Isaac Asimov's *I, Robot*, William Faulkner's *A Rose for Emily*, Maxim Gorky's *Twenty-Six Men and a Girl*, and Jeffrey Eugenides' *The Virgin Suicides* all use first-person plural narration. Author Kurt Vonnegut is the first-person narrator in his semi-autobiographical novel *Timequake*. Also unusual, but effective, is a **first-person omniscient** (rather than the more common third-person omniscient) narrator, like Death in Markus Zusak's *The Book Thief* and the ghost in Alice Sebold's *The Lovely Bones*.

SECOND-PERSON NARRATION

While **second-person** address is very commonplace in popular song lyrics, it is the least used form of narrative voice in literary works. Popular serial books of the 1980s like *Fighting Fantasy* or *Choose Your Own Adventure* employed second-person narratives. In some cases, a narrative combines both second-person and first-person voices, using the pronouns *you* and *I*. This can draw readers into the story, and it can also enable the authors to compare directly "your" and "my" feelings, thoughts, and actions. When the narrator is also a character in the story, as in Edgar Allan Poe's short story "The Tell-Tale Heart" or Jay McInerney's novel *Bright Lights, Big City*, the narrative is better defined as first-person despite it also addressing "you."

THIRD-PERSON NARRATION

Narration in the third person is the most prevalent type, as it allows authors the most flexibility. It is so common that readers simply assume without needing to be informed that the narrator is not a character in the story, or involved in its events. **Third-person singular** is used more frequently than **third-person plural**, though some authors have also effectively used plural. However, both singular and plural are most often included in stories according to which characters are being described. The third-person narrator may be either objective or subjective, and either omniscient or limited. **Objective third-person** narration does not include what the characters described are thinking or feeling, while **subjective third-person** narration does. The **third-person omniscient** narrator knows everything about all characters, including their thoughts and emotions, and all related places, times, and events. However, the **third-person limited** narrator may know

everything about a particular character, but is limited to that character. In other words, the narrator cannot speak about anything that character does not know.

ALTERNATING-PERSON NARRATION

Although authors more commonly write stories from one point of view, there are also instances wherein they alternate the narrative voice within the same book. For example, they may sometimes use an omniscient third-person narrator and a more intimate first-person narrator at other times. In J. K. Rowling's series of *Harry Potter* novels, she often writes in a third-person limited narrative, but sometimes changes to narration by characters other than the protagonist. George R. R. Martin's series *A Song of Ice and Fire* changes the point of view to coincide with divisions between chapters. The same technique is used by Erin Hunter (a pseudonym for several authors of the *Warriors, Seekers,* and *Survivors* book series). Authors using first-person narrative sometimes switch to third-person to describe significant action scenes, especially those where the narrator was absent or uninvolved, as Barbara Kingsolver does in her novel *The Poisonwood Bible*.

HISTORICAL AND SOCIAL CONTEXT

Fiction that is heavily influenced by a historical or social context cannot be comprehended as the author intended if the reader does not keep this context in mind. Many important elements of the text will be influenced by any context, including symbols, allusions, settings, and plot events. These contexts, as well as the identity of the work's author, can help to inform the reader about the author's concerns and intended meanings. For example, George Orwell published his novel *1984* in the year 1949, soon after the end of World War II. At that time, following the defeat of the Nazis, the Cold War began between the Western Allied nations and the Eastern Soviet Communists. People were therefore concerned about the conflict between the freedoms afforded by Western democracies versus the oppression represented by Communism. Orwell had also previously fought in the Spanish Civil War against a Spanish regime that he and his fellows viewed as oppressive. From this information, readers can infer that Orwell was concerned about oppression by totalitarian governments. This informs *1984*'s story of Winston Smith's rebellion against the oppressive "Big Brother" government, of the fictional dictatorial state of Oceania, and his capture, torture, and ultimate conversion by that government. Some literary theories also seek to use historical and social contexts to reveal deeper meanings and implications in a text.

TEXTUAL EVIDENCE

No literary analysis is complete without textual evidence. Summaries, paraphrases, and quotes are all forms of textual evidence, but direct quotes from the text are the most effective form of evidence. The best textual evidence is relevant, accurate, and clearly supports the writer's claim. This can include pieces of descriptions, dialogue, or exposition that shows the applicability of the analysis to the text. Analysis that is average, or sufficient, shows an understanding of the text; contains supporting textual evidence that is relevant and accurate, if not strong; and shows a specific and clear response. Analysis that partially meets criteria also shows understanding, but the textual evidence is generalized, incomplete, only partly relevant or accurate, or connected only weakly. Inadequate analysis is vague, too general, or incorrect. It may give irrelevant or incomplete textual evidence, or may simply summarize the plot rather than analyzing the work. It is important to incorporate textual evidence from the work being analyzed and any supplemental materials and to provide appropriate attribution for these sources.

Themes and Plots in Literature

THEMES IN LITERATURE

When we read parables, their themes are the lessons they aim to teach. When we read fables, the moral of each story is its theme. When we read fictional works, the authors' perspectives regarding life and human behavior are their themes. Unlike in parables and fables, themes in literary fiction are usually not meant to preach or teach the readers a lesson. Hence, themes in fiction are not as explicit as they are in parables or fables. Instead, they are implicit, and the reader only infers them. By analyzing the fictional characters through thinking about their actions and behavior, understanding the setting of the story, and reflecting on how its plot develops, the reader comes to infer the main theme of the work. When writers succeed, they communicate with their readers such that common ground is established between author and audience. While a reader's individual experience may differ in its details from the author's written story, both may share universal underlying truths which allow author and audience to connect.

DETERMINING THEME

In well-crafted literature, theme, structure, and plot are interdependent and inextricable: each element informs and reflects the others. The structure of a work is how it is organized. The theme is the central idea or meaning found in it. The plot is what happens in the story. Titles can also inform us of a work's theme. For instance, the title of Edgar Allan Poe's "The Tell-Tale Heart" informs readers of the story's theme of guilt before they even read about the repeated heartbeat the protagonist hears immediately before and constantly after committing and hiding a murder. Repetitive patterns of events or behaviors also give clues to themes. The same is true of symbols. For example, in F. Scott Fitzgerald's *The Great Gatsby,* for Jay Gatsby the green light at the end of the dock symbolizes Daisy Buchanan and his own dreams for the future. More generally, it is also understood as a symbol of the American Dream, and narrator Nick Carraway explicitly compares it to early settlers' sight of America rising from the ocean.

THEMATIC DEVELOPMENT
THEME IN THE GREAT GATSBY

In *The Great Gatsby*, F. Scott Fitzgerald portrayed 1920s America as greedy, cynical, and rife with moral decay. Jay Gatsby's lavish weekly parties symbolize the reckless excesses of the Jazz Age. The growth of bootlegging and organized crime in reaction to Prohibition is symbolized by the character of Meyer Wolfsheim and by Gatsby's own ill-gotten wealth. Fitzgerald symbolized social divisions using geography. The "old money" aristocrats like the Buchanans lived on East Egg, while the "new money" bourgeois like Gatsby lived on West Egg. Fitzgerald also used weather, as many authors have, to reinforce narrative and emotional tones in the novel. Just as in *Romeo and Juliet*, where William Shakespeare set the confrontation of Tybalt and Mercutio and its deadly consequences on the hottest summer day under a burning sun, in *The Great Gatsby*, Fitzgerald did the same with Tom Wilson's deadly confrontation with Gatsby. Both works are ostensible love stories carrying socially critical themes about the destructiveness of pointless and misguided behaviors—family feuds in the former, pursuit of money in the latter.

> **Review Video: Thematic Development**
> Visit mometrix.com/academy and enter code: 576507

THEME IN LES MISÉRABLES

In Victor Hugo's novel *Les Misérables*, the overall metamorphosis of protagonist Jean Valjean from a cynical ex-convict into a noble benefactor demonstrates Hugo's theme of the importance of love and

compassion for others. Hugo also reflects this in more specific plot events. For example, Valjean's love for Cosette sustains him through many difficult periods and trying events. Hugo illustrates how love and compassion for others beget the same in them: Bishop Myriel's kindness to Valjean eventually inspires him to become honest. Years later, Valjean, as M. Madeleine, has rescued Fauchelevent from under a fallen carriage, Fauchelevent returns the compassionate act by giving Valjean sanctuary in the convent. M. Myriel's kindness also ultimately enables Valjean to rescue Cosette from the Thénardiers. Receiving Valjean's father-like love enables Cosette to fall in love with and marry Marius, and the love between Cosette and Marius enables the couple to forgive Valjean for his past crimes when they are revealed.

THEME IN "THE TELL-TALE HEART"

In one of his shortest stories, "The Tell-Tale Heart," Poe used economy of language to emphasize the murderer-narrator's obsessive focus on bare details like the victim's cataract-milky eye, the sound of a heartbeat, and insistence he is sane. The narrator begins by denying he is crazy, even citing his extreme agitation as proof of sanity. Contradiction is then extended: the narrator loves the old man, yet kills him. His motives are irrational—not greed or revenge, but to relieve the victim of his "evil eye." Because "eye" and "I" are homonyms, readers may infer that eye/I symbolizes the old man's identity, contradicting the killer's delusion that he can separate them. The narrator distances himself from the old man by perceiving his eye as separate, and dismembering his dead body. This backfires when he imagines the victim's heartbeat, which is really his own, just before he kills him and frequently afterward. Guilty and paranoid, he gives himself away. Poe predated Freud in exploring the paradox of killing those we love and the concept of projecting our own processes onto others.

THEME IN THE WORKS OF WILLIAM FAULKNER AND CHARLES DICKENS

William Faulkner contrasts the traditions of the antebellum South with the rapid changes of post-Civil War industrialization in his short story "A Rose for Emily." Living inside the isolated world of her house, Emily Grierson denies the reality of modern progress. Contradictorily, she is both a testament to time-honored history and a mysterious, eccentric, unfathomable burden. Faulkner portrays her with deathlike imagery even in life, comparing her to a drowned woman and referring to her skeleton. Emily symbolizes the Old South; as her social status is degraded, so is the antebellum social order. Like Miss Havisham in Charles Dickens' *Great Expectations,* Emily preserves her bridal bedroom, denying change and time's passage. Emily tries to control death through denial, shown in her necrophilia with her father's corpse and her killing of Homer Barron to stop him from leaving her, then also denying his death. Faulkner uses the motif of dust throughout to represent not only the decay of Emily, her house, and Old Southern traditions, but also how her secrets are obscured from others.

THEME IN MOBY-DICK

The great White Whale in *Moby-Dick* plays various roles to different characters. In Captain Ahab's obsessive, monomaniacal quest to kill it, the whale represents all evil, and Ahab believes it his duty and destiny to rid the world of it. Ishmael attempts through multiple scientific disciplines to understand the whale objectively, but fails—it is hidden underwater and mysterious to humans— reinforcing Melville's theme that humans can never know everything; here the whale represents the unknowable. Melville reverses white's usual connotation of purity in Ishmael's dread of white, associated with crashing waves, polar animals, albinos—all frightening and unnatural. White is often viewed as an absence of color, yet white light is the sum total of all colors in the spectrum. In the same way, white can signify both absence of meaning, and totality of meaning incomprehensible to humans. As a creature of nature, the whale also symbolizes how 19th-century white men's exploitative expansionistic actions were destroying the natural environment.

THEME IN THE OLD MAN AND THE SEA

Because of the old fisherman Santiago's struggle to capture a giant marlin, some people characterize Ernest Hemingway's *The Old Man and the Sea* as telling of man against nature. However, it can more properly be interpreted as telling of man's role as part of nature. Both man and fish are portrayed as brave, proud, and honorable. In Hemingway's world, all creatures, including humans, must either kill or be killed. Santiago reflects, "man can be destroyed but not defeated," following this principle in his life. As heroes are often created through their own deaths, Hemingway seems to believe that while being destroyed is inevitable, destruction enables living beings to transcend it by fighting bravely with honor and dignity. Hemingway echoes Romantic poet John Keats' contention that only immediately before death can we understand beauty as it is about to be destroyed. He also echoes ancient Greek and Roman myths and the Old Testament with the tragic flaw of overweening pride or overreaching. Like Icarus, Prometheus, and Adam and Eve, the old man "went out too far."

UNIVERSAL THEMES

The Old Testament book of Genesis, the Quran, and the Epic of Gilgamesh all contain flood stories. Versions differ somewhat, yet marketed similarities also exist. Genesis describes a worldwide flood, attributing it to God's decision that mankind, his creation, had become incontrovertibly wicked in spirit and must be destroyed for the world to start anew. The Quran describes the flood as regional, caused by Allah after sending Nuh (notice the similarity in name to Noah) as a messenger to his people to cease their evil. The Quran stipulates that Allah only destroys those who deny or ignore messages from his messengers. In the Gilgamesh poems Utnapishtim, like Noah, is instructed to build a ship to survive the flood. Both men also send out birds afterward as tests, using doves and a raven, though with different outcomes. Many historians and archeologists believe a Middle Eastern tidal wave was a real basis for these stories. However, their universal themes remain the same: the flood was seen as God's way of wiping out humans whose behavior had become ungodly.

THEME OF OVERREACHING

A popular theme throughout literature is the human trait of **reaching too far** or **presuming too much**. In Greek mythology, Daedalus constructed wings of feathers and wax that men might fly like birds. He permitted his son Icarus to try them, but cautioned the boy not to fly too close to the sun. The impetuous youth (in what psychologist David Elkind later named adolescence's myth of invincibility) ignored this, flying too close to the sun. The wax melted, the wings disintegrated, and Icarus fell into the sea and perished. In the Old Testament, God warned Adam and Eve not to eat fruit from the tree of knowledge of good and evil. Because they ignored this command, they were banished from Eden's eternal perfection, condemning them to mortality and suffering. The Romans were themselves examples of overreaching in their conquest and assimilation of most of the then-known world and their ultimate demise. In Christopher Marlowe's *Dr. Faustus* and Johann Wolfgang von Goethe's *Faust*, the protagonist sells his soul to the Devil for unlimited knowledge and success, ultimately leading to his own tragic end.

STORY VS. DISCOURSE

In terms of plot, "story" is the characters, places, and events originating in the author's mind, while "discourse" is how the author arranges and sequences events—which may be chronological or not. Story is imaginary; discourse is words on the page. Discourse allows a story to be told in different ways. One element of plot structure is relating events differently from the order in which they occurred. This is easily done with cause-and-effect; for example, in the sentence, "He died following a long illness," we know the illness preceded the death, but the death precedes the illness in words. In Kate Chopin's short story "The Story of an Hour" (1894), she tells some of the events out of chronological order, which has the effect of amplifying the surprise of the ending for the reader. Another element of plot structure is selection. Chopin omits some details, such as Mr. Mallard's trip home; this allows readers to be as surprised at his arrival as Mrs. Mallard is.

PLOT AND MEANING

Novelist E. M. Forster has made the distinction between story as relating a series of events, such as a king dying and then his queen dying, versus plot as establishing motivations for actions and causes for events, such as a king dying and then his queen dying from grief over his death. Thus, plot fulfills the function of helping readers understand cause-and-effect in events and underlying motivations in characters' actions, which in turn helps them understand life. This affects a work's meaning by supporting its ability to explain why things happen, why people do things, and ultimately the meaning of life. Some authors find that while story events convey meaning, they do not tell readers there is any one meaning in life or way of living, but rather are mental experiments with various meanings, enabling readers to explore. Hence stories may not necessarily be constructed to impose one definitive meaning, but rather to find some shape, direction, and meaning within otherwise random events.

CLASSIC ANALYSIS OF PLOT STRUCTURE

In *Poetics,* Aristotle defined plot as "the arrangement of the incidents." He meant not the story, but how it is structured for presentation. In tragedies, Aristotle found results driven by chains of cause and effect preferable to those driven by the protagonist's personality or character. He identified "unity of action" as necessary for a plot's wholeness, meaning its events must be internally connected, not episodic or relying on *deus ex machina* or other external intervention. A plot must have a beginning, middle, and end. Gustav Freytag adapted Aristotle's ideas into his Pyramid (1863). The beginning, today called the exposition, incentive, or inciting moment, emphasizes causes and de-emphasizes effects. Aristotle called the ensuing cause and effect *desis*, or tying up, today called complications which occur during the rising action. These culminate in a crisis or climax, Aristotle's *peripateia*. This occurs at the plot's middle, where cause and effect are both emphasized. The falling action, which Aristotle called the *lusis* or unraveling, is today called the dénouement. The resolution comes at the catastrophe, outcome, or end, when causes are emphasized and effects de-emphasized.

> **Review Video: Plot Line**
> Visit mometrix.com/academy and enter code: 944011

ANALYSIS OF PLOT STRUCTURES THROUGH RECURRING PATTERNS

Authors of fiction select characters, places, and events from their imaginations and arrange them to create a story that will affect their readers. One way to analyze plot structure is to compare and contrast different events in a story. For example, in Kate Chopin's "The Story of an Hour," a very simple but key pattern of repetition is the husband's leaving and then returning. Such patterns fulfill the symmetrical aspect that Aristotle said was required of sound plot structure. In James Baldwin's short story, "Sonny's Blues," the narrator is Sonny's brother. In an encounter with one of Sonny's old friends early in the story, the brother initially disregards his communication. In a subsequent flashback, Baldwin informs us that this was the same way he had treated Sonny. In Nathaniel Hawthorne's "Young Goodman Brown," a pattern is created by the protagonist's recurrent efforts not to go farther into the wood. In Herman Melville's "Bartleby the Scrivener" and in William Faulkner's "Barn Burning," patterns are also created by repetition such as Bartleby's repeated refusals and the history of barn-burning episodes, respectively.

LITERARY THEORIES AND CRITICISM AND INTERPRETATION

Literary theory includes ideas that guide readers through the process of interpreting literature. Literary theory, as a subject, encompasses several specific, focused theories that lead readers to interpret or analyze literature through the context of the theory using the subjects and elements it involves. Some commonly used and discussed literary theories include **postcolonial theory, gender and feminist theory, structuralism, new historicism, reader-response theory**, and **sociological criticism**.

- **Postcolonial theory** involves the historical and geographical context of a work and leads readers to consider how colonization informs the plot, characters, setting, and other elements in the work.
- **Gender and feminist theory** invites readers to interpret a text by looking at its treatment of and suggestions about women and a culture's treatment of women. As with most literary theories, this information can be clearly stated or strongly implied in a work, but it may also be gleaned through looking closely at symbols, characters, and plot elements in a work.
- **Structuralism** uses the structure and organization of a work and the foundations of language to examine how and what a text conveys about the human experience and how those findings connect to common human experiences.
- **New historicism** heavily relies on the cultural and historical context of a work, including when it was written, where the author lives or lived, the culture and history of that location, and other works from the same culture. New historical readings seek to examine these details to expose the ideologies of the location and culture that influenced the work.
- **Reader-response theory** uses the individual reader's response to the text and experience while reading the text to examine the meaning of the reader's relationship with the text and what that relationship suggests about the reader or the factors impacting their experience.
- **Sociological criticism** considers the societies that are relevant to a text. The author's society and any reader's society are important to the text, as sociological criticism seeks to uncover what the text implies or reveals about those societies. This method of criticism can also involve studying the presentation of a society within the text and applying it to the author's society or their other writings.

Reading Comprehension

UNDERSTANDING A PASSAGE

One of the most important skills in reading comprehension is the identification of **topics** and **main ideas**. There is a subtle difference between these two features. The topic is the subject of a text (i.e., what the text is all about). The main idea, on the other hand, is the most important point being made by the author. The topic is usually expressed in a few words at the most while the main idea often needs a full sentence to be completely defined. As an example, a short passage might be written on the topic of penguins, and the main idea could be written as *Penguins are different from other birds in many ways*. In most nonfiction writing, the topic and the main idea will be **stated directly** and often appear in a sentence at the very beginning or end of the text. When being tested on an understanding of the author's topic, you may be able to skim the passage for the general idea by reading only the first sentence of each paragraph. A body paragraph's first sentence is often—but not always—the main **topic sentence** which gives you a summary of the content in the paragraph.

However, there are cases in which the reader must figure out an **unstated** topic or main idea. In these instances, you must read every sentence of the text and try to come up with an overarching idea that is supported by each of those sentences.

Note: The main idea should not be confused with the thesis statement. While the main idea gives a brief, general summary of a text, the thesis statement provides a **specific perspective** on an issue that the author supports with evidence.

> **Review Video: <u>Topics and Main Ideas</u>**
> Visit mometrix.com/academy and enter code: 407801

Supporting details are smaller pieces of evidence that provide backing for the main point. In order to show that a main idea is correct or valid, an author must add details that prove their point. All texts contain details, but they are only classified as supporting details when they serve to reinforce some larger point. Supporting details are most commonly found in informative and persuasive texts. In some cases, they will be clearly indicated with terms like *for example* or *for instance*, or they will be enumerated with terms like *first*, *second*, and *last*. However, you need to be prepared for texts that do not contain those indicators. As a reader, you should consider whether the author's supporting details really back up his or her main point. Details can be factual and correct, yet they may not be **relevant** to the author's point. Conversely, details can be relevant, but be ineffective because they are based on opinion or assertions that cannot be proven.

> **Review Video: <u>Supporting Details</u>**
> Visit mometrix.com/academy and enter code: 396297

An example of a main idea is: *Giraffes live in the Serengeti of Africa*. A supporting detail about giraffes could be: *A giraffe in this region benefits from a long neck by reaching twigs and leaves on tall trees*. The main idea gives the general idea that the text is about giraffes. The supporting detail gives a specific fact about how the giraffes eat.

ORGANIZATION OF THE TEXT

The way a text is organized can help readers understand the author's intent and his or her conclusions. There are various ways to organize a text, and each one has a purpose and use. Usually, authors will organize information logically in a passage so the reader can follow and locate the

55

information within the text. However, since not all passages are written with the same logical structure, you need to be familiar with several different types of passage structure.

CHRONOLOGICAL

When using **chronological** order, the author presents information in the order that it happened. For example, biographies are typically written in chronological order. The subject's birth and childhood are presented first, followed by their adult life, and lastly the events leading up to the person's death.

CAUSE AND EFFECT

One of the most common text structures is **cause and effect**. A **cause** is an act or event that makes something happen, and an **effect** is the thing that happens as a result of the cause. A cause-and-effect relationship is not always explicit, but there are some terms in English that signal causes, such as *since, because,* and *due to*. Furthermore, terms that signal effects include *consequently, therefore, this leads to.* As an example, consider the sentence *Because the sky was clear, Ron did not bring an umbrella.* The cause is the clear sky, and the effect is that Ron did not bring an umbrella. However, readers may find that sometimes the cause-and-effect relationship will not be clearly noted. For instance, the sentence *He was late and missed the meeting* does not contain any signaling words, but the sentence still contains a cause (he was late) and an effect (he missed the meeting).

MULTIPLE EFFECTS

Be aware of the possibility for a single cause to have **multiple effects.** (e.g., *Single cause*: Because you left your homework on the table, your dog engulfed the assignment. *Multiple effects*: As a result, you receive a failing grade, your parents do not allow you to go out with your friends, you miss out on the new movie, and one of your classmates spoils it for you before you have another chance to watch it).

MULTIPLE CAUSES

Also, there is the possibility for a single effect to have **multiple causes.** (e.g., *Single effect*: Alan has a fever. *Multiple causes*: An unexpected cold front came through the area, and Alan forgot to take his multi-vitamin to avoid getting sick.) Additionally, an effect can in turn be the cause of another effect, in what is known as a cause-and-effect chain. (e.g., As a result of her disdain for procrastination, Lynn prepared for her exam. This led to her passing her test with high marks. Hence, her resume was accepted and her application was approved.)

CAUSE AND EFFECT IN PERSUASIVE ESSAYS

Persuasive essays, in which an author tries to make a convincing argument and change the minds of readers, usually include cause-and-effect relationships. However, these relationships should not always be taken at face value. Frequently, an author will assume a cause or take an effect for granted. To read a persuasive essay effectively, readers need to judge the cause-and-effect relationships that the author is presenting. For instance, imagine an author wrote the following: *The parking deck has been unprofitable because people would prefer to ride their bikes.* The relationship is clear: the cause is that people prefer to ride their bikes, and the effect is that the parking deck has been unprofitable. However, readers should consider whether this argument is conclusive. Perhaps

56

there are other reasons for the failure of the parking deck: a down economy, excessive fees, etc. Too often, authors present causal relationships as if they are fact rather than opinion. Readers should be on the alert for these dubious claims.

PROBLEM-SOLUTION

Some nonfiction texts are organized to **present a problem** followed by a solution. For this type of text, the problem is often explained before the solution is offered. In some cases, as when the problem is well known, the solution may be introduced briefly at the beginning. Other passages may focus on the solution, and the problem will be referenced only occasionally. Some texts will outline multiple solutions to a problem, leaving readers to choose among them. If the author has an interest or an allegiance to one solution, he or she may fail to mention or describe accurately some of the other solutions. Readers should be careful of the author's agenda when reading a problem-solution text. Only by understanding the author's perspective and interests can one develop a proper judgment of the proposed solution.

COMPARE AND CONTRAST

Many texts follow the **compare-and-contrast** model in which the similarities and differences between two ideas or things are explored. Analysis of the similarities between ideas is called **comparison**. In an ideal comparison, the author places ideas or things in an equivalent structure, i.e., the author presents the ideas in the same way. If an author wants to show the similarities between cricket and baseball, then he or she may do so by summarizing the equipment and rules for each game. Be mindful of the similarities as they appear in the passage and take note of any differences that are mentioned. Often, these small differences will only reinforce the more general similarity.

> **Review Video: Compare and Contrast Essays**
> Visit mometrix.com/academy and enter code: 798319

Thinking critically about ideas and conclusions can seem like a daunting task. One way to ease this task is to understand the basic elements of ideas and writing techniques. Looking at the ways different ideas relate to each other can be a good way for readers to begin their analysis. For instance, sometimes authors will write about two ideas that are in opposition to each other. Or, one author will provide his or her ideas on a topic, and another author may respond in opposition. The analysis of these opposing ideas is known as **contrast**. Contrast is often marred by the author's obvious partiality to one of the ideas. A discerning reader will be put off by an author who does not engage in a fair fight. In an analysis of opposing ideas, both ideas should be presented in clear and reasonable terms. If the author does prefer a side, you need to read carefully to determine the areas where the author shows or avoids this preference. In an analysis of opposing ideas, you should proceed through the passage by marking the major differences point by point with an eye that is looking for an explanation of each side's view. For instance, in an analysis of capitalism and communism, there is an importance in outlining each side's view on labor, markets, prices, personal responsibility, etc. Additionally, as you read through the passages, you should note whether the opposing views present each side in a similar manner.

SEQUENCE

Readers must be able to identify a text's **sequence**, or the order in which things happen. Often, when the sequence is very important to the author, the text is indicated with signal words like *first, then, next,* and *last*. However, a sequence can be merely implied and must be noted by the reader. Consider the sentence *He walked through the garden and gave water and fertilizer to the plants.* Clearly, the man did not walk through the garden before he collected water and fertilizer for the plants. So, the implied sequence is that he first collected water, then he collected fertilizer, next he walked through the garden, and last he gave water or fertilizer as necessary to the plants. Texts do not always proceed in an orderly sequence from first to last. Sometimes they begin at the end and start over at the beginning. As a reader, you can enhance your understanding of the passage by taking brief notes to clarify the sequence.

MAKING CONNECTIONS TO ENHANCE COMPREHENSION

Reading involves thinking. For good comprehension, readers make **text-to-self**, **text-to-text**, and **text-to-world connections**. Making connections helps readers understand text better and predict what might occur next based on what they already know, such as how characters in the story feel or what happened in another text. Text-to-self connections with the reader's life and experiences make literature more personally relevant and meaningful to readers. Readers can make connections before, during, and after reading—including whenever the text reminds them of something similar they have encountered in life or other texts. The genre, setting, characters, plot elements, literary structure and devices, and themes an author uses allow a reader to make connections to other works of literature or to people and events in their own lives. Venn diagrams and other graphic organizers help visualize connections. Readers can also make double-entry notes: key content, ideas, events, words, and quotations on one side, and the connections with these on the other.

SUMMARIZING LITERATURE TO SUPPORT COMPREHENSION

When reading literature, especially demanding works, **summarizing** helps readers identify important information and organize it in their minds. They can also identify themes, problems, and solutions, and can sequence the story. Readers can summarize before, during, and after they read. They should use their own words, as they do when describing a personal event or giving directions. Previewing a text's organization before reading by examining the book cover, table of contents, and illustrations also aids summarizing. Making notes of key words and ideas in a graphic organizer while reading can benefit readers in the same way. Graphic organizers are another useful method; readers skim the text to determine main ideas and then narrow the list with the aid of the organizer. Unimportant details should be omitted in summaries. Summaries can be organized using description, problem-solution, comparison-contrast, sequence, main ideas, or cause-and-effect.

> **Review Video: Summarizing Text**
> Visit mometrix.com/academy and enter code: 172903

PARAPHRASING

Paraphrasing is another method that the reader can use to aid in comprehension. When paraphrasing, one puts what they have read into their own words by rephrasing what the author has written, or one "translates" all of what the author shared into their own words by including as many details as they can.

Making Predictions and Inferences

MAKING PREDICTIONS

When we read literature, **making predictions** about what will happen in the writing reinforces our purpose for reading and prepares us mentally. A **prediction** is a guess about what will happen next. Readers constantly make predictions based on what they have read and what they already know. We can make predictions before we begin reading and during our reading. Consider the following sentence: *Staring at the computer screen in shock, Kim blindly reached over for the brimming glass of water on the shelf to her side.* The sentence suggests that Kim is distracted, and that she is not looking at the glass that she is going to pick up. So, a reader might predict that Kim is going to knock over the glass. Of course, not every prediction will be accurate: perhaps Kim will pick the glass up cleanly. Nevertheless, the author has certainly created the expectation that the water might be spilled.

As we read on, we can test the accuracy of our predictions, revise them in light of additional reading, and confirm or refute our predictions. Predictions are always subject to revision as the reader acquires more information. A reader can make predictions by observing the title and illustrations; noting the structure, characters, and subject; drawing on existing knowledge relative to the subject; and asking "why" and "who" questions. Connecting reading to what we already know enables us to learn new information and construct meaning. For example, before third-graders read a book about Johnny Appleseed, they may start a KWL chart—a list of what they *Know*, what they *Want* to know or learn, and what they have *Learned* after reading. Activating existing background knowledge and thinking about the text before reading improves comprehension.

> **Review Video: Predictive Reading**
> Visit mometrix.com/academy and enter code: 437248

Test-taking tip: To respond to questions requiring future predictions, your answers should be based on evidence of past or present behavior and events.

EVALUATING PREDICTIONS

When making predictions, readers should be able to explain how they developed their prediction. One way readers can defend their thought process is by citing textual evidence. Textual evidence to evaluate reader predictions about literature includes specific synopses of the work, paraphrases of the work or parts of it, and direct quotations from the work. These references to the text must support the prediction by indicating, clearly or unclearly, what will happen later in the story. A text may provide these indications through literary devices such as foreshadowing. Foreshadowing is anything in a text that gives the reader a hint about what is to come by emphasizing the likelihood of an event or development. Foreshadowing can occur through descriptions, exposition, and dialogue. Foreshadowing in dialogue usually occurs when a character gives a warning or expresses a strong feeling that a certain event will occur. Foreshadowing can also occur through irony. However, unlike other forms of foreshadowing, the events that seem the most likely are the opposite of what actually happens. Instances of foreshadowing and irony can be summarized, paraphrased, or quoted to defend a reader's prediction.

> **Review Video: Textual Evidence for Predictions**
> Visit mometrix.com/academy and enter code: 261070

DRAWING CONCLUSIONS FROM INFERENCES

Inferences about literary text are logical conclusions that readers make based on their observations and previous knowledge. An inference is based on both what is found in a passage or a story and what is known from personal experience. For instance, a story may say that a character is frightened and can hear howling in the distance. Based on both what is in the text and personal knowledge, it is a logical conclusion that the character is frightened because he hears the sound of wolves. A good inference is supported by the information in a passage.

IMPLICIT AND EXPLICIT INFORMATION

By inferring, readers construct meanings from text that are personally relevant. By combining their own schemas or concepts and their background information pertinent to the text with what they read, readers interpret it according to both what the author has conveyed and their own unique perspectives. Inferences are different from **explicit information**, which is clearly stated in a passage. Authors do not always explicitly spell out every meaning in what they write; many meanings are implicit. Through inference, readers can comprehend implied meanings in the text, and also derive personal significance from it, making the text meaningful and memorable to them. Inference is a natural process in everyday life. When readers infer, they can draw conclusions about what the author is saying, predict what may reasonably follow, amend these predictions as they continue to read, interpret the import of themes, and analyze the characters' feelings and motivations through their actions.

EXAMPLE OF DRAWING CONCLUSIONS FROM INFERENCES

Read the excerpt and decide why Jana finally relaxed.

> Jana loved her job, but the work was very demanding. She had trouble relaxing. She called a friend, but she still thought about work. She ordered a pizza, but eating it did not help. Then, her kitten jumped on her lap and began to purr. Jana leaned back and began to hum a little tune. She felt better.

You can draw the conclusion that Jana relaxed because her kitten jumped on her lap. The kitten purred, and Jana leaned back and hummed a tune. Then she felt better. The excerpt does not explicitly say that this is the reason why she was able to relax. The text leaves the matter unclear, but the reader can infer or make a "best guess" that this is the reason she is relaxing. This is a logical conclusion based on the information in the passage. It is the best conclusion a reader can make based on the information he or she has read. Inferences are based on the information in a passage, but they are not directly stated in the passage.

Test-taking tip: While being tested on your ability to make correct inferences, you must look for **contextual clues**. An answer can be true, but not the best or most correct answer. The contextual clues will help you find the answer that is the **best answer** out of the given choices. Be careful in your reading to understand the context in which a phrase is stated. When asked for the implied meaning of a statement made in the passage, you should immediately locate the statement and read the **context** in which the statement was made. Also, look for an answer choice that has a similar phrase to the statement in question.

Review Video: Inference Visit mometrix.com/academy and enter code: 379203 **Review Video: Identifying Logical Conclusions** Visit mometrix.com/academy and enter code: 281653

Interactions with Texts

PURPOSES FOR WRITING

In order to be an effective reader, one must pay attention to the author's **position** and **purpose**. Even those texts that seem objective and impartial, like textbooks, have a position and bias. Readers need to take these positions into account when considering the author's message. When an author uses emotional language or clearly favors one side of an argument, his or her position is clear. However, the author's position may be evident not only in what he or she writes, but also in what he or she doesn't write. In a normal setting, a reader would want to review some other texts on the same topic in order to develop a view of the author's position. If this was not possible, then you would want to at least acquire some background about the author. However, since you are in the middle of an exam and the only source of information is the text, you should look for language and argumentation that seems to indicate a particular stance on the subject.

> **Review Video: Author's Position**
> Visit mometrix.com/academy and enter code: 827954

Usually, identifying the author's **purpose** is easier than identifying his or her position. In most cases, the author has no interest in hiding his or her purpose. A text that is meant to entertain, for instance, should be written to please the reader. Most narratives, or stories, are written to entertain, though they may also inform or persuade. Informative texts are easy to identify, while the most difficult purpose of a text to identify is persuasion because the author has an interest in making this purpose hard to detect. When a reader discovers that the author is trying to persuade, he or she should be skeptical of the argument. For this reason, persuasive texts often try to establish an entertaining tone and hope to amuse the reader into agreement. On the other hand, an informative tone may be implemented to create an appearance of authority and objectivity.

An author's purpose is evident often in the organization of the text (e.g., section headings in bold font points to an informative text). However, you may not have such organization available to you in your exam. Instead, if the author makes his or her main idea clear from the beginning, then the likely purpose of the text is to inform. If the author begins by making a claim and provides various arguments to support that claim, then the purpose is probably to persuade. If the author tells a story or wants to gain the reader's attention more than to push a particular point or deliver information, then his or her purpose is most likely to entertain. As a reader, you must judge authors on how well they accomplish their purpose. In other words, you need to consider the type of passage (e.g., technical, persuasive, etc.) that the author has written and if the author has followed the requirements of the passage type.

> **Review Video: Purpose**
> Visit mometrix.com/academy and enter code: 511819

MAKING LOGICAL CONCLUSIONS ABOUT A PASSAGE

A reader should always be drawing conclusions from the text. Sometimes conclusions are **implied** from written information, and other times the information is **stated directly** within the passage. One should always aim to draw conclusions from information stated within a passage, rather than to draw them from mere implications. At times an author may provide some information and then describe a counterargument. Readers should be alert for direct statements that are subsequently rejected or weakened by the author. Furthermore, you should always read through the entire passage before drawing conclusions. Many readers are trained to expect the author's conclusions at either the beginning or the end of the passage, but many texts do not adhere to this format.

61

Drawing conclusions from information implied within a passage requires confidence on the part of the reader. **Implications** are things that the author does not state directly, but readers can assume based on what the author does say. Consider the following passage: *I stepped outside and opened my umbrella. By the time I got to work, the cuffs of my pants were soaked.* The author never states that it is raining, but this fact is clearly implied. Conclusions based on implication must be well supported by the text. In order to draw a solid conclusion, readers should have **multiple pieces of evidence**. If readers have only one piece, they must be assured that there is no other possible explanation than their conclusion. A good reader will be able to draw many conclusions from information implied by the text, which will be a great help on the exam.

DRAWING CONCLUSIONS

A common type of inference that a reader has to make is **drawing a conclusion**. The reader makes this conclusion based on the information provided within a text. Certain facts are included to help a reader come to a specific conclusion. For example, a story may open with a man trudging through the snow on a cold winter day, dragging a sled behind him. The reader can logically **infer** from the setting of the story that the man is wearing heavy winter clothes in order to stay warm. Information is implied based on the setting of a story, which is why **setting** is an important element of the text. If the same man in the example was trudging down a beach on a hot summer day, dragging a surf board behind him, the reader would assume that the man is not wearing heavy clothes. The reader makes inferences based on their own experiences and the information presented to them in the story.

Test-taking tip: When asked to identify a conclusion that may be drawn, look for critical "hedge" phrases, such as *likely*, *may*, *can*, and *will often*, among many others. When you are being tested on this knowledge, remember the question that writers insert into these hedge phrases to cover every possibility. Often an answer will be wrong simply because there is no room for exception. Extreme positive or negative answers (such as always or never) are usually not correct. When answering these questions, the reader **should not** use any outside knowledge that is not gathered directly or reasonably inferred from the passage. Correct answers can be derived straight from the passage.

EXAMPLE

Read the following sentence from *Little Women* by Louisa May Alcott and draw a conclusion based upon the information presented:

> *You know the reason Mother proposed not having any presents this Christmas was because it is going to be a hard winter for everyone; and she thinks we ought not to spend money for pleasure, when our men are suffering so in the army.*

Based on the information in the sentence, the reader can conclude, or **infer**, that the men are away at war while the women are still at home. The pronoun *our* gives a clue to the reader that the character is speaking about men she knows. In addition, the reader can assume that the character is speaking to a brother or sister, since the term "Mother" is used by the character while speaking to another person. The reader can also come to the conclusion that the characters celebrate Christmas, since it is mentioned in the **context** of the sentence. In the sentence, the mother is presented as an unselfish character who is opinionated and thinks about the wellbeing of other people.

> **Review Video: Drafting Conclusions**
> Visit mometrix.com/academy and enter code: 209408

COMPARING TWO STORIES

When presented with two different stories, there will be **similarities** and **differences** between the two. A reader needs to make a list, or other graphic organizer, of the points presented in each story. Once the reader has written down the main point and supporting points for each story, the two sets of ideas can be compared. The reader can then present each idea and show how it is the same or different in the other story. This is called **comparing and contrasting ideas**.

The reader can compare ideas by stating, for example: "In Story 1, the author believes that humankind will one day land on Mars, whereas in Story 2, the author believes that Mars is too far away for humans to ever step foot on." Note that the two viewpoints are different in each story that the reader is comparing. A reader may state that: "Both stories discussed the likelihood of humankind landing on Mars." This statement shows how the viewpoint presented in both stories is based on the same topic, rather than how each viewpoint is different. The reader will complete a comparison of two stories with a conclusion.

> **Review Video: Comparing Two Stories**
> Visit mometrix.com/academy and enter code: 833765

OUTLINING A PASSAGE

As an aid to drawing conclusions, **outlining** the information contained in the passage should be a familiar skill to readers. An effective outline will reveal the structure of the passage and will lead to solid conclusions. An effective outline will have a title that refers to the basic subject of the text, though the title does not need to restate the main idea. In most outlines, the main idea will be the first major section. Each major idea in the passage will be established as the head of a category. For instance, the most common outline format calls for the main ideas of the passage to be indicated with Roman numerals. In an effective outline of this kind, each of the main ideas will be represented by a Roman numeral and none of the Roman numerals will designate minor details or secondary ideas. Moreover, all supporting ideas and details should be placed in the appropriate place on the outline. An outline does not need to include every detail listed in the text, but it should feature all of those that are central to the argument or message. Each of these details should be listed under the corresponding main idea.

> **Review Video: Outlining**
> Visit mometrix.com/academy and enter code: 584445

USING GRAPHIC ORGANIZERS

Ideas from a text can also be organized using **graphic organizers**. A graphic organizer is a way to simplify information and take key points from the text. A graphic organizer such as a timeline may have an event listed for a corresponding date on the timeline, while an outline may have an event listed under a key point that occurs in the text. Each reader needs to create the type of graphic organizer that works the best for him or her in terms of being able to recall information from a story. Examples include a spider-map, which takes a main idea from the story and places it in a bubble with supporting points branching off the main idea. An outline is useful for diagramming the main and supporting points of the entire story, and a Venn diagram compares and contrasts characteristics of two or more ideas.

> **Review Video: Graphic Organizers**
> Visit mometrix.com/academy and enter code: 665513

SUMMARIZING

A helpful tool is the ability to **summarize** the information that you have read in a paragraph or passage format. This process is similar to creating an effective outline. First, a summary should accurately define the main idea of the passage, though the summary does not need to explain this main idea in exhaustive detail. The summary should continue by laying out the most important supporting details or arguments from the passage. All of the significant supporting details should be included, and none of the details included should be irrelevant or insignificant. Also, the summary should accurately report all of these details. Too often, the desire for brevity in a summary leads to the sacrifice of clarity or accuracy. Summaries are often difficult to read because they omit all of the graceful language, digressions, and asides that distinguish great writing. However, an effective summary should communicate the same overall message as the original text.

EVALUATING A PASSAGE

It is important to understand the logical conclusion of the ideas presented in an informational text. **Identifying a logical conclusion** can help you determine whether you agree with the writer or not. Coming to this conclusion is much like making an inference: the approach requires you to combine the information given by the text with what you already know and make a logical conclusion. If the author intended for the reader to draw a certain conclusion, then you can expect the author's argumentation and detail to be leading in that direction.

One way to approach the task of drawing conclusions is to make brief **notes** of all the points made by the author. When the notes are arranged on paper, they may clarify the logical conclusion. Another way to approach conclusions is to consider whether the reasoning of the author raises any pertinent questions. Sometimes you will be able to draw several conclusions from a passage. On occasion these will be conclusions that were never imagined by the author. Therefore, be aware that these conclusions must be **supported directly by the text**.

EVALUATION OF SUMMARIES

A summary of a literary passage is a condensation in the reader's own words of the passage's main points. Several guidelines can be used in evaluating a summary. The summary should be complete yet concise. It should be accurate, balanced, fair, neutral, and objective, excluding the reader's own opinions or reactions. It should reflect in similar proportion how much each point summarized was covered in the original passage. Summary writers should include tags of attribution, like "Macaulay argues that" to reference the original author whose ideas are represented in the summary. Summary writers should not overuse quotations; they should only quote central concepts or phrases they cannot precisely convey in words other than those of the original author. Another aspect of evaluating a summary is considering whether it can stand alone as a coherent, unified composition. In addition, evaluation of a summary should include whether its writer has cited the original source of the passage they have summarized so that readers can find it.

Language and Dialect

DIVERSITY AND SITUATIONAL NATURE OF LANGUAGE

Language is a diverse tool that allows people to communicate. However, language is often impacted and molded by the culture that uses it. This can make it difficult to learn and use a new language, since not all native speakers of the language will use it or interpret it the same way. For example, English is spoken all over America, but Americans in various regions of the country speak using different **dialects**. Other differences in speech include **accents** and **rhythm of speech**. Language is also manipulated by situations. Some terms and phrases have multiple meanings. A word's meaning often depends on the **context** in which the word or phrase is used, meaning that non-native speakers must learn to interpret situations to understand messages.

FACTORS OF LANGUAGE AND COMMUNICATION

INFLUENCES ON LANGUAGE

While dialect and diction are heavily influenced by an individual's culture and the location and history of the place they live, other personal factors can also impact language. A person's ethnicity, religious beliefs or background, and gender can influence the way they use and understand language. **Ethnicity** impacts language by incorporating a group's communication norms into an individual's speech and behavior. These norms may affect a speaker's tone, volume, or pace. These factors may lead others outside of that group to misinterpret the speaker's message, depending on their understanding of how those factors are used in speech. A person's **religious beliefs** can also affect their use of language. Religious beliefs and practices may lead an individual to abstain from using certain terms and may change the context in which a speaker uses specific words, or change their understanding of the word's usage. Additionally, a person may use language differently depending on their gender. **Gender's** influence on communication varies by region and industry. A region or industry's treatment of gender roles often impacts language use among its members. This can lead members of one gender group to be more assertive or submissive or to use different terms and phrases.

CULTURE AND COMMUNICATION

Individuals from different countries and cultures communicate differently. Not only do many people speak different languages, but they also speak using different inflections, volumes, tones, and dialects. These factors can have a significant impact on communication, even if the communicators speak the same language. In different cultures, certain behaviors are associated with different meanings and implications. When communicators from different cultures have a conversation, these expectations and associations may lead to misunderstanding. For example, Americans are considered to be louder and more demonstrative than people from other countries. Someone from a country where people speak more quietly who is not aware of this characterization may perceive an American's volume or large gestures as an indication of anger, when in reality, the American speaker is calm. The American may similarly perceive the other person as sad or shy due to their quiet voice, when the speaker is actually happy and comfortable in the conversation. Awareness of these factors and effects promotes respect for others and helps speakers understand the reasons for differences in communication, rather than allowing these differences to create division or conflict.

LANGUAGE VS. DIALECT

Languages are distinct and structured forms of verbal communication. Languages have cohesive sets of rules and words that are shared between the majority of that language's users. The main identifier of a language is that members of one language group are incapable of communicating fluently with members of another language group. New languages are formed as different dialects grow further apart until the members of each dialect can no longer innately communicate with each other.

Dialects are subsets of languages that do not violate the rules of the language as a whole, but which vary from other dialects in vocabulary usage, grammar forms, pronunciation, and spelling. Two major groupings of dialects are American and British English. Most American English and British English speakers can communicate with relative ease with one another, though the pronunciation, vocabulary (torch vs. flashlight; trunk vs. boot), spelling (meter vs. metre; color vs. colour), and grammar (in American English, collective nouns are always considered singular, but can be singular or plural in British English).

DEVELOPMENT OF DIALECTS OVER TIME

Dialects are formed primarily through the influences of location and time, but can be the result of other elements of **social stratification** as well (economic, ethnic, religious, etc.). As one group of a language's speakers is separated from another, in British and American English speakers for example, the language develops in isolated locations at the same time, resulting in distinct dialects. Language changes continuously over time as new words and phrases are adopted and others are phased out. Eventually, these small changes result culminate into enough grammar and vocabulary changes that the speakers of the distinct dialects cannot easily communicate with one another. The dialects can then be recognized as distinct languages.

USE OF DIALECT IN MEDIA

Literary authors often use dialect when writing dialogue to illustrate the social and geographical backgrounds of specific characters, which supports character development. For example, in *The Adventures of Huckleberry Finn* (1885), Mark Twain's novel is written in the dialect of a young, uneducated, white, Southern character, opening with this sentence: "You don't know about me without you have read a book by the name of The Adventures of Tom Sawyer, but that ain't no matter." Twain uses a different and exaggerated dialect to represent the speech of the African-American slave Jim: "We's safe, Huck, we's safe! Jump up and crack yo' heels. Dat's de good ole Cairo at las', I jis knows it."

In *To Kill a Mockingbird,* author Harper Lee used dialect in the characters' dialogue to portray an uneducated boy in the American South: "Reckon I have. Almost died the first year I come to school and et them pecans—folks say he pizened 'em." Lee also uses many Southern regional expressions, such as "right stove up," "What in the sam holy hill?", "sit a spell," "fess" (meaning "confess"), "jim-dandy," and "hush your fussing." These contribute to Lee's characterization of the people she describes, who live in a small town in Alabama circa the 1930s. In *Wuthering Heights* (1847), Emily Bronte reproduces Britain's 18th–19th-century Yorkshire dialect in the speech of servant Joseph: "Running after t'lads, as usuald!... If I war yah, maister, I'd just slam t'boards i' their faces all on 'em, gentle and simple! Never a day ut yah're off, but yon cat o' Linton comes sneaking hither; and Miss Nelly, shoo's a fine lass!"

DIALECT VS. DICTION

When written as characters' dialogue in literary works, dialect represents the particular pronunciation, grammar, and figurative expressions used by certain groups of people based on their geographic region, social class, and cultural background. For example, when a character says, "There's gold up in them thar hills," the author is using dialect to add to the characterization of that individual. Diction is more related to individual characters than to groups of people. The way in which a specific character speaks, including his or her choice of words, manner of expressing

66

himself or herself, and use of grammar all represent individual types of diction. For example, two characters in the same novel might describe the same action or event using different diction: One says "I'm heading uptown for the evening," and the other says "I'm going out for a night on the town." These convey the same literal meaning, but due to their variations in diction, the speakers are expressing themselves in slightly different ways.

> **Review Video: Dialogue, Paradox, and Dialect**
> Visit mometrix.com/academy and enter code: 684341

INFLUENCES ON REGIONAL DIALECT

Linguistic researchers have identified regional variations in vocabulary choices, which have evolved because of differences in local climates and how they influence human behaviors. For example, in the Southern United States, the Linguistic Atlas of the Gulf States (LAGS) Project by Dr. Lee Pederson of Emory University discovered and documented that people living in the northern or Upland section of the Piedmont plateau region call the fungal infection commonly known as athlete's foot "toe itch," but people living in the southern or Lowland section call it "ground itch." The explanation for this difference is that in the north, temperatures are cooler and people wear shoes accordingly, so they associate the itching with the feet in their description, but in the south, temperatures are hotter and people often went barefoot, so they associated the itching with the ground that presumably transmitted the infection.

USING DIALECT IN WRITING

Dialect is most appropriate for informal or creative writing. Using dialectal writing when communicating casually or informally, such as in a text message or a quick email to a peer, is acceptable. However, in academic and professional contexts, writing using indications of dialect is inappropriate and often unacceptable. If the audience includes individuals who have a higher rank than the author, or authority over the author, it is best not to write in a way that suggests a dialect.

World Literature

AMERICAN LITERARY PERIODS
DARK ROMANTICS

In American literature, a group of late Romantic writers are recognized as **Dark Romantics**. These authors' works may be associated with both the Romantic and Gothic movements. These works emphasize nature and emotion, aligning them with Romanticism, and include dark themes and tones, aligning them with Gothic literature. However, these works do not all feature the historically inspired characteristics of Gothic literature, and their morals or outcomes more closely resemble those of Romantic literature. The Dark Romantics include writers such as Edgar Allan Poe, Nathaniel Hawthorne, Emily Dickinson, and Herman Melville.

TRANSCENDENTALISM

Transcendentalism was a smaller movement that occurred alongside the American Romantic movement. The **transcendentalists** shared the Romantic emphasis on emotion and also focused heavily on how a person experiences life through their senses. They extended these sentiments to suggest that through embracing one's senses, an individual could transcend, or experience a state of being above physical humanity. They also extended the Romantic emphasis on subjectivity through their praise of self-sufficiency, as exemplified through Ralph Waldo Emerson's *Self-Reliance*. Emerson was a prominent transcendentalist. His writings included an essay titled *Nature*, which explains a progression from the use of the senses to the achievement of transcendence. Transcendentalist literature includes several essays that discuss the value of the senses and emotions or the process of transcendence. Transcendentalists also wrote poetry that includes the frequent use of imagery, metaphors, and references to nature. These elements reflect the ideas of transcendentalism and create a resemblance to the alleged experience of transcendence. Ralph Waldo Emerson, Henry David Thoreau, and Walt Whitman were all prominent writers in this movement.

COLONIAL AMERICA

The **colonial era** in America was influenced by immigration from England to what is now New England. These immigrants were mainly Puritans who centered their society in New England on their religious beliefs, allowing those beliefs to inform all aspects of their lives. This is apparent in the literature of the time, as much of it includes essays and sermons that discuss religion or the way the Puritans believed one should live and conduct themselves. Colonial literature also includes many poems, and these works also discuss or reference religious ideas and themes. There was not much fiction written in Colonial America, as most of the literature was written to inform or persuade.

ROMANTIC PERIOD

The **American Romantic** movement is also known as the American Renaissance. This movement yielded several notable American writers and works that began characterizing American literature and differentiating it from British literature. This literature, written after the American Revolutionary War and until the end of the Civil War, praised individualism and featured an expression of national pride and patriotism. The transcendentalists' extreme ideas about self-sufficiency and subjectivity reiterated this individualism, and their recommendations about society and its structure furthered the separation of American literature from British literature. While this period shaped the definition of American literature, it is criticized for featuring a narrow view of American politics and social issues at the time, as well as promoting a small group of similar writers.

HARLEM RENAISSANCE

The **Harlem Renaissance** took place in America during the 1920s and 1930s. The changing economy and opportunities led African Americans in the south to seek new lifestyles in other parts of America at the beginning of the 20th century. Many moved to Harlem, a small area in New York City. This group of African Americans yielded highly influential scholarly and artistic works, including poetry, fiction, music, and plays. The Harlem Renaissance marked an opportunity for these intellectuals and artists, who were largely ignored in the aftermath of the Civil War, to use their talents and express themselves through their works. While artists often featured personal expression in their works, the Harlem Renaissance was unique in its volume of culturally expressive works. This cultural expression and the movement's main ideas also contributed to the Civil Rights movement by promoting a spirit of unity among African Americans. The Harlem Renaissance eventually ended in the wake of the stock market crash in 1929. As the Great Depression began, financial support for the arts dwindled, making it difficult for many artists to succeed financially. Some members of the Harlem Renaissance who influenced American literature include Langston Hughes, Zora Neale Hurston, and Paul Robeson.

BRITISH LITERARY PERIODS

NEOCLASSICAL

The **British Neoclassical** period began in the middle of the 17th century and ended in the late 18th century. The latter part of the movement also took place alongside the Enlightenment, a period of scientific discovery and study that influenced many Western cultures. The Enlightenment's concern with intellectual pursuits and improvement increased discussions of introspection, or an individual's analysis of their own behavior, thoughts, and self. These ideas also affected society in England, as they contributed to a general attitude of complacency and a desire to ignore the past. The period saw a slightly increased acceptance of female writers, as their works were viewed as a method of self-reflection and improvement. The changes in British society allowed several new forms of literature to gain popularity and acceptance, usually for their introspective qualities. Essays, diaries, and letters all displayed the author's thoughts and experience, aligning them with the culture's values. Novels also gained popularity, as many were fictional diaries or epistolary novels. Journalism flourished during the Neoclassical period, leading to the creation of the newspaper. Literary criticism also gained popularity, though it was used to criticize an author and their style rather than examine or analyze the content of the work.

VICTORIAN

The **Victorian Era** in England was influenced by a variety of events and ideas, many of which were influenced by the Victorians' economy. The Industrial Revolution in England changed the circumstances of work for the Victorians. The changing industries and lack of labor laws led to several problems and a wide division between Victorian social classes. These factors inspired and saturated much of Victorian literature. Many novels' plots and characters were heavily influenced by social and economic issues, and many poems referenced and criticized specific events that occurred during this period.

While the structure of Victorian society was a major influence on literature, there were other popular topics that appeared in literature. Topics like evolution, psychology, and colonization frequently appeared in Victorian literature, reflecting the concerns and interests of the Victorian culture. The Victorian society was also characterized by a strict moral code that supported the view of women as homemakers and criticized the idea of female writers. Not only did this affect the portrayal of women in literature, but it also led some female novelists, such as the Bronte sisters, to write under a pseudonym and present their works as having been written by a man. Victorian literature also popularized forms of literature, including the novel and the dramatic monologue, a

69

poetic form developed by Robert Browning. Victorian writers include Charles Dickens, Oscar Wilde, Elizabeth Barrett Browning, Emily Bronte, Matthew Arnold, and Thomas Hardy.

WORLD LITERARY CHARACTERISTICS AND PERIODS

While many other nations shared literary movements with America and England, there are numerous literary movements that are unique to other countries and cultures. Some of these literary movements can be understood as variations of movements like Romanticism or modernism, since they occurred at similar times and feature similar elements, but the political and cultural events of each country shaped their version of each movement. Most regions also have some type of mythology, and while different mythologies have similar characters and events, each region's mythology is unique and significant to the region's literature. Another common feature of world literature is colonialism. Many nations are former colonies of European countries, and the effects of colonization are present in modern literature from countries worldwide, making it a key feature of many regions' body of literature.

AFRICAN LITERATURE

Literature from some cultures was not recorded until the 19th century, causing any movements and trends to be informed by ideas told aloud. This is true of African literature, where stories and ideas were spoken and passed down through the generations. Early African poetry was often metaphorical, structured or written to form a paradox, and included a riddle or puzzling statement. Proverbs and didactic tales were also told frequently, reflecting the dominant religions in a given region and time period. These poems and stories also reflect the variety of languages spoken in Africa and the shifts in each language's usage. Early African literature, once people began writing it down, included stories and proverbs that had been passed down, translations of religious texts, and descriptions of the way of life in different African cultures or groups. These cultures and the events specific to each of them produce a unique body of literature that places emphasis on certain topics and ideas. For example, much of the modern literature written in South Africa discusses politics and issues of race, since the country's history is characterized by events and movements that revolved around these topics.

ASIAN LITERATURE

Asian literature features writings from several different countries and languages and has spanned many centuries. Many popular forms of writing have come from Asia, such as the haiku. A couple of significant literary movements include The Hungry Generation in South Asia and the Misty Poets in China. The Hungry Generation is a literary movement involving literature written in the Bengali language, spoken mainly in West Bengal and Bangladesh. The literature is characterized by unique and innovative writing, which impacted the use of figurative language in the region. The Hungry Generation also discussed cultural issues, particularly colonization in the region, and many participants were arrested for their work. The Misty Poets in China were characterized by their expressive use of abstractions. Their name, Misty Poets, comes from their writings, which were difficult to interpret due to their use of abstract language and ambiguity. This movement was partly inspired by the Misty Poets' distaste for literary realism, though its influence is detectable within their poetry. Many of the Misty Poets were punished for their poetry, since the poetry of this movement was also politically critical.

LATIN AMERICAN LITERATURE

Latin American literature has several literary movements, many of which occurred near the same time as American and British literary movements and share ideas and trends with their English counterparts. Despite these similarities, each of these movements is distinguishable as its own movement with unique impacts of Latin American literature. By the 17th century, written language

70

was in use in Mexico, and Latin American literary trends and figures had been recognized. During the 18th century, Latin American literature featured a variety of ideas and themes within each form of literature. By the 19th century, literary themes were more unified throughout popular Latin American literature. In the early 19th century, Latin American literature embraced the Romantic movement as it came to an end in England and the United States. Several Latin American countries were also fighting for independence during this time, amplifying the Romantic idea of national pride and identity.

In the wake of the Romantic movement, Latin American literature introduced the unique *Modernismo* movement, which yielded a large volume of poetry and is characterized by the use of whimsical imagery and discussions of spiritual ideas. Following *Modernismo* was the *Vanguardia* movement, which was created to introduce diversity within Latin American literature after modernism permeated the literature of the time. *Vanguardia* involved writers taking risks in their writing and breaking the mold from typical Latin American literature. In the 20th century, *Estridentismo* followed the *Vanguardia* movement, marrying the *Vanguardia* movement with the European Avant-Garde movement. Other 20th century movements functioned similarly by adapting literary movements from other regions to suit the themes and trends in Latin American literature, reflect Latin American cultures, and set their literature apart from other cultures.

Literary Periods and Movements

OLD ENGLISH

The English language developed over a long period of time through interactions between different groups in Europe, including the Romans, the Germans, and the Celtics. The Anglo-Saxons, a group that left what is now Germany and settled in England, further established the English language by using what is now called **Old English**. While Old English laid foundations for modern English, its usage fundamentally differs from the way English is used today. For example, Old English relied on inflections to create meaning, placing little importance on the order of the words in the sentence. Its use of verbs and tenses also differs from modern English grammar. The Anglo-Saxons also used kennings, or compound words that functioned as figurative language.

Old English, as a language influenced by several cultures, had dialects from its inception. Differences in usage also came from the division between secular and religious cultures. This division heavily influenced Old English literature, as most of the literature from the time is categorized according to the set of beliefs it reflects. Most of the influential literature of the time includes riddles, poems, or translations of religious texts. Surviving Old English poetry mainly discusses real heroes and battles or provides a narrative about a fictional hero. Many of these fictional poems are considered *lays*, or *lais*, which are narrative poems that are structured using couplets of lines containing eight syllables each. The translations were often of passages from the Christian Bible, adaptations of Biblical passages, or copies of Christian hymns. Old English persisted until the 12th century, where it was eventually replaced with Middle English. Influential literature from this period includes *Beowulf*, "The Wanderer," "The Wife's Lament," and "The Seafarer."

MIDDLE ENGLISH

Old English was replaced by **Middle English**, which was used from the 12th century to the 16th century. Old English was not governed by a consistent set of grammatical rules until the Norse people, their language, and its structure influenced the integration of grammar into English, leading to Middle English. Middle English relied less on inflections than Old English, instead creating variations by using affixes and synonyms. The development of grammar was further facilitated by the printing press, which made it easier for writers to comply with grammar rules since the printing of identical copies reduced variation between texts.

Old English's evolution into Middle English can be narrowed down to three stages: Early, Central, and Late Middle English. Early Middle English, though it showed a change in the language, maintained the writing style of Old English. Central Middle English is characterized by the development of dialects within written communication, which is partly due to scribes who translated texts or parts of texts using terms from their own dialect, rather than the source. Late Middle English includes numerous developments that created the foundation for Modern English. *The Canterbury Tales*, "Sir Gawain and the Green Knight," and "Le Morte d'Arthur" are all Middle English texts that are still read and studied today.

THE RENAISSANCE

The **Renaissance** swept through Europe and lasted for multiple centuries, bringing many developments in culture, the arts, education, and philosophy. The Renaissance in England did not begin until the late 15th century. Though ideas and cultures of the past, especially those of the ancient Greeks and Romans, inspired the Renaissance, the period saw innumerable developments in the English language and literature. The Renaissance was characterized by a focus on the humanities, allowing the arts, including literature, to flourish. At the time, drama was possibly the most popular form of literature, as the popularity of plays and theatrical performances greatly

72

increased. Much of Renaissance literature is still studied today, maintaining its influence on Western literature. Poetry was also popular, and the period saw the development of new forms of poetry, such as the sonnet. Sonnets are often recognized according to one of four styles, each of which was popularized by a Renaissance writer. Lyrical poetry, which discusses emotions and is often written using first-person point of view, was also popular during the Renaissance.

In addition to new forms and literary trends, the Renaissance period also impacted English literature by facilitating discussion over the translation of the Bible. Education at the time often included instruction in Greek and Latin, allowing those with an education to read ancient texts in their original language. However, this instruction did not reach the majority of the public. The Protestant Reformation encouraged discussions about translating the Bible to make it accessible to more people. This suggestion was challenged by those who doubted the ability of the English language to fully reflect the original text. Eventually, the Bible was translated to English, and William Tyndale's partial translation became especially influential for later translations and the continuing development of the English language. Influential writers of the English Renaissance include William Shakespeare, John Donne, John Milton, Edmund Spenser, and Christopher Marlowe.

GOTHIC

The Gothic literary movement, beginning in the 18th century and persisting through the 19th century, took inspiration from the architecture and cultures of the Late Middle Ages in Europe. The Late Middle Ages saw the popularity of Gothic architecture, most prominently in places of worship. These structures inspired many of the settings in **Gothic literature**, as a large volume of Gothic literature takes place in an impressive location, such as a castle or ornate mansion. Gothic works also are often set in the past, long before the time the story was written. This aligns with prominent themes in Gothic literature, as several pieces are informed by an event that occurred before the story begins or a character who died before the plot's first event.

Another common characteristic of Gothic literature is its eerie, dark, suspenseful tone. Authors of Gothic literature often created this tone by setting their works in secluded and strange locations and incorporating intense, unsettling, or even supernatural events and scenarios into the plot. This tone is also created through the theme of death or mortality that often appears in Gothic literature. These characteristics support the aim of many Gothic writers to create fiction that evokes a certain emotion from the reader or shapes their reading experience. Well-known authors of Gothic literature include Horace Walpole, Ann Radcliffe, Edgar Allan Poe, and Nathaniel Hawthorne. While the Gothic literary movement took place in the 18th and 19th centuries, many works have been published in more recent centuries that have several characteristics of Gothic literature and may be included within the overall Gothic genre.

NATURALISM

Naturalism was an active literary movement in the late 19th century, taking place alongside movements such as realism and modernism. **Naturalism**, like realism, rejected the emotional focus and sentimentality of Romanticism and provided a type of social commentary. However, the naturalist movement stretched the ideas of realism, promoting literature that authentically depicts the life of the common man and criticizing the influence of morality on such literature. Naturalist literature often includes characters who belong to a lower class and experience circumstances beyond their own control and takes place in urban settings. Prominent themes in naturalist literature include nature as an apathetic force, the influence of heredity, and life as something to be endured and survived. One of the most influential naturalist writers is French writer Emile Zola. Influential American Naturalists include Stephen Crane, Hamlin Garland, and Theodore Dreiser.

MODERNISM

The Modernist literary movement was largely influenced by industrialization, which heavily impacted both the Unites States and England, primarily in the 19th century. **Modernism** in literature was characterized by an attempt to turn away from the norms and traditions of literature and use new techniques and methods. Modernist literature was often written in first person and used literary devices and techniques to reveal problems within society. For the American modernists, these societal changes came from industrialization and the first World War, which effected the general view of human nature and reliability. In England, there were additional factors contributing to this shift. Modernism began during Queen Victoria's reign, which defined the period known as the Victorian Era. The Victorian society was characterized by a strict moral code that permeated England's society at the time. This moral code was incompatible with the Modernist's desire to turn away from tradition, but the changes that accompanied Victoria's death in 1901 enabled the Modernist movement to grow in England. American Modernist writers include Ezra Pound, William Carlos Williams, and Gertrude Stein. British Modernist writers include Matthew Arnold, William Butler Yeats, T. S. Eliot, and Joseph Conrad.

POSTMODERNISM

Postmodernism grew out of Modernism's reliance on science and universal assertions, but emphasized the individual's subjective perception of reality, as it is often more authentic to an individual's experience than a universally applied statement. Postmodernism asserts that since each person creates their own version of reality, fully and accurately defining reality is futile and impossible. Due to this skepticism, postmodern writers use many concrete details, rather than abstract details, because they can be objectively observed and are not left up to the individual. The postmodernist literary movement began around the 1960s. The literary movement included a variety of new genres and techniques, reflecting the postmodernist idea that things like art cannot be truly defined or simplified. Notable American writers of the postmodernist movement include Kurt Vonnegut, John Barth, and Thomas Pynchon. British postmodernist writers include John Fowles and Julian Barnes.

Public Speaking

SPEECHES

Speeches are written to be delivered in spoken language in public, to various groups of people, at formal or informal events. Some generic types include welcome speeches, thank-you speeches, keynote addresses, position papers, commemorative and dedication speeches, and farewell speeches. Speeches are commonly written in present tense and usually begin with an introduction greeting the audience. At official functions, specific audience members are named ("Chairperson [name]," "Principal [name], teachers, and students," etc.) and when audiences include a distinguished guest, he or she is often named as well. Then the speaker introduces him or herself by name, position, and department or organization as applicable. After the greeting, the speaker then introduces the topic and states the purpose of the speech. The body of the speech follows, similarly to the body of an essay, stating its main points, an explanation of each point, and supporting evidence. Finally, in the conclusion, the speaker states his or her hope for accomplishing the speech's purpose and thanks the audience for attending and listening to the speech.

CLEARLY WRITTEN PROSE AND SPEECHES

To achieve **clarity**, a writer or speaker must first define his or her purpose carefully. The speech should be organized logically, so that sentences make sense and follow each other in an understandable order. Sentences must also be constructed well, with carefully chosen words and structure. Organizing a speech in advance using an outline provides the writer or speaker with a blueprint, directing and focusing the composition to meet its intended purpose. Organized speeches enable audiences to comprehend and retain the presented information more easily. Humans naturally seek to impose order on the world by seeking patterns. Hence, when ideas in a speech are well-organized and adhere to a consistent pattern, the speaker communicates better with listeners and is more convincing. Speechwriters can use chronological patterns to organize events, sequential patterns to organize processes by their steps, and spatial patterns to help audiences visualize geographical locations and movements or physical scenarios. Also, comparison-contrast patterns give audiences insight about similarities and differences between and among topics, especially when listeners are more familiar with one than the other.

EVALUATING SPEECHES FOR CONCISE INFORMATION

To convince or persuade listeners or reinforce a message, speeches must be succinct. Audiences can become confused by excessive anecdotes and details. If a speaker takes three minutes or more to get to the point, audience members' attention will start to fade and will only worsen when details deviate from the main subject. When answering a question, the asker and speaker may even forget the original question if the speaker takes too long. Speakers should practice not only rehearsing written speeches, but also developing skill for spontaneous question-and-answer sessions after speeches. Speakers should differentiate necessary from simply interesting information because audiences can become overwhelmed by too much information. Speakers should know what points they wish to make. They should not be afraid to pause before responding to questions, which indicates thoughtfulness and control rather than lack of knowledge. Restating questions increases comprehension and appropriate responses, and allows time to form answers mentally.

ORGANIZATIONAL PATTERNS FOR SPEECHES

A speechwriter who uses an **advantages-disadvantages** pattern of organization presents the audience with the pros and cons of a topic. This aids writers in discussing two sides of an issue objectively without an argumentative position, enabling listeners to weigh both aspects. When a speechwriter uses a **cause-and-effect** pattern, it can help to persuade audiences to agree with an action or solution by showing significant relationships between factors. Writers may separate an

75

outline into two main "cause" and "effect" sections or into separate sections for each cause, including the effect for each. Persuasive writing also benefits from **problem-solution** patterns: by establishing the existence of a problem, writers induce audiences to realize a need for change. By supplying a solution and supporting its superiority above other solutions, the writer convinces audiences of the value of that solution. When none of these patterns—or **chronological**, **sequential**, **spatial**, or **comparison-contrast** patterns—applies, speechwriters often use topical patterns. These organize information by various subtopics and types within the main topic or category.

EFFECTIVE SPEECH DELIVERY

Speakers should deliver speeches in a natural, conversational manner rather than being rigidly formal or theatrical. Effective delivery is also supported by confidence. Speakers should be direct, building audience rapport through personal connection and vivid imagery. Speakers should be mindful of the occasion, subject, and audience of their speeches and take care to use appropriate language. Good speakers learn vocal control, including volume, speed, pitch, use of pauses, tonal variety, correct pronunciation, and clear articulation. They can express enthusiasm and emphasize important points with their voices. Nonverbal behaviors, such as eye contact, facial expressions, gestures, good posture, and body movements clarify communication, stress important ideas, and influence perceptions that the speaker is trustworthy, competent, and credible. Nonverbal communications should seem as spontaneous and natural as vocal or verbal ones. Speakers should know their speeches well and practice frequently, taking care to avoid nervous or irrelevant movements such as tapping or pacing.

Media Types

MEDIA AND FORMAT CHOICES

Effective communication depends on choosing the correct method. Media and format choices are influenced by the target audience, the budget, and the needs of the audience.

INSTRUCTIONAL VIDEOS

Instructional videos have potential for excellent two-way communication because questions and feedback can be built in. Videos can be targeted to particular audiences, and they can be paused for discussion or replayed to reinforce concepts. Viewers can see processes, including "before," "during," and "after" phases. Videos are accessible because most communities have at least one DVD player or computer. Moreover, video players and computers are continually becoming less expensive to buy and use. Disadvantages include the necessity of editing software and equipment in some cases, as well as the need for support from other print materials. There is also danger of overuse, if other media or methods are more appropriate, and higher up-front costs. Producers of instructional videos must account for the costs of script development and hiring local performers as needed.

DVDS AND CDS

Interactive DVDs and CDs, such as games, give viewers the opportunity to actively participate as they learn information. Additionally, videos are considered to be a professional method of sharing information. Compared to many other media formats, discs are comparatively inexpensive to make and are easy to transport due to their small size and weight. They are more resistant to damage and aging than older videotape technology, making them more durable. Some disadvantages include needing access to technology to play what is stored on the disc and access to certain software programs to add new content to a disc, especially if the producer wants to include video animation or audio commentary. Producers must also consider expenses concerning paid staff and production and labeling expenses. Content that would appear on DVDs and CDs can alternatively be shared through streaming services or digital files stored on a computer or other compatible device.

TELEVISION AND RADIO

Both television and radio are forms of mass media that reach many people. TV has the broadest reach and can market to the general public or be customized for target audiences, while radio only tends to reach specific target audiences. TV has the advantage of video plus audio, while radio broadcasts only feature audio. However, access to television programs is more expensive than access to radio broadcasts. A shared disadvantage is that TV and radio audiences can only interact directly during call-in programs. Additionally, programming times may be inconvenient, but tape, digital sound, and digital video recording (DVR) can remedy this. Many streaming services also provide access to these programs. Both television and radio are useful for communicating simple slogans and messages, and both can generate awareness, interest, and excitement.

NEWSPAPERS

Except for the occasional community columns, news releases, and letters to the editor, newspaper pages and features afford little opportunity for audience input or participation. However, they do reach and appeal to the general public. Cost is an advantage: hiring a PR writer and paying for a news advertisement costs much less than a radio or TV spot. Additionally, newspaper features are high-status, and audiences can reread and review them as often as they like. However, newspaper ads may have difficulty affecting the reader as deeply without audio or video, and they require a literate audience. Their publication is also subject to editors' whims and biases. Newspaper pieces combining advertising and editorial content—"advertorials"—provide inclusion of paid material, but are viewed as medium-status and cost more.

WEBSITES, BLOGS, MOBILE PHONES, AND TEXT MESSAGING

Computer literacy is required for online material, but participation potential is high via websites, e-networking, and blogging. Mobile phones and text messaging are used for enormous direct, public, two-way and one-on-one communication, with timely information and reminders. Web media need a literate public and can be tailored for specific audiences. They afford global information, are accessible by increasingly technology-literate populations, and are high-status. Web media disadvantages include the necessity of computers and people to design, manage, and supply content, as well as to provide technical support. Mobile and text media are globally popular, but appeal especially to certain demographics like teens and young adults. They are increasingly available, especially in rural regions, and are decreasing in cost. Mobile and text media disadvantages include required brevity in texts and provider messaging charges. Links to related websites and pages within existing sites are also advantages of digital media.

PUBLIC PRESENTATIONS AND SLIDESHOWS

Public presentations have great potential for audience participation and can directly target various audiences. They can encourage the establishment of partnerships and groups, stimulate local ownership of issues and projects, and make information public. A drawback to public presentations is that they are limited to nights, weekends, or whenever audiences are available and do not always attract the intended audience.

Another method of presentation is to use **slideshows**. These presentations are best for sophisticated audiences like professionals, civil servants, and service organizations. Well-designed slideshows are good for stimulating audience interest, selling ideas, and marketing products. Also, they are accessible online as well as in-person so they can reach a broader audience. Slideshow disadvantages include the necessity of projectors and other equipment. They are also limited to communicating more general points, outlines, and summaries rather than conveying a multitude of information in more detail.

POSTERS AND BROCHURES

Both **posters** and **brochures** can target audiences of the general public and more specific public sectors. Posters are better for communicating simple slogans and messages, while brochures can include more detail and are better for printing instructional information. Both can be inexpensive to produce, especially if printed only as needed and in-house. Posters can often be printed in-house without using outside printing companies. However, it is difficult to get feedback on both posters and brochures—unless they have been broadly tested, or if their publication is accompanied by workshops and other participatory events. A disadvantage of using posters is that they are designed to draw attention and communicate quickly, as they are mostly viewed in passing. This means that their messages must be simple and communicate efficiently. A disadvantage of using brochures is that they can only be distributed to a specific, limited group or area. Posters and brochures are also only understood when audiences are literate in both written language and visual elements.

FLYERS AND FACT SHEETS

Flyers and fact sheets have one-way communication potential because readers cannot give feedback. Their target audiences are general. Some advantages of using this form of media include flexibility: people can distribute them at meetings or events, put them on car windshields in parking lots, leave them in stores or on bulletin boards at community agencies and schools, hand them out from booths and other displays, or mail them. When printed in black and white, they can be very inexpensive. They afford recipients the convenience of being able to review them at their leisure. Organizations and individuals can produce flyers and fact sheets in-house, or even at home with desktop publishing software. Disadvantages include their limitation to single facts or tips and specific information on specified topics.

EVALUATING MEDIA INFORMATION SOURCES

With the wealth of media in different formats available today, users are more likely to take media at face value. However, to understand the content of media, consumers must **critically evaluate each source**.

Users should ask themselves the following questions about media sources:

- Who is delivering this message and why?
- What methods do a media source's publishers employ to gain and maintain users' attention?
- Which points of view is the media source representing?
- What are the various ways this message could be interpreted?
- What information is missing from the message?
- Is the source scholarly, i.e., peer-reviewed?
- Does it include author names and their credentials as they relate to the topic?
- Who publishes it and why?
- Who is the target audience?
- Is the language technically specific or non-technical?
- Are sources cited, research claims documented, conclusions based on furnished evidence, and references provided?
- Is the publication current?

OTHER CONSIDERATIONS FOR THE VALIDITY OF SOURCES

For books, consider whether information is **up-to-date** and whether **historical perspectives** apply. Content is more likely to be **scholarly** if publishers are universities, government, or professional organizations. Book reviews can also provide useful information. For articles, identify the author, publisher, frequency of the periodical's publication, and what kind of advertising, if any, is included. Looking for book reviews also informs users. For articles, look for biographical author information, publisher name, frequency of the periodical's publication, and whether advertising is included and, if so, whether it is for certain occupations or disciplines. For web pages, check their domain names, identify publishers or sponsors, look for the author or publisher's contact information, check dates of most recent page updates, be alert to biases, and verify the validity of the information on the webpage. The quality and accuracy of web pages located through search engines rather than library databases varies widely and requires careful user inspection. Web page recommendations from reliable sources like university faculties can help indicate quality and accuracy. Citations of websites by credible or scholarly sources also show reliability. Authors' names, relevant credentials, affiliations, and contact information support their authority. Site functionality, such as ease of navigation, ability to search, site maps, and indexes, is also a criterion to consider.

PERSUASIVE MEDIA

Advertising, public relations, and advocacy media all use **persuasion**. Advertisers use persuasion to sell goods and services. The public relations field uses persuasion to give good impressions of companies, governments, or organizations. Advocacy groups use persuasion to garner support or votes. Persuasion can come through commercials, public service announcements, speeches, websites, and newsletters, among other channels. Activists, lobbyists, government officials, and politicians use political rhetoric involving persuasive techniques. Basic techniques include using celebrity spokespersons, whom consumers admire or aspire to resemble, or conversely, "everyday people" (albeit often portrayed by actors) with whom consumers identify. Using expert testimonials lends credibility. Explicit claims of content, effectiveness, quality, and reliability—which often cannot be proven or disproven—are used to persuade. While news and advocacy messages mostly eschew humor for credibility's sake (except in political satire), advertising often persuades via humor, which gets consumer attention and associates its pleasure with advertised products and services. Qualifiers and other misleading terms, sometimes called "Weasel words," are often combined with exaggerated claims. Intensifiers, such as hyperboles, superlatives, repetitions, and sentimental appeals are also persuasive.

INTERMEDIATE TECHNIQUES

Dangerous propagandist Adolf Hitler said people suspect little lies more than big ones; hence the "Big Lie" is a persuasion method that cannot be identified without consumers' keen critical thinking. A related method is **charisma**, which can induce people to believe messages they would otherwise reject. **Euphemisms** substitute abstract, vague, or bland terms in place of more graphic, clear, and unpleasant ones. For example, the terms "layoffs" and "firing" are replaced by "downsizing," and "torture" is replaced with "intensive interrogation techniques." **Extrapolation** bases sweeping conclusions on small amounts of minor information to appeal to what consumers wish or hope. Flattery appeals to consumer self-esteem needs, such as L'Oréal's "You're worth it." Flattery is sometimes accomplished through contrast, like ads showing others' mistakes to make consumers feel superior and smarter. "Glittering generalities" refer to claims based on concepts such as beauty, love, health, democracy, freedom, and science. Persuaders use this tactic to gain consumer acceptance without consumers questioning what they mean. The opposite is name-calling to persuade consumers to reject someone or something.

American citizens love new ideas and technology. Persuaders exploit this by emphasizing the **newness** of products, services, and candidates. Conversely, they also use **nostalgia** to evoke consumers' happy memories, which they often remember more than unhappy ones. Citing "scientific evidence" is an intermediate version of the basic technique of expert testimonials. Consumers may accept this as proof, but some advertisers, politicians, and other persuaders may present inaccurate or misleading "evidence." Another intermediate technique is the "simple solution." Although the natures of people and life are complex, when consumers feel overwhelmed by complexity, persuaders exploit this by offering policies, products, or services they claim will solve complicated problems by simple means. Persuaders also use symbols, images, words, and names we associate with more general, emotional concepts like lifestyle, country, family, religion, and gender. While symbols have power, their significance also varies across individuals. For example, some consumers regard the Hummer SUV as a prestigious status symbol, while others regard it as environmentally harmful and irresponsible.

ADVANCED TECHNIQUES

Ad hominem, Latin for "against the man" attacks the person behind an idea rather than criticizing the idea itself. It operates by association: if a person is considered immoral or uneducated, then his or her ideas must be bad as well. **"Stacking the deck"** misleads by presenting only selected information that supports one position. **Apophasis**, or a false denial, allows the speaker or writer to indirectly bring attention to a flaw in an opponent's credibility. For example, a politician saying, "I won't mention my opponent's tax evasion issues" manages to mention them while seeming less accusatory. Persuaders may also use **majority belief**, making statements such as "Four out of five dentists recommend this brand" or "[insert number] people can't be wrong." In an intensified version, persuaders exploit group dynamics at rallies, speeches, and other live-audience events where people are vulnerable to surrounding crowd influences. **Scapegoating**, blaming one person or group for complex problems, is a form of the intermediate "simple solution" technique, a practice common in politics. **Timing** also persuades, like advertising flowers and candy in the weeks preceding Valentine's Day, ad campaigns preceding new technology rollouts, and politician speeches following big news events.

VISUAL MEDIA

Some images have the power to communicate more information than an entire paragraph. Images can contain several elements and be interpreted different ways, making them an effective vessel for abstract and emotionally appealing ideas. Humans are also able to understand images before they fully acquire language, meaning that images can reach more people than language can at any time. Images are also more quickly comprehended than text, making them a highly efficient method of communication. People can remember or memorize images more easily than text, also. Historically, images have been used for propaganda and subliminal messaging. Images are also used by different companies as an effective technique to entice customers to buy their products. Though images do not always contain text, they can still convey explicit and implicit meanings. An image's explicit meaning would be the most recognizable shape or concept in the image. The implicit meaning may be obscured within the image through the use of negative space, background images, or out-of-focus shapes.

INTERPRETING AND EVALUATING PERSUASIVE MEDIA

Most messages can be interpreted in different ways. They can be interpreted explicitly, where the literal meaning of the words in the message creates the meaning of the message, and no context is considered. Alternatively, other contexts can be considered alongside the explicit meaning of the message. These create alternative, not clearly stated meanings called **implicit meanings**. Politics, current events, regional norms, and even emotions are examples of contexts that can add implicit meanings to a message. These implicit meanings can change the effect a message has on its recipient. Many products have slogans with both implicit and explicit meanings. These implicit meanings must be considered to fully interpret a message.

Messages come in different forms, and each form has a unique way of communicating both explicit and implicit meanings. Images can come with captions that communicate a message, but some images carry subliminal messages. This means that their implicit meaning is received by the viewer, but the viewer is not aware of it. The term **propaganda** describes messages that advocate for a specific opinion or way of thinking. Most propaganda is politically driven and has been used during historical periods, most notably World War II. Unlike messages with hidden or veiled implicit meanings, most propaganda aggressively communicates its entire meaning and is difficult to misinterpret. Documentaries are another prominent form of communication. Documentaries are informational videos that focus on a specific figure, subject, phenomenon, or time period. While documentaries are primarily fact based and contain excerpts from interviews and testimonials, documentaries feature a limited view of their subject and sometimes attempt to persuade viewers to take action or embrace their central message. While some documentaries communicate this clearly, some hide an implicit meaning through the way they present each piece of information.

Writing

Parts of Speech

THE EIGHT PARTS OF SPEECH
NOUNS

When you talk about a person, place, thing, or idea, you are talking about a **noun**. The two main types of nouns are **common** and **proper** nouns. Also, nouns can be abstract (i.e., general) or concrete (i.e., specific).

COMMON NOUNS

Common nouns are generic names for people, places, and things. Common nouns are not usually capitalized.

Examples of common nouns:

> *People*: boy, girl, worker, manager
>
> *Places*: school, bank, library, home
>
> *Things*: dog, cat, truck, car

PROPER NOUNS

Proper nouns name specific people, places, or things. All proper nouns are capitalized.

Examples of proper nouns:

> *People*: Abraham Lincoln, George Washington, Martin Luther King, Jr.
>
> *Places*: Los Angeles, California; New York; Asia
>
> *Things*: Statue of Liberty, Earth, Lincoln Memorial

Note: When referring to the planet that we live on, capitalize *Earth*. When referring to the dirt, rocks, or land, lowercase *earth*.

GENERAL AND SPECIFIC NOUNS

General nouns are the names of conditions or ideas. **Specific nouns** name people, places, and things that are understood by using your senses.

General nouns:

> *Condition*: beauty, strength
>
> *Idea*: truth, peace

Specific nouns:

People: baby, friend, father

Places: town, park, city hall

Things: rainbow, cough, apple, silk, gasoline

<u>COLLECTIVE NOUNS</u>

Collective nouns are the names for a group of people, places, or things that may act as a whole. The following are examples of collective nouns: *class, company, dozen, group, herd, team,* and *public*. Collective nouns usually require an article, which denotes the noun as being a single unit. For instance, a choir is a group of singers. Even though there are many singers in a choir, the word choir is grammatically treated as a single unit. If we refer to the members of the group, and not the group itself, it is no longer a collective noun.

Incorrect: The *choir are* going to compete nationally this year.

Correct: The *choir is* going to compete nationally this year.

Incorrect: The *members* of the choir *is* competing nationally this year.

Correct: The *members* of the choir *are* competing nationally this year.

PRONOUNS

Pronouns are words that are used to stand in for nouns. A pronoun may be classified as personal, intensive, relative, interrogative, demonstrative, indefinite, and reciprocal.

Personal: *Nominative* is the case for nouns and pronouns that are the subject of a sentence. *Objective* is the case for nouns and pronouns that are an object in a sentence. *Possessive* is the case for nouns and pronouns that show possession or ownership.

Singular

	Nominative	Objective	Possessive
First Person	I	me	my, mine
Second Person	you	you	your, yours
Third Person	he, she, it	him, her, it	his, her, hers, its

Plural

	Nominative	Objective	Possessive
First Person	we	us	our, ours
Second Person	you	you	your, yours
Third Person	they	them	their, theirs

Intensive: I myself, you yourself, he himself, she herself, the (thing) itself, we ourselves, you yourselves, they themselves

Relative: which, who, whom, whose

Interrogative: what, which, who, whom, whose

83

Demonstrative: this, that, these, those

Indefinite: all, any, each, everyone, either/neither, one, some, several

Reciprocal: each other, one another

VERBS

If you want to write a sentence, then you need a verb. Without a verb, you have no sentence. The verb of a sentence indicates action or being. In other words, the verb shows something's action or state of being or the action that has been done to something.

TRANSITIVE AND INTRANSITIVE VERBS

A **transitive verb** is a verb whose action (e.g., drive, run, jump) indicates a receiver (e.g., car, dog, kangaroo). **Intransitive verbs** do not indicate a receiver of an action. In other words, the action of the verb does not point to a subject or object.

Transitive: He plays the piano. | The piano was played by him.

Intransitive: He plays. | John plays well.

A dictionary will tell you whether a verb is transitive or intransitive. Some verbs can be transitive and intransitive.

ACTION VERBS AND LINKING VERBS

Action verbs show what the subject is doing. In other words, an action verb shows action. Unlike most types of words, a single action verb, in the right context, can be an entire sentence. **Linking verbs** link the subject of a sentence to a noun or pronoun, or they link a subject with an adjective. You always need a verb if you want a complete sentence. However, linking verbs on their own cannot be a complete sentence.

Common linking verbs include *appear, be, become, feel, grow, look, seem, smell, sound,* and *taste*. However, any verb that shows a condition and connects to a noun, pronoun, or adjective that describes the subject of a sentence is a linking verb.

Action: He sings. | Run! | Go! | I talk with him every day. | She reads.

Linking:

Incorrect: I am.

Correct: I am John. | I smell roses. | I feel tired.

Note: Some verbs are followed by words that look like prepositions, but they are a part of the verb and a part of the verb's meaning. These are known as phrasal verbs, and examples include *call off, look up,* and *drop off*.

VOICE

Transitive verbs come in active or passive **voice**. If something does an action or is acted upon, then you will know whether a verb is active or passive. When the subject of the sentence is doing the action, the verb is in **active voice**. When the subject is acted upon, the verb is in **passive voice**.

> **Active**: Jon drew the picture. (The subject *Jon* is doing the action of *drawing a picture*.)

> **Passive**: The picture is drawn by Jon. (The subject *picture* is receiving the action from Jon.)

VERB TENSES

A verb **tense** shows the different form of a verb to point to the time of an action. The present and past tense are indicated by the verb's form. An action in the present, *I talk*, can change form for the past: *I talked*. However, for the other tenses, an auxiliary (i.e., helping) verb is needed to show the change in form. These helping verbs include *am, are, is | have, has, had | was, were, will* (or *shall*).

Present: I talk	Present perfect: I have talked
Past: I talked	Past perfect: I had talked
Future: I will talk	Future perfect: I will have talked

Present: The action happens at the current time.

> Example: He *walks* to the store every morning.

To show that something is happening right now, use the progressive present tense: I *am walking*.

Past: The action happened in the past.

> Example: He *walked* to the store an hour ago.

Future: The action is going to happen later.

> Example: I *will walk* to the store tomorrow.

Present perfect: The action started in the past and continues into the present or took place previously at an unspecified time

> Example: I *have walked* to the store three times today.

Past perfect: The second action happened in the past. The first action came before the second.

> Example: Before I walked to the store (Action 2), I *had walked* to the library (Action 1).

Future perfect: An action that uses the past and the future. In other words, the action is complete before a future moment.

> Example: When she comes for the supplies (future moment), I *will have walked* to the store (action completed before the future moment).

CONJUGATING VERBS

When you need to change the form of a verb, you are **conjugating** a verb. The key forms of a verb are singular, present tense (dream); singular, past tense (dreamed); and the past participle (have dreamed). Note: the past participle needs a helping verb to make a verb tense. For example, I *have dreamed* of this day. The following tables demonstrate some of the different ways to conjugate a verb:

Singular

Tense	First Person	Second Person	Third Person
Present	I dream	You dream	He, she, it dreams
Past	I dreamed	You dreamed	He, she, it dreamed
Past Participle	I have dreamed	You have dreamed	He, she, it has dreamed

Plural

Tense	First Person	Second Person	Third Person
Present	We dream	You dream	They dream
Past	We dreamed	You dreamed	They dreamed
Past Participle	We have dreamed	You have dreamed	They have dreamed

MOOD

There are three **moods** in English: the indicative, the imperative, and the subjunctive.

The **indicative mood** is used for facts, opinions, and questions.

Fact: You can do this.

Opinion: I think that you can do this.

Question: Do you know that you can do this?

The **imperative** is used for orders or requests.

Order: You are going to do this!

Request: Will you do this for me?

The **subjunctive mood** is for wishes and statements that go against fact.

Wish: I wish that I were famous.

Statement against fact: If I were you, I would do this. (This goes against fact because I am not you. You have the chance to do this, and I do not have the chance.)

> **Review Video: <u>Present Perfect, Past Perfect, and Future Perfect Verb Tenses</u>**
> Visit mometrix.com/academy and enter code: 269472

ADJECTIVES

An **adjective** is a word that is used to modify a noun or pronoun. An adjective answers a question: *Which one? What kind?* or *How many?* Usually, adjectives come before the words that they modify, but they may also come after a linking verb.

>Which one? The *third* suit is my favorite.

>What kind? This suit is *navy blue*.

>How many? I am going to buy *four* pairs of socks to match the suit.

ARTICLES

Articles are adjectives that are used to distinguish nouns as definite or indefinite. **Definite** nouns are preceded by the article *the* and indicate a specific person, place, thing, or idea. **Indefinite** nouns are preceded by *a* or *an* and do not indicate a specific person, place, thing, or idea. *A*, *an*, and *the* are the only articles. Note: *An* comes before words that start with a vowel sound. For example, "Are you going to get an **u**mbrella?"

>**Definite**: I lost *the* bottle that belongs to me.

>**Indefinite**: Does anyone have *a* bottle to share?

COMPARISON WITH ADJECTIVES

Some adjectives are relative and other adjectives are absolute. Adjectives that are **relative** can show the comparison between things. **Absolute** adjectives can also show comparison, but they do so in a different way. Let's say that you are reading two books. You think that one book is perfect, and the other book is not exactly perfect. It is not possible for one book to be more perfect than the other. Either you think that the book is perfect, or you think that the book is imperfect. In this case, perfect and imperfect are absolute adjectives.

Relative adjectives will show the different **degrees** of something or someone to something else or someone else. The three degrees of adjectives include positive, comparative, and superlative.

The **positive** degree is the normal form of an adjective.

>Example: This work is *difficult*. | She is *smart*.

The **comparative** degree compares one person or thing to another person or thing.

>Example: This work is *more difficult* than your work. | She is *smarter* than me.

The **superlative** degree compares more than two people or things.

>Example: This is the *most difficult* work of my life. | She is the *smartest* lady in school.

>**Review Video: Adjectives**
>Visit mometrix.com/academy and enter code: 470154

ADVERBS

An **adverb** is a word that is used to **modify** a verb, adjective, or another adverb. Usually, adverbs answer one of these questions: *When? Where? How?* and *Why?* The negatives *not* and *never* are

considered adverbs. Adverbs that modify adjectives or other adverbs **strengthen** or **weaken** the words that they modify.

Examples:

He walks *quickly* through the crowd.

The water flows *smoothly* on the rocks.

Note: Adverbs are usually indicated by the morpheme *-ly*, which has been added to the root word. For instance, *quick* can be made into an adverb by adding *-ly* to construct *quickly*. Some words that end in *-ly* do not follow this rule and can behave as other parts of speech. Examples of adjectives ending in *-ly* include: *early, friendly, holy, lonely, silly*, and *ugly*. To know if a word that ends in *-ly* is an adjective or adverb, check your dictionary. Also, while many adverbs end in *-ly*, you need to remember that not all adverbs end in *-ly*.

Examples:

He is *never* angry.

You walked *across* the bridge.

COMPARISON WITH ADVERBS

The rules for comparing adverbs are the same as the rules for adjectives.

The **positive** degree is the standard form of an adverb.

Example: He arrives *soon*. | She speaks *softly* to her friends.

The **comparative** degree compares one person or thing to another person or thing.

Example: He arrives *sooner* than Sarah. | She speaks *more softly* than him.

The **superlative** degree compares more than two people or things.

Example: He arrives *soonest* of the group. | She speaks the *most softly* of any of her friends.

> **Review Video: Adverbs**
> Visit mometrix.com/academy and enter code: 713951

PREPOSITIONS

A **preposition** is a word placed before a noun or pronoun that shows the relationship between an object and another word in the sentence.

Common prepositions:

about	before	during	on	under
after	beneath	for	over	until
against	between	from	past	up
among	beyond	in	through	with
around	by	of	to	within
at	down	off	toward	without

Examples:

> The napkin is *in* the drawer.

> The Earth rotates *around* the Sun.

> The needle is *beneath* the haystack.

> Can you find "me" *among* the words?

CONJUNCTIONS

Conjunctions join words, phrases, or clauses and they show the connection between the joined pieces. **Coordinating conjunctions** connect equal parts of sentences. **Correlative conjunctions** show the connection between pairs. **Subordinating conjunctions** join subordinate (i.e., dependent) clauses with independent clauses.

COORDINATING CONJUNCTIONS

The **coordinating conjunctions** include: *and, but, yet, or, nor, for,* and *so*

Examples:

> The rock was small, *but* it was heavy.

> She drove in the night, *and* he drove in the day.

CORRELATIVE CONJUNCTIONS

The **correlative conjunctions** are: *either...or* | *neither...nor* | *not only...but also*

Examples:

> *Either* you are coming *or* you are staying.

> He *not only* ran three miles *but also* swam 200 yards.

SUBORDINATING CONJUNCTIONS

Common **subordinating conjunctions** include:

after	since	whenever
although	so that	where
because	unless	wherever
before	until	whether
in order that	when	while

Examples:

I am hungry *because* I did not eat breakfast.

He went home *when* everyone left.

Review Video: Subordinating Conjunctions
Visit mometrix.com/academy and enter code: 958913

INTERJECTIONS

Interjections are words of exclamation (i.e., audible expression of great feeling) that are used alone or as a part of a sentence. Often, they are used at the beginning of a sentence for an introduction. Sometimes, they can be used in the middle of a sentence to show a change in thought or attitude.

Common Interjections: Hey! | Oh, | Ouch! | Please! | Wow!

Agreement and Sentence Structure

SUBJECTS AND PREDICATES

SUBJECTS

The **subject** of a sentence names who or what the sentence is about. The subject may be directly stated in a sentence, or the subject may be the implied *you*. The **complete subject** includes the simple subject and all of its modifiers. To find the complete subject, ask *Who* or *What* and insert the verb to complete the question. The answer, including any modifiers (adjectives, prepositional phrases, etc.), is the complete subject. To find the **simple subject**, remove all of the modifiers in the complete subject. Being able to locate the subject of a sentence helps with many problems, such as those involving sentence fragments and subject-verb agreement.

Examples:

simple
subject

The small, red car is the one that he wants for Christmas.

complete
subject

simple
subject

The young artist is coming over for dinner.

complete
subject

> **Review Video: Subjects**
> Visit mometrix.com/academy and enter code: 444771

In **imperative** sentences, the verb's subject is understood (e.g., [You] Run to the store), but is not actually present in the sentence. Normally, the subject comes before the verb. However, the subject comes after the verb in sentences that begin with *There are* or *There was*.

Direct:

John knows the way to the park.	Who knows the way to the park?	John
The cookies need ten more minutes.	What needs ten minutes?	The cookies
By five o'clock, Bill will need to leave.	Who needs to leave?	Bill
There are five letters on the table for him.	What is on the table?	Five letters
There were coffee and doughnuts in the house.	What was in the house?	Coffee and doughnuts

Implied:

| Go to the post office for me. | Who is going to the post office? | You |
| Come and sit with me, please? | Who needs to come and sit? | You |

PREDICATES

In a sentence, you always have a predicate and a subject. The subject tells what the sentence is about, and the **predicate** explains or describes the subject.

Think about the sentence *He sings*. In this sentence, we have a subject (He) and a predicate (sings). This is all that is needed for a sentence to be complete. Most sentences contain more information, but if this is all the information that you are given, then you have a complete sentence.

Now, let's look at another sentence: *John and Jane sing on Tuesday nights at the dance hall.*

subject   predicate

John and Jane sing on Tuesday nights at the dance hall.

SUBJECT-VERB AGREEMENT

Verbs **agree** with their subjects in number. In other words, singular subjects need singular verbs. Plural subjects need plural verbs. **Singular** is for **one** person, place, or thing. **Plural** is for **more than one** person, place, or thing. Subjects and verbs must also share the same point of view, as in first, second, or third person. The present tense ending *-s* is used on a verb if its subject is third person singular; otherwise, the verb's ending is not modified.

> **Review Video: Subject-Verb Agreement**
> Visit mometrix.com/academy and enter code: 479190

NUMBER AGREEMENT EXAMPLES:

singular singular
subject   verb

Single Subject and Verb: Dan calls home.

Dan is one person. So, the singular verb *calls* is needed.

plural   plural
subject   verb

Plural Subject and Verb: Dan and Bob call home.

More than one person needs the plural verb *call*.

PERSON AGREEMENT EXAMPLES:

First Person: I *am* walking.

Second Person: You *are* walking.

Third Person: He *is* walking.

COMPLICATIONS WITH SUBJECT-VERB AGREEMENT

WORDS BETWEEN SUBJECT AND VERB

Words that come between the simple subject and the verb have no bearing on subject-verb agreement.

Examples:

singular   singular
subject   verb

The joy of my life returns home tonight.

The phrase *of my life* does not influence the verb *returns*.

The question that still remains unanswered is "Who are you?"

[singular subject — question; singular verb — is]

Don't let the phrase "*that still remains…*" trouble you. The subject *question* goes with *is*.

COMPOUND SUBJECTS

A compound subject is formed when two or more nouns joined by *and*, *or*, or *nor* jointly act as the subject of the sentence.

JOINED BY AND

When a compound subject is joined by *and*, it is treated as a plural subject and requires a plural verb.

Examples:

[plural subject] You and Jon *[plural verb]* are invited to come to my house.

[plural subject] The pencil and paper *[plural verb]* belong to me.

JOINED BY OR/NOR

For a compound subject joined by *or* or *nor*, the verb must agree in number with the part of the subject that is closest to the verb (italicized in the examples below).

Examples:

[subject] Today or tomorrow *[verb]* is the day.

[subject] Stan or Phil *[verb]* wants to read the book.

[subject] Neither the pen nor the book *[verb]* is on the desk.

[subject] Either the blanket or pillows *[verb]* arrive this afternoon.

INDEFINITE PRONOUNS AS SUBJECT

An indefinite pronoun is a pronoun that does not refer to a specific noun. Different indefinite pronouns may only function as a singular noun, only function as a plural noun, or change depending on how they are used.

ALWAYS SINGULAR

Pronouns such as *each, either, everybody, anybody, somebody,* and *nobody* are always singular.

Examples:

singular subject   singular verb

Each of the runners has a different bib number.

singular verb   singular subject

Is either of you ready for the game?

Note: The words *each* and *either* can also be used as adjectives (e.g., *each* person is unique). When one of these adjectives modifies the subject of a sentence, it is always a singular subject.

singular subject   singular verb

Everybody grows a day older every day.

singular subject   singular verb

Anybody is welcome to bring a tent.

ALWAYS PLURAL

Pronouns such as *both, several,* and *many* are always plural.

Examples:

plural subject   plural verb

Both of the siblings were too tired to argue.

plural subject   plural verb

Many have tried, but none have succeeded.

DEPEND ON CONTEXT

Pronouns such as *some, any, all, none, more,* and *most* can be either singular or plural depending on what they are representing in the context of the sentence.

Examples:

singular subject   singular verb

All of my dog's food was still there in his bowl.

plural subject   plural verb

By the end of the night, all of my guests were already excited about coming to my next party.

OTHER CASES INVOLVING PLURAL OR IRREGULAR FORM

Some nouns are **singular in meaning but plural in form**: news, mathematics, physics, and economics.

> The *news is* coming on now.

> *Mathematics is* my favorite class.

Some nouns are plural in form and meaning, and have **no singular equivalent**: scissors and pants.

> Do these *pants come* with a shirt?

> The *scissors are* for my project.

Mathematical operations are **irregular** in their construction, but are normally considered to be **singular in meaning**.

> *One plus one is* two.

> *Three times three is* nine.

Note: Look to your **dictionary** for help when you aren't sure whether a noun with a plural form has a singular or plural meaning.

COMPLEMENTS

A complement is a noun, pronoun, or adjective that is used to give more information about the subject or verb in the sentence.

DIRECT OBJECTS

A direct object is a noun or pronoun that takes or receives the **action** of a verb. (Remember: a complete sentence does not need a direct object, so not all sentences will have them. A sentence needs only a subject and a verb.) When you are looking for a direct object, find the verb and ask *who* or *what*.

Examples:

> I took *the blanket*.

> Jane read *books*.

INDIRECT OBJECTS

An indirect object is a word or group of words that show how an action had an **influence** on someone or something. If there is an indirect object in a sentence, then you always have a direct object in the sentence. When you are looking for the indirect object, find the verb and ask *to/for whom or what*.

Examples:

indirect direct
object object
We taught the old dog a new trick.

indirect direct
object object
I gave them a math lesson.

> **Review Video: Direct and Indirect Objects**
> Visit mometrix.com/academy and enter code: 817385

PREDICATE NOMINATIVES AND PREDICATE ADJECTIVES

As we looked at previously, verbs may be classified as either action verbs or linking verbs. A linking verb is so named because it links the subject to words in the predicate that describe or define the subject. These words are called predicate nominatives (if nouns or pronouns) or predicate adjectives (if adjectives).

Examples:

subject predicate
nominative
My father is a lawyer.

subject predicate
adjective
Your mother is patient.

PRONOUN USAGE

The **antecedent** is the noun that has been replaced by a pronoun. A pronoun and its antecedent **agree** when they have the same number (singular or plural) and gender (male, female, or neutral).

Examples:

antecedent pronoun
Singular agreement: John came into town, and he played for us.

antecedent pronoun
Plural agreement: John and Rick came into town, and they played for us.

To determine which is the correct pronoun to use in a compound subject or object, try each pronoun **alone** in place of the compound in the sentence. Your knowledge of pronouns will tell you which one is correct.

Example:

Bob and (I, me) will be going.

Test: (1) *I will be going* or (2) *Me will be going*. The second choice cannot be correct because *me* cannot be used as the subject of a sentence. Instead, *me* is used as an object.

Answer: Bob and I will be going.

When a pronoun is used with a noun immediately following (as in "we boys"), try the sentence **without the added noun**.

Example:

(We/Us) boys played football last year.

Test: (1) *We played football last year* or (2) *Us played football last year*. Again, the second choice cannot be correct because *us* cannot be used as a subject of a sentence. Instead, *us* is used as an object.

Answer: We boys played football last year.

> **Review Video: Pronoun Usage**
> Visit mometrix.com/academy and enter code: 666500

A pronoun should point clearly to the **antecedent**. Here is how a pronoun reference can be unhelpful if it is puzzling or not directly stated.

            antecedent   pronoun
Unhelpful: Ron and Jim went to the store, and he bought soda.

Who bought soda? Ron or Jim?

          antecedent   pronoun
Helpful: Jim went to the store, and he bought soda.

The sentence is clear. Jim bought the soda.

Some pronouns change their form by their placement in a sentence. A pronoun that is a **subject** in a sentence comes in the **subjective case**. Pronouns that serve as **objects** appear in the **objective case**. Finally, the pronouns that are used as **possessives** appear in the **possessive case**.

Examples:

Subjective case: *He* is coming to the show.

The pronoun *He* is the subject of the sentence.

Objective case: Josh drove *him* to the airport.

The pronoun *him* is the object of the sentence.

Possessive case: The flowers are *mine*.

The pronoun *mine* shows ownership of the flowers.

The word *who* is a subjective-case pronoun that can be used as a **subject**. The word *whom* is an objective-case pronoun that can be used as an **object**. The words *who* and *whom* are common in subordinate clauses or in questions.

Examples:

subject   verb
He knows who wants to come.

object   verb
He knows the man whom we want at the party.

CLAUSES

A clause is a group of words that contains both a subject and a predicate (verb). There are two types of clauses: independent and dependent. An **independent clause** contains a complete thought, while a **dependent (or subordinate) clause** does not. A dependent clause includes a subject and a verb, and may also contain objects or complements, but it cannot stand as a complete thought without being joined to an independent clause. Dependent clauses function within sentences as adjectives, adverbs, or nouns.

Example:

independent   dependent
clause   clause
I am running because I want to stay in shape.

The clause *I am running* is an independent clause: it has a subject and a verb, and it gives a complete thought. The clause *because I want to stay in shape* is a dependent clause: it has a subject and a verb, but it does not express a complete thought. It adds detail to the independent clause to which it is attached.

> **Review Video: Independent and Dependent Clauses**
> Visit mometrix.com/academy and enter code: 556903

TYPES OF DEPENDENT CLAUSES

ADJECTIVE CLAUSES

An **adjective clause** is a dependent clause that modifies a noun or a pronoun. Adjective clauses begin with a relative pronoun (*who, whose, whom, which,* and *that*) or a relative adverb (*where, when,* and *why*).

Also, adjective clauses come after the noun that the clause needs to explain or rename. This is done to have a clear connection to the independent clause.

Examples:

independent   adjective
clause   clause
I learned the reason why I won the award.

independent   adjective
clause   clause
This is the place where I started my first job.

An adjective clause can be an essential or nonessential clause. An essential clause is very important to the sentence. **Essential clauses** explain or define a person or thing. **Nonessential clauses** give more information about a person or thing but are not necessary to define them. Nonessential clauses are set off with commas while essential clauses are not.

Examples:

essential
clause

A person who works hard at first can often rest later in life.

nonessential
clause

Neil Armstrong , who walked on the moon, is my hero.

ADVERB CLAUSES

An **adverb clause** is a dependent clause that modifies a verb, adjective, or adverb. In sentences with multiple dependent clauses, adverb clauses are usually placed immediately before or after the independent clause. An adverb clause is introduced with words such as *after, although, as, before, because, if, since, so, unless, when, where*, and *while*.

Examples:

adverb
clause

When you walked outside, I called the manager.

adverb
clause

I will go with you unless you want to stay.

NOUN CLAUSES

A **noun clause** is a dependent clause that can be used as a subject, object, or complement. Noun clauses begin with words such as *how, that, what, whether, which, who*, and *why*. These words can also come with an adjective clause. Unless the noun clause is being used as the subject of the sentence, it should come after the verb of the independent clause.

Examples:

noun
clause

The real mystery is how you avoided serious injury.

noun
clause

What you learn from each other depends on your honesty with others.

SUBORDINATION

When two related ideas are not of equal importance, the ideal way to combine them is to make the more important idea an independent clause and the less important idea a dependent or subordinate clause. This is called **subordination**.

Example:

Separate ideas: The team had a perfect regular season. The team lost the championship.

Subordinated: Despite having a perfect regular season, *the team lost the championship.*

PHRASES

A phrase is a group of words that functions as a single part of speech, usually a noun, adjective, or adverb. A **phrase** is not a complete thought, but it adds detail or explanation to a sentence, or renames something within the sentence.

PREPOSITIONAL PHRASES

One of the most common types of phrases is the prepositional phrase. A **prepositional phrase** begins with a preposition and ends with a noun or pronoun that is the object of the preposition. Normally, the prepositional phrase functions as an **adjective** or an **adverb** within the sentence.

Examples:

prepositional
phrase
The picnic is on the blanket.

prepositional
phrase
I am sick with a fever today.

prepositional
phrase
Among the many flowers, John found a four-leaf clover.

VERBAL PHRASES

A **verbal** is a word or phrase that is formed from a verb but does not function as a verb. Depending on its particular form, it may be used as a noun, adjective, or adverb. A verbal does **not** replace a verb in a sentence.

Examples:

verb
Correct: Walk a mile daily.

This is a complete sentence with the implied subject *you*.

verbal
Incorrect: To walk a mile.

This is not a sentence since there is no functional verb.

There are three types of verbal: **participles**, **gerunds**, and **infinitives**. Each type of verbal has a corresponding **phrase** that consists of the verbal itself along with any complements or modifiers.

PARTICIPLES

A **participle** is a type of verbal that always functions as an adjective. The present participle always ends with *-ing*. Past participles end with *-d, -ed, -n,* or *-t.*

verb | present participle | past participle
Examples: dance | dancing | danced

Participial phrases most often come right before or right after the noun or pronoun that they modify.

Examples:

participial
phrase

Shipwrecked on an island, the boys started to fish for food.

participial
phrase

Having been seated for five hours, we got out of the car to stretch our legs.

participial
phrase

Praised for their work, the group accepted the first-place trophy.

GERUNDS

A **gerund** is a type of verbal that always functions as a **noun**. Like present participles, gerunds always end with -*ing*, but they can be easily distinguished from one another by the part of speech they represent (participles always function as adjectives). Since a gerund or gerund phrase always functions as a noun, it can be used as the subject of a sentence, the predicate nominative, or the object of a verb or preposition.

Examples:

gerund

We want to be known for teaching the poor.

object of preposition

gerund

Coaching this team is the best job of my life.

subject

gerund

We like practicing our songs in the basement.

object of verb

INFINITIVES

An **infinitive** is a type of verbal that can function as a noun, an adjective, or an adverb. An infinitive is made of the word *to* and the basic form of the verb. As with all other types of verbal phrases, an infinitive phrase includes the verbal itself and all of its complements or modifiers.

Examples:

infinitive
To join the team is my goal in life.
noun

infinitive
The animals have enough food to eat for the night.
adjective

infinitive
People lift weights to exercise their muscles.
adverb

> **Review Video: Gerunds, Infinitives, and Participles**
> Visit mometrix.com/academy and enter code: 634263

APPOSITIVE PHRASES

An **appositive** is a word or phrase that is used to explain or rename nouns or pronouns. Noun phrases, gerund phrases, and infinitive phrases can all be used as appositives.

Examples:

appositive
Terriers, hunters at heart, have been dressed up to look like lap dogs.

The noun phrase *hunters at heart* renames the noun *terriers*.

appositive
His plan, to save and invest his money, was proven as a safe approach.

The infinitive phrase explains what the plan is.

Appositive phrases can be **essential** or **nonessential**. An appositive phrase is essential if the person, place, or thing being described or renamed is too general for its meaning to be understood without the appositive.

Examples:

essential
Two of America's Founding Fathers, George Washington and Thomas Jefferson, served as presidents.

nonessential
George Washington and Thomas Jefferson, two Founding Fathers, served as presidents.

ABSOLUTE PHRASES

An absolute phrase is a phrase that consists of **a noun followed by a participle**. An absolute phrase provides **context** to what is being described in the sentence, but it does not modify or explain any particular word; it is essentially independent.

102

Examples:

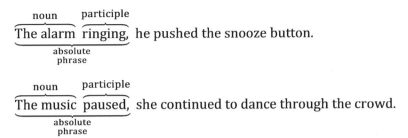

noun   participle
The alarm ringing, he pushed the snooze button.
    absolute
    phrase

noun   participle
The music paused, she continued to dance through the crowd.
    absolute
    phrase

PARALLELISM

When multiple items or ideas are presented in a sentence in series, such as in a list, the items or ideas must be stated in grammatically equivalent ways. In other words, if one idea is stated in gerund form, the second cannot be stated in infinitive form. For example, to write, *I enjoy reading and to study* would be incorrect. An infinitive and a gerund are not equivalent. Instead, you should write *I enjoy reading and studying*. In lists of more than two, all items must be parallel.

Example:

Incorrect: He stopped at the office, grocery store, and the pharmacy before heading home.

The first and third items in the list of places include the article *the*, so the second item needs it as well.

Correct: He stopped at the office, *the* grocery store, and the pharmacy before heading home.

Example:

Incorrect: While vacationing in Europe, she went biking, skiing, and climbed mountains.

The first and second items in the list are gerunds, so the third item must be as well.

Correct: While vacationing in Europe, she went biking, skiing, and *mountain climbing*.

> **Review Video: Parallel Construction**
> Visit mometrix.com/academy and enter code: 831988

SENTENCE PURPOSE

There are four types of sentences: declarative, imperative, interrogative, and exclamatory.

A **declarative** sentence states a fact and ends with a period.

The football game starts at seven o'clock.

An **imperative** sentence tells someone to do something and generally ends with a period. An urgent command might end with an exclamation point instead.

Don't forget to buy your ticket.

An **interrogative** sentence asks a question and ends with a question mark.

Are you going to the game on Friday?

103

An **exclamatory** sentence shows strong emotion and ends with an exclamation point.

I can't believe we won the game!

Review Video: Functions of a Sentence
Visit mometrix.com/academy and enter code: 475974

SENTENCE STRUCTURE

Sentences are classified by structure based on the type and number of clauses present. The four classifications of sentence structure are the following:

Simple: A simple sentence has one independent clause with no dependent clauses. A simple sentence may have **compound elements** (i.e., compound subject or verb).

Examples:

single subject · single verb
Judy watered the lawn.

compound subject · single verb
Judy and Alan watered the lawn.

single subject · compound verb · compound verb
Judy watered the lawn and pulled weeds.

compound subject · compound verb · compound verb
Judy and Alan watered the lawn and pulled weeds.

Compound: A compound sentence has two or more independent clauses with no dependent clauses. Usually, the independent clauses are joined with a comma and a coordinating conjunction or with a semicolon.

Examples:

independent clause · independent clause
The time has come, and we are ready.

independent clause · independent clause
I woke up at dawn; the sun was just coming up.

Complex: A complex sentence has one independent clause and at least one dependent clause.

Examples:

dependent clause · independent clause
Although he had the flu, Harry went to work.

independent clause · dependent clause
Marcia got married, after she finished college.

104

Compound-Complex: A compound-complex sentence has at least two independent clauses and at least one dependent clause.

Examples:

independent clause — dependent clause — independent clause
John is my friend who went to India, and he brought back souvenirs.

independent clause — independent clause — dependent clause
You may not realize this, but we heard the music that you played last night.

> **Review Video: Sentence Structure**
> Visit mometrix.com/academy and enter code: 700478

Sentence variety is important to consider when writing an essay or speech. A variety of sentence lengths and types creates rhythm, makes a passage more engaging, and gives writers an opportunity to demonstrate their writing style. Writing that uses the same length or type of sentence without variation can be boring or difficult to read. To evaluate a passage for effective sentence variety, it is helpful to note whether the passage contains diverse sentence structures and lengths. It is also important to pay attention to the way each sentence starts and avoid beginning with the same words or phrases.

SENTENCE FRAGMENTS

Recall that a group of words must contain at least one **independent clause** in order to be considered a sentence. If it doesn't contain even one independent clause, it is called a **sentence fragment**.

The appropriate process for **repairing** a sentence fragment depends on what type of fragment it is. If the fragment is a dependent clause, it can sometimes be as simple as removing a subordinating word (e.g., when, because, if) from the beginning of the fragment. Alternatively, a dependent clause can be incorporated into a closely related neighboring sentence. If the fragment is missing some required part, like a subject or a verb, the fix might be as simple as adding the missing part.

Examples:

Fragment: Because he wanted to sail the Mediterranean.

Removed subordinating word: He wanted to sail the Mediterranean.

Combined with another sentence: Because he wanted to sail the Mediterranean, he booked a Greek island cruise.

RUN-ON SENTENCES

Run-on sentences consist of multiple independent clauses that have not been joined together properly. Run-on sentences can be corrected in several different ways:

Join clauses properly: This can be done with a comma and coordinating conjunction, with a semicolon, or with a colon or dash if the second clause is explaining something in the first.

Example:

Incorrect: I went on the trip, we visited lots of castles.

Corrected: I went on the trip, and we visited lots of castles.

Split into separate sentences: This correction is most effective when the independent clauses are very long or when they are not closely related.

Example:

Incorrect: The drive to New York takes ten hours, my uncle lives in Boston.

Corrected: The drive to New York takes ten hours. My uncle lives in Boston.

Make one clause dependent: This is the easiest way to make the sentence correct and more interesting at the same time. It's often as simple as adding a subordinating word between the two clauses or before the first clause.

Example:

Incorrect: I finally made it to the store and I bought some eggs.

Corrected: When I finally made it to the store, I bought some eggs.

Reduce to one clause with a compound verb: If both clauses have the same subject, remove the subject from the second clause, and you now have just one clause with a compound verb.

Example:

Incorrect: The drive to New York takes ten hours, it makes me very tired.

Corrected: The drive to New York takes ten hours and makes me very tired.

Note: While these are the simplest ways to correct a run-on sentence, often the best way is to completely reorganize the thoughts in the sentence and rewrite it.

Review Video: Fragments and Run-on Sentences
Visit mometrix.com/academy and enter code: 541989

DANGLING AND MISPLACED MODIFIERS

DANGLING MODIFIERS

A dangling modifier is a dependent clause or verbal phrase that does not have a clear logical connection to a word in the sentence.

Example:

dangling
modifier

Incorrect: Reading each magazine article, the stories caught my attention.

The word *stories* cannot be modified by *Reading each magazine article*. People can read, but stories cannot read. Therefore, the subject of the sentence must be a person.

dependent
clause

Corrected: Reading each magazine article, I was entertained by the stories.

Example:

dangling
modifier

Incorrect: Ever since childhood, my grandparents have visited me for Christmas.

The speaker in this sentence can't have been visited by her grandparents when *they* were children, since she wouldn't have been born yet. Either the modifier should be clarified or the sentence should be rearranged to specify whose childhood is being referenced.

dependent
clause

Clarified: Ever since I was a child, my grandparents have visited for Christmas.

dependent
clause

Rearranged: I have enjoyed my grandparents visiting for Christmas, ever since childhood.

MISPLACED MODIFIERS

Because modifiers are grammatically versatile, they can be put in many different places within the structure of a sentence. The danger of this versatility is that a modifier can accidentally be placed where it is modifying the wrong word or where it is not clear which word it is modifying.

Example:

modifier

Incorrect: She read the book to a crowd that was filled with beautiful pictures.

The book was filled with beautiful pictures, not the crowd.

modifier

Corrected: She read the book that was filled with beautiful pictures to a crowd.

Example:

modifier
Ambiguous: Derek saw a bus nearly hit a man on his way to work.

Was Derek on his way to work or was the other man?

modifier
Derek: On his way to work, Derek saw a bus nearly hit a man.

modifier
The other man: Derek saw a bus nearly hit a man who was on his way to work.

SPLIT INFINITIVES

A split infinitive occurs when a modifying word comes between the word *to* and the verb that pairs with *to*.

Example: To *clearly* explain vs. To *explain* clearly | To *softly* sing vs. To *sing* softly

Though considered improper by some, split infinitives may provide better clarity and simplicity in some cases than the alternatives. As such, avoiding them should not be considered a universal rule.

DOUBLE NEGATIVES

Standard English allows **two negatives** only when a **positive** meaning is intended. For example, *The team was not displeased with their performance.* Double negatives to emphasize negation are not used in standard English.

Negative modifiers (e.g., never, no, and not) should not be paired with other negative modifiers or negative words (e.g., none, nobody, nothing, or neither). The modifiers *hardly, barely*, and *scarcely* are also considered negatives in standard English, so they should not be used with other negatives.

Punctuation

END PUNCTUATION

PERIODS

Use a period to end all sentences except direct questions and exclamations. Periods are also used for abbreviations.

Examples: 3 p.m. | 2 a.m. | Mr. Jones | Mrs. Stevens | Dr. Smith | Bill, Jr. | Pennsylvania Ave.

Note: An abbreviation is a shortened form of a word or phrase.

QUESTION MARKS

Question marks should be used following a **direct question**. A polite request can be followed by a period instead of a question mark.

Direct Question: What is for lunch today? | How are you? | Why is that the answer?

Polite Requests: Can you please send me the item tomorrow. | Will you please walk with me on the track.

> **Review Video: Question Marks**
> Visit mometrix.com/academy and enter code: 118471

EXCLAMATION MARKS

Exclamation marks are used after a word group or sentence that shows much feeling or has special importance. Exclamation marks should not be overused. They are saved for proper **exclamatory interjections**.

Example: We're going to the finals! | You have a beautiful car! | "That's crazy!" she yelled.

> **Review Video: Exclamation Points**
> Visit mometrix.com/academy and enter code: 199367

COMMAS

The comma is a punctuation mark that can help you understand connections in a sentence. Not every sentence needs a comma. However, if a sentence needs a comma, you need to put it in the

right place. A comma in the wrong place (or an absent comma) will make a sentence's meaning unclear. These are some of the rules for commas:

Use Case	Example
Before a **coordinating conjunction** joining independent clauses	Bob caught three fish, and I caught two fish.
After an **introductory phrase**	After the final out, we went to a restaurant to celebrate.
After an **adverbial clause**	Studying the stars, I was awed by the beauty of the sky.
Between **items in a series**	I will bring the turkey, the pie, and the coffee.
For **interjections**	Wow, you know how to play this game.
After *yes* and *no* responses	No, I cannot come tomorrow.
Separate **nonessential modifiers**	John Frank, who coaches the team, was promoted today.
Separate **nonessential appositives**	Thomas Edison, an American inventor, was born in Ohio.
Separate **nouns of direct address**	You, John, are my only hope in this moment.
Separate **interrogative tags**	This is the last time, correct?
Separate **contrasts**	You are my friend, not my enemy.
Writing **dates**	July 4, 1776, is an important date to remember.
Writing **addresses**	He is meeting me at 456 Delaware Avenue, Washington, D.C., tomorrow morning.
Writing **geographical names**	Paris, France, is my favorite city.
Writing **titles**	John Smith, PhD, will be visiting your class today.
Separate **expressions like *he said***	"You can start," she said, "with an apology."

Also, you can use a comma **between coordinate adjectives** not joined with *and*. However, not all adjectives are coordinate (i.e., equal or parallel).

Incorrect: The kind, brown dog followed me home.

Correct: The kind, loyal dog followed me home.

There are two simple ways to know if your adjectives are coordinate. One, you can join the adjectives with *and*: *The kind and loyal dog*. Two, you can change the order of the adjectives: *The loyal, kind dog*.

> **Review Video: Commas**
> Visit mometrix.com/academy and enter code: 786797

SEMICOLONS

The semicolon is used to connect major sentence pieces of equal value. Some rules for semicolons include:

Use Case	Example
Between closely connected independent clauses **not connected with a coordinating conjunction**	You are right; we should go with your plan.
Between independent clauses **linked with a transitional word**	I think that we can agree on this; however, I am not sure about my friends.
Between items in a **series that has internal punctuation**	I have visited New York, New York; Augusta, Maine; and Baltimore, Maryland.

> **Review Video: Semicolon Usage**
> Visit mometrix.com/academy and enter code: 370605

COLONS

The colon is used to call attention to the words that follow it. A colon must come after a **complete independent clause**. The rules for colons are as follows:

Use Case	Example
After an independent clause to **make a list**	I want to learn many languages: Spanish, German, and Italian.
For **explanations**	There is one thing that stands out on your resume: responsibility.
To give a **quote**	He started with an idea: "We are able to do more than we imagine."
After the **greeting in a formal letter**	To Whom It May Concern:
Show **hours and minutes**	It is 3:14 p.m.
Separate a **title and subtitle**	The essay is titled "America: A Short Introduction to a Modern Country."

> **Review Video: Colons**
> Visit mometrix.com/academy and enter code: 868673

PARENTHESES

Parentheses are used for additional information. Also, they can be used to put labels for letters or numbers in a series. Parentheses should be not be used very often. If they are overused, parentheses can be a distraction instead of a help.

Examples:

> **Extra Information**: The rattlesnake (see Image 2) is a dangerous snake of North and South America.

> **Series**: Include in the email (1) your name, (2) your address, and (3) your question for the author.

> **Review Video: Parentheses**
> Visit mometrix.com/academy and enter code: 947743

111

QUOTATION MARKS

Use quotation marks to close off **direct quotations** of a person's spoken or written words. Do not use quotation marks around indirect quotations. An indirect quotation gives someone's message without using the person's exact words. Use **single quotation marks** to close off a quotation inside a quotation.

Direct Quote: Nancy said, "I am waiting for Henry to arrive."

Indirect Quote: Henry said that he is going to be late to the meeting.

Quote inside a Quote: The teacher asked, "Has everyone read 'The Gift of the Magi'?"

Quotation marks should be used around the titles of **short works**: newspaper and magazine articles, poems, short stories, songs, television episodes, radio programs, and subdivisions of books or websites.

Examples:

"Rip Van Winkle" (short story by Washington Irving)

"O Captain! My Captain!" (poem by Walt Whitman)

Although it is not standard usage, quotation marks are sometimes used to highlight **irony** or the use of words to mean something other than their dictionary definition. This type of usage should be employed sparingly, if at all.

Examples:

| The boss warned Frank that he was walking on "thin ice." | Frank is not walking on real ice. Instead, he is being warned to avoid mistakes. |
| The teacher thanked the young man for his "honesty." | The quotation marks around *honesty* show that the teacher does not believe the young man's explanation. |

| **Review Video: Quotation Marks** |
| Visit mometrix.com/academy and enter code: 884918 |

Periods and commas are put **inside** quotation marks. Colons and semicolons are put **outside** the quotation marks. Question marks and exclamation points are placed inside quotation marks when they are part of a quote. When the question or exclamation mark goes with the whole sentence, the mark is left outside of the quotation marks.

Examples:

Period and comma	We read "The Gift of the Magi," "The Skylight Room," and "The Cactus."
Semicolon	They watched "The Nutcracker"; then, they went home.
Exclamation mark that is a part of a quote	The crowd cheered, "Victory!"
Question mark that goes with the whole sentence	Is your favorite short story "The Tell-Tale Heart"?

112

APOSTROPHES

An apostrophe is used to show **possession** or the **deletion of letters in contractions**. An apostrophe is not needed with the possessive pronouns *his, hers, its, ours, theirs, whose,* and *yours.*

Singular Nouns: David's car | a book's theme | my brother's board game

Plural Nouns that end with *-s*: the scissors' handle | boys' basketball

Plural Nouns that end without *-s*: Men's department | the people's adventure

> **Review Video: When to Use an Apostrophe**
> Visit mometrix.com/academy and enter code: 213068
>
> **Review Video: Punctuation Errors in Possessive Pronouns**
> Visit mometrix.com/academy and enter code: 221438

HYPHENS

Hyphens are used to **separate compound words**. Use hyphens in the following cases:

Use Case	Example
Compound numbers from 21 to 99 when written out in words	This team needs twenty-five points to win the game.
Written-out fractions that are used as adjectives	The recipe says that we need a three-fourths cup of butter.
Compound adjectives that come before a noun	The well-fed dog took a nap.
Unusual compound words that would be hard to read or easily confused with other words	This is the best anti-itch cream on the market.

Note: This is not a complete set of the rules for hyphens. A dictionary is the best tool for knowing if a compound word needs a hyphen.

> **Review Video: Hyphens**
> Visit mometrix.com/academy and enter code: 981632

DASHES

Dashes are used to show a **break** or a **change in thought** in a sentence or to act as parentheses in a sentence. When typing, use two hyphens to make a dash. Do not put a space before or after the dash. The following are the functions of dashes:

Use Case	Example
Set off parenthetical statements or an **appositive with internal punctuation**	The three trees—oak, pine, and magnolia—are coming on a truck tomorrow.
Show a **break or change in tone or thought**	The first question—how silly of me—does not have a correct answer.

ELLIPSIS MARKS

The ellipsis mark has **three** periods (...) to show when **words have been removed** from a quotation. If a **full sentence or more** is removed from a quoted passage, you need to use **four** periods to show the removed text and the end punctuation mark. The ellipsis mark should not be

used at the beginning of a quotation. The ellipsis mark should also not be used at the end of a quotation unless some words have been deleted from the end of the final sentence.

Example:

"Then he picked up the groceries...paid for them...later he went home."

BRACKETS

There are two main reasons to use brackets:

Use Case	Example
Placing **parentheses inside of parentheses**	The hero of this story, Paul Revere (a silversmith and industrialist [see Ch. 4]), rode through towns of Massachusetts to warn of advancing British troops.
Adding **clarification or detail to a quotation** that is not part of the quotation	The father explained, "My children are planning to attend my alma mater [State University]."

Review Video: Brackets
Visit mometrix.com/academy and enter code: 727546

Common Usage Mistakes

WORD CONFUSION
WHICH, THAT, AND WHO

The words *which, that,* and *who* can act as **relative pronouns** to help clarify or describe a noun.

Which is used for things only.

Example: Andrew's car, *which is old and rusty,* broke down last week.

That is used for people or things. *That* is usually informal when used to describe people.

Example: Is this the only book *that Louis L'Amour wrote?*

Example: Is Louis L'Amour the author *that wrote Western novels?*

Who is used for people or for animals that have an identity or personality.

Example: Mozart was the composer *who wrote those operas.*

Example: John's dog, *who is called Max,* is large and fierce.

HOMOPHONES

Homophones are words that sound alike (or similar) but have different **spellings** and **definitions**. A homophone is a type of **homonym**, which is a pair or group of words that are pronounced or spelled the same, but do not mean the same thing.

TO, TOO, AND TWO

To can be an adverb or a preposition for showing direction, purpose, and relationship. See your dictionary for the many other ways to use *to* in a sentence.

Examples: I went to the store. | I want to go with you.

Too is an adverb that means *also, as well, very,* or *in excess.*

Examples: I can walk a mile too. | You have eaten too much.

Two is a number.

Example: You have two minutes left.

THERE, THEIR, AND THEY'RE

There can be an adjective, adverb, or pronoun. Often, *there* is used to show a place or to start a sentence.

Examples: I went there yesterday. | There is something in his pocket.

Their is a pronoun that is used to show ownership.

Examples: He is their father. | This is their fourth apology this week.

They're is a contraction of *they are.*

Example: Did you know that they're in town?

115

KNEW AND NEW

Knew is the past tense of *know*.

>Example: I knew the answer.

New is an adjective that means something is current, has not been used, or is modern.

>Example: This is my new phone.

THEN AND THAN

Then is an adverb that indicates sequence or order:

>Example: I'm going to run to the library and then come home.

Than is special-purpose word used only for comparisons:

>Example: Susie likes chips more than candy.

ITS AND IT'S

Its is a pronoun that shows ownership.

>Example: The guitar is in its case.

It's is a contraction of *it is*.

>Example: It's an honor and a privilege to meet you.

Note: The *h* in honor is silent, so *honor* starts with the vowel sound *o*, which must have the article *an*.

YOUR AND YOU'RE

Your is a pronoun that shows ownership.

>Example: This is your moment to shine.

You're is a contraction of *you are*.

>Example: Yes, you're correct.

SAW AND SEEN

Saw is the past-tense form of *see*.

>Example: I saw a turtle on my walk this morning.

Seen is the past participle of *see*.

>Example: I have seen this movie before.

AFFECT AND EFFECT

There are two main reasons that *affect* and *effect* are so often confused: 1) both words can be used as either a noun or a verb, and 2) unlike most homophones, their usage and meanings are closely related to each other. Here is a quick rundown of the four usage options:

Affect (n): feeling, emotion, or mood that is displayed

> Example: The patient had a flat *affect*. (i.e., his face showed little or no emotion)

Affect (v): to alter, to change, to influence

> Example: The sunshine *affects* the plant's growth.

Effect (n): a result, a consequence

> Example: What *effect* will this weather have on our schedule?

Effect (v): to bring about, to cause to be

> Example: These new rules will *effect* order in the office.

The noun form of *affect* is rarely used outside of technical medical descriptions, so if a noun form is needed on the test, you can safely select *effect*. The verb form of *effect* is not as rare as the noun form of *affect*, but it's still not all that likely to show up on your test. If you need a verb and you can't decide which to use based on the definitions, choosing *affect* is your best bet.

HOMOGRAPHS

Homographs are words that share the same spelling, but have different meanings and sometimes different pronunciations. To figure out which meaning is being used, you should be looking for context clues. The context clues give hints to the meaning of the word. For example, the word *spot* has many meanings. It can mean "a place" or "a stain or blot." In the sentence "After my lunch, I saw a spot on my shirt," the word *spot* means "a stain or blot." The context clues of "After my lunch" and "on my shirt" guide you to this decision. A homograph is another type of homonym.

BANK

> (noun): an establishment where money is held for savings or lending

> (verb): to collect or pile up

CONTENT

> (noun): the topics that will be addressed within a book

> (adjective): pleased or satisfied

> (verb): to make someone pleased or satisfied

FINE

> (noun): an amount of money that acts a penalty for an offense

> (adjective): very small or thin

> (adverb): in an acceptable way

> (verb): to make someone pay money as a punishment

INCENSE

> (noun): a material that is burned in religious settings and makes a pleasant aroma

> (verb): to frustrate or anger

LEAD

(noun): the first or highest position

(noun): a heavy metallic element

(verb): to direct a person or group of followers

(adjective): containing lead

OBJECT

(noun): a lifeless item that can be held and observed

(verb): to disagree

PRODUCE

(noun): fruits and vegetables

(verb): to make or create something

REFUSE

(noun): garbage or debris that has been thrown away

(verb): to not allow

SUBJECT

(noun): an area of study

(verb): to force or subdue

TEAR

(noun): a fluid secreted by the eyes

(verb): to separate or pull apart

The Writing Process

BRAINSTORMING

Brainstorming is a technique that is used to find a creative approach to a subject. This can be accomplished by simple **free-association** with a topic. For example, with paper and pen, write every thought that you have about the topic in a word or phrase. This is done without critical thinking. You should put everything that comes to your mind about the topic on your scratch paper. Then, you need to read the list over a few times. Next, look for patterns, repetitions, and clusters of ideas. This allows a variety of fresh ideas to come as you think about the topic.

FREE WRITING

Free writing is a more structured form of brainstorming. The method involves taking a limited amount of time (e.g., 2 to 3 minutes) to write everything that comes to mind about the topic in complete sentences. When time expires, review everything that has been written down. Many of your sentences may make little or no sense, but the insights and observations that can come from free writing make this method a valuable approach. Usually, free writing results in a fuller expression of ideas than brainstorming because thoughts and associations are written in complete sentences. However, both techniques can be used to complement each other.

PLANNING

Planning is the process of organizing a piece of writing before composing a draft. Planning can include creating an outline or a graphic organizer, such as a Venn diagram, a spider-map, or a flowchart. These methods should help the writer identify their topic, main ideas, and the general organization of the composition. Preliminary research can also take place during this stage. Planning helps writers organize all of their ideas and decide if they have enough material to begin their first draft. However, writers should remember that the decisions they make during this step will likely change later in the process, so their plan does not have to be perfect.

DRAFTING

Writers may then use their plan, outline, or graphic organizer to compose their first draft. They may write subsequent drafts to improve their writing. Writing multiple drafts can help writers consider different ways to communicate their ideas and address errors that may be difficult to correct without rewriting a section or the whole composition. Most writers will vary in how many drafts they choose to write, as there is no "right" number of drafts. Writing drafts also takes away the pressure to write perfectly on the first try, as writers can improve with each draft they write.

REVISING, EDITING, AND PROOFREADING

Once a writer completes a draft, they can move on to the revising, editing, and proofreading steps to improve their draft. These steps begin with making broad changes that may apply to large sections of a composition and then making small, specific corrections. **Revising** is the first and broadest of these steps. Revising involves ensuring that the composition addresses an appropriate audience, includes all necessary material, maintains focus throughout, and is organized logically. Revising may occur after the first draft to ensure that the following drafts improve upon errors from the first draft. Some revision should occur between each draft to avoid repeating these errors. The **editing** phase of writing is narrower than the revising phase. Editing a composition should include steps such as improving transitions between paragraphs, ensuring each paragraph is on topic, and improving the flow of the text. The editing phase may also include correcting grammatical errors that cannot be fixed without significantly altering the text. **Proofreading** involves fixing misspelled words, typos, other grammatical errors, and any remaining surface-level flaws in the composition.

119

RECURSIVE WRITING PROCESS

However you approach writing, you may find comfort in knowing that the revision process can occur in any order. The **recursive writing process** is not as difficult as the phrase may make it seem. Simply put, the recursive writing process means that you may need to revisit steps after completing other steps. It also implies that the steps are not required to take place in any certain order. Indeed, you may find that planning, drafting, and revising can all take place at about the same time. The writing process involves moving back and forth between planning, drafting, and revising, followed by more planning, more drafting, and more revising until the writing is satisfactory.

> **Review Video: Recursive Writing Process**
> Visit mometrix.com/academy and enter code: 951611

TECHNOLOGY IN THE WRITING PROCESS

Modern technology has yielded several tools that can be used to make the writing process more convenient and organized. Word processors and online tools, such as databases and plagiarism detectors, allow much of the writing process to be completed in one place, using one device.

TECHNOLOGY FOR PLANNING AND DRAFTING

For the planning and drafting stages of the writing process, word processors are a helpful tool. These programs also feature formatting tools, allowing users to create their own planning tools or create digital outlines that can be easily converted into sentences, paragraphs, or an entire essay draft. Online databases and references also complement the planning process by providing convenient access to information and sources for research. Word processors also allow users to keep up with their work and update it more easily than if they wrote their work by hand. Online word processors often allow users to collaborate, making group assignments more convenient. These programs also allow users to include illustrations or other supplemental media in their compositions.

TECHNOLOGY FOR REVISING, EDITING, AND PROOFREADING

Word processors also benefit the revising, editing, and proofreading stages of the writing process. Most of these programs indicate errors in spelling and grammar, allowing users to catch minor errors and correct them quickly. There are also websites designed to help writers by analyzing text for deeper errors, such as poor sentence structure, inappropriate complexity, lack of sentence variety, and style issues. These websites can help users fix errors they may not know to look for or may have simply missed. As writers finish these steps, they may benefit from checking their work for any plagiarism. There are several websites and programs that compare text to other documents and publications across the internet and detect any similarities within the text. These websites show the source of the similar information, so users know whether or not they referenced the source and unintentionally plagiarized its contents.

TECHNOLOGY FOR PUBLISHING

Technology also makes managing written work more convenient. Digitally storing documents keeps everything in one place and is easy to reference. Digital storage also makes sharing work easier, as documents can be attached to an email or stored online. This also allows writers to publish their work easily, as they can electronically submit it to other publications or freely post it to a personal blog, profile, or website.

Outlining and Organizing Ideas

MAIN IDEAS, SUPPORTING DETAILS, AND OUTLINING A TOPIC

A writer often begins the first paragraph of a paper by stating the **main idea** or point, also known as the **topic sentence**. The rest of the paragraph supplies particular details that develop and support the main point. One way to visualize the relationship between the main point and supporting information is by considering a table: the tabletop is the main point, and each of the table's legs is a supporting detail or group of details. Both professional authors and students can benefit from planning their writing by first making an outline of the topic. Outlines facilitate quick identification of the main point and supporting details without having to wade through the additional language that will exist in the fully developed essay, article, or paper. Outlining can also help readers to analyze a piece of existing writing for the same reason. The outline first summarizes the main idea in one sentence. Then, below that, it summarizes the supporting details in a numbered list. Writing the paper then consists of filling in the outline with detail, writing a paragraph for each supporting point, and adding an introduction and conclusion.

INTRODUCTION

The purpose of the introduction is to capture the reader's attention and announce the essay's main idea. Normally, the introduction contains 50-80 words, or 3-5 sentences. An introduction can begin with an interesting quote, a question, or a strong opinion—something that will **engage** the reader's interest and prompt them to keep reading. If you are writing your essay to a specific prompt, your introduction should include a **restatement or summarization** of the prompt so that the reader will have some context for your essay. Finally, your introduction should briefly state your **thesis or main idea**: the primary thing you hope to communicate to the reader through your essay. Don't try to include all of the details and nuances of your thesis, or all of your reasons for it, in the introduction. That's what the rest of the essay is for!

> **Review Video: Introduction**
> Visit mometrix.com/academy and enter code: 961328

THESIS STATEMENT

The thesis is the main idea of the essay. A temporary thesis, or working thesis, should be established early in the writing process because it will serve to keep the writer focused as ideas develop. This temporary thesis is subject to change as you continue to write.

The temporary thesis has two parts: a **topic** (i.e., the focus of your essay based on the prompt) and a **comment**. The comment makes an important point about the topic. A temporary thesis should be interesting and specific. Also, you need to limit the topic to a manageable scope. These three questions are useful tools to measure the effectiveness of any temporary thesis:

- Does the focus of my essay have enough interest to hold an audience?
- Is the focus of my essay specific enough to generate interest?
- Is the focus of my essay manageable for the time limit? Too broad? Too narrow?

The thesis should be a generalization rather than a fact because the thesis prepares readers for facts and details that support the thesis. The process of bringing the thesis into sharp focus may help in outlining major sections of the work. Once the thesis and introduction are complete, you can address the body of the work.

> **Review Video: Thesis Statements**
> Visit mometrix.com/academy and enter code: 691033

SUPPORTING THE THESIS

Throughout your essay, the thesis should be **explained clearly and supported** adequately by additional arguments. The thesis sentence needs to contain a clear statement of the purpose of your essay and a comment about the thesis. With the thesis statement, you have an opportunity to state what is noteworthy of this particular treatment of the prompt. Each sentence and paragraph should build on and support the thesis.

When you respond to the prompt, use parts of the passage to support your argument or defend your position. Using supporting evidence from the passage strengths your argument because readers can see your attention to the entire passage and your response to the details and facts within the passage. You can use facts, details, statistics, and direct quotations from the passage to uphold your position. Be sure to point out which information comes from the original passage and base your argument around that evidence.

BODY

In an essay's introduction, the writer establishes the thesis and may indicate how the rest of the piece will be structured. In the body of the piece, the writer **elaborates** upon, **illustrates**, and **explains** the **thesis statement**. How writers arrange supporting details and their choices of paragraph types are development techniques. Writers may give examples of the concept introduced in the thesis statement. If the subject includes a cause-and-effect relationship, the author may explain its causality. A writer will explain or analyze the main idea of the piece throughout the body, often by presenting arguments for the veracity or credibility of the thesis statement. Writers may use development to define or clarify ambiguous terms. Paragraphs within the body may be organized using natural sequences, like space and time. Writers may employ **inductive reasoning**, using multiple details to establish a generalization or causal relationship, or **deductive reasoning**, proving a generalized hypothesis or proposition through a specific example or case.

> **Review Video: Drafting Body Paragraphs**
> Visit mometrix.com/academy and enter code: 724590

PARAGRAPHS

After the introduction of a passage, a series of body paragraphs will carry a message through to the conclusion. Each paragraph should be **unified around a main point**. Normally, a good topic sentence summarizes the paragraph's main point. A topic sentence is a general sentence that gives an introduction to the paragraph.

The sentences that follow support the topic sentence. However, though it is usually the first sentence, the topic sentence can come as the final sentence to the paragraph if the earlier sentences give a clear explanation of the paragraph's topic. This allows the topic sentence to function as a concluding sentence. Overall, the paragraphs need to stay true to the main point. This means that any unnecessary sentences that do not advance the main point should be removed.

The main point of a paragraph requires adequate development (i.e., a substantial paragraph that covers the main point). A paragraph of two or three sentences does not cover a main point. This is especially true when the main point of the paragraph gives strong support to the argument of the thesis. An occasional short paragraph is fine as a transitional device. However, a well-developed argument will have paragraphs with more than a few sentences.

METHODS OF DEVELOPING PARAGRAPHS

Common methods of adding substance to paragraphs include examples, illustrations, analogies, and cause and effect.

- **Examples** are supporting details to the main idea of a paragraph or a passage. When authors write about something that their audience may not understand, they can provide an example to show their point. When authors write about something that is not easily accepted, they can give examples to prove their point.
- **Illustrations** are extended examples that require several sentences. Well-selected illustrations can be a great way for authors to develop a point that may not be familiar to their audience.
- **Analogies** make comparisons between items that appear to have nothing in common. Analogies are employed by writers to provoke fresh thoughts about a subject. These comparisons may be used to explain the unfamiliar, to clarify an abstract point, or to argue a point. Although analogies are effective literary devices, they should be used carefully in arguments. Two things may be alike in some respects but completely different in others.
- **Cause and effect** is an excellent device to explain the connection between an action or situation and a particular result. One way that authors can use cause and effect is to state the effect in the topic sentence of a paragraph and add the causes in the body of the paragraph. This method can give an author's paragraphs structure, which always strengthens writing.

TYPES OF PARAGRAPHS

A **paragraph of narration** tells a story or a part of a story. Normally, the sentences are arranged in chronological order (i.e., the order that the events happened). However, flashbacks (i.e., an anecdote from an earlier time) can be included.

A **descriptive paragraph** makes a verbal portrait of a person, place, or thing. When specific details are used that appeal to one or more of the senses (i.e., sight, sound, smell, taste, and touch), authors give readers a sense of being present in the moment.

A **process paragraph** is related to time order (i.e., First, you open the bottle. Second, you pour the liquid, etc.). Usually, this describes a process or teaches readers how to perform a process.

Comparing two things draws attention to their similarities and indicates a number of differences. When authors contrast, they focus only on differences. Both comparing and contrasting may be done point-by-point, noting both the similarities and differences of each point, or in sequential paragraphs, where you discuss all the similarities and then all the differences, or vice versa.

BREAKING TEXT INTO PARAGRAPHS

For most forms of writing, you will need to use multiple paragraphs. As such, determining when to start a new paragraph is very important. Reasons for starting a new paragraph include:

- To mark off the introduction and concluding paragraphs
- To signal a shift to a new idea or topic
- To indicate an important shift in time or place
- To explain a point in additional detail
- To highlight a comparison, contrast, or cause and effect relationship

PARAGRAPH LENGTH

Most readers find that their comfort level for a paragraph is between 100 and 200 words. Shorter paragraphs cause too much starting and stopping and give a choppy effect. Paragraphs that are too long often test the attention span of readers. Two notable exceptions to this rule exist. In scientific or scholarly papers, longer paragraphs suggest seriousness and depth. In journalistic writing, constraints are placed on paragraph size by the narrow columns in a newspaper format.

The first and last paragraphs of a text will usually be the introduction and conclusion. These special-purpose paragraphs are likely to be shorter than paragraphs in the body of the work. Paragraphs in the body of the essay follow the subject's outline (e.g., one paragraph per point in short essays and a group of paragraphs per point in longer works). Some ideas require more development than others, so it is good for a writer to remain flexible. A paragraph of excessive length may be divided, and shorter ones may be combined.

COHERENT PARAGRAPHS

A smooth flow of sentences and paragraphs without gaps, shifts, or bumps will lead to paragraph **coherence**. Ties between old and new information can be smoothed using several methods:

- **Linking ideas clearly**, from the topic sentence to the body of the paragraph, is essential for a smooth transition. The topic sentence states the main point, and this should be followed by specific details, examples, and illustrations that support the topic sentence. The support may be direct or indirect. In **indirect support**, the illustrations and examples may support a sentence that in turn supports the topic directly.
- The **repetition of key words** adds coherence to a paragraph. To avoid dull language, variations of the key words may be used.
- **Parallel structures** are often used within sentences to emphasize the similarity of ideas and connect sentences giving similar information.
- Maintaining a **consistent verb tense** throughout the paragraph helps. Shifting tenses affects the smooth flow of words and can disrupt the coherence of the paragraph.

> **Review Video: How to Write a Good Paragraph**
> Visit mometrix.com/academy and enter code: 682127

SEQUENCE WORDS AND PHRASES

When a paragraph opens with the topic sentence, the second sentence may begin with a phrase like *first of all*, introducing the first supporting detail or example. The writer may introduce the second supporting item with words or phrases like *also*, *in addition*, and *besides*. The writer might introduce succeeding pieces of support with wording like, *another thing*, *moreover*, *furthermore*, or *not only that, but*. The writer may introduce the last piece of support with *lastly*, *finally*, or *last but not least*. Writers get off the point by presenting off-target items not supporting the main point. For example, a main point *my dog is not smart* is supported by the statement, *he's six years old and still doesn't answer to his name*. But *he cries when I leave for school* is not supportive, as it does not indicate lack of intelligence. Writers stay on point by presenting only supportive statements that are directly relevant to and illustrative of their main point.

TRANSITIONS

Transitions between sentences and paragraphs guide readers from idea to idea and indicate relationships between sentences and paragraphs. Writers should be judicious in their use of transitions, inserting them sparingly. They should also be selected to fit the author's purpose— transitions can indicate time, comparison, and conclusion, among other purposes. Tone is also important to consider when using transitional phrases, varying the tone for different audiences. For example, in a scholarly essay, *in summary* would be preferable to the more informal *in short*.

When working with transitional words and phrases, writers usually find a natural flow that indicates when a transition is needed. In reading a draft of the text, it should become apparent where the flow is disrupted. At this point, the writer can add transitional elements during the revision process. Revising can also afford an opportunity to delete transitional devices that seem heavy handed or unnecessary.

> **Review Video: Transitions in Writing**
> Visit mometrix.com/academy and enter code: 233246

TYPES OF TRANSITIONAL WORDS

Time	Afterward, immediately, earlier, meanwhile, recently, lately, now, since, soon, when, then, until, before, etc.
Sequence	too, first, second, further, moreover, also, again, and, next, still, besides, finally
Comparison	similarly, in the same way, likewise, also, again, once more
Contrasting	but, although, despite, however, instead, nevertheless, on the one hand... on the other hand, regardless, yet, in contrast.
Cause and Effect	because, consequently, thus, therefore, then, to this end, since, so, as a result, if... then, accordingly
Examples	for example, for instance, such as, to illustrate, indeed, in fact, specifically
Place	near, far, here, there, to the left/right, next to, above, below, beyond, opposite, beside
Concession	granted that, naturally, of course, it may appear, although it is true that
Repetition, Summary, or Conclusion	as mentioned earlier, as noted, in other words, in short, on the whole, to summarize, therefore, as a result, to conclude, in conclusion
Addition	and, also, furthermore, moreover
Generalization	in broad terms, broadly speaking, in general

> **Review Video: Transitional Words and Phrases**
> Visit mometrix.com/academy and enter code: 197796
>
> **Review Video: Transitions**
> Visit mometrix.com/academy and enter code: 707563

CONCLUSION

Two important principles to consider when writing a conclusion are strength and closure. A strong conclusion gives the reader a sense that the author's main points are meaningful and important, and that the supporting facts and arguments are convincing, solid, and well developed. When a conclusion achieves closure, it gives the impression that the writer has stated all necessary information and points and completed the work, rather than simply stopping after a specified length. Some things to avoid when writing concluding paragraphs include:

- Introducing a completely new idea
- Beginning with obvious or unoriginal phrases like "In conclusion" or "To summarize"
- Apologizing for one's opinions or writing

- Repeating the thesis word for word rather than rephrasing it
- Believing that the conclusion must always summarize the piece

Review Video: <u>Drafting Conclusions</u>
Visit mometrix.com/academy and enter code: 209408

Writing Style and Form

WRITING STYLE AND LINGUISTIC FORM

Linguistic form encodes the literal meanings of words and sentences. It comes from the phonological, morphological, syntactic, and semantic parts of a language. **Writing style** consists of different ways of encoding the meaning and indicating figurative and stylistic meanings. An author's writing style can also be referred to as his or her **voice**.

Writers' stylistic choices accomplish three basic effects on their audiences:

- They **communicate meanings** beyond linguistically dictated meanings,
- They communicate the **author's attitude**, such as persuasive or argumentative effects accomplished through style, and
- They communicate or **express feelings**.

Within style, component areas include:

- Narrative structure
- Viewpoint
- Focus
- Sound patterns
- Meter and rhythm
- Lexical and syntactic repetition and parallelism
- Writing genre
- Representational, realistic, and mimetic effects
- Representation of thought and speech
- Meta-representation (representing representation)
- Irony
- Metaphor and other indirect meanings
- Representation and use of historical and dialectal variations
- Gender-specific and other group-specific speech styles, both real and fictitious
- Analysis of the processes for inferring meaning from writing

LEVEL OF FORMALITY

The relationship between writer and reader is important in choosing a **level of formality** as most writing requires some degree of formality. **Formal writing** is for addressing a superior in a school or work environment. Business letters, textbooks, and newspapers use a moderate to high level of formality. **Informal writing** is appropriate for private letters, personal emails, and business correspondence between close associates.

For your exam, you will want to be aware of informal and formal writing. One way that this can be accomplished is to watch for shifts in point of view in the essay. For example, unless writers are using a personal example, they will rarely refer to themselves (e.g., "*I* think that *my* point is very clear.") to avoid being informal when they need to be formal.

Also, be mindful of an author who addresses his or her audience **directly** in their writing (e.g., "Readers, *like you*, will understand this argument.") as this can be a sign of informal writing. Good writers understand the need to be consistent with their level of formality. Shifts in levels of formality or point of view can confuse readers and cause them to discount the message.

CLICHÉS

Clichés are phrases that have been **overused** to the point that the phrase has no importance or has lost the original meaning. These phrases have no originality and add very little to a passage. Therefore, most writers will avoid the use of clichés. Another option is to make changes to a cliché so that it is not predictable and empty of meaning.

Examples:

When life gives you lemons, make lemonade.

Every cloud has a silver lining.

JARGON

Jargon is **specialized vocabulary** that is used among members of a certain trade or profession. Since jargon is understood by only a small audience, writers will use jargon in passages that will only be read by a specialized audience. For example, medical jargon should be used in a medical journal but not in a New York Times article. Jargon includes exaggerated language that tries to impress rather than inform. Sentences filled with jargon are not precise and are difficult to understand.

Examples:

"He is going to *toenail* these frames for us." (Toenail is construction jargon for nailing at an angle.)

"They brought in a *kip* of material today." (Kip refers to 1000 pounds in architecture and engineering.)

SLANG

Slang is an **informal** and sometimes private language that is understood by some individuals. Slang terms have some usefulness, but they can have a small audience. So, most formal writing will not include this kind of language.

Examples:

"Yes, the event was a blast!" (In this sentence, *blast* means that the event was a great experience.)

"That attempt was an epic fail." (By *epic fail*, the speaker means that his or her attempt was not a success.)

COLLOQUIALISM

A colloquialism is a word or phrase that is found in informal writing. Unlike slang, **colloquial language** will be familiar to a greater range of people. However, colloquialisms are still considered inappropriate for formal writing. Colloquial language can include some slang, but these are limited to contractions for the most part.

Examples:

"Can *y'all* come back another time?" (Y'all is a contraction of "you all.")

"Will you stop him from building this *castle in the air*?" (A "castle in the air" is an improbable or unlikely event.)

ACADEMIC LANGUAGE

In educational settings, students are often expected to use academic language in their schoolwork. Academic language is also commonly found in dissertations and theses, texts published by academic journals, and other forms of academic research. Academic language conventions may vary between fields, but general academic language is free of slang, regional terminology, and noticeable grammatical errors. Specific terms may also be used in academic language, and it is important to understand their proper usage. A writer's command of academic language impacts their ability to communicate in an academic or professional context. While it is acceptable to use colloquialisms, slang, improper grammar, or other forms of informal speech in social settings or at home, it is inappropriate to practice non-academic language in academic contexts.

TONE

Tone may be defined as the writer's **attitude** toward the topic, and to the audience. This attitude is reflected in the language used in the writing. The tone of a work should be **appropriate to the topic** and to the intended audience. While it may be fine to use slang or jargon in some pieces, other texts should not contain such terms. Tone can range from humorous to serious and any level in between. It may be more or less formal, depending on the purpose of the writing and its intended audience. All these nuances in tone can flavor the entire writing and should be kept in mind as the work evolves.

WORD SELECTION

A writer's choice of words is a signature of their style. Careful thought about the use of words can improve a piece of writing. A passage can be an exciting piece to read when attention is given to the use of vivid or specific nouns rather than general ones.

Example:

> General: His kindness will never be forgotten.

> Specific: His thoughtful gifts and bear hugs will never be forgotten.

Attention should also be given to the kind of verbs that are used in sentences. Active verbs (e.g., run, swim) are about an action. Whenever possible, an **active verb should replace a linking verb** to provide clear examples for arguments and to strengthen a passage overall. When using an active verb, one should be sure that the verb is used in the active voice instead of the passive voice. Verbs are in the active voice when the subject is the one doing the action. A verb is in the passive voice when the subject is the recipient of an action.

Example:

> Passive: The winners were called to the stage by the judges.

> Active: The judges called the winners to the stage.

> **Review Video: Word Usage**
> Visit mometrix.com/academy and enter code: 197863

129

CONCISENESS

Conciseness is writing that communicates a message in the fewest words possible. Writing concisely is valuable because short, uncluttered messages allow the reader to understand the author's message more easily and efficiently. Planning is important in writing concise messages. If you have in mind what you need to write beforehand, it will be easier to make a message short and to the point. Do not state the obvious.

Revising is also important. After the message is written, make sure you have effective, pithy sentences that efficiently get your point across. When reviewing the information, imagine a conversation taking place, and concise writing will likely result.

APPROPRIATE KINDS OF WRITING FOR DIFFERENT TASKS, PURPOSES, AND AUDIENCES

When preparing to write a composition, consider the audience and purpose to choose the best type of writing. Three common types of writing are persuasive, expository, and narrative. **Persuasive**, or argumentative writing, is used to convince the audience to take action or agree with the author's claims. **Expository** writing is meant to inform the audience of the author's observations or research on a topic. **Narrative** writing is used to tell the audience a story and often allows more room for creativity. While task, purpose, and audience inform a writer's mode of writing, these factors also impact elements such as tone, vocabulary, and formality.

For example, students who are writing to persuade their parents to grant them some additional privilege, such as permission for a more independent activity, should use more sophisticated vocabulary and diction that sounds more mature and serious to appeal to the parental audience. However, students who are writing for younger children should use simpler vocabulary and sentence structure, as well as choose words that are more vivid and entertaining. They should treat their topics more lightly, and include humor when appropriate. Students who are writing for their classmates may use language that is more informal, as well as age-appropriate.

> **Review Video: Writing Purpose and Audience**
> Visit mometrix.com/academy and enter code: 146627

Modes of Writing

ESSAYS

Essays usually focus on one topic, subject, or goal. There are several types of essays, including informative, persuasive, and narrative. An essay's structure and level of formality depend on the type of essay and its goal. While narrative essays typically do not include outside sources, other types of essays often require some research and the integration of primary and secondary sources.

The basic format of an essay typically has three major parts: the introduction, the body, and the conclusion. The body is further divided into the writer's main points. Short and simple essays may have three main points, while essays covering broader ranges and going into more depth can have almost any number of main points, depending on length.

An essay's introduction should answer three questions:

1. What is the **subject** of the essay?

   If a student writes an essay about a book, the answer would include the title and author of the book and any additional information needed—such as the subject or argument of the book.

2. How does the essay **address** the subject?

   To answer this, the writer identifies the essay's organization by briefly summarizing main points and the evidence supporting them.

3. What will the essay **prove**?

   This is the thesis statement, usually the opening paragraph's last sentence, clearly stating the writer's message.

The body elaborates on all the main points related to the thesis, introducing one main point at a time, and includes supporting evidence with each main point. Each body paragraph should state the point in a topic sentence, which is usually the first sentence in the paragraph. The paragraph should then explain the point's meaning, support it with quotations or other evidence, and then explain how this point and the evidence are related to the thesis. The writer should then repeat this procedure in a new paragraph for each additional main point.

The conclusion reiterates the content of the introduction, including the thesis, to remind the reader of the essay's main argument or subject. The essay writer may also summarize the highlights of the argument or description contained in the body of the essay, following the same sequence originally used in the body. For example, a conclusion might look like: Point 1 + Point 2 + Point 3 = Thesis, or Point 1 → Point 2 → Point 3 → Thesis Proof. Good organization makes essays easier for writers to compose and provides a guide for readers to follow. Well-organized essays hold attention better and are more likely to get readers to accept their theses as valid.

INFORMATIVE VS. PERSUASIVE WRITING

Informative writing, also called explanatory or expository writing, begins with the basis that something is true or factual, while **persuasive** writing strives to prove something that may or may not be true or factual. Whereas argumentative text is written to **persuade** readers to agree with the author's position, informative text merely **provides information and insight** to readers. Informative writing concentrates on **informing** readers about why or how something is as it is. This can include offering new information, explaining how a process works, and developing a concept for readers. To accomplish these objectives, the essay may name and distinguish various things within a category, provide definitions, provide details about the parts of something, explain a particular function or behavior, and give readers explanations for why a fact, object, event, or process exists or occurs.

> **Review Video: Informative Text**
> Visit mometrix.com/academy and enter code: 924964
>
> **Review Video: Argumentative Writing**
> Visit mometrix.com/academy and enter code: 561544

NARRATIVE WRITING

Put simply, **narrative** writing tells a story. The most common examples of literary narratives are novels. Non-fictional biographies, autobiographies, memoirs, and histories are also narratives. Narratives should tell stories in such a way that the readers learn something or gain insight or understanding. Students can write more interesting narratives by describing events or experiences that were meaningful to them. Narratives should start with the story's actions or events, rather than long descriptions or introductions. Students should ensure that there is a point to each story by describing what they learned from the experience they narrate. To write an effective description, students should include sensory details, asking themselves what they saw, heard, felt or touched, smelled, and tasted during the experiences they describe. In narrative writing, the details should be **concrete** rather than **abstract**. Using concrete details enables readers to imagine everything that the writer describes.

> **Review Video: Narratives**
> Visit mometrix.com/academy and enter code: 280100

SENSORY DETAILS

Students need to use vivid descriptions when writing descriptive essays. Narratives should also include descriptions of characters, things, and events. Students should remember to describe not only the visual detail of what someone or something looks like, but details from other senses, as well. For example, they can contrast the feeling of a sea breeze to that of a mountain breeze, describe how they think something inedible would taste, and compare sounds they hear in the same location at different times of day and night. Readers have trouble visualizing images or imagining sensory impressions and feelings from abstract descriptions, so concrete descriptions make these more real.

CONCRETE VS. ABSTRACT DESCRIPTIONS IN NARRATIVE

Concrete language provides information that readers can grasp and may empathize with, while **abstract language**, which is more general, can leave readers feeling disconnected, empty, or even confused. "It was a lovely day" is abstract, but "The sun shone brightly, the sky was blue, the air felt warm, and a gentle breeze wafted across my skin" is concrete. "Ms. Couch was a good teacher" uses abstract language, giving only a general idea of the writer's opinion. But "Ms. Couch is excellent at helping us take our ideas and turn them into good essays and stories" uses concrete language, giving more specific examples of what makes Ms. Couch a good teacher. "I like writing poems but not essays" gives readers a general idea that the student prefers one genre over another, but not why. But when reading, "I like writing short poems with rhythm and rhyme, but I hate writing five-page essays that go on and on about the same ideas," readers understand that the student prefers the brevity, rhyme, and meter of short poetry over the length and redundancy of longer prose.

AUTOBIOGRAPHICAL NARRATIVES

Autobiographical narratives are narratives written by an author about an event or period in their life. Autobiographical narratives are written from one person's perspective, in first person, and often include the author's thoughts and feelings alongside their description of the event or period. Structure, style, or theme varies between different autobiographical narratives, since each narrative is personal and specific to its author and his or her experience.

REFLECTIVE ESSAY

A less common type of essay is the reflective essay. **Reflective essays** allow the author to reflect, or think back, on an experience and analyze what they recall. They should consider what they learned from the experience, what they could have done differently, what would have helped them during the experience, or anything else that they have realized from looking back on the experience. Reflection essays incorporate both objective reflection on one's own actions and subjective explanation of thoughts and feelings. These essays can be written for a number of experiences in a formal or informal context.

JOURNALS AND DIARIES

A **journal** is a personal account of events, experiences, feelings, and thoughts. Many people write journals to express their feelings and thoughts or to help them process experiences they have had. Since journals are **private documents** not meant to be shared with others, writers may not be concerned with grammar, spelling, or other mechanics. However, authors may write journals that they expect or hope to publish someday; in this case, they not only express their thoughts and feelings and process their experiences, but they also attend to their craft in writing them. Some authors compose journals to record a particular time period or a series of related events, such as a cancer diagnosis, treatment, surviving the disease, and how these experiences have changed or affected them. Other experiences someone might include in a journal are recovering from addiction, journeys of spiritual exploration and discovery, time spent in another country, or anything else someone wants to personally document. Journaling can also be therapeutic, as some people use journals to work through feelings of grief over loss or to wrestle with big decisions.

EXAMPLES OF DIARIES IN LITERATURE

The Diary of a Young Girl by Dutch Jew Anne Frank (1947) contains her life-affirming, nonfictional diary entries from 1942-1944 while her family hid in an attic from World War II's genocidal Nazis. *Go Ask Alice* (1971) by Beatrice Sparks is a cautionary, fictional novel in the form of diary entries by Alice, an unhappy, rebellious teen who takes LSD, runs away from home and lives with hippies, and eventually returns home. Frank's writing reveals an intelligent, sensitive, insightful girl, raised by intellectual European parents—a girl who believes in the goodness of human nature despite surrounding atrocities. Alice, influenced by early 1970s counterculture, becomes less optimistic. However, similarities can be found between them: Frank dies in a Nazi concentration camp while the fictitious Alice dies from a drug overdose. Both young women are also unable to escape their surroundings. Additionally, adolescent searches for personal identity are evident in both books.

> **Review Video: Journals, Diaries, Letters, and Blogs**
> Visit mometrix.com/academy and enter code: 432845

LETTERS

Letters are messages written to other people. In addition to letters written between individuals, some writers compose letters to the editors of newspapers, magazines, and other publications, while some write "Open Letters" to be published and read by the general public. Open letters, while

133

intended for everyone to read, may also identify a group of people or a single person whom the letter directly addresses. In everyday use, the most-used forms are business letters and personal or friendly letters. Both kinds share common elements: business or personal letterhead stationery; the writer's return address at the top; the addressee's address next; a salutation, such as "Dear [name]" or some similar opening greeting, followed by a colon in business letters or a comma in personal letters; the body of the letter, with paragraphs as indicated; and a closing, like "Sincerely/Cordially/Best regards/etc." or "Love," in intimate personal letters.

EARLY LETTERS

The Greek word for "letter" is *epistolē*, which became the English word "epistle." The earliest letters were called epistles, including the New Testament's epistles from the apostles to the Christians. In ancient Egypt, the writing curriculum in scribal schools included the epistolary genre. Epistolary novels frame a story in the form of letters. Examples of noteworthy epistolary novels include:

- *Pamela* (1740), by 18th-century English novelist Samuel Richardson
- *Shamela* (1741), Henry Fielding's satire of *Pamela* that mocked epistolary writing.
- *Lettres persanes* (1721) by French author Montesquieu
- *The Sorrows of Young Werther* (1774) by German author Johann Wolfgang von Goethe
- *The History of Emily Montague* (1769), the first Canadian novel, by Frances Brooke
- *Dracula* (1897) by Bram Stoker
- *Frankenstein* (1818) by Mary Shelley
- *The Color Purple* (1982) by Alice Walker

BLOGS

The word "blog" is derived from "weblog" and refers to writing done exclusively on the internet. Readers of reputable newspapers expect quality content and layouts that enable easy reading. These expectations also apply to blogs. For example, readers can easily move visually from line to line when columns are narrow, while overly wide columns cause readers to lose their places. Blogs must also be posted with layouts enabling online readers to follow them easily. However, because the way people read on computer, tablet, and smartphone screens differs from how they read print on paper, formatting and writing blog content is more complex than writing newspaper articles. Two major principles are the bases for blog-writing rules: The first is while readers of print articles skim to estimate their length, online they must scroll down to scan; therefore, blog layouts need more subheadings, graphics, and other indications of what information follows. The second is onscreen reading can be harder on the eyes than reading printed paper, so legibility is crucial in blogs.

RULES AND RATIONALES FOR WRITING BLOGS

1. Format all posts for smooth page layout and easy scanning.
2. Column width should not be too wide, as larger lines of text can be difficult to read
3. Headings and subheadings separate text visually, enable scanning or skimming, and encourage continued reading.
4. Bullet-pointed or numbered lists enable quick information location and scanning.
5. Punctuation is critical, so beginners should use shorter sentences until confident in their knowledge of punctuation rules.
6. Blog paragraphs should be far shorter—two to six sentences each—than paragraphs written on paper to enable "chunking" because reading onscreen is more difficult.
7. Sans-serif fonts are usually clearer than serif fonts, and larger font sizes are better.
8. Highlight important material and draw attention with **boldface**, but avoid overuse. Avoid hard-to-read *italics* and ALL CAPITALS.

9. Include enough blank spaces: overly busy blogs tire eyes and brains. Images not only break up text but also emphasize and enhance text and can attract initial reader attention.
10. Use background colors judiciously to avoid distracting the eye or making it difficult to read.
11. Be consistent throughout posts, since people read them in different orders.
12. Tell a story with a beginning, middle, and end.

SPECIALIZED MODES OF WRITING

EDITORIALS

Editorials are articles in newspapers, magazines, and other serial publications. Editorials express an opinion or belief belonging to the majority of the publication's leadership. This opinion or belief generally refers to a specific issue, topic, or event. These articles are authored by a member, or a small number of members, of the publication's leadership and are often written to affect their readers, such as persuading them to adopt a stance or take a particular action.

RESUMES

Resumes are brief, but formal, documents that outline an individual's experience in a certain area. Resumes are most often used for job applications. Such resumes will list the applicant's work experience, certification, and achievements or qualifications related to the position. Resumes should only include the most pertinent information. They should also use strategic formatting to highlight the applicant's most impressive experiences and achievements, to ensure the document can be read quickly and easily, and to eliminate both visual clutter and excessive negative space.

REPORTS

Reports summarize the results of research, new methodology, or other developments in an academic or professional context. Reports often include details about methodology and outside influences and factors. However, a report should focus primarily on the results of the research or development. Reports are objective and deliver information efficiently, sacrificing style for clear and effective communication.

MEMORANDA

A memorandum, also called a memo, is a formal method of communication used in professional settings. Memoranda are printed documents that include a heading listing the sender and their job title, the recipient and their job title, the date, and a specific subject line. Memoranda often include an introductory section explaining the reason and context for the memorandum. Next, a memorandum includes a section with details relevant to the topic. Finally, the memorandum will conclude with a paragraph that politely and clearly defines the sender's expectations of the recipient.

Research Writing

RESEARCH WRITING

Writing for research is essentially writing to answer a question or a problem about a particular **research topic**. A **problem statement** is written to clearly define the problem with a topic before asking about how to solve the problem. A **research question** serves to ask what can be done to address the problem. Before a researcher should try to solve a problem, the researcher should spend significant time performing a **literature review** to find out what has already been learned about the topic and if there are already solutions in place. The literature review can help to re-evaluate the research question as well. If the question has not been thoroughly answered, then it is proper to do broader research to learn about the topic and build up the body of literature. If the literature review provides plenty of background, but no practical solutions to the problem, then the research question should be targeted at solving a problem more directly. After the research has been performed, a **thesis** can act as a proposal for a solution or as a recommendation to future researchers to continue to learn more about the topic. The thesis should then be supported by significant contributing evidence to help support the proposed solution.

EXAMPLE OF RESEARCH WRITING ELEMENTS

Topic	The general idea the research is about. This is usually broader than the problem itself. <u>Example</u>: Clean Water
Problem Statement	A problem statement is a brief, clear description of a problem with the topic. <u>Example</u>: Not all villages in third-world countries have ready access to clean water.
Research Question	A research question asks a specific question about what needs to be learned or done about the problem statement. <u>Example</u>: What can local governments do to improve access to clean water?
Literature Review	A review of the body of literature by the researcher to show what is already known about the topic and the problem. If the literature review shows that the research question has already been thoroughly answered, the researcher should consider changing problem statements to something that has not been solved.
Thesis	A brief proposal of a solution to a problem. Theses do not include their own support, but are supported by later evidence. <u>Example</u>: Local governments can improve access to clean water by installing sealed rain-water collection units.
Body Paragraphs	Paragraphs focused on the primary supporting evidence for the main idea of the thesis. There are usually three body paragraphs, but there can be more if needed.
Conclusion	A final wrap-up of the research project. The conclusion should reiterate the problem, question, thesis, and briefly mention how the main evidences support the thesis.

THE RESEARCH PROCESS

Researchers should prepare some information before gathering sources. Researchers who have chosen a **research question** should choose key words or names that pertain to their question. They should also identify what type of information and sources they are looking for. Researchers should consider whether secondary or primary sources will be most appropriate for their research project. As researchers find credible and appropriate sources, they should be prepared to adjust the scope of their research question or topic in response to the information and insights they gather.

USING SOURCES AND SYNTHESIZING INFORMATION

As researchers find potential sources for their research project, it is important to keep a **record** of the material they find and note how each source may impact their work. When taking these notes, researchers should keep their research question or outline in mind and consider how their chosen references would complement their discussion. **Literature reviews** and **annotated bibliographies** are helpful tools for evaluating sources, as they require the researcher to consider the qualities and offerings of the sources they choose to use. These tools also help researchers synthesize the information they find.

SYNTHESIZING INFORMATION

Synthesizing information requires the researcher to integrate sources and their own thoughts by quoting, paraphrasing, or summarizing outside information in their research project. Synthesizing information indicates that the research complements the writer's claims, ensures that the ideas in the composition flow logically, and makes including small details and quotes easier. Paraphrasing is one of the simplest ways to integrate a source. **Paraphrasing** allows the writer to support their ideas with research while presenting the information in their own words, rather than using the source's original wording. Paraphrasing also allows the writer to reference the source's main ideas instead of specific details. While paraphrasing does not require the writer to quote the source, it still entails a direct reference to the source, meaning that any paraphrased material still requires a citation.

CITING SOURCES

While researchers should combine research with their own ideas, the information and ideas that come from outside sources should be attributed to the author of the source. When conducting research, it is helpful to record the publication information for each source so that **citations** can be easily added within the composition. Keeping a close record of the source of each idea in a composition or project is helpful for avoiding plagiarism, as both direct and indirect references require documentation.

PLAGIARISM

Understanding what is considered to be plagiarism is important to preventing unintentional plagiarism. Using another person's work in any way without proper attribution is **plagiarism**. However, it is easy to mistakenly commit plagiarism by improperly citing a source or creating a citation that is not intended for the way the source was used. Even when an honest attempt to attribute information is made, small errors can still result in plagiarized content. For this reason, it is important to create citations carefully and review citations before submitting or publishing research. It is also possible to plagiarize one's own work. This occurs when a writer has published work with one title and purpose and then attempts to publish it again as new material under a new title or purpose.

LITERATURE REVIEW

One of the two main parts of a literature review is searching through existing literature. The other is actually writing the review. Researchers must take care not to get lost in the information and inhibit progress toward their research goal. A good precaution is to write out the research question and keep it nearby. It is also wise to make a search plan and establish a time limit in advance. Finding a seemingly endless number of references indicates a need to revisit the research question because the topic is too broad. Finding too little material means that the research topic is too narrow. With new or cutting-edge research, one may find that nobody has investigated this particular question. This requires systematic searching, using abstracts in periodicals for an overview of available literature, research papers or other specific sources to explore its reference, and references in books and other sources.

When searching published literature on a research topic, one must take thorough notes. It is common to find a reference that could be useful later in the research project, but is not needed yet. In situations like this, it is helpful to make a note of the reference so it will be easy to find later. These notes can be grouped in a word processing document, which also allows for easy compiling of links and quotes from internet research. Researchers should explore the internet regularly, view resources for their research often, learn how to use resources correctly and efficiently, experiment with resources available within the disciplines, open and examine databases, become familiar with reference desk materials, find publications with abstracts of articles and books on one's topic, use papers' references to locate the most useful journals and important authors, identify keywords for refining and narrowing database searches, and peruse library catalogues online for available sources—all while taking notes.

As one searches for references, one will gradually develop an overview of the body of literature available for his or her subject. This signals the time to prepare for writing the literature review. The researcher should assemble his or her notes along with copies of all the journal articles and all the books he or she has acquired. Then one should write the research question again at the top of a page and list below it all of the author names and keywords discovered while searching. It is also helpful to observe whether any groups or pairs of these stand out. These activities are parts of structuring one's literature review—the first step for writing a thesis, dissertation, or research paper. Writers should rewrite their work as necessary rather than expecting to write only one draft. However, stopping to edit along the way can distract from the momentum of writing the first draft. If the writer is dissatisfied with a certain part of the draft, it may be better to skip to a later portion of the paper and revisit the problem section at another time.

BODY AND CONCLUSION IN LITERATURE REVIEW

The first step of a literature review paper is to create a rough draft. The next step is to edit: rewrite for clarity, eliminate unnecessary verbiage, and change terminology that could confuse readers. After editing, a writer should ask others to read and give feedback. Additionally, the writer should read the paper aloud to hear how it sounds, editing as needed. Throughout a literature review, the writer should not only summarize and comment on each source reviewed, but should also relate these findings to the original research question. The writer should explicitly state in the conclusion how the research question and pertinent literature interaction is developed throughout the body, reflecting on insights gained through the process.

> **Review Video: Drafting Conclusions**
> Visit mometrix.com/academy and enter code: 209408

SUMMARIES AND ABSTRACTS

When preparing to submit or otherwise publish research, it may be necessary to compose a summary or abstract to accompany the research composition.

A summary is a brief description of the contents of a longer work that provides an overview of the work and may include its most important details. One common type of summary is an abstract. Abstracts are specialized summaries that are most commonly used in the context of research. Abstracts may include details such as the purpose for the research, the researcher's methodology, and the most significant results of the research. Abstracts sometimes include sections and headings, where most summaries are limited to one or a few paragraphs with no special groupings.

138

EDITING AND REVISING

After composing a rough draft of a research paper, the writer should **edit** it. The purpose of the paper is to communicate the answer to one's research question in an efficient and effective manner. The writing should be as **concise** and **clear** as possible, and the style should also be consistent. Editing is often easier to do after writing the first draft rather than during it, as taking time between writing and editing allows writers to be more objective. If the paper includes an abstract and an introduction, the writer should compose these after writing the rest, when he or she will have a better grasp of the theme and arguments. Not all readers understand technical terminology or long words, so writers should use these sparingly. Finally, writers should consult a writing and style guide to address any industry- or institution-specific issues that may arise as they edit.

> **Review Video: <u>Revising and Editing</u>**
> Visit mometrix.com/academy and enter code: 674181

139

Information Sources

PRIMARY SOURCES

In literature review, one may examine both primary and secondary sources. Primary sources contain original information that was witnessed, gathered, or otherwise produced by the source's author. **Primary sources** can include firsthand accounts, found in sources such as books, autobiographies, transcripts, speeches, videos, photos, and personal journals or diaries. Primary sources may also include records of information, such as government documents, or personally-conducted research in sources like reports and essays. They may be found in academic books, journals and other periodicals, and authoritative databases. Using primary sources allows researchers to develop their own conclusions about the subject. Primary sources are also reliable for finding information about a person or their personal accounts and experiences. Primary sources such as photos, videos, audio recordings, transcripts, and government documents are often reliable, as they are usually objective and can be used to confirm information from other sources.

SECONDARY SOURCES

Secondary sources are sources that reference information originally provided by another source. The original source may be cited, quoted, paraphrased, or described in a secondary source. **Secondary sources** may be articles, essays, videos, or books found in periodicals, magazines, newspapers, films, databases, or websites. A secondary source can be used to reference another researcher's analysis or conclusion from a primary source. This information can inform the researcher of the existing discussions regarding their subject. These types of sources may also support the researcher's claims by providing a credible argument that contributes to the researcher's argument. Secondary sources may also highlight connections between primary sources or criticize both primary and other secondary sources. These types of secondary sources are valuable because they provide information and conclusions the researcher may not have considered or found, otherwise.

> **Review Video: Primary and Secondary Sources**
> Visit mometrix.com/academy and enter code: 383328

TYPES OF SOURCES

- **Textbooks** are specialized materials that are designed to thoroughly instruct readers on a particular topic. Textbooks often include features such as a table of contents, visuals, an index, a glossary, headings, and practice questions and exercises.
- **Newspapers** are collections of several written pieces and are primarily used to distribute news stories to their audience. In addition to news articles, newspapers may also include advertisements or pieces meant to entertain their audience, such as comic strips, columns, and letters from readers. Newspapers are written for a variety of audiences, as they are published on both the local and national levels.
- **Manuals** are instructional documents that accompany a product or explain an important procedure. Manuals include a table of contents, guidelines, and instructional content. Instructional manuals often include information about safe practices, risks, and product warranty. The instructions in manuals are often presented as step-by-step instructions, as they are meant to help users properly use a product or complete a task.

- **Electronic texts** are written documents that are read digitally and are primarily accessed online or through a network. Many electronic texts have characteristics similar to printed texts, such as a table of contents, publication information, a main text, and supplemental materials. However, electronic texts are more interactive and can be navigated more quickly. Electronic texts can also provide more accessibility, as they can be easily resized or narrated by text-to-speech software.

FINDING SOURCES

Finding sources for a research project may be intimidating or difficult. There are numerous sources available, and several research tools to help researchers find them. Starting with one of these tools can help narrow down the number of sources a researcher is working with at one time.

- **Libraries** house independent, printed publications that are organized by subject. This makes finding sources easy, since researchers can visit sections with sources relevant to their topic and immediately see what sources are available. Many libraries also offer printed journals and collections that include sources related to a common subject or written by the same author.
- **Databases** offer digital access to sources from a wide variety of libraries and online containers. To use a database, users search for keywords related to their topic or the type of source they want to use. The database then lists results related to or featuring those key words. Users can narrow their results using filters that will limit their results based on factors such as publication year, source type, or whether the sources are peer-reviewed. Database search results also list individual articles and methods of accessing the article directly. While databases help users find sources, they do not guarantee users access to each source.
- **Academic Journals** are collections of articles that cover a particular topic or fit within a certain category. These journals are often offered both online and in print. Academic journals typically contain peer-reviewed works or works that have undergone another type of reviewing process.

CREDIBILITY

There are innumerable primary and secondary sources available in print and online. However, not every published or posted source is appropriate for a research project. When finding sources, the researcher must know how to evaluate each source for credibility and relevance. Not only must the sources be reliable and relevant to the research subject, but they must also be appropriate and help form an answer to the research question. As researchers progress in their research and composition, the relevance of each source will become clear. Appropriate sources will contribute valuable information and arguments to the researcher's own thoughts and conclusions, providing useful evidence to bolster the researcher's claims. The researcher has the freedom to choose which sources they reference or even change their research topic and question in response to the sources they find. However, the researcher should not use unreliable sources, and determining a source's credibility is not always easy.

CONSIDERATIONS FOR EVALUATING THE CREDIBILITY OF A SOURCE

- The author and their purpose for writing the source
- The author's qualifications to write on the topic
- Whether the source is peer-reviewed or included in a scholarly publication
- The publisher
- The target audience

- The jargon or dialect the source is written in (e.g., academic, technical)
- The presence of bias or manipulation of information
- The date of publication
- The author's use of other sources to support their claims
- Whether any outside sources are cited appropriately in the source
- The accuracy of information presented

AUTHOR'S PURPOSE AND CREDIBILITY

Knowing who wrote a source and why they wrote it is important to determine whether a source is appropriate for a research project. The author should be qualified to write on the subject of the material. Their purpose may be to inform their audience of information, to present and defend an analysis, or even to criticize a work or other argument. The researcher must decide whether the author's purpose makes the source appropriate to use. The source's container and publisher are important to note because they indicate the source's reputability and whether other qualified individuals have reviewed the information in the source. Credible secondary sources should also reference other sources, primary or secondary, that support or inform the source's content. Evaluating the accuracy of the information or the presence of bias in a source will require careful reading and critical thinking on the part of the researcher. However, a source with excellent credentials may still contain pieces of inaccurate information or bias, so it is the researcher's responsibility to be careful in their use of each source.

INTEGRATING REFERENCES AND QUOTATIONS

In research papers, one can include studies whose conclusions agree with one's position (Reed 284; Becker and Fagen 93), as well as studies that disagree (Limbaugh 442, Beck 69) by including parenthetical citations as demonstrated in this sentence. Quotations should be selective: writers should compose an original sentence and incorporate only a few words from a research source. If students cannot use more original words than quotation, they are likely padding their compositions. However, including quotations appropriately increases the credibility of the writer and their argument.

PROPERLY INTEGRATING QUOTATIONS

When using sources in a research paper, it is important to integrate information so that the flow of the composition is not interrupted as the two compositions are combined. When quoting outside sources, it is necessary to lead into the quote and ensure that the whole sentence is logical, is grammatically correct, and flows well. Below is an example of an incorrectly integrated quote.

> During the Industrial Revolution, many unions organized labor strikes "child labor, unregulated working conditions, and excessive working hours" in America.

Below is the same sentence with a properly integrated quote..

> During the Industrial Revolution, many unions organized labor strikes to protest the presence of "child labor, unregulated working conditions, and excessive working hours" in America.

In the first example, the connection between "strikes" and the quoted list is unclear. In the second example, the phrase "to protest the presence of" link the ideas together and successfully creates a suitable place for the quotation.

When quoting sources, writers should work quotations and references seamlessly into their sentences instead of interrupting the flow of their own argument to summarize a source.

Summarizing others' content is often a ploy to bolster word counts. Writing that analyzes the content, evaluates it, and synthesizes material from various sources demonstrates critical thinking skills and is thus more valuable.

PROPERLY INCORPORATING OUTSIDE SOURCES

Writers do better to include short quotations rather than long. For example, quoting six to eight long passages in a 10-page paper is excessive. It is also better to avoid wording like "This quotation shows," "As you can see from this quotation," or "It talks about." These are amateur, feeble efforts to interact with other authors' ideas. Also, writing about sources and quotations wastes words that should be used to develop one's own ideas. Quotations should be used to stimulate discussion rather than taking its place. Ending a paragraph, section, or paper with a quotation is not incorrect per se, but using it to prove a point, without including anything more in one's own words regarding the point or subject, suggests a lack of critical thinking about the topic and consideration of multiple alternatives. It can also be a tactic to dissuade readers from challenging one's propositions. Writers should include references and quotations that challenge as well as support their thesis statements. Presenting evidence on both sides of an issue makes it easier for reasonably skeptical readers to agree with a writer's viewpoint.

CITING SOURCES

Formal research writers must **cite all sources used**—books, articles, interviews, conversations, and anything else that contributed to the research. One reason is to **avoid plagiarism** and give others credit for their ideas. Another reason is to help readers find the sources consulted in the research and access more information about the subject for further reading and research. Additionally, citing sources helps to make a paper academically authoritative. To prepare, research writers should keep a running list of sources consulted, in an electronic file or on file cards. For every source used, the writer needs specific information. For books, a writer needs to record the author's and editor's names, book title, publication date, city, and publisher name. For articles, one needs the author's name, article title, journal (or magazine or newspaper) name, volume and issue number, publication date, and page numbers. For electronic resources, a writer will need the author's name, article information plus the URL, database name, name of the database's publisher, and the date of access.

COMMON REFERENCE STYLES

Three common reference styles are **MLA** (Modern Language Association), **APA** (American Psychological Association), and **Turabian** (created by author Kate Turabian, also known as the Chicago Manual of Style). Each style formats citation information differently. Professors and instructors often specify that students use one of these. Generally, APA style is used in psychology and sociology papers, and MLA style is used in English literature papers and similar scholarly projects. To understand how these styles differ, consider an imaginary article cited in each of these styles. This article is titled "Ten Things You Won't Believe Dragons Do," written by author Andra Gaines, included in the journal *Studies in Fantasy Fiction*, and published by Quest for Knowledge Publishing.

MLA:

Gaines, Andra. "Ten Things You Won't Believe Dragons Do." Studies in Fantasy Fiction, vol. 3, no. 8, Quest for Knowledge Publishing, 21 Aug. 2019.

APA:

Gaines, A. (2019). Ten Things You Won't Believe Dragons Do. *Studies in Fantasy Fiction, 3(8)*, 42-65.

CHICAGO:

Gaines, Andra. "Ten Things You Won't Believe Dragons Do," *Studies in Fantasy Fiction* 3, no. 8 (2019): 42-65.

Within each of these styles, citations, though they vary according to the type of source and how its used, generally follow a structure and format similar to those above. For example, citations for whole books will probably not include a container title or a volume number, but will otherwise look very similar.

> **Review Video: <u>Citing Sources</u>**
> Visit mometrix.com/academy and enter code: 993637

Vocabulary and Word Relationships

SYNONYMS AND ANTONYMS

When you understand how words relate to each other, you will discover more in a passage. This is explained by understanding **synonyms** (e.g., words that mean the same thing) and **antonyms** (e.g., words that mean the opposite of one another). As an example, *dry* and *arid* are synonyms, and *dry* and *wet* are antonyms.

There are many pairs of words in English that can be considered synonyms, despite having slightly different definitions. For instance, the words *friendly* and *collegial* can both be used to describe a warm interpersonal relationship, and one would be correct to call them synonyms. However, *collegial* (kin to *colleague*) is often used in reference to professional or academic relationships, and *friendly* has no such connotation.

If the difference between the two words is too great, then they should not be called synonyms. *Hot* and *warm* are not synonyms because their meanings are too distinct. A good way to determine whether two words are synonyms is to substitute one word for the other word and verify that the meaning of the sentence has not changed. Substituting *warm* for *hot* in a sentence would convey a different meaning. Although warm and hot may seem close in meaning, warm generally means that the temperature is moderate, and hot generally means that the temperature is excessively high.

Antonyms are words with opposite meanings. *Light* and *dark*, *up* and *down*, *right* and *left*, *good* and *bad*: these are all sets of antonyms. Be careful to distinguish between antonyms and pairs of words that are simply different. *Black* and *gray*, for instance, are not antonyms because gray is not the opposite of black. *Black* and *white*, on the other hand, are antonyms.

Not every word has an antonym. For instance, many nouns do not. What would be the antonym of *chair*? During your exam, the questions related to antonyms are more likely to concern adjectives. You will recall that adjectives are words that describe a noun. Some common adjectives include *purple*, *fast*, *skinny*, and *sweet*. From those four adjectives, *purple* is the item that lacks a group of obvious antonyms.

> **Review Video: <u>What Are Synonyms and Antonyms?</u>**
> Visit mometrix.com/academy and enter code: 105612

AFFIXES

Affixes in the English language are morphemes that are added to words to create related but different words. Derivational affixes form new words based on and related to the original words. For example, the affix *–ness* added to the end of the adjective *happy* forms the noun *happiness.* Inflectional affixes form different grammatical versions of words. For example, the plural affix *–s* changes the singular noun *book* to the plural noun *books*, and the past tense affix *–ed* changes the present tense verb *look* to the past tense *looked.* Prefixes are affixes placed in front of words. For example, *heat* means to make hot; *preheat* means to heat in advance. Suffixes are affixes placed at the ends of words. The *happiness* example above contains the suffix *–ness.* Circumfixes add parts both before and after words, such as how *light* becomes *enlighten* with the prefix *en-* and the suffix *–en.* Interfixes create compound words via central affixes: *speed* and *meter* become *speedometer* via the interfix *–o–.*

> **Review Video: <u>Affixes</u>**
> Visit mometrix.com/academy and enter code: 782422

WORD ROOTS, PREFIXES, AND SUFFIXES TO HELP DETERMINE MEANINGS OF WORDS

Many English words were formed from combining multiple sources. For example, the Latin *habēre* means "to have," and the prefixes *in-* and *im-* mean a lack or prevention of something, as in *insufficient* and *imperfect*. Latin combined *in-* with *habēre* to form *inhibēre,* whose past participle was *inhibitus*. This is the origin of the English word *inhibit,* meaning to prevent from having. Hence by knowing the meanings of both the prefix and the root, one can decipher the word meaning. In Greek, the root *enkephalo-* refers to the brain. Many medical terms are based on this root, such as encephalitis and hydrocephalus. Understanding the prefix and suffix meanings (*-itis* means inflammation; *hydro-* means water) allows a person to deduce that encephalitis refers to brain inflammation and hydrocephalus refers to water (or other fluid) in the brain.

> **Review Video: Determining Word Meanings**
> Visit mometrix.com/academy and enter code: 894894

PREFIXES

While knowing prefix meanings helps ESL and beginning readers learn new words, other readers take for granted the meanings of known words. However, prefix knowledge will also benefit them for determining meanings or definitions of unfamiliar words. For example, native English speakers and readers familiar with recipes know what *preheat* means. Knowing that *pre-* means in advance can also inform them that *presume* means to assume in advance, that *prejudice* means advance judgment, and that this understanding can be applied to many other words beginning with *pre-*. Knowing that the prefix *dis-* indicates opposition informs the meanings of words like *disbar, disagree, disestablish,* and many more. Knowing *dys-* means bad, impaired, abnormal, or difficult informs *dyslogistic, dysfunctional, dysphagia,* and *dysplasia.*

SUFFIXES

In English, certain suffixes generally indicate both that a word is a noun, and that the noun represents a state of being or quality. For example, *-ness* is commonly used to change an adjective into its noun form, as with *happy* and *happiness, nice* and *niceness,* and so on. The suffix *–tion* is commonly used to transform a verb into its noun form, as with *converse* and *conversation or move* and *motion.* Thus, if readers are unfamiliar with the second form of a word, knowing the meaning of the transforming suffix can help them determine meaning.

PREFIXES FOR NUMBERS

Prefix	Definition	Examples
bi-	two	bisect, biennial
mono-	one, single	monogamy, monologue
poly-	many	polymorphous, polygamous
semi-	half, partly	semicircle, semicolon
uni-	one	uniform, unity

PREFIXES FOR TIME, DIRECTION, AND SPACE

Prefix	Definition	Examples
a-	in, on, of, up, to	abed, afoot
ab-	from, away, off	abdicate, abjure
ad-	to, toward	advance, adventure
ante-	before, previous	antecedent, antedate
anti-	against, opposing	antipathy, antidote
cata-	down, away, thoroughly	catastrophe, cataclysm
circum-	around	circumspect, circumference
com-	with, together, very	commotion, complicate
contra-	against, opposing	contradict, contravene
de-	from	depart
dia-	through, across, apart	diameter, diagnose
dis-	away, off, down, not	dissent, disappear
epi-	upon	epilogue
ex-	out	extract, excerpt
hypo-	under, beneath	hypodermic, hypothesis
inter-	among, between	intercede, interrupt
intra-	within	intramural, intrastate
ob-	against, opposing	objection
per-	through	perceive, permit
peri-	around	periscope, perimeter
post-	after, following	postpone, postscript
pre-	before, previous	prevent, preclude
pro-	forward, in place of	propel, pronoun
retro-	back, backward	retrospect, retrograde
sub-	under, beneath	subjugate, substitute
super-	above, extra	supersede, supernumerary
trans-	across, beyond, over	transact, transport
ultra-	beyond, excessively	ultramodern, ultrasonic

NEGATIVE PREFIXES

Prefix	Definition	Examples
a-	without, lacking	atheist, agnostic
in-	not, opposing	incapable, ineligible
non-	not	nonentity, nonsense
un-	not, reverse of	unhappy, unlock

Extra Prefixes

Prefix	Definition	Examples
belli-	war, warlike	bellicose
bene-	well, good	benefit, benefactor
equi-	equal	equivalent, equilibrium
for-	away, off, from	forget, forswear
fore-	previous	foretell, forefathers
homo-	same, equal	homogenized, homonym
hyper-	excessive, over	hypercritical, hypertension
in-	in, into	intrude, invade
magn-	large	magnitude, magnify
mal-	bad, poorly, not	malfunction, malpractice
mis-	bad, poorly, not	misspell, misfire
mor-	death	mortality, mortuary
neo-	new	Neolithic, neoconservative
omni-	all, everywhere	omniscient, omnivore
ortho-	right, straight	orthogonal, orthodox
over-	above	overbearing, oversight
pan-	all, entire	panorama, pandemonium
para-	beside, beyond	parallel, paradox
phil-	love, like	philosophy, philanthropic
prim-	first, early	primitive, primary
re-	backward, again	revoke, recur
sym-	with, together	sympathy, symphony
vis-	to see	visage, visible

Below is a list of common suffixes and their meanings:

Adjective Suffixes

Suffix	Definition	Examples
-able (-ible)	capable of being	tolerable, edible
-esque	in the style of, like	picturesque, grotesque
-ful	filled with, marked by	thankful, zestful
-ific	make, cause	terrific, beatific
-ish	suggesting, like	churlish, childish
-less	lacking, without	hopeless, countless
-ous	marked by, given to	religious, riotous

NOUN SUFFIXES

Suffix	Definition	Examples
-acy	state, condition	accuracy, privacy
-ance	act, condition, fact	acceptance, vigilance
-ard	one that does excessively	drunkard, sluggard
-ation	action, state, result	occupation, starvation
-dom	state, rank, condition	serfdom, wisdom
-er (-or)	office, action	teacher, elevator, honor
-ess	feminine	waitress, duchess
-hood	state, condition	manhood, statehood
-ion	action, result, state	union, fusion
-ism	act, manner, doctrine	barbarism, socialism
-ist	worker, follower	monopolist, socialist
-ity (-ty)	state, quality, condition	acidity, civility, twenty
-ment	result, action	Refreshment
-ness	quality, state	greatness, tallness
-ship	position	internship, statesmanship
-sion (-tion)	state, result	revision, expedition
-th	act, state, quality	warmth, width
-tude	quality, state, result	magnitude, fortitude

VERB SUFFIXES

Suffix	Definition	Examples
-ate	having, showing	separate, desolate
-en	cause to be, become	deepen, strengthen
-fy	make, cause to have	glorify, fortify
-ize	cause to be, treat with	sterilize, mechanize

Review Video: English Root Words
Visit mometrix.com/academy and enter code: 896380

DENOTATIVE VS. CONNOTATIVE MEANING

The **denotative** meaning of a word is the literal meaning. The **connotative** meaning goes beyond the denotative meaning to include the emotional reaction that a word may invoke. The connotative meaning often takes the denotative meaning a step further due to associations the reader makes with the denotative meaning. Readers can differentiate between the denotative and connotative meanings by first recognizing how authors use each meaning. Most non-fiction, for example, is fact-based and authors do not use flowery, figurative language. The reader can assume that the writer is using the denotative meaning of words. In fiction, the author may use the connotative meaning. Readers can determine whether the author is using the denotative or connotative meaning of a word by implementing context clues.

Review Video: Denotation and Connotation
Visit mometrix.com/academy and enter code: 310092

NUANCES OF WORD MEANING RELATIVE TO CONNOTATION, DENOTATION, DICTION, AND USAGE

A word's denotation is simply its objective dictionary definition. However, its connotation refers to the subjective associations, often emotional, that specific words evoke in listeners and readers. Two

149

or more words can have the same dictionary meaning, but very different connotations. Writers use diction (word choice) to convey various nuances of thought and emotion by selecting synonyms for other words that best communicate the associations they want to trigger for readers. For example, a car engine is naturally greasy; in this sense, "greasy" is a neutral term. But when a person's smile, appearance, or clothing is described as "greasy," it has a negative connotation. Some words have even gained additional or different meanings over time. For example, *awful* used to be used to describe things that evoked a sense of awe. When *awful* is separated into its root word, awe, and suffix, -ful, it can be understood to mean "full of awe." However, the word is now commonly used to describe things that evoke repulsion, terror, or another intense, negative reaction.

> **Review Video: Word Usage**
> Visit mometrix.com/academy and enter code: 197863

CONTEXT CLUES

Readers of all levels will encounter words that they have either never seen or have encountered only on a limited basis. The best way to define a word in **context** is to look for nearby words that can assist in revealing the meaning of the word. For instance, unfamiliar nouns are often accompanied by examples that provide a definition. Consider the following sentence: *Dave arrived at the party in hilarious garb: a leopard-print shirt, buckskin trousers, and bright green sneakers.* If a reader was unfamiliar with the meaning of garb, he or she could read the examples (i.e., a leopard-print shirt, buckskin trousers, and high heels) and quickly determine that the word means *clothing*. Examples will not always be this obvious. Consider this sentence: *Parsley, lemon, and flowers were just a few of the items he used as garnishes.* Here, the word *garnishes* is exemplified by parsley, lemon, and flowers. Readers who have eaten in a variety of restaurants will probably be able to identify a garnish as something used to decorate a plate.

> **Review Video: Context**
> Visit mometrix.com/academy and enter code: 613660

USING CONTRAST IN CONTEXT CLUES

In addition to looking at the context of a passage, readers can use contrast to define an unfamiliar word in context. In many sentences, the author will not describe the unfamiliar word directly; instead, he or she will describe the opposite of the unfamiliar word. Thus, you are provided with some information that will bring you closer to defining the word. Consider the following example: *Despite his intelligence, Hector's low brow and bad posture made him look obtuse.* The author writes that Hector's appearance does not convey intelligence. Therefore, *obtuse* must mean unintelligent. Here is another example: *Despite the horrible weather, we were beatific about our trip to Alaska.* The word *despite* indicates that the speaker's feelings were at odds with the weather. Since the weather is described as *horrible*, then *beatific* must mean something positive.

SUBSTITUTION TO FIND MEANING

In some cases, there will be very few contextual clues to help a reader define the meaning of an unfamiliar word. When this happens, one strategy that readers may employ is **substitution**. A good reader will brainstorm some possible synonyms for the given word, and he or she will substitute these words into the sentence. If the sentence and the surrounding passage continue to make sense, then the substitution has revealed at least some information about the unfamiliar word. Consider the sentence: *Frank's admonition rang in her ears as she climbed the mountain.* A reader unfamiliar with *admonition* might come up with some substitutions like *vow, promise, advice, complaint*, or *compliment*. All of these words make general sense of the sentence, though their meanings are diverse. However, this process has suggested that an admonition is some sort of message. The substitution strategy is rarely able to pinpoint a precise definition, but this process can be effective as a last resort.

Occasionally, you will be able to define an unfamiliar word by looking at the descriptive words in the context. Consider the following sentence: *Fred dragged the recalcitrant boy kicking and screaming up the stairs.* The words *dragged*, *kicking*, and *screaming* all suggest that the boy does not want to go up the stairs. The reader may assume that *recalcitrant* means something like unwilling or protesting. In this example, an unfamiliar adjective was identified.

Additionally, using description to define an unfamiliar noun is a common practice compared to unfamiliar adjectives, as in this sentence: *Don's wrinkled frown and constantly shaking fist identified him as a curmudgeon of the first order.* Don is described as having a *wrinkled frown and constantly shaking fist*, suggesting that a *curmudgeon* must be a grumpy person. Contrasts do not always provide detailed information about the unfamiliar word, but they at least give the reader some clues.

WORDS WITH MULTIPLE MEANINGS

When a word has more than one meaning, readers can have difficulty determining how the word is being used in a given sentence. For instance, the verb *cleave*, can mean either *join* or *separate*. When readers come upon this word, they will have to select the definition that makes the most sense. Consider the following sentence: *Hermione's knife cleaved the bread cleanly.* Since a knife cannot join bread together, the word must indicate separation. A slightly more difficult example would be the sentence: *The birds cleaved to one another as they flew from the oak tree.* Immediately, the presence of the words *to one another* should suggest that in this sentence *cleave* is being used to mean *join*. Discovering the intent of a word with multiple meanings requires the same tricks as defining an unknown word: look for contextual clues and evaluate the substituted words.

CONTEXT CLUES TO HELP DETERMINE MEANINGS OF WORDS

If readers simply bypass unknown words, they can reach unclear conclusions about what they read. However, looking for the definition of every unfamiliar word in the dictionary can slow their reading progress. Moreover, the dictionary may list multiple definitions for a word, so readers must search the word's context for meaning. Hence context is important to new vocabulary regardless of reader methods. Four types of context clues are examples, definitions, descriptive words, and opposites. Authors may use a certain word, and then follow it with several different examples of what it describes. Sometimes authors actually supply a definition of a word they use, which is especially true in informational and technical texts. Authors may use descriptive words that elaborate upon a vocabulary word they just used. Authors may also use opposites with negation that help define meaning.

EXAMPLES AND DEFINITIONS

An author may use a word and then give examples that illustrate its meaning. Consider this text: "Teachers who do not know how to use sign language can help students who are deaf or hard of hearing understand certain instructions by using gestures instead, like pointing their fingers to indicate which direction to look or go; holding up a hand, palm outward, to indicate stopping; holding the hands flat, palms up, curling a finger toward oneself in a beckoning motion to indicate 'come here'; or curling all fingers toward oneself repeatedly to indicate 'come on', 'more', or 'continue.'" The author of this text has used the word "gestures" and then followed it with examples, so a reader unfamiliar with the word could deduce from the examples that "gestures" means "hand motions." Readers can find examples by looking for signal words "for example," "for instance," "like," "such as," and "e.g."

While readers sometimes have to look for definitions of unfamiliar words in a dictionary or do some work to determine a word's meaning from its surrounding context, at other times an author may make it easier for readers by defining certain words. For example, an author may write, "The company did not have sufficient capital, that is, available money, to continue operations." The author defined "capital" as "available money," and heralded the definition with the phrase "that is." Another way that authors supply word definitions is with appositives. Rather than being introduced by a signal phrase like "that is," "namely," or "meaning," an appositive comes after the vocabulary word it defines and is enclosed within two commas. For example, an author may write, "The Indians introduced the Pilgrims to pemmican, cakes they made of lean meat dried and mixed with fat, which proved greatly beneficial to keep settlers from starving while trapping." In this example, the appositive phrase following "pemmican" and preceding "which" defines the word "pemmican."

DESCRIPTIONS

When readers encounter a word they do not recognize in a text, the author may expand on that word to illustrate it better. While the author may do this to make the prose more picturesque and vivid, the reader can also take advantage of this description to provide context clues to the meaning of the unfamiliar word. For example, an author may write, "The man sitting next to me on the airplane was obese. His shirt stretched across his vast expanse of flesh, strained almost to bursting." The descriptive second sentence elaborates on and helps to define the previous sentence's word "obese" to mean extremely fat. A reader unfamiliar with the word "repugnant" can decipher its meaning through an author's accompanying description: "The way the child grimaced and shuddered as he swallowed the medicine showed that its taste was particularly repugnant."

OPPOSITES

Text authors sometimes introduce a contrasting or opposing idea before or after a concept they present. They may do this to emphasize or heighten the idea they present by contrasting it with something that is the reverse. However, readers can also use these context clues to understand familiar words. For example, an author may write, "Our conversation was not cheery. We sat and talked very solemnly about his experience and a number of similar events." The reader who is not familiar with the word "solemnly" can deduce by the author's preceding use of "not cheery" that "solemn" means the opposite of cheery or happy, so it must mean serious or sad. Or if someone writes, "Don't condemn his entire project because you couldn't find anything good to say about it," readers unfamiliar with "condemn" can understand from the sentence structure that it means the opposite of saying anything good, so it must mean reject, dismiss, or disapprove. "Entire" adds another context clue, meaning total or complete rejection.

SYNTAX TO DETERMINE PART OF SPEECH AND MEANINGS OF WORDS

Syntax refers to sentence structure and word order. Suppose that a reader encounters an unfamiliar word when reading a text. To illustrate, consider an invented word like "splunch." If this word is used in a sentence like "Please splunch that ball to me," the reader can assume from syntactic context that "splunch" is a verb. We would not use a noun, adjective, adverb, or preposition with the object "that ball," and the prepositional phrase "to me" further indicates "splunch" represents an action. However, in the sentence, "Please hand that splunch to me," the reader can assume that "splunch" is a noun. Demonstrative adjectives like "that" modify nouns. Also, we hand someone some*thing*—a thing being a noun; we do not hand someone a verb, adjective, or adverb. Some sentences contain further clues. For example, from the sentence, "The princess wore the glittering splunch on her head," the reader can deduce that it is a crown, tiara, or something similar from the syntactic context, without knowing the word.

SYNTAX TO INDICATE DIFFERENT MEANINGS OF SIMILAR SENTENCES

The syntax, or structure, of a sentence affords grammatical cues that aid readers in comprehending the meanings of words, phrases, and sentences in the texts that they read. Seemingly minor differences in how the words or phrases in a sentence are ordered can make major differences in meaning. For example, two sentences can use exactly the same words but have different meanings based on the word order:

- "The man with a broken arm sat in a chair.
- "The man sat in a chair with a broken arm."

While both sentences indicate that a man sat in a chair, differing syntax indicates whether the man's or chair's arm was broken.

DETERMINING MEANING OF PHRASES AND PARAGRAPHS

Like unknown words, the meanings of phrases, paragraphs, and entire works can also be difficult to discern. Each of these can be better understood with added context. However, for larger groups of words, more context is needed. Unclear phrases are similar to unclear words, and the same methods can be used to understand their meaning. However, it is also important to consider how the individual words in the phrase work together. Paragraphs are a bit more complicated. Just as words must be compared to other words in a sentence, paragraphs must be compared to other paragraphs in a composition or a section.

DETERMINING MEANING IN VARIOUS TYPES OF COMPOSITIONS

To understand the meaning of an entire composition, the type of composition must be considered. **Expository writing** is generally organized so that each paragraph focuses on explaining one idea, or part of an idea, and its relevance. **Persuasive writing** uses paragraphs for different purposes to organize the parts of the argument. **Unclear paragraphs** must be read in the context of the paragraphs around them for their meaning to be fully understood. The meaning of full texts can also be unclear at times. The purpose of composition is also important for understanding the meaning of a text. To quickly understand the broad meaning of a text, look to the introductory and concluding paragraphs. Fictional texts are different. Some fictional works have implicit meanings, but some do not. The target audience must be considered for understanding texts that do have an implicit meaning, as most children's fiction will clearly state any lessons or morals. For other fiction, the application of literary theories and criticism may be helpful for understanding the text.

ADDITIONAL RESOURCES FOR DETERMINING WORD MEANING AND USAGE

While these strategies are useful for determining the meaning of unknown words and phrases, sometimes additional resources are needed to properly use the terms in different contexts. Some words have multiple definitions, and some words are inappropriate in particular contexts or modes of writing. The following tools are helpful for understanding all meanings and proper uses for words and phrases.

- **Dictionaries** provide the meaning of a multitude of words in a language. Many dictionaries include additional information about each word, such as its etymology, its synonyms, or variations of the word.
- **Glossaries** are similar to dictionaries, as they provide the meanings of a variety of terms. However, while dictionaries typically feature an extensive list of words and comprise an entire publication, glossaries are often included at the end of a text and only include terms and definitions that are relevant to the text they follow.

- **Spell Checkers** are used to detect spelling errors in typed text. Some spell checkers may also detect the misuse of plural or singular nouns, verb tenses, or capitalization. While spell checkers are a helpful tool, they are not always reliable or attuned to the author's intent, so it is important to review the spell checker's suggestions before accepting them.
- **Style Manuals** are guidelines on the preferred punctuation, format, and grammar usage according to different fields or organizations. For example, the Associated Press Stylebook is a style guide often used for media writing. The guidelines within a style guide are not always applicable across different contexts and usages, as the guidelines often cover grammatical or formatting situations that are not objectively correct or incorrect.

Figurative Language

LITERAL AND FIGURATIVE MEANING

When language is used **literally**, the words mean exactly what they say and nothing more. When language is used **figuratively**, the words mean something beyond their literal meaning. For example, "The weeping willow tree has long, trailing branches and leaves" is a literal description. But "The weeping willow tree looks as if it is bending over and crying" is a figurative description—specifically, a **simile** or stated comparison. Another figurative language form is **metaphor**, or an implied comparison. A good example is the metaphor of a city, state, or city-state as a ship, and its governance as sailing that ship. Ancient Greek lyrical poet Alcaeus is credited with first using this metaphor, and ancient Greek tragedian Aeschylus then used it in *Seven Against Thebes,* and then Plato used it in the *Republic.*

FIGURES OF SPEECH

A **figure of speech** is a verbal expression whose meaning is figurative rather than literal. For example, the phrase "butterflies in the stomach" does not refer to actual butterflies in a person's stomach. It is a metaphor representing the fluttery feelings experienced when a person is nervous or excited—or when one "falls in love," which does not mean physically falling. "Hitting a sales target" does not mean physically hitting a target with arrows as in archery; it is a metaphor for meeting a sales quota. "Climbing the ladder of success" metaphorically likens advancing in one's career to ascending ladder rungs. Similes, such as "light as a feather" (meaning very light, not a feather's actual weight), and hyperbole, like "I'm starving/freezing/roasting," are also figures of speech. Figures of speech are often used and crafted for emphasis, freshness of expression, or clarity.

> **Review Video: Figure of Speech**
> Visit mometrix.com/academy and enter code: 111295

FIGURATIVE LANGUAGE

Figurative language extends past the literal meanings of words. It offers readers new insight into the people, things, events, and subjects covered in a work of literature. Figurative language also enables readers to feel they are sharing the authors' experiences. It can stimulate the reader's senses, make comparisons that readers find intriguing or even startling, and enable readers to view the world in different ways. When looking for figurative language, it is important to consider the context of the sentence or situation. Phrases that appear out of place or make little sense when read literally are likely instances of figurative language. Once figurative language has been recognized, context is also important to determining the type of figurative language being used and its function. For example, when a comparison is being made, a metaphor or simile is likely being used. This means the comparison may emphasize or create irony through the things being compared. Seven specific types of figurative language include: alliteration, onomatopoeia, personification, imagery, similes, metaphors, and hyperbole.

> **Review Video: Figurative Language**
> Visit mometrix.com/academy and enter code: 584902

ALLITERATION AND ONOMATOPOEIA

Alliteration describes a series of words beginning with the same sounds. **Onomatopoeia** uses words imitating the sounds of things they name or describe. For example, in his poem "Come Down, O Maid," Alfred Tennyson writes of "The moan of doves in immemorial elms, / And murmuring of

155

innumerable bees." The word "moan" sounds like some sounds doves make, "murmuring" represents the sounds of bees buzzing. Onomatopoeia also includes words that are simply meant to represent sounds, such as "meow," "kaboom," and "whoosh."

PERSONIFICATION

Another type of figurative language is **personification**. This is describing a non-human thing, like an animal or an object, as if it were human. The general intent of personification is to describe things in a manner that will be comprehensible to readers. When an author states that a tree *groans* in the wind, he or she does not mean that the tree is emitting a low, pained sound from a mouth. Instead, the author means that the tree is making a noise similar to a human groan. Of course, this personification establishes a tone of sadness or suffering. A different tone would be established if the author said that the tree was *swaying* or *dancing*. Alfred Tennyson's poem "The Eagle" uses all of these types of figurative language: "He clasps the crag with crooked hands." Tennyson used alliteration, repeating /k/ and /kr/ sounds. These hard-sounding consonants reinforce the imagery, giving visual and tactile impressions of the eagle.

SIMILES AND METAPHORS

Similes are stated comparisons using "like" or "as." Similes can be used to stimulate readers' imaginations and appeal to their senses. Because a simile includes *like* or *as,* the device creates more space between the description and the thing being described than a metaphor does. If an author says that *a house was like a shoebox*, then the tone is different than the author saying that the house *was* a shoebox. Authors will choose between a metaphor and a simile depending on their intended tone.

Similes also help compare fictional characters to well-known objects or experiences, so the reader can better relate to them. William Wordsworth's poem about "Daffodils" begins, "I wandered lonely as a cloud." This simile compares his loneliness to that of a cloud. It is also personification, giving a cloud the human quality loneliness. In his novel *Lord Jim* (1900), Joseph Conrad writes in Chapter 33, "I would have given anything for the power to soothe her frail soul, tormenting itself in its invincible ignorance like a small bird beating about the cruel wires of a cage." Conrad uses the word "like" to compare the girl's soul to a small bird. His description of the bird beating at the cage shows the similar helplessness of the girl's soul to gain freedom.

A **metaphor** is a type of figurative language in which the writer equates something with another thing that is not particularly similar, instead of using *like* or *as*. For instance, *the bird was an arrow arcing through the sky*. In this sentence, the arrow is serving as a metaphor for the bird. The point of a metaphor is to encourage the reader to consider the item being described in a *different way*. Let's continue with this metaphor for a flying bird. You are asked to envision the bird's flight as being similar to the arc of an arrow. So, you imagine the flight to be swift and bending. Metaphors are a way for the author to describe an item *without being direct and obvious*. This literary device is a lyrical and suggestive way of providing information. Note that the reference for a metaphor will not always be mentioned explicitly by the author. Consider the following description of a forest in winter: *Swaying skeletons reached for the sky and groaned as the wind blew through them.* In this example, the author is using *skeletons* as a metaphor for leafless trees. This metaphor creates a spooky tone while inspiring the reader's imagination.

LITERARY EXAMPLES OF METAPHOR

A **metaphor** is an implied comparison, i.e., it compares something to something else without using "like", "as", or other comparative words. For example, in "The Tyger" (1794), William Blake writes, "Tyger Tyger, burning bright, / In the forests of the night." Blake compares the tiger to a flame not by saying it is like a fire, but by simply describing it as "burning." Henry Wadsworth Longfellow's poem "O Ship of State" (1850) uses an extended metaphor by referring consistently throughout the entire poem to the state, union, or republic as a seagoing vessel, referring to its keel, mast, sail, rope, anchors, and to its braving waves, rocks, gale, tempest, and "false lights on the shore." Within the extended metaphor, Wordsworth uses a specific metaphor: "the anchors of thy hope!"

TED HUGHES' ANIMAL METAPHORS

Ted Hughes frequently used animal metaphors in his poetry. In "The Thought Fox," a model of concise, structured beauty, Hughes characterizes the poet's creative process with succinct, striking imagery of an idea entering his head like a wild fox. Repeating "loneliness" in the first two stanzas emphasizes the poet's lonely work: "Something else is alive / Beside the clock's loneliness." He treats an idea's arrival as separate from himself. Three stanzas detail in vivid images a fox's approach from the outside winter forest at starless midnight—its nose, "Cold, delicately" touching twigs and leaves; "neat" paw prints in snow; "bold" body; brilliant green eyes; and self-contained, focused progress—"Till, with a sudden sharp hot stink of fox," he metaphorically depicts poetic inspiration as the fox's physical entry into "the dark hole of the head." Hughes ends by summarizing his vision of a poet as an interior, passive idea recipient, with the outside world unchanged: "The window is starless still; the clock ticks, / The page is printed."

> **Review Video: Metaphor**
> Visit mometrix.com/academy and enter code: 133295

HYPERBOLE

Hyperbole is excessive exaggeration used for humor or emphasis rather than for literal meaning. For example, in *To Kill a Mockingbird*, Harper Lee wrote, "People moved slowly then. There was no hurry, for there was nowhere to go, nothing to buy and no money to buy it with, nothing to see outside the boundaries of Maycomb County." This was not literally true; Lee exaggerates the scarcity of these things for emphasis. In "Old Times on the Mississippi," Mark Twain wrote, "I... could have hung my hat on my eyes, they stuck out so far." This is not literal, but makes his description vivid and funny. In his poem "As I Walked Out One Evening", W. H. Auden wrote, "I'll love you, dear, I'll love you / Till China and Africa meet, / And the river jumps over the mountain / And the salmon sing in the street." He used things not literally possible to emphasize the duration of his love.

> **Review Video: Hyperbole and Understatement**
> Visit mometrix.com/academy and enter code: 308470

LITERARY IRONY

In literature, irony demonstrates the opposite of what is said or done. The three types of irony are **verbal irony**, **situational irony**, and **dramatic irony**. Verbal irony uses words opposite to the meaning. Sarcasm may use verbal irony. One common example is describing something that is confusing as "clear as mud." For example, in his 1986 movie *Hannah and Her Sisters,* author, director, and actor Woody Allen says to his character's date, "I had a great evening; it was like the Nuremburg Trials." Notice these employ similes. In situational irony, what happens contrasts with what was expected. O. Henry's short story *The Gift of the Magi* uses situational irony: a husband and wife each sacrifice their most prized possession to buy each other a Christmas present. The irony is that she sells her long hair to buy him a watch fob, while he sells his heirloom pocket-watch to buy her the jeweled combs for her hair she had long wanted; in the end, neither of them can use their gifts. In dramatic irony, narrative informs audiences of more than its characters know. For example, in *Romeo and Juliet,* the audience is made aware that Juliet is only asleep, while Romeo believes her to be dead, which then leads to Romeo's death.

> **Review Video: <u>Irony</u>**
> Visit mometrix.com/academy and enter code: 374204

IDIOMS

Idioms create comparisons, and often take the form of similes or metaphors. Idioms are always phrases and are understood to have a meaning that is different from its individual words' literal meaning. For example, "break a leg" is a common idiom that is used to wish someone luck or tell them to perform well. Literally, the phrase "break a leg" means to injure a person's leg, but the phrase takes on a different meaning when used as an idiom. Another example is "call it a day," which means to temporarily stop working on a task, or find a stopping point, rather than literally referring to something as "a day." Many idioms are associated with a region or group. For example, an idiom commonly used in the American South is "'til the cows come home." This phrase is often used to indicate that something will take or may last for a very long time, but not that it will literally last until the cows return to where they reside.

Mathematics

Numbers

CLASSIFICATIONS OF NUMBERS

Numbers are the basic building blocks of mathematics. Specific features of numbers are identified by the following terms:

Integer – any positive or negative whole number, including zero. Integers do not include fractions $\left(\frac{1}{3}\right)$, decimals (0.56), or mixed numbers $\left(7\frac{3}{4}\right)$.

Prime number – any whole number greater than 1 that has only two factors, itself and 1; that is, a number that can be divided evenly only by 1 and itself.

Composite number – any whole number greater than 1 that has more than two different factors; in other words, any whole number that is not a prime number. For example: The composite number 8 has the factors of 1, 2, 4, and 8.

Even number – any integer that can be divided by 2 without leaving a remainder. For example: 2, 4, 6, 8, and so on.

Odd number – any integer that cannot be divided evenly by 2. For example: 3, 5, 7, 9, and so on.

Decimal number – any number that uses a decimal point to show the part of the number that is less than one. Example: 1.234.

Decimal point – a symbol used to separate the ones place from the tenths place in decimals or dollars from cents in currency.

Decimal place – the position of a number to the right of the decimal point. In the decimal 0.123, the 1 is in the first place to the right of the decimal point, indicating tenths; the 2 is in the second place, indicating hundredths; and the 3 is in the third place, indicating thousandths.

The **decimal**, or base 10, system is a number system that uses ten different digits (0, 1, 2, 3, 4, 5, 6, 7, 8, 9). An example of a number system that uses something other than ten digits is the **binary**, or base 2, number system, used by computers, which uses only the numbers 0 and 1. It is thought that the decimal system originated because people had only their 10 fingers for counting.

Rational numbers include all integers, decimals, and fractions. Any terminating or repeating decimal number is a rational number.

Irrational numbers cannot be written as fractions or decimals because the number of decimal places is infinite and there is no recurring pattern of digits within the number. For example, pi (π) begins with 3.141592 and continues without terminating or repeating, so pi is an irrational number.

Real numbers are the set of all rational and irrational numbers.

THE NUMBER LINE

A number line is a graph to see the distance between numbers. Basically, this graph shows the relationship between numbers. So a number line may have a point for zero and may show negative numbers on the left side of the line. Also, any positive numbers are placed on the right side of the line. For example, consider the points labeled on the following number line:

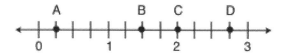

We can use the dashed lines on the number line to identify each point. Each dashed line between two whole numbers is $\frac{1}{4}$. The line halfway between two numbers is $\frac{1}{2}$.

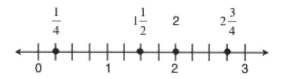

NUMBERS IN WORD FORM AND PLACE VALUE

When writing numbers out in word form or translating word form to numbers, it is essential to understand how a place value system works. In the decimal or base-10 system, each digit of a number represents how many of the corresponding place value—a specific factor of 10—are contained in the number being represented. To make reading numbers easier, every three digits to the left of the decimal place is preceded by a comma. The following table demonstrates some of the place values:

Power of 10	10^3	10^2	10^1	10^0	10^{-1}	10^{-2}	10^{-3}
Value	1,000	100	10	1	0.1	0.01	0.001
Place	thousands	hundreds	tens	ones	tenths	hundredths	thousandths

Mometrix

For example, consider the number 4,546.09, which can be separated into each place value like this:

4: thousands
5: hundreds
4: tens
6: ones
0: tenths
9: hundredths

This number in word form would be *four thousand five hundred forty-six and nine hundredths.*

Review Video: Number Place Value
Visit mometrix.com/academy and enter code: 205433

ABSOLUTE VALUE

A precursor to working with negative numbers is understanding what **absolute values** are. A number's absolute value is simply the distance away from zero a number is on the number line. The absolute value of a number is always positive and is written $|x|$. For example, the absolute value of 3, written as $|3|$, is 3 because the distance between 0 and 3 on a number line is three units. Likewise, the absolute value of –3, written as $|-3|$, is 3 because the distance between 0 and –3 on a number line is three units. So $|3| = |-3|$.

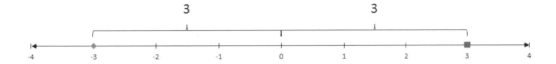

Review Video: Absolute Value
Visit mometrix.com/academy and enter code: 314669

PRACTICE

P1. Write the place value of each digit in 14,059.826

P2. Write out each of the following in words:

(a) 29
(b) 478
(c) 98,542
(d) 0.06
(e) 13.113

P3. Write each of the following in numbers:

(a) nine thousand four hundred thirty-five
(b) three hundred two thousand eight hundred seventy-six
(c) nine hundred one thousandths
(d) nineteen thousandths
(e) seven thousand one hundred forty-two and eighty-five hundredths

161

Mometrix

Practice Solutions

P1. The place value for each digit would be as follows:

Digit	Place Value
1	ten-thousands
4	thousands
0	hundreds
5	tens
9	ones
8	tenths
2	hundredths
6	thousandths

P2. Each written out in words would be:

(a) twenty-nine
(b) four hundred seventy-eight
(c) ninety-eight thousand five hundred forty-two
(d) six hundredths
(e) thirteen and one hundred thirteen thousandths

P3. Each in numeric form would be:

(a) 9,435
(b) 302876
(c) 0.901
(d) 0.019
(e) 7,142.85

162

Operations

OPERATIONS

An **operation** is simply a mathematical process that takes some value(s) as input(s) and produces an output. Elementary operations are often written in the following form: *value operation value*. For instance, in the expression $1 + 2$ the values are 1 and 2 and the operation is addition. Performing the operation gives the output of 3. In this way we can say that $1 + 2$ and 3 are equal, or $1 + 2 = 3$.

ADDITION

Addition increases the value of one quantity by the value of another quantity (both called **addends**). Example: $2 + 4 = 6$ or $8 + 9 = 17$. The result is called the **sum**. With addition, the order does not matter, $4 + 2 = 2 + 4$.

When adding signed numbers, if the signs are the same simply add the absolute values of the addends and apply the original sign to the sum. For example, $(+4) + (+8) = +12$ and $(-4) + (-8) = -12$. When the original signs are different, take the absolute values of the addends and subtract the smaller value from the larger value, then apply the original sign of the larger value to the difference. Example: $(+4) + (-8) = -4$ and $(-4) + (+8) = +4$.

SUBTRACTION

Subtraction is the opposite operation to addition; it decreases the value of one quantity (the **minuend**) by the value of another quantity (the **subtrahend**). For example, $6 - 4 = 2$ or $17 - 8 = 9$. The result is called the **difference**. Note that with subtraction, the order does matter, $6 - 4 \neq 4 - 6$.

For subtracting signed numbers, change the sign of the subtrahend and then follow the same rules used for addition. Example: $(+4) - (+8) = (+4) + (-8) = -4$

MULTIPLICATION

Multiplication can be thought of as repeated addition. One number (the **multiplier**) indicates how many times to add the other number (the **multiplicand**) to itself. Example: $3 \times 2 = 2 + 2 + 2 = 6$. With multiplication, the order does not matter, $2 \times 3 = 3 \times 2$ or $3 + 3 = 2 + 2 + 2$, either way the result (the **product**) is the same.

If the signs are the same, the product is positive when multiplying signed numbers. Example: $(+4) \times (+8) = +32$ and $(-4) \times (-8) = +32$. If the signs are opposite, the product is negative. Example: $(+4) \times (-8) = -32$ and $(-4) \times (+8) = -32$. When more than two factors are multiplied together, the sign of the product is determined by how many negative factors are present. If there are an odd number of negative factors then the product is negative, whereas an even number of negative factors indicates a positive product. Example: $(+4) \times (-8) \times (-2) = +64$ and $(-4) \times (-8) \times (-2) = -64$.

DIVISION

Division is the opposite operation to multiplication; one number (the **divisor**) tells us how many parts to divide the other number (the **dividend**) into. The result of division is called the **quotient**. Example: $20 \div 4 = 5$. If 20 is split into 4 equal parts, each part is 5. With division, the order of the numbers does matter, $20 \div 4 \neq 4 \div 20$.

The rules for dividing signed numbers are similar to multiplying signed numbers. If the dividend and divisor have the same sign, the quotient is positive. If the dividend and divisor have opposite signs, the quotient is negative. Example: $(-4) \div (+8) = -0.5$.

> **Review Video: Mathematical Operations**
> Visit mometrix.com/academy and enter code: 208095

PARENTHESES

Parentheses are used to designate which operations should be done first when there are multiple operations. Example: $4 - (2 + 1) = 1$; the parentheses tell us that we must add 2 and 1, and then subtract the sum from 4, rather than subtracting 2 from 4 and then adding 1 (this would give us an answer of 3).

> **Review Video: Mathematical Parentheses**
> Visit mometrix.com/academy and enter code: 978600

EXPONENTS

An **exponent** is a superscript number placed next to another number at the top right. It indicates how many times the base number is to be multiplied by itself. Exponents provide a shorthand way to write what would be a longer mathematical expression, Example: $2^4 = 2 \times 2 \times 2 \times 2$. A number with an exponent of 2 is said to be "squared," while a number with an exponent of 3 is said to be "cubed." The value of a number raised to an exponent is called its power. So 8^4 is read as "8 to the 4th power," or "8 raised to the power of 4."

The properties of exponents are as follows:

Property	Description
$a^1 = a$	Any number to the power of 1 is equal to itself
$1^n = 1$	The number 1 raised to any power is equal to 1
$a^0 = 1$	Any number raised to the power of 0 is equal to 1
$a^n \times a^m = a^{n+m}$	Add exponents to multiply powers of the same base number
$a^n \div a^m = a^{n-m}$	Subtract exponents to divide powers of the same base number
$(a^n)^m = a^{n \times m}$	When a power is raised to a power, the exponents are multiplied
$(a \times b)^n = a^n \times b^n$ $(a \div b)^n = a^n \div b^n$	Multiplication and division operations inside parentheses can be raised to a power. This is the same as each term being raised to that power.
$a^{-n} = \dfrac{1}{a^n}$	A negative exponent is the same as the reciprocal of a positive exponent

Note that exponents do not have to be integers. Fractional or decimal exponents follow all the rules above as well. Example: $5^{\frac{1}{4}} \times 5^{\frac{3}{4}} = 5^{\frac{1}{4}+\frac{3}{4}} = 5^1 = 5$.

> **Review Video: Exponents**
> Visit mometrix.com/academy and enter code: 600998
>
> **Review Video: Laws of Exponents**
> Visit mometrix.com/academy and enter code: 532558

ROOTS

A **root**, such as a square root, is another way of writing a fractional exponent. Instead of using a superscript, roots use the radical symbol ($\sqrt{\ }$) to indicate the operation. A radical will have a number underneath the bar, and may sometimes have a number in the upper left: $\sqrt[n]{a}$, read as "the nth root of a." The relationship between radical notation and exponent notation can be described by this equation:

$$\sqrt[n]{a} = a^{\frac{1}{n}}$$

The two special cases of $n = 2$ and $n = 3$ are called square roots and cube roots. If there is no number to the upper left, the radical is understood to be a square root ($n = 2$). Nearly all of the roots you encounter will be square roots. A square root is the same as a number raised to the one-half power. When we say that a is the square root of b ($a = \sqrt{b}$), we mean that a multiplied by itself equals b: ($a \times a = b$).

A **perfect square** is a number that has an integer for its square root. There are 10 perfect squares from 1 to 100: 1, 4, 9, 16, 25, 36, 49, 64, 81, 100 (the squares of integers 1 through 10).

> **Review Video: Roots**
> Visit mometrix.com/academy and enter code: 795655

ORDER OF OPERATIONS

Order of operations is a set of rules that dictates the order in which we must perform each operation in an expression so that we will evaluate it accurately. If we have an expression that includes multiple different operations, order of operations tells us which operations to do first. The most common mnemonic for order of operations is **PEMDAS**, or "Please Excuse My Dear Aunt Sally." PEMDAS stands for parentheses, exponents, multiplication, division, addition, and subtraction. It is important to understand that multiplication and division have equal precedence, as do addition and subtraction, so those pairs of operations are simply worked from left to right in order.

For example, evaluating the expression $5 + 20 \div 4 \times (2 + 3)^2 - 6$ using the correct order of operations would be done like this:

- **P:** Perform the operations inside the parentheses: $(2 + 3) = 5$
- **E:** Simplify the exponents: $(5)^2 = 5 \times 5 = 25$
  - The equation now looks like this: $5 + 20 \div 4 \times 25 - 6$
- **MD:** Perform multiplication and division from left to right: $20 \div 4 = 5$; then $5 \times 25 = 125$
  - The equation now looks like this: $5 + 125 - 6$
- **AS:** Perform addition and subtraction from left to right: $5 + 125 = 130$; then $130 - 6 = 124$

> **Review Video: Order of Operations**
> Visit mometrix.com/academy and enter code: 259675

SUBTRACTION WITH REGROUPING

A great way to make use of some of the features built into the decimal system would be regrouping when attempting longform subtraction operations. When subtracting within a place value, sometimes the minuend is smaller than the subtrahend, **regrouping** enables you to 'borrow' a unit from a place value to the left in order to get a positive difference. For example, consider subtracting 189 from 525 with regrouping.

First, set up the subtraction problem in vertical form:

```
   525
 − 189
```

Notice that the numbers in the ones and tens columns of 525 are smaller than the numbers in the ones and tens columns of 189. This means you will need to use regrouping to perform subtraction:

```
   5   2   5
 − 1   8   9
```

To subtract 9 from 5 in the ones column you will need to borrow from the 2 in the tens columns:

```
   5   1   15
 − 1   8    9
            6
```

Next, to subtract 8 from 1 in the tens column you will need to borrow from the 5 in the hundreds column:

```
   4   11   15
 − 1    8    9
        3    6
```

Last, subtract the 1 from the 4 in the hundreds column:

```
   4   11   15
 − 1    8    9
   3    3    6
```

WORD PROBLEMS AND MATHEMATICAL SYMBOLS

When working on word problems, you must be able to translate verbal expressions or "math words" into math symbols. This chart contains several "math words" and their appropriate symbols:

Phrase	Symbol
equal, is, was, will be, has, costs, gets to, is the same as, becomes	=
times, of, multiplied by, product of, twice, doubles, halves, triples	×
divided by, per, ratio of/to, out of	÷
plus, added to, sum, combined, and, more than, totals of	+
subtracted from, less than, decreased by, minus, difference between	−
what, how much, original value, how many, a number, a variable	x, n, etc.

EXAMPLES OF TRANSLATED MATHEMATICAL PHRASES

- The phrase four more than twice a number can be written algebraically as $2x + 4$.

- The phrase half a number decreased by six can be written algebraically as $\frac{1}{2}x - 6$.
- The phrase the sum of a number and the product of five and that number can be written algebraically as $x + 5x$.
- You may see a test question that says, "Olivia is constructing a bookcase from seven boards. Two of them are for vertical supports and five are for shelves. The height of the bookcase is twice the width of the bookcase. If the seven boards total 36 feet in length, what will be the height of Olivia's bookcase?" You would need to make a sketch and then create the equation to determine the width of the shelves. The height can be represented as double the width. (If x represents the width of the shelves in feet, then the height of the bookcase is $2x$. Since the seven boards total 36 feet, $2x + 2x + x + x + x + x + x = 36$ or $9x = 36$; $x = 4$. The height is twice the width, or 8 feet.)

PRACTICE

P1. Demonstrate how to subtract 477 from 620 using regrouping.

P2. Simplify the following expressions with exponents:

(a) 37^0
(b) 1^{30}
(c) $2^3 \times 2^4 \times 2^x$
(d) $(3^x)^3$
(e) $(12 \div 3)^2$

Practice Solutions

P1. First, set up the subtraction problem in vertical form:

$$
\begin{array}{ccc}
 & 6 & 2 & 0 \\
- & 4 & 7 & 7 \\
\hline
\end{array}
$$

To subtract 7 from 0 in the ones column you will need to borrow from the 2 in the tens column:

$$
\begin{array}{ccc}
 & 6 & 1 & 10 \\
- & 4 & 7 & 7 \\
\hline
 & & & 3 \\
\end{array}
$$

Next, to subtract 7 from the 1 that's still in the tens column you will need to borrow from the 6 in the hundreds column:

$$
\begin{array}{ccc}
 & 5 & 11 & 10 \\
- & 4 & 7 & 7 \\
\hline
 & & 4 & 3 \\
\end{array}
$$

Lastly, subtract 4 from the 5 remaining in the hundreds column:

$$
\begin{array}{ccc}
 & 5 & 11 & 10 \\
- & 4 & 7 & 7 \\
\hline
 & 1 & 4 & 3 \\
\end{array}
$$

P2. Using the properties of exponents and the proper order of operations:

    (a) Any number raised to the power of 0 is equal to 1: $37^0 = 1$
    (b) The number 1 raised to any power is equal to 1: $1^{30} = 1$
    (c) Add exponents to multiply powers of the same base: $2^3 \times 2^4 \times 2^x = 2^{(3+4+x)} = 2^{(7+x)}$
    (d) When a power is raised to a power, the exponents are multiplied: $(3^x)^3 = 3^{3x}$
    (e) Perform the operation inside the parentheses first: $(12 \div 3)^2 = 4^2 = 16$

Factoring

FACTORS AND GREATEST COMMON FACTOR

Factors are numbers that are multiplied together to obtain a **product**. For example, in the equation $2 \times 3 = 6$, the numbers 2 and 3 are factors. A **prime number** has only two factors (1 and itself), but other numbers can have many factors.

A **common factor** is a number that divides exactly into two or more other numbers. For example, the factors of 12 are 1, 2, 3, 4, 6, and 12, while the factors of 15 are 1, 3, 5, and 15. The common factors of 12 and 15 are 1 and 3.

A **prime factor** is also a prime number. Therefore, the prime factors of 12 are 2 and 3. For 15, the prime factors are 3 and 5.

The **greatest common factor (GCF)** is the largest number that is a factor of two or more numbers. For example, the factors of 15 are 1, 3, 5, and 15; the factors of 35 are 1, 5, 7, and 35. Therefore, the greatest common factor of 15 and 35 is 5.

> **Review Video: Factors**
> Visit mometrix.com/academy and enter code: 920086
>
> **Review Video: Greatest Common Factor (GCF)**
> Visit mometrix.com/academy and enter code: 838699

MULTIPLES AND LEAST COMMON MULTIPLE

Often listed out in multiplication tables, **multiples** are integer increments of a given factor. In other words, dividing a multiple by the factor will result in an integer. For example, the multiples of 7 include: $1 \times 7 = 7, 2 \times 7 = 14, 3 \times 7 = 21, 4 \times 7 = 28, 5 \times 7 = 35$. Dividing 7, 14, 21, 28, or 35 by 7 will result in the integers 1, 2, 3, 4, and 5, respectively.

The least common multiple (**LCM**) is the smallest number that is a multiple of two or more numbers. For example, the multiples of 3 include 3, 6, 9, 12, 15, etc.; the multiples of 5 include 5, 10, 15, 20, etc. Therefore, the least common multiple of 3 and 5 is 15.

> **Review Video: Multiples**
> Visit mometrix.com/academy and enter code: 626738

Rational Numbers

FRACTIONS

A **fraction** is a number that is expressed as one integer written above another integer, with a dividing line between them $\left(\frac{x}{y}\right)$. It represents the **quotient** of the two numbers "x divided by y." It can also be thought of as x out of y equal parts.

The top number of a fraction is called the **numerator**, and it represents the number of parts under consideration. The 1 in $\frac{1}{4}$ means that 1 part out of the whole is being considered in the calculation. The bottom number of a fraction is called the **denominator**, and it represents the total number of equal parts. The 4 in $\frac{1}{4}$ means that the whole consists of 4 equal parts. A fraction cannot have a denominator of zero; this is referred to as "*undefined.*"

Fractions can be manipulated, without changing the value of the fraction, by multiplying or dividing (but not adding or subtracting) both the numerator and denominator by the same number. If you divide both numbers by a common factor, you are **reducing** or simplifying the fraction. Two fractions that have the same value but are expressed differently are known as **equivalent fractions**. For example, $\frac{2}{10}, \frac{3}{15}, \frac{4}{20}$, and $\frac{5}{25}$ are all equivalent fractions. They can also all be reduced or simplified to $\frac{1}{5}$.

When two fractions are manipulated so that they have the same denominator, this is known as finding a **common denominator**. The number chosen to be that common denominator should be the least common multiple of the two original denominators. Example: $\frac{3}{4}$ and $\frac{5}{6}$; the least common multiple of 4 and 6 is 12. Manipulating to achieve the common denominator: $\frac{3}{4} = \frac{9}{12}$; $\frac{5}{6} = \frac{10}{12}$.

PROPER FRACTIONS AND MIXED NUMBERS

A fraction whose denominator is greater than its numerator is known as a **proper fraction**, while a fraction whose numerator is greater than its denominator is known as an **improper fraction**. Proper fractions have values *less than one* and improper fractions have values *greater than one*.

A **mixed number** is a number that contains both an integer and a fraction. Any improper fraction can be rewritten as a mixed number. Example: $\frac{8}{3} = \frac{6}{3} + \frac{2}{3} = 2 + \frac{2}{3} = 2\frac{2}{3}$. Similarly, any mixed number can be rewritten as an improper fraction. Example: $1\frac{3}{5} = 1 + \frac{3}{5} = \frac{5}{5} + \frac{3}{5} = \frac{8}{5}$.

> **Review Video: <u>Improper Fractions and Mixed Numbers</u>**
> Visit mometrix.com/academy and enter code: 211077
>
> **Review Video: <u>Fractions</u>**
> Visit mometrix.com/academy and enter code: 262335

ADDING AND SUBTRACTING FRACTIONS

If two fractions have a common denominator, they can be added or subtracted simply by adding or subtracting the two numerators and retaining the same denominator. If the two fractions do not already have the same denominator, one or both of them must be manipulated to achieve a common denominator before they can be added or subtracted. Example: $\frac{1}{2} + \frac{1}{4} = \frac{2}{4} + \frac{1}{4} = \frac{3}{4}$.

> **Review Video: Adding and Subtracting Fractions**
> Visit mometrix.com/academy and enter code: 378080

MULTIPLYING FRACTIONS

Two fractions can be multiplied by multiplying the two numerators to find the new numerator and the two denominators to find the new denominator. Example: $\frac{1}{3} \times \frac{2}{3} = \frac{1 \times 2}{3 \times 3} = \frac{2}{9}$.

DIVIDING FRACTIONS

Two fractions can be divided by flipping the numerator and denominator of the second fraction and then proceeding as though it were a multiplication problem. Example: $\frac{2}{3} \div \frac{3}{4} = \frac{2}{3} \times \frac{4}{3} = \frac{8}{9}$.

> **Review Video: Multiplying and Dividing Fractions**
> Visit mometrix.com/academy and enter code: 473632

MULTIPLYING A MIXED NUMBER BY A WHOLE NUMBER OR A DECIMAL

When multiplying a mixed number by something, it is usually best to convert it to an improper fraction first. Additionally, if the multiplicand is a decimal, it is most often simplest to convert it to a fraction. For instance, to multiply $4\frac{3}{8}$ by 3.5, begin by rewriting each quantity as a whole number plus a proper fraction. Remember, a mixed number is a fraction added to a whole number and a decimal is a representation of the sum of fractions, specifically tenths, hundredths, thousandths, and so on:

$$4\frac{3}{8} \times 3.5 = \left(4 + \frac{3}{8}\right) \times \left(3 + \frac{1}{2}\right)$$

Next, the quantities being added need to be expressed with the same denominator. This is achieved by multiplying and dividing the whole number by the denominator of the fraction. Recall that a whole number is equivalent to that number divided by 1:

$$= \left(\frac{4}{1} \times \frac{8}{8} + \frac{3}{8}\right) \times \left(\frac{3}{1} \times \frac{2}{2} + \frac{1}{2}\right)$$

When multiplying fractions, remember to multiply the numerators and denominators separately:

$$= \left(\frac{4 \times 8}{1 \times 8} + \frac{3}{8}\right) \times \left(\frac{3 \times 2}{1 \times 2} + \frac{1}{2}\right)$$

$$= \left(\frac{32}{8} + \frac{3}{8}\right) \times \left(\frac{6}{2} + \frac{1}{2}\right)$$

Now that the fractions have the same denominators, they can be added:

$$= \frac{35}{8} \times \frac{7}{2}$$

171

Finally, perform the last multiplication and then simplify:

$$= \frac{35 \times 7}{8 \times 2} = \frac{245}{16} = \frac{240}{16} + \frac{5}{16} = 15\frac{5}{16}$$

DECIMALS

Decimals are one way to represent parts of a whole. Using the place value system, each digit to the right of a decimal point denotes the number of units of a corresponding *negative* power of ten. For example, consider the decimal 0.24. We can use a model to represent the decimal. Since a dime is worth one-tenth of a dollar and a penny is worth one-hundredth of a dollar, one possible model to represent this fraction is to have 2 dimes representing the 2 in the tenths place and 4 pennies representing the 4 in the hundredths place:

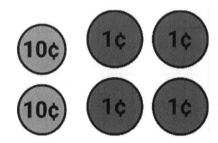

To write the decimal as a fraction, put the decimal in the numerator with 1 in the denominator. Multiply the numerator and denominator by tens until there are no more decimal places. Then simplify the fraction to lowest terms. For example, converting 0.24 to a fraction:

$$0.24 = \frac{0.24}{1} = \frac{0.24 \times 100}{1 \times 100} = \frac{24}{100} = \frac{6}{25}$$

> **Review Video: Decimals**
> Visit mometrix.com/academy and enter code: 837268

OPERATIONS WITH DECIMALS
ADDING AND SUBTRACTING DECIMALS
When adding and subtracting decimals, the decimal points must always be aligned. Adding decimals is just like adding regular whole numbers. Example: $4.5 + 2.0 = 6.5$.

If the problem-solver does not properly align the decimal points, an incorrect answer of 4.7 may result. An easy way to add decimals is to align all of the decimal points in a vertical column visually. This will allow one to see exactly where the decimal should be placed in the final answer. Begin adding from right to left. Add each column in turn, making sure to carry the number to the left if a column adds up to more than 9. The same rules apply to the subtraction of decimals.

> **Review Video: Adding and Subtracting Decimals**
> Visit mometrix.com/academy and enter code: 381101

MULTIPLYING DECIMALS
A simple multiplication problem has two components: a **multiplicand** and a **multiplier**. When multiplying decimals, work as though the numbers were whole rather than decimals. Once the final product is calculated, count the number of places to the right of the decimal in both the multiplicand and the multiplier. Then, count that number of places from the right of the product and place the decimal in that position.

For example, 12.3 × 2.56 has a total of three places to the right of the respective decimals. Multiply 123 × 256 to get 31,488. Now, beginning on the right, count three places to the left and insert the decimal. The final product will be 31,488.

DIVIDING DECIMALS

Every division problem has a **divisor** and a **dividend**. The dividend is the number that is being divided. In the problem 14 ÷ 7, 14 is the dividend and 7 is the divisor. In a division problem with decimals, the divisor must be converted into a whole number. Begin by moving the decimal in the divisor to the right until a whole number is created. Next, move the decimal in the dividend the same number of spaces to the right. For example, 4.9 into 24.5 would become 49 into 245. The decimal was moved one space to the right to create a whole number in the divisor, and then the same was done for the dividend. Once the whole numbers are created, the problem is carried out normally: 245 ÷ 49 = 5.

PERCENTAGES

Percentages can be thought of as fractions that are based on a whole of 100; that is, one whole is equal to 100%. The word **percent** means "per hundred." Percentage problems are often presented in three main ways:

- Find what percentage of some number another number is.
  - Example: What percentage of 40 is 8?
- Find what number is some percentage of a given number.
  - Example: What number is 20% of 40?
- Find what number another number is a given percentage of.
  - Example: What number is 8 20% of?

There are three components in each of these cases: a **whole** (W), a **part** (P), and a **percentage** (%). These are related by the equation: $P = W \times \%$. This can easily be rearranged into other forms that may suit different questions better: $\% = \frac{P}{W}$ and $W = \frac{P}{\%}$. Percentage problems are often also word problems. As such, a large part of solving them is figuring out which quantities are what. For example, consider the following word problem:

In a school cafeteria, 7 students choose pizza, 9 choose hamburgers, and 4 choose tacos. What percentage of student choose tacos?

To find the whole, you must first add all of the parts: $7 + 9 + 4 = 20$. The percentage can then be found by dividing the part by the whole $\left(\% = \frac{P}{W}\right)$: $\frac{4}{20} = \frac{20}{100} = 20\%$.

CONVERTING BETWEEN PERCENTAGES, FRACTIONS, AND DECIMALS

Converting decimals to percentages and percentages to decimals is as simple as moving the decimal point. To *convert from a decimal to a percentage*, move the decimal point **two places to the right**. To *convert from a percentage to a decimal*, move it **two places to the left**. It may be helpful to remember that the percentage number will always be larger than the equivalent decimal number. Example:

$$0.23 = 23\% \quad 5.34 = 534\% \quad 0.007 = 0.7\%$$
$$700\% = 7.00 \quad 86\% = 0.86 \quad 0.15\% = 0.0015$$

To convert a fraction to a decimal, simply divide the numerator by the denominator in the fraction. To convert a decimal to a fraction, put the decimal in the numerator with 1 in the denominator. Multiply the numerator and denominator by tens until there are no more decimal places. Then simplify the fraction to lowest terms. For example, converting 0.24 to a fraction:

$$0.24 = \frac{0.24}{1} = \frac{0.24 \times 100}{1 \times 100} = \frac{24}{100} = \frac{6}{25}$$

Fractions can be converted to a percentage by finding equivalent fractions with a denominator of 100. Example:

$$\frac{7}{10} = \frac{70}{100} = 70\% \quad \frac{1}{4} = \frac{25}{100} = 25\%$$

To convert a percentage to a fraction, divide the percentage number by 100 and reduce the fraction to its simplest possible terms. Example:

$$60\% = \frac{60}{100} = \frac{3}{5} \quad 96\% = \frac{96}{100} = \frac{24}{25}$$

RATIONAL NUMBERS

The term **rational** means that the number can be expressed as a ratio or fraction. That is, a number, r, is rational if and only if it can be represented by a fraction $\frac{a}{b}$ where a and b are integers and b does not equal 0. The set of rational numbers includes integers and decimals. If there is no finite

way to represent a value with a fraction of integers, then the number is **irrational**. Common examples of irrational numbers include: $\sqrt{5}$, $\left(1 + \sqrt{2}\right)$, and π.

Review Video: Rational and Irrational Numbers
Visit mometrix.com/academy and enter code: 280645

PRACTICE

P1. What is 30% of 120?

P2. What is 150% of 20?

P3. What is 14.5% of 96?

P4. Simplify the following expressions:

(a) $\frac{2}{5} \div \frac{4}{7}$

(b) $\frac{7}{8} - \frac{8}{16}$

(c) $\frac{1}{2} + \left(3\left(\frac{3}{4}\right) - 2\right) + 4$

(d) $0.22 + 0.5 - (5.5 + 3.3 \div 3)$

(e) $\frac{3}{2} + (4(0.5) - 0.75) + 2$

P5. Convert the following to a fraction and to a decimal: **(a)** 15%; **(b)** 24.36%

P6. Convert the following to a decimal and to a percentage. **(a)** $\frac{4}{5}$; **(b)** $3\frac{2}{5}$

P7. A woman's age is thirteen more than half of 60. How old is the woman?

P8. A patient was given pain medicine at a dosage of 0.22 grams. The patient's dosage was then increased to 0.80 grams. By how much was the patient's dosage increased?

P9. At a hotel, $\frac{3}{4}$ of the 100 rooms are occupied today. Yesterday, $\frac{4}{5}$ of the 100 rooms were occupied. On which day were more of the rooms occupied and by how much more?

P10. At a school, 40% of the teachers teach English. If 20 teachers teach English, how many teachers work at the school?

P11. A patient was given blood pressure medicine at a dosage of 2 grams. The patient's dosage was then decreased to 0.45 grams. By how much was the patient's dosage decreased?

P12. Two weeks ago, $\frac{2}{3}$ of the 60 customers at a skate shop were male. Last week, $\frac{3}{6}$ of the 80 customers were male. During which week were there more male customers?

P13. Jane ate lunch at a local restaurant. She ordered a $4.99 appetizer, a $12.50 entrée, and a $1.25 soda. If she wants to tip her server 20%, how much money will she spend in all?

P14. According to a survey, about 82% of engineers were highly satisfied with their job. If 145 engineers were surveyed, how many reported that they were highly satisfied?

P15. A patient was given 40 mg of a certain medicine. Later, the patient's dosage was increased to 45 mg. What was the percent increase in his medication?

P16. Order the following rational numbers from least to greatest: 0.55, 17%, $\sqrt{25}$, $\frac{64}{4}$, $\frac{25}{50}$, 3.

P17. Order the following rational numbers from greatest to least: 0.3, 27%, $\sqrt{100}$, $\frac{72}{9}$, $\frac{1}{9}$, 4.5

P18. Perform the following multiplication. Write each answer as a mixed number.

(a) $\left(1\frac{11}{16}\right) \times 4$

(b) $\left(12\frac{1}{3}\right) \times 1.1$

(c) $3.71 \times \left(6\frac{1}{5}\right)$

P19. Suppose you are making doughnuts and you want to triple the recipe you have. If the following list is the original amounts for the ingredients, what would be the amounts for the tripled recipe?

$1\frac{3}{4}$	cup	Flour	$1\frac{1}{2}$	Tbsp	Butter
$1\frac{1}{4}$	tsp	Baking powder	2	large	Eggs
$\frac{3}{4}$	tsp	Salt	$\frac{3}{4}$	tsp	Vanilla extract
$\frac{3}{8}$	cup	Sugar	$\frac{3}{8}$	cup	Sour cream

PRACTICE SOLUTIONS

P1. The word *of* indicates multiplication, so 30% of 120 is found by multiplying 120 by 30%. Change 30% to a decimal, then multiply: $120 \times 0.3 = 36$

P2. The word *of* indicates multiplication, so 150% of 20 is found by multiplying 20 by 150%. Change 150% to a decimal, then multiply: $20 \times 1.5 = 30$

P3. Change 14.5% to a decimal before multiplying. $0.145 \times 96 = 13.92$.

P4. Follow the order of operations and utilize properties of fractions to solve each:

(a) Rewrite the problem as a multiplication problem: $\frac{2}{5} \times \frac{7}{4} = \frac{2 \times 7}{5 \times 4} = \frac{14}{20}$. Make sure the fraction is reduced to lowest terms. Both 14 and 20 can be divided by 2.

$$\frac{14}{20} = \frac{14 \div 2}{20 \div 2} = \frac{7}{10}$$

(b) The denominators of $\frac{7}{8}$ and $\frac{8}{16}$ are 8 and 16, respectively. The lowest common denominator of 8 and 16 is 16 because 16 is the least common multiple of 8 and 16. Convert the first fraction to its equivalent with the newly found common denominator of 16: $\frac{7 \times 2}{8 \times 2} = \frac{14}{16}$. Now that the fractions have the same denominator, you can subtract them.

$$\frac{14}{16} - \frac{8}{16} = \frac{6}{16} = \frac{3}{8}$$

(c) When simplifying expressions, first perform operations within groups. Within the set of parentheses are multiplication and subtraction operations. Perform the multiplication first to get $\frac{1}{2} + \left(\frac{9}{4} - 2\right) + 4$. Then, subtract two to obtain $\frac{1}{2} + \frac{1}{4} + 4$. Finally, perform addition from left to right:

$$\frac{1}{2} + \frac{1}{4} + 4 = \frac{2}{4} + \frac{1}{4} + \frac{16}{4} = \frac{19}{4} = 4\frac{3}{4}$$

(d) First, evaluate the terms in the parentheses $(5.5 + 3.3 \div 3)$ using order of operations. $3.3 \div 3 = 1.1$, and $5.5 + 1.1 = 6.6$. Next, rewrite the problem: $0.22 + 0.5 - 6.6$. Finally, add and subtract from left to right: $0.22 + 0.5 = 0.72$; $0.72 - 6.6 = -5.88$. The answer is -5.88.

(e) First, simplify within the parentheses, then change the fraction to a decimal and perform addition from left to right:

$$\frac{3}{2} + (2 - 0.75) + 2 =$$
$$\frac{3}{2} + 1.25 + 2 =$$
$$1.5 + 1.25 + 2 = 4.75$$

P5. (a) 15% can be written as $\frac{15}{100}$. Both 15 and 100 can be divided by 5: $\frac{15 \div 5}{100 \div 5} = \frac{3}{20}$

When converting from a percentage to a decimal, drop the percent sign and move the decimal point two places to the left: $15\% = 0.15$

(b) 24.36% written as a fraction is $\frac{24.36}{100}$, or $\frac{2436}{10,000}$, which reduces to $\frac{609}{2500}$. 24.36% written as a decimal is 0.2436. Recall that dividing by 100 moves the decimal two places to the left.

P6. (a) Recall that in the decimal system the first decimal place is one tenth: $\frac{4 \times 2}{5 \times 2} = \frac{8}{10} = 0.8$

Percent means "per hundred." $\frac{4 \times 20}{5 \times 20} = \frac{80}{100} = 80\%$

(b) The mixed number $3\frac{2}{5}$ has a whole number and a fractional part. The fractional part $\frac{2}{5}$ can be written as a decimal by dividing 5 into 2, which gives 0.4. Adding the whole to the part gives 3.4.

To find the equivalent percentage, multiply the decimal by 100. $3.4(100) = 340\%$. Notice that this percentage is greater than 100%. This makes sense because the original mixed number $3\frac{2}{5}$ is greater than 1.

P7. "More than" indicates addition, and "of" indicates multiplication. The expression can be written as $\frac{1}{2}(60) + 13$. So, the woman's age is equal to $\frac{1}{2}(60) + 13 = 30 + 13 = 43$. The woman is 43 years old.

P8. The first step is to determine what operation (addition, subtraction, multiplication, or division) the problem requires. Notice the keywords and phrases "by how much" and "increased."

"Increased" means that you go from a smaller amount to a larger amount. This change can be found by subtracting the smaller amount from the larger amount: 0.80 grams– 0.22 grams = 0.58 grams.

Remember to line up the decimal when subtracting:

$$
\begin{array}{r}
0.80 \\
-\ 0.22 \\
\hline
0.58
\end{array}
$$

P9. First, find the number of rooms occupied each day. To do so, multiply the fraction of rooms occupied by the number of rooms available:

$$\text{Number occupied} = \text{Fraction occupied} \times \text{Total number}$$

$$\text{Number of rooms occupied today} = \frac{3}{4} \times 100 = 75$$

$$\text{Number of rooms occupied} = \frac{4}{5} \times 100 = 80$$

The difference in the number of rooms occupied is: $80 - 75 = 5$ rooms

P10. To answer this problem, first think about the number of teachers that work at the school. Will it be more or less than the number of teachers who work in a specific department such as English? More teachers work at the school, so the number you find to answer this question will be greater than 20.

40% of the teachers are English teachers. "Of" indicates multiplication, and words like "is" and "are" indicate equivalence. Translating the problem into a mathematical sentence gives $40\% \times t = 20$, where t represents the total number of teachers. Solving for t gives $t = \frac{20}{40\%} = \frac{20}{0.40} = 50$. Fifty teachers work at the school.

P11. The decrease is represented by the difference between the two amounts:

$$2 \text{ grams} - 0.45 \text{ grams} = 1.55 \text{ grams}.$$

Remember to line up the decimal point before subtracting.

$$
\begin{array}{r}
2.00 \\
-\ 0.45 \\
\hline
1.55
\end{array}
$$

P12. First, you need to find the number of male customers that were in the skate shop each week. You are given this amount in terms of fractions. To find the actual number of male customers, multiply the fraction of male customers by the number of customers in the store.

$$\text{Actual number of male customers} = \text{fraction of male customers} \times \text{total customers}$$

$$\text{Number of male customers two weeks ago} = \frac{2}{3} \times 60 = \frac{120}{3} = 40$$

$$\text{Number of male customers last week} = \frac{3}{6} \times 80 = \frac{1}{2} \times 80 = \frac{80}{2} = 40$$

The number of male customers was the same both weeks.

P13. To find total amount, first find the sum of the items she ordered from the menu and then add 20% of this sum to the total.

$$\$4.99 + \$12.50 + \$1.25 = \$18.74$$

$$\$18.74 \times 20\% = (0.20)(\$18.74) = \$3.748 \approx \$3.75$$

$$\text{Total} = \$18.74 + \$3.75 = \$22.49$$

P14. 82% of 145 is $0.82 \times 145 = 118.9$. Because you can't have 0.9 of a person, we must round up to say that 119 engineers reported that they were highly satisfied with their jobs.

P15. To find the percent increase, first compare the original and increased amounts. The original amount was 40 mg, and the increased amount is 45 mg, so the dosage of medication was increased by 5 mg ($45 - 40 = 5$). Note, however, that the question asks not by how much the dosage increased but by what percentage it increased.

$$\text{Percent increase} = \frac{\text{new amount} - \text{original amount}}{\text{original amount}} \times 100\%$$

$$= \frac{45 \text{ mg} - 40 \text{ mg}}{40 \text{ mg}} \times 100\% = \frac{5}{40} \times 100\% = 0.125 \times 100\% = 12.5\%$$

P16. Recall that the term rational simply means that the number can be expressed as a ratio or fraction. Notice that each of the numbers in the problem can be written as a decimal or integer:

$$17\% = 0.1717$$

$$\sqrt{25} = 5$$

$$\frac{64}{4} = 16$$

$$\frac{25}{50} = \frac{1}{2} = 0.5$$

So, the answer is $17\%, \frac{25}{50}, 0.55, 3, \sqrt{25}, \frac{64}{4}$.

P17. Converting all the numbers to integers and decimals makes it easier to compare the values:

$$27\% = 0.27$$

$$\sqrt{100} = 10$$

$$\frac{72}{9} = 8$$

$$\frac{1}{9} \approx 0.11$$

So, the answer is $\sqrt{100}, \frac{72}{9}, 4.5, 0.3, 27\%, \frac{1}{9}$.

> **Review Video: <u>Ordering Rational Numbers</u>**
> Visit mometrix.com/academy and enter code: 419578

P18. For each, convert improper fractions, adjust to a common denominator, perform the operations, and then simplify:

(a) Sometimes, you can skip converting the denominator and just distribute the multiplication.

$$\left(1\frac{11}{16}\right) \times 4 = \left(1 + \frac{11}{16}\right) \times 4$$

$$= 1 \times 4 + \frac{11}{16} \times 4$$

$$= 4 + \frac{11}{16} \times \frac{4}{1}$$

$$= 4 + \frac{44}{16} = 4 + \frac{11}{4} = 4 + 2\frac{3}{4} = 6\frac{3}{4}$$

(b)

$$\left(12\frac{1}{3}\right) \times 1.1 = \left(12 + \frac{1}{3}\right) \times \left(1 + \frac{1}{10}\right)$$

$$= \left(\frac{12}{1} \times \frac{3}{3} + \frac{1}{3}\right) \times \left(\frac{10}{10} + \frac{1}{10}\right)$$

$$= \left(\frac{36}{3} + \frac{1}{3}\right) \times \frac{11}{10}$$

$$= \frac{37}{3} \times \frac{11}{10}$$

$$= \frac{407}{30} = \frac{390}{30} + \frac{17}{30} = 13\frac{17}{30}$$

(c)

$$3.71 \times \left(6\frac{1}{5}\right) = \left(3 + \frac{71}{100}\right) \times \left(6 + \frac{1}{5}\right)$$

$$= \left(\frac{300}{100} + \frac{71}{100}\right) \times \left(\frac{6}{1} \times \frac{5}{5} + \frac{1}{5}\right)$$

$$= \frac{371}{100} \times \left(\frac{30}{5} + \frac{1}{5}\right)$$

$$= \frac{371}{100} \times \frac{31}{5}$$

$$= \frac{11501}{500} = \frac{11500}{500} + \frac{1}{500} = 23\frac{1}{500}$$

P19. Fortunately, some of the amounts are duplicated, so we do not need to convert every amount.

$$1\frac{3}{4} \times 3 = (1 \times 3) + \left(\frac{3}{4} \times 3\right)$$
$$= 3 + \frac{9}{4}$$
$$= 3 + 2\frac{1}{4}$$
$$= 5\frac{1}{4}$$

$$1\frac{1}{4} \times 3 = (1 \times 3) + \left(\frac{1}{4} \times 3\right)$$
$$= 3 + \frac{3}{4}$$
$$= 3\frac{3}{4}$$

$$\frac{3}{4} \times 3 = \frac{3}{4} \times 3$$
$$= \frac{9}{4}$$
$$= 2\frac{1}{4}$$

$$\frac{3}{8} \times 3 = \frac{3}{8} \times 3$$
$$= \frac{9}{8}$$
$$= 1\frac{1}{8}$$

$$1\frac{1}{2} \times 3 = 1 \times 3 + \frac{1}{2} \times 3$$
$$= 3 + \frac{3}{2}$$
$$= 3 + 1\frac{1}{2}$$
$$= 4\frac{1}{2}$$

$$2 \times 3 = 6$$

So, the result for the triple recipe is:

$5\frac{1}{4}$	cup	Flour	$4\frac{1}{2}$	Tbsp	Butter
$3\frac{3}{4}$	tsp	Baking powder	6	large	Eggs
$2\frac{1}{4}$	tsp	Salt	$2\frac{1}{4}$	tsp	Vanilla extract
$1\frac{1}{8}$	cup	Sugar	$1\frac{1}{8}$	cup	Sour cream

Proportions and Ratios

PROPORTIONS

A proportion is a relationship between two quantities that dictates how one changes when the other changes. A **direct proportion** describes a relationship in which a quantity increases by a set amount for every increase in the other quantity, or decreases by that same amount for every decrease in the other quantity. Example: Assuming a constant driving speed, the time required for a car trip increases as the distance of the trip increases. The distance to be traveled and the time required to travel are directly proportional.

Inverse proportion is a relationship in which an increase in one quantity is accompanied by a decrease in the other, or vice versa. Example: the time required for a car trip decreases as the speed increases and increases as the speed decreases, so the time required is inversely proportional to the speed of the car.

> **Review Video: Proportions**
> Visit mometrix.com/academy and enter code: 505355

RATIOS

A **ratio** is a comparison of two quantities in a particular order. Example: If there are 14 computers in a lab, and the class has 20 students, there is a student to computer ratio of 20 to 14, commonly written as 20: 14. Ratios are normally reduced to their smallest whole number representation, so 20: 14 would be reduced to 10: 7 by dividing both sides by 2.

> **Review Video: Ratios**
> Visit mometrix.com/academy and enter code: 996914

CONSTANT OF PROPORTIONALITY

When two quantities have a proportional relationship, there exists a **constant of proportionality** between the quantities; the product of this constant and one of the quantities is equal to the other quantity. For example, if one lemon costs $0.25, two lemons cost $0.50, and three lemons cost $0.75, there is a proportional relationship between the total cost of lemons and the number of lemons purchased. The constant of proportionality is the **unit price**, namely $0.25/lemon. Notice that the total price of lemons, t, can be found by multiplying the unit price of lemons, p, and the number of lemons, n: $t = pn$.

WORK/UNIT RATE

Unit rate expresses a quantity of one thing in terms of one unit of another. For example, if you travel 30 miles every two hours, a unit rate expresses this comparison in terms of one hour: in one hour you travel 15 miles, so your unit rate is 15 miles per hour. Other examples are how much one ounce of food costs (price per ounce) or figuring out how much one egg costs out of the dozen (price per 1 egg, instead of price per 12 eggs). The denominator of a unit rate is always 1. Unit rates are used to compare different situations to solve problems. For example, to make sure you get the best deal when deciding which kind of soda to buy, you can find the unit rate of each. If soda #1 costs $1.50 for a 1-liter bottle, and soda #2 costs $2.75 for a 2-liter bottle, it would be a better deal to buy soda #2, because its unit rate is only $1.375 per 1-liter, which is cheaper than soda #1. Unit rates can also help determine the length of time a given event will take. For example, if you can paint 2 rooms in 4.5 hours, you can determine how long it will take you to paint 5 rooms by solving for the unit rate per room and then multiplying that by 5.

SLOPE

On a graph with two points, (x_1, y_1) and (x_2, y_2), the **slope** is found with the formula $m = \frac{y_2 - y_1}{x_2 - x_1}$; where $x_1 \neq x_2$ and m stands for slope. If the value of the slope is **positive**, the line has an *upward direction* from left to right. If the value of the slope is **negative**, the line has a *downward direction* from left to right. Consider the following example:

A new book goes on sale in bookstores and online stores. In the first month, 5,000 copies of the book are sold. Over time, the book continues to grow in popularity. The data for the number of copies sold is in the table below.

# of Months on Sale	1	2	3	4	5
# of Copies Sold (In Thousands)	5	10	15	20	25

So, the number of copies that are sold and the time that the book is on sale is a proportional relationship. In this example, an equation can be used to show the data: $y = 5x$, where x is the number of months that the book is on sale. Also, y is the number of copies sold. So, the slope of the corresponding line is $\frac{\text{rise}}{\text{run}} = \frac{5}{1} = 5$.

FINDING AN UNKNOWN IN EQUIVALENT EXPRESSIONS

It is often necessary to apply information given about a rate or proportion to a new scenario. For example, if you know that Jedha can run a marathon (26.2 miles) in 3 hours, how long would it take her to run 10 miles at the same pace? Start by setting up equivalent expressions:

$$\frac{26.2 \text{ mi}}{3 \text{ hr}} = \frac{10 \text{ mi}}{x \text{ hr}}$$

Now, cross multiply and solve for x:

$$26.2x = 30$$
$$x = \frac{30}{26.2} = \frac{15}{13.1}$$
$$x \approx 1.15 \text{ hrs } or \text{ 1 hr 9 min}$$

So, at this pace, Jedha could run 10 miles in about 1.15 hours or about 1 hour and 9 minutes.

PRACTICE

P1. Solve the following for x.

(a) $\frac{45}{12} = \frac{15}{x}$

(b) $\frac{0.50}{2} = \frac{1.50}{x}$

(c) $\frac{40}{8} = \frac{x}{24}$

P2. At a school, for every 20 female students there are 15 male students. This same student ratio happens to exist at another school. If there are 100 female students at the second school, how many male students are there?

P3. In a hospital emergency room, there are 4 nurses for every 12 patients. What is the ratio of nurses to patients? If the nurse-to-patient ratio remains constant, how many nurses must be present to care for 24 patients?

P4. In a bank, the banker-to-customer ratio is $1:2$. If seven bankers are on duty, how many customers are currently in the bank?

P5. Janice made $40 during the first 5 hours she spent babysitting. She will continue to earn money at this rate until she finishes babysitting in 3 more hours. Find how much money Janice earns per hour and the total she earned babysitting.

P6. The McDonalds are taking a family road trip, driving 300 miles to their cabin. It took them 2 hours to drive the first 120 miles. They will drive at the same speed all the way to their cabin. Find the speed at which the McDonalds are driving and how much longer it will take them to get to their cabin.

P7. It takes Andy 10 minutes to read 6 pages of his book. He has already read 150 pages in his book that is 210 pages long. Find how long it takes Andy to read 1 page and also find how long it will take him to finish his book if he continues to read at the same speed.

PRACTICE SOLUTIONS

P1. Cross multiply, then solve for x:

(a)

$$45x = 12 \times 15$$
$$45x = 180$$
$$x = \frac{180}{45} = 4$$

(b)

$$0.5x = 1.5 \times 2$$
$$0.5x = 3$$
$$x = \frac{3}{0.5} = 6$$

(c)

$$8x = 40 \times 24$$
$$8x = 960$$
$$x = \frac{960}{8} = 120$$

P2. One way to find the number of male students is to set up and solve a proportion.

$$\frac{\text{number of female students}}{\text{number of male students}} = \frac{20}{15} = \frac{100}{\text{number of male students}}$$

Represent the unknown number of male students as the variable x: $\frac{20}{15} = \frac{100}{x}$

Cross multiply and then solve for x:

$$20x = 15 \times 100$$
$$x = \frac{1500}{20}$$
$$x = 75$$

P3. The ratio of nurses to patients can be written as 4 to 12, 4 : 12, or $\frac{4}{12}$. Because four and twelve have a common factor of four, the ratio should be reduced to 1 : 3, which means that there is one nurse present for every three patients. If this ratio remains constant, there must be eight nurses present to care for 24 patients.

P4. Use proportional reasoning or set up a proportion to solve. Because there are twice as many customers as bankers, there must be fourteen customers when seven bankers are on duty. Setting up and solving a proportion gives the same result:

$$\frac{\text{number of bankers}}{\text{number of customers}} = \frac{1}{2} = \frac{7}{\text{number of customers}}$$

Represent the unknown number of patients as the variable x: $\frac{1}{2} = \frac{7}{x}$.

To solve for x, cross multiply: $1 \times x = 7 \times 2$, so $x = 14$.

P5. Janice earns $8 per hour. This can be found by taking her initial amount earned, $40, and dividing it by the number of hours worked, 5. Since $\frac{40}{5} = 8$, Janice makes $8 in one hour. This can also be found by finding the unit rate, money earned per hour: $\frac{40}{5} = \frac{x}{1}$. Since cross multiplying yields $5x = 40$, and division by 5 shows that $x = 8$, Janice earns $8 per hour.

Janice will earn $64 babysitting in her 8 total hours (adding the first 5 hours to the remaining 3 gives the 8-hour total). Since Janice earns $8 per hour and she worked 8 hours, $\frac{\$8}{\text{hr}} \times 8 \text{ hrs} = \$64$.

This can also be found by setting up a proportion comparing money earned to babysitting hours. Since she earns $40 for 5 hours and since the rate is constant, she will earn a proportional amount in 8 hours: $\frac{40}{5} = \frac{x}{8}$. Cross multiplying will yield $5x = 320$, and division by 5 shows that $x = 64$.

P6. The McDonalds are driving 60 miles per hour. This can be found by setting up a proportion to find the unit rate, the number of miles they drive per one hour: $\frac{120}{2} = \frac{x}{1}$. Cross multiplying yields $2x = 120$ and division by 2 shows that $x = 60$.

Since the McDonalds will drive this same speed, it will take them another 3 hours to get to their cabin. This can be found by first finding how many miles the McDonalds have left to drive, which is $300 - 120 = 180$. The McDonalds are driving at 60 miles per hour, so a proportion can be set up to determine how many hours it will take them to drive 180 miles: $\frac{180}{x} = \frac{60}{1}$. Cross multiplying yields $60x = 180$, and division by 60 shows that $x = 3$. This can also be found by using the formula $D = r \times t$ (or distance = rate × time), where $180 = 60 \times t$, and division by 60 shows that $t = 3$.

P7. It takes Andy 10 minutes to read 6 pages, $\frac{10}{6} = 1\frac{2}{3}$ minutes, which is 1 minute and 40 seconds.

Next, determine how many pages Andy has left to read, $210 - 150 = 60$. Since it is now known that it takes him $1\frac{2}{3}$ minutes to read each page, that rate must be multiplied by however many pages he has left to read (60) to find the time he'll need: $60 \times 1\frac{2}{3} = 100$, so it will take him 100 minutes, or 1 hour and 40 minutes, to read the rest of his book.

Expressions

TERMS AND COEFFICIENTS

Mathematical expressions consist of a combination of one or more values arranged in terms that are added together. As such, an expression could be just a single number, including zero. A **variable term** is the product of a real number, also called a **coefficient**, and one or more variables, each of which may be raised to an exponent. Expressions may also include numbers without a variable, called **constants** or **constant terms**. The expression $6s^2$, for example, is a single term where the coefficient is the real number 6 and the variable term is s^2. Note that if a term is written as simply a variable to some exponent, like t^2, then the coefficient is 1, because $t^2 = 1t^2$.

LINEAR EXPRESSIONS

A **single variable linear expression** is the sum of a single variable term, where the variable has no exponent, and a constant, which may be zero. For instance, the expression $2w + 7$ has $2w$ as the variable term and 7 as the constant term. It is important to realize that terms are separated by addition or subtraction. Since an expression is a sum of terms, expressions such as $5x - 3$ can be written as $5x + (-3)$ to emphasize that the constant term is negative. A real-world example of a single variable linear expression is the perimeter of a square, four times the side length, often expressed: $4s$.

In general, a **linear expression** is the sum of any number of variable terms so long as none of the variables have an exponent. For example, $3m + 8n - \frac{1}{4}p + 5.5q - 1$ is a linear expression, but $3y^3$ is not. In the same way, the expression for the perimeter of a general triangle, the sum of the side lengths $(a + b + c)$ is considered to be linear, but the expression for the area of a square, the side length squared (s^2) is not.

M�⊘metrix

Equations

LINEAR EQUATIONS

Equations that can be written as $ax + b = 0$, where $a \neq 0$, are referred to as **one variable linear equations**. A solution to such an equation is called a **root**. In the case where we have the equation $5x + 10 = 0$, if we solve for x we get a solution of $x = -2$. In other words, the root of the equation is -2. This is found by first subtracting 10 from both sides, which gives $5x = -10$. Next, simply divide both sides by the coefficient of the variable, in this case 5, to get $x = -2$. This can be checked by plugging -2 back into the original equation $(5)(-2) + 10 = -10 + 10 = 0$.

The **solution set** is the set of all solutions of an equation. In our example, the solution set would simply be -2. If there were more solutions (there usually are in multivariable equations) then they would also be included in the solution set. When an equation has no true solutions, it is referred to as an **empty set**. Equations with identical solution sets are **equivalent equations**. An **identity** is a term whose value or determinant is equal to 1.

Linear equations can be written many ways. Below is a list of some forms linear equations can take:

- **Standard Form**: $Ax + By = C$; the slope is $\frac{-A}{B}$ and the y-intercept is $\frac{C}{B}$
- **Slope Intercept Form**: $y = mx + b$, where m is the slope and b is the y-intercept
- **Point-Slope Form**: $y - y_1 = m(x - x_1)$, where m is the slope and (x_1, y_1) is a point on the line
- **Two-Point Form**: $\frac{y - y_1}{x - x_1} = \frac{y_2 - y_1}{x_2 - x_1}$, where (x_1, y_1) and (x_2, y_2) are two points on the given line
- **Intercept Form**: $\frac{x}{x_1} + \frac{y}{y_1} = 1$, where $(x_1, 0)$ is the point at which a line intersects the x-axis, and $(0, y_1)$ is the point at which the same line intersects the y-axis

> **Review Video: <u>Slope-Intercept and Point-Slope Forms</u>**
> Visit mometrix.com/academy and enter code: 113216

SOLVING ONE-VARIABLE LINEAR EQUATIONS

Multiply all terms by the lowest common denominator to eliminate any fractions. Look for addition or subtraction to undo so you can isolate the variable on one side of the equal sign. Divide both sides by the coefficient of the variable. When you have a value for the variable, substitute this value into the original equation to make sure you have a true equation. Consider the following example:

Kim's savings are represented by the table below. Represent her savings, using an equation.

X (Months)	Y (Total Savings)
2	$1,300
5	$2,050
9	$3,050
11	$3,550
16	$4,800

The table shows a function with a constant rate of change, or slope, of 250. Given the points on the table, the slopes can be calculated as $\frac{(2,050 - 1300)}{(5 - 2)}$, $\frac{(3,050 - 2,050)}{(9 - 5)}$, $\frac{(3,550 - 3,050)}{(11 - 9)}$, and $\frac{(4,800 - 3,550)}{(16 - 11)}$, each of

189

which equals 250. Thus, the table shows a constant rate of change, indicating a linear function. The slope-intercept form of a linear equation is written as $y = mx + b$, where m represents the slope and b represents the y-intercept. Substituting the slope into this form gives $y = 250x + b$. Substituting corresponding x- and y-values from any point into this equation will give the y-intercept, or b. Using the point, $(2, 1,300)$, gives $1,300 = 250(2) + b$, which simplifies as $b = 800$. Thus, her savings may be represented by the equation, $y = 250x + 800$.

RULES FOR MANIPULATING EQUATIONS
LIKE TERMS

Like terms are terms in an equation that have the same variable, regardless of whether or not they also have the same coefficient. This includes terms that *lack* a variable; all constants (i.e., numbers without variables) are considered like terms. If the equation involves terms with a variable raised to different powers, the like terms are those that have the variable raised to the same power.

For example, consider the equation $x^2 + 3x + 2 = 2x^2 + x - 7 + 2x$. In this equation, 2 and –7 are like terms; they are both constants. $3x$, x, and $2x$ are like terms, they all include the variable x raised to the first power. x^2 and $2x^2$ are like terms, they both include the variable x, raised to the second power. $2x$ and $2x^2$ are not like terms; although they both involve the variable x, the variable is not raised to the same power in both terms. The fact that they have the same coefficient, 2, is not relevant.

> **Review Video: Rules for Manipulating Equations**
> Visit mometrix.com/academy and enter code: 838871

CARRYING OUT THE SAME OPERATION ON BOTH SIDES OF AN EQUATION

When solving an equation, the general procedure is to carry out a series of operations on both sides of an equation, choosing operations that will tend to simplify the equation when doing so. The reason why the same operation must be carried out on both sides of the equation is because that leaves the meaning of the equation unchanged, and yields a result that is equivalent to the original equation. This would not be the case if we carried out an operation on one side of an equation and not the other. Consider what an equation means: it is a statement that two values or expressions are equal. If we carry out the same operation on both sides of the equation—add 3 to both sides, for example—then the two sides of the equation are changed in the same way, and so remain equal. If we do that to only one side of the equation—add 3 to one side but not the other—then that wouldn't be true; if we change one side of the equation but not the other then the two sides are no longer equal.

ADVANTAGE OF COMBINING LIKE TERMS

Combining like terms refers to adding or subtracting like terms—terms with the same variable—and therefore reducing sets of like terms to a single term. The main advantage of doing this is that it simplifies the equation. Often, combining like terms can be done as the first step in solving an equation, though it can also be done later, such as after distributing terms in a product.

For example, consider the equation $2(x + 3) + 3(2 + x + 3) = -4$. The 2 and the 3 in the second set of parentheses are like terms, and we can combine them, yielding $2(x + 3) + 3(x + 5) = -4$. Now we can carry out the multiplications implied by the parentheses, distributing the outer 2 and 3 accordingly: $2x + 6 + 3x + 15 = -4$. The $2x$ and the $3x$ are like terms, and we can add them together: $5x + 6 + 15 = -4$. Now, the constants 6, 15, and –4 are also like terms, and we can combine them as well: subtracting 6 and 15 from both sides of the equation, we get $5x = -4 - 6 - 15$, or $5x = -25$, which simplifies further to $x = -5$.

CANCELING TERMS ON OPPOSITE SIDES OF AN EQUATION

Two terms on opposite sides of an equation can be canceled if and only if they *exactly* match each other. They must have the same variable raised to the same power and the same coefficient. For example, in the equation $3x + 2x^2 + 6 = 2x^2 - 6$, $2x^2$ appears on both sides of the equation and can be canceled, leaving $3x + 6 = -6$. The 6 on each side of the equation *cannot* be canceled, because it is added on one side of the equation and subtracted on the other. While they cannot be canceled, however, the 6 and –6 are like terms and can be combined, yielding $3x = -12$, which simplifies further to $x = -4$.

It's also important to note that the terms to be canceled must be independent terms and cannot be part of a larger term. For example, consider the equation $2(x + 6) = 3(x + 4) + 1$. We cannot cancel the x's, because even though they match each other they are part of the larger terms $2(x + 6)$ and $3(x + 4)$. We must first distribute the 2 and 3, yielding $2x + 12 = 3x + 12 + 1$. Now we see that the terms with the x's do not match, but the 12s do, and can be canceled, leaving $2x = 3x + 1$, which simplifies to $x = -1$.

PROCESS FOR MANIPULATING EQUATIONS

ISOLATING VARIABLES

To **isolate a variable** means to manipulate the equation so that the variable appears by itself on one side of the equation, and does not appear at all on the other side. Generally, an equation or inequality is considered to be solved once the variable is isolated and the other side of the equation or inequality is simplified as much as possible. In the case of a two-variable equation or inequality, only one variable needs to be isolated; it will not usually be possible to simultaneously isolate both variables.

For a linear equation—an equation in which the variable only appears raised to the first power—isolating a variable can be done by first moving all the terms with the variable to one side of the equation and all other terms to the other side. (*Moving* a term really means adding the inverse of the term to both sides; when a term is *moved* to the other side of the equation its sign is flipped.) Then combine like terms on each side. Finally, divide both sides by the coefficient of the variable, if applicable. The steps need not necessarily be done in this order, but this order will always work.

EQUATIONS WITH MORE THAN ONE SOLUTION

Some types of non-linear equations, such as equations involving squares of variables, may have more than one solution. For example, the equation $x^2 = 4$ has two solutions: 2 and –2. Equations with absolute values can also have multiple solutions: $|x| = 1$ has the solutions $x = 1$ and $x = -1$.

It is also possible for a linear equation to have more than one solution, but only if the equation is true regardless of the value of the variable. In this case, the equation is considered to have infinitely many solutions, because any possible value of the variable is a solution. We know a linear equation has infinitely many solutions if when we combine like terms the variables cancel, leaving a true statement. For example, consider the equation $2(3x + 5) = x + 5(x + 2)$. Distributing, we get $6x + 10 = x + 5x + 10$; combining like terms gives $6x + 10 = 6x + 10$, and the $6x$-terms cancel to leave $10 = 10$. This is clearly true, so the original equation is true for any value of x. We could also have canceled the 10s leaving $0 = 0$, but again this is clearly true—in general if both sides of the equation match exactly, it has infinitely many solutions.

EQUATIONS WITH NO SOLUTION

Some types of non-linear equations, such as equations involving squares of variables, may have no solution. For example, the equation $x^2 = -2$ has no solutions in the real numbers, because the square of any real number must be positive. Similarly, $|x| = -1$ has no solution, because the absolute value of a number is always positive.

It is also possible for an equation to have no solution even if does not involve any powers greater than one, absolute values, or other special functions. For example, the equation $2(x + 3) + x = 3x$ has no solution. We can see that if we try to solve it: first we distribute, leaving $2x + 6 + x = 3x$. But now if we try to combine all the terms with the variable, we find that they cancel: we have $3x$ on the left and $3x$ on the right, canceling to leave us with $6 = 0$. This is clearly false. In general, whenever the variable terms in an equation cancel leaving different constants on both sides, it means that the equation has no solution. (If we are left with the *same* constant on both sides, the equation has infinitely many solutions instead.)

FEATURES OF EQUATIONS THAT REQUIRE SPECIAL TREATMENT

LINEAR EQUATIONS

A linear equation is an equation in which variables only appear by themselves: not multiplied together, not with exponents other than one, and not inside absolute value signs or any other functions. For example, the equation $x + 1 - 3x = 5 - x$ is a linear equation; while x appears multiple times, it never appears with an exponent other than one, or inside any function. The two-variable equation $2x - 3y = 5 + 2x$ is also a linear equation. In contrast, the equation $x^2 - 5 = 3x$ is *not* a linear equation, because it involves the term x^2. $\sqrt{x} = 5$ is not a linear equation, because it involves a square root. $(x - 1)^2 = 4$ is not a linear equation because even though there's no exponent on the x directly, it appears as part of an expression that is squared. The two-variable equation $x + xy - y = 5$ is not a linear equation because it includes the term xy, where two variables are multiplied together.

Linear equations can always be solved (or shown to have no solution) by combining like terms and performing simple operations on both sides of the equation. Some non-linear equations can be solved by similar methods, but others may require more advanced methods of solution, if they can be solved analytically at all.

SOLVING EQUATIONS INVOLVING ROOTS

In an equation involving roots, the first step is to isolate the term with the root, if possible, and then raise both sides of the equation to the appropriate power to eliminate it. Consider an example equation, $2\sqrt{x + 1} - 1 = 3$. In this case, begin by adding 1 to both sides, yielding $2\sqrt{x + 1} = 4$, and then dividing both sides by 2, yielding $\sqrt{x + 1} = 2$. Now square both sides, yielding $x + 1 = 4$. Finally, subtracting 1 from both sides yields $x = 3$.

Squaring both sides of an equation may, however, yield a spurious solution—a solution to the squared equation that is *not* a solution of the original equation. It's therefore necessary to plug the solution back into the original equation to make sure it works. In this case, it does: $2\sqrt{3 + 1} - 1 = 2\sqrt{4} - 1 = 2(2) - 1 = 4 - 1 = 3$.

The same procedure applies for other roots as well. For example, given the equation $3 + \sqrt[3]{2x} = 5$, we can first subtract 3 from both sides, yielding $\sqrt[3]{2x} = 2$ and isolating the root. Raising both sides to the third power yields $2x = 2^3$; i.e., $2x = 8$. We can now divide both sides by 2 to get $x = 4$.

> **Review Video: Solving Equations Involving Roots**
> Visit mometrix.com/academy and enter code: 297670

SOLVING EQUATIONS WITH EXPONENTS

To solve an equation involving an exponent, the first step is to isolate the variable with the exponent. We can then take the appropriate root of both sides to eliminate the exponent. For instance, for the equation $2x^3 + 17 = 5x^3 - 7$, we can subtract $5x^3$ from both sides to get $-3x^3 + 17 = -7$, and then subtract 17 from both sides to get $-3x^3 = -24$. Finally, we can divide both sides by –3 to get $x^3 = 8$. Finally, we can take the cube root of both sides to get $x = \sqrt[3]{8} = 2$.

One important but often overlooked point is that equations with an exponent greater than 1 may have more than one answer. The solution to $x^2 = 9$ isn't simply $x = 3$; it's $x = \pm 3$ (that is, $x = 3$ or $x = -3$). For a slightly more complicated example, consider the equation $(x - 1)^2 - 1 = 3$. Adding 1 to both sides yields $(x - 1)^2 = 4$; taking the square root of both sides yields $x - 1 = 2$. We can then add 1 to both sides to get $x = 3$. However, there's a second solution. We also have the possibility that $x - 1 = -2$, in which case $x = -1$. Both $x = 3$ and $x = -1$ are valid solutions, as can be verified by substituting them both into the original equation.

> **Review Video: Solving Equations with Exponents**
> Visit mometrix.com/academy and enter code: 514557

SOLVING EQUATIONS WITH ABSOLUTE VALUES

When solving an equation with an absolute value, the first step is to isolate the absolute value term. We then consider two possibilities: when the expression inside the absolute value is positive or when it is negative. In the former case, the expression in the absolute value equals the expression on the other side of the equation; in the latter, it equals the additive inverse of that expression—the expression times negative one. We consider each case separately and finally check for spurious solutions.

For instance, consider solving $|2x - 1| + x = 5$ for x. We can first isolate the absolute value by moving the x to the other side: $|2x - 1| = -x + 5$. Now, we have two possibilities. First, that $2x - 1$ is positive, and hence $2x - 1 = -x + 5$. Rearranging and combining like terms yields $3x = 6$, and hence $x = 2$. The other possibility is that $2x - 1$ is negative, and hence $2x - 1 = -(-x + 5) = x - 5$. In this case, rearranging and combining like terms yields $x = -4$. Substituting $x = 2$ and $x = -4$ back into the original equation, we see that they are both valid solutions.

Note that the absolute value of a sum or difference applies to the sum or difference as a whole, not to the individual terms; in general, $|2x - 1|$ is not equal to $|2x + 1|$ or to $|2x| - 1$.

> **Review Video: Solving Absolute Value Inequalities**
> Visit mometrix.com/academy and enter code: 997008

SPURIOUS SOLUTIONS

A **spurious solution** may arise when we square both sides of an equation as a step in solving it or under certain other operations on the equation. It is a solution to the squared or otherwise modified equation that is *not* a solution of the original equation. To identify a spurious solution, it's useful when you solve an equation involving roots or absolute values to plug the solution back into the original equation to make sure it's valid.

CHOOSING WHICH VARIABLE TO ISOLATE IN TWO-VARIABLE EQUATIONS

Similar to methods for a one-variable equation, solving a two-variable equation involves isolating a variable: manipulating the equation so that a variable appears by itself on one side of the equation, and not at all on the other side. However, in a two-variable equation, you will usually only be able to isolate one of the variables; the other variable may appear on the other side along with constant terms, or with exponents or other functions.

Often one variable will be much more easily isolated than the other, and therefore that's the variable you should choose. If one variable appears with various exponents, and the other is only raised to the first power, the latter variable is the one to isolate: given the equation $a^2 + 2b = a^3 + b + 3$, the b only appears to the first power, whereas a appears squared and cubed, so b is the variable that can be solved for: combining like terms and isolating the b on the left side of the equation, we get $b = a^3 - a^2 + 3$. If both variables are equally easy to isolate, then it's best to isolate the independent variable, if one is defined; if the two variables are x and y, the convention is that y is the independent variable.

PRACTICE

P1. Seeing the equation $2x + 4 = 4x + 7$, a student divides the first terms on each side by 2, yielding $x + 4 = 2x + 7$, and then combines like terms to get $x = -3$. However, this is incorrect, as can be seen by substituting –3 into the original equation. Explain what is wrong with the student's reasoning.

P2. Describe the steps necessary to solve the equation $2x + 1 - x = 4 + 3x + 7$.

P3. Describe the steps necessary to solve the equation $2(x + 5) = 7(4 - x)$.

P4. Find all real solutions to the equation $1 - \sqrt{x} = 2$.

P5. Find all real solutions to the equation $|x + 1| = 2x + 5$.

P6. Solve for x: $-x + 2\sqrt{x + 5} + 1 = 3$.

P7. Ray earns \$10 an hour at his job. Write an equation for his earnings as a function of time spent working. Determine how long Ray has to work in order to earn \$360.

P8. Simplify the following: $3x + 2 + 2y = 5y - 7 + |2x - 1|$

PRACTICE SOLUTIONS

P1. As stated, it's easy to verify that the student's solution is incorrect: $2(-3) + 4 = -2$ and $4(-3) + 7 = -5$; clearly $-2 \neq -5$. The mistake was in the first step, which illustrates a common type of error in solving equations. The student tried to simplify the two variable terms by dividing them by 2. However, it's not valid to multiply or divide only one term on each side of an equation by a number; when multiplying or dividing, the operation must be applied to *every* term in the equation. So, dividing by 2 would yield not $x + 4 = 2x + 7$, but $x + 2 = 2x + \frac{7}{2}$. While this is now valid, that fraction is inconvenient to work with, so this may not be the best first step in solving the equation. Rather, it may have been better to first combine like terms. Subtracting $4x$ from both sides yields $-2x + 4 = 7$; subtracting 4 from both sides yields $-2x = 3$; *now* we can divide both sides by -2 to get $x = -\frac{3}{2}$.

P2. Our ultimate goal is to isolate the variable, x. To that end we first move all the terms containing x to the left side of the equation, and all the constant terms to the right side. Note that when we move a term to the other side of the equation its sign changes. We are therefore now left with $2x - x - 3x = 4 + 7 - 1$.

Next, we combine the like terms on each side of the equation, adding and subtracting the terms as appropriate. This leaves us with $-2x = 10$.

At this point, we're almost done; all that remains is to divide both sides by -2 to leave the x by itself. We now have our solution, $x = -5$. We can verify that this is a correct solution by substituting it back into the original equation.

P3. Generally, in equations that have a sum or difference of terms multiplied by another value or expression, the first step is to multiply those terms, distributing as necessary: $2(x + 5) = 2(x) + 2(5) = 2x + 10$, and $7(4 - x) = 7(4) - 7(x) = 28 - 7x$. So, the equation becomes $2x + 10 = 28 - 7x$. We can now add $7x$ to both sides to eliminate the variable from the right-hand side: $9x + 10 = 28$. Similarly, we can subtract 10 from both sides to move all the constants to the right: $9x = 18$. Finally, we can divide both sides by 9, yielding the final answer, $x = 2$.

P4. It's not hard to isolate the root: subtract one from both sides, yielding $-\sqrt{x} = 1$. Finally, multiply both sides by -1, yielding $\sqrt{x} = -1$. Squaring both sides of the equation yields $x = 1$. However, if we plug this back into the original equation, we get $1 - \sqrt{1} = 2$, which is false. Therefore $x = 1$ is a spurious solution, and the equation has no real solutions.

P5. This equation has two possibilities: $x + 1 = 2x + 5$, which simplifies to $x = -4$; or $x + 1 = -(2x + 5) = -2x - 5$, which simplifies to $x = -2$. However, if we try substituting both values back into the original equation, we see that only $x = -2$ yields a true statement. $x = -4$ is a spurious solution; $x = -2$ is the only valid solution to the equation.

P6. Start by isolating the term with the root. We can do that by moving the $-x$ and the 1 to the other side, yielding $2\sqrt{x + 5} = 3 + x - 1$, or $2\sqrt{x + 5} = x + 2$. Dividing both sides of the equation by 2 would give us a fractional term that could be messy to deal with, so we won't do that for now. Instead, we square both sides of the equation; note that on the left-hand side the 2 is outside the square root sign, so we have to square it. As a result, we get $4(x + 5) = (x + 2)^2$. Expanding both sides gives us $4x + 20 = x^2 + 4x + 4$. In this case, we see that we have $4x$ on both sides, so we can cancel the $4x$ (which is what allows us to solve this equation despite the different powers of x). We now have $20 = x^2 + 4$, or $x^2 = 16$. Since the variable is raised to an even power, we need to take the positive and negative roots, so $x = \pm 4$: that is, $x = 4$ or $x = -4$. Substituting both values into the original equation, we see that $x = 4$ satisfies the equation but $x = -4$ does not; hence $x = -4$ is a spurious solution, and the only solution to the equation is $x = 4$.

P7. The number of dollars that Ray earns is dependent on the number of hours he works, so earnings will be represented by the dependent variable y and hours worked will be represented by the independent variable x. He earns 10 dollars per hour worked, so his earnings can be calculated as $y = 10x$. To calculate the number of hours Ray must work in order to earn \$360, plug in 360 for y and solve for x:

$$360 = 10x$$
$$x = \frac{360}{10} = 36$$

P8. To simplify this equation, we must isolate one of its variables on one side of the equation. In this case, the x appears under an absolute value sign, which makes it difficult to isolate. The y, on the other hand, only appears without an exponent—the equation is linear in y. We will therefore choose to isolate the y. The first step, then, is to move all the terms with y to the left side of the equation, which we can do by subtracting $5y$ from both sides:

$$3x + 2 - 3y = -7 + |2x - 1|$$

We can then move all the terms that do *not* include y to the right side of the equation, by subtracting $3x$ and 2 from both sides of the equation:

$$-3y = -3x - 9 + |2x - 1|$$

Finally, we can isolate the y by dividing both sides by –3.

$$y = x + 3 - \frac{1}{3}|2x - 1|$$

This is as far as we can simplify the equation; we cannot combine the terms inside and outside the absolute value sign. We can therefore consider the equation to be solved.

Inequalities

WORKING WITH INEQUALITIES

Commonly in algebra and other upper-level fields of math you find yourself working with mathematical expressions that do not equal each other. The statement comparing such expressions with symbols such as $<$ (less than) or $>$ (greater than) is called an *inequality*. An example of an inequality is $7x > 5$. To solve for x, simply divide both sides by 7 and the solution is shown to be $x > \frac{5}{7}$. Graphs of the solution set of inequalities are represented on a number line. Open circles are used to show that an expression approaches a number but is never quite equal to that number.

> **Review Video: Inequalities**
> Visit mometrix.com/academy and enter code: 347842

Conditional inequalities are those with certain values for the variable that will make the condition true and other values for the variable where the condition will be false. **Absolute inequalities** can have any real number as the value for the variable to make the condition true, while there is no real number value for the variable that will make the condition false. Solving inequalities is done by following the same rules for solving equations with the exception that when multiplying or dividing by a negative number the direction of the inequality sign must be flipped or reversed. **Double inequalities** are situations where two inequality statements apply to the same variable expression. Example: $-c < ax + b < c$.

DETERMINING SOLUTIONS TO INEQUALITIES

To determine whether a coordinate is a solution of an inequality, you can substitute the values of the coordinate into the inequality, simplify, and check whether the resulting statement holds true. For instance, to determine whether $(-2,4)$ is a solution of the inequality $y \geq -2x + 3$, substitute the values into the inequality, $4 \geq -2(-2) + 3$. Simplify the right side of the inequality and the result is $4 \geq 7$, which is a false statement. Therefore, the coordinate is not a solution of the inequality. You can also use this method to determine which part of the graph of an inequality is shaded. The graph of $y \geq -2x + 3$ includes the solid line $y = -2x + 3$ and, since it excludes the point $(-2,4)$ to the left of the line, it is shaded to the right of the line.

FLIPPING INEQUALITY SIGNS

When given an inequality, we can always turn the entire inequality around, swapping the two sides of the inequality and changing the inequality sign. For instance, $x + 2 > 2x - 3$ is equivalent to $2x - 3 < x + 2$. Aside from that, normally the inequality does not change if we carry out the same operation on both sides of the inequality. There is, however, one principal exception: if we *multiply* or *divide* both sides of the inequality by a *negative number*, the inequality is flipped. For example, if we take the inequality $-2x < 6$ and divide both sides by –2, the inequality flips and we are left with $x > -3$. This *only* applies to multiplication and division, and only with negative numbers. Multiplying or dividing both sides by a positive number, or adding or subtracting any number regardless of sign, does not flip the inequality.

COMPOUND INEQUALITIES

A **compound inequality** is an equality that consists of two inequalities combined with *and* or *or*. The two components of a proper compound inequality must be of opposite type: that is, one must be greater than (or greater than or equal to), the other less than (or less than or equal to). For instance, "$x + 1 < 2$ or $x + 1 > 3$" is a compound inequality, as is "$2x \geq 4$ and $2x \leq 6$." An *and* inequality can be written more compactly by having one inequality on each side of the common part: "$2x \geq 1$ and $2x \leq 6$," can also be written as $1 \leq 2x \leq 6$.

In order for the compound inequality to be meaningful, the two parts of an *and* inequality must overlap; otherwise, no numbers satisfy the inequality. On the other hand, if the two parts of an *or* inequality overlap, then *all* numbers satisfy the inequality and as such the inequality is usually not meaningful.

Solving a compound inequality requires solving each part separately. For example, given the compound inequality "$x + 1 < 2$ or $x + 1 > 3$," the first inequality, $x + 1 < 2$, reduces to $x < 1$, and the second part, $x + 1 > 3$, reduces to $x > 2$, so the whole compound inequality can be written as "$x < 1$ or $x > 2$." Similarly, $1 \leq 2x \leq 6$ can be solved by dividing each term by 2, yielding $\frac{1}{2} \leq x \leq 3$.

SOLVING INEQUALITIES INVOLVING ABSOLUTE VALUES

To solve an inequality involving an absolute value, first isolate the term with the absolute value. Then proceed to treat the two cases separately as with an absolute value equation, but flipping the inequality in the case where the expression in the absolute value is negative (since that essentially involves multiplying both sides by –1.) The two cases are then combined into a compound inequality; if the absolute value is on the greater side of the inequality, then it is an *or* compound inequality, if on the lesser side, then it's an *and*.

Consider the inequality $2 + |x - 1| \geq 3$. We can isolate the absolute value term by subtracting 2 from both sides: $|x - 1| \geq 1$. Now, we're left with the two cases $x - 1 \geq 1$ or $x - 1 \leq -1$: note that in the latter, negative case, the inequality is flipped. $x - 1 \geq 1$ reduces to $x \geq 2$, and $x - 1 \leq -1$ reduces to $x \leq 0$. Since in the inequality $|x - 1| \geq 1$ the absolute value is on the greater side, the two cases combine into an *or* compound inequality, so the final, solved inequality is "$x \leq 0$ or $x \geq 2$."

> **Review Video: Solving Absolute Value Inequalities**
> Visit mometrix.com/academy and enter code: 997008

SOLVING INEQUALITIES INVOLVING SQUARE ROOTS

Solving an inequality with a square root involves two parts. First, we solve the inequality as if it were an equation, isolating the square root and then squaring both sides of the equation. Second, we restrict the solution to the set of values of x for which the value inside the square root sign is non-negative.

For example, in the inequality, $\sqrt{x - 2} + 1 < 5$, we can isolate the square root by subtracting 1 from both sides, yielding $\sqrt{x - 2} < 4$. Squaring both sides of the inequality yields $x - 2 < 16$, so $x < 18$. Since we can't take the square root of a negative number, we also require the part inside the square root to be non-negative. In this case, that means $x - 2 \geq 0$. Adding 2 to both sides of the inequality yields $x \geq 2$. Our final answer is a compound inequality combining the two simple inequalities: $x \geq 2$ and $x < 18$, or $2 \leq x < 18$.

Note that we only get a compound inequality if the two simple inequalities are in opposite directions; otherwise, we take the one that is more restrictive.

The same technique can be used for other even roots, such as fourth roots. It is *not*, however, used for cube roots or other odd roots—negative numbers *do* have cube roots, so the condition that the quantity inside the root sign cannot be negative does not apply.

> **Review Video: Solving Inequalities Involving Square Roots**
> Visit mometrix.com/academy and enter code: 800288

SPECIAL CIRCUMSTANCES

Sometimes an inequality involving an absolute value or an even exponent is true for all values of x, and we don't need to do any further work to solve it. This is true if the inequality, once the absolute value or exponent term is isolated, says that term is greater than a negative number (or greater than or equal to zero). Since an absolute value or a number raised to an even exponent is *always* non-negative, this inequality is always true.

GRAPHICAL SOLUTIONS TO EQUATIONS AND INEQUALITIES

When equations are shown graphically, they are usually shown on a **Cartesian coordinate plane**. The Cartesian coordinate plane consists of two number lines placed perpendicular to each other and intersecting at the zero point, also known as the origin. The horizontal number line is known as the x-axis, with positive values to the right of the origin, and negative values to the left of the origin. The vertical number line is known as the y-axis, with positive values above the origin, and negative values below the origin. Any point on the plane can be identified by an ordered pair in the form (x, y), called coordinates. The x-value of the coordinate is called the abscissa, and the y-value of the coordinate is called the ordinate. The two number lines divide the plane into **four quadrants**: I, II, III, and IV.

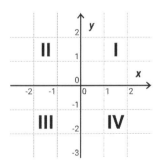

Note that in quadrant I $x > 0$ and $y > 0$, in quadrant II $x < 0$ and $y > 0$, in quadrant III $x < 0$ and $y < 0$, and in quadrant IV $x > 0$ and $y < 0$.

Recall that if the value of the slope of a line is positive, the line slopes upward from left to right. If the value of the slope is negative, the line slopes downward from left to right. If the y-coordinates are the same for two points on a line, the slope is 0 and the line is a **horizontal line**. If the x-coordinates are the same for two points on a line, there is no slope and the line is a **vertical line**. Two or more lines that have equivalent slopes are **parallel lines**. **Perpendicular lines** have slopes that are negative reciprocals of each other, such as $\frac{a}{b}$ and $\frac{-b}{a}$.

GRAPHING SIMPLE INEQUALITIES

To graph a simple inequality, we first mark on the number line the value that signifies the end point of the inequality. If the inequality is strict (involves a less than or greater than), we use a hollow circle; if it is not strict (less than or equal to or greater than or equal to), we use a solid circle. We then fill in the part of the number line that satisfies the inequality: to the left of the marked point for less than (or less than or equal to), to the right for greater than (or greater than or equal to).

For example, we would graph the inequality $x < 5$ by putting a hollow circle at 5 and filling in the part of the line to the left:

GRAPHING COMPOUND INEQUALITIES

To graph a compound inequality, we fill in both parts of the inequality for an *or* inequality, or the overlap between them for an *and* inequality. More specifically, we start by plotting the endpoints of each inequality on the number line. For an *or* inequality, we then fill in the appropriate side of the line for each inequality. Typically, the two component inequalities do not overlap, which means the shaded part is *outside* the two points. For an *and* inequality, we instead fill in the part of the line that meets both inequalities.

For the inequality "$x \leq -3$ or $x > 4$," we first put a solid circle at –3 and a hollow circle at 4. We then fill the parts of the line *outside* these circles:

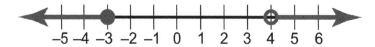

GRAPHING INEQUALITIES INCLUDING ABSOLUTE VALUES

An inequality with an absolute value can be converted to a compound inequality. To graph the inequality, first convert it to a compound inequality, and then graph that normally. If the absolute value is on the greater side of the inequality, we end up with an *or* inequality; we plot the endpoints of the inequality on the number line and fill in the part of the line *outside* those points. If the absolute value is on the smaller side of the inequality, we end up with an *and* inequality; we plot the endpoints of the inequality on the number line and fill in the part of the line *between* those points.

For example, the inequality $|x + 1| \geq 4$ can be rewritten as $x \geq 3$ or $x \leq -5$. We place solid circles at the points 3 and –5 and fill in the part of the line *outside* them:

GRAPHING EQUATIONS IN TWO VARIABLES

One way of graphing an equation in two variables is to plot enough points to get an idea for its shape and then draw the appropriate curve through those points. A point can be plotted by substituting in a value for one variable and solving for the other. If the equation is linear, we only need two points and can then draw a straight line between them.

For example, consider the equation $y = 2x - 1$. This is a linear equation—both variables only appear raised to the first power—so we only need two points. When $x = 0, y = 2(0) - 1 = -1$.

When $x = 2$, $y = 2(2) - 1 = 3$. We can therefore choose the points $(0, -1)$ and $(2, 3)$, and draw a line between them:

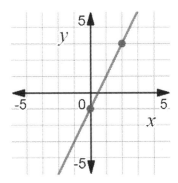

GRAPHING INEQUALITIES IN TWO VARIABLES

To graph an inequality in two variables, we first graph the border of the inequality. This means graphing the equation that we get if we replace the inequality sign with an equals sign. If the inequality is strict ($>$ or $<$), we graph the border with a dashed or dotted line; if it is not strict ($\geq$ or $\leq$), we use a solid line. We can then test any point not on the border to see if it satisfies the inequality. If it does, we shade in that side of the border; if not, we shade in the other side. As an example, consider $y > 2x + 2$. To graph this inequality, we first graph the border, $y = 2x + 2$. Since it is a strict inequality, we use a dashed line. Then, we choose a test point. This can be any point not on the border; in this case, we will choose the origin, $(0,0)$. (This makes the calculation easy and is generally a good choice unless the border passes through the origin.) Putting this into the original inequality, we get $0 > 2(0) + 2$, i.e., $0 > 2$. This is *not* true, so we shade in the side of the border that does *not* include the point $(0,0)$:

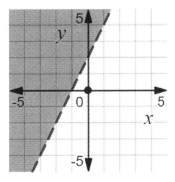

GRAPHING COMPOUND INEQUALITIES IN TWO VARIABLES

One way to graph a compound inequality in two variables is to first graph each of the component inequalities. For an *and* inequality, we then shade in only the parts where the two graphs overlap; for an *or* inequality, we shade in any region that pertains to either of the individual inequalities.

Consider the graph of "$y \geq x - 1$ and $y \leq -x$":

We first shade in the individual inequalities:

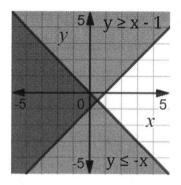

Now, since the compound inequality has an *and*, we only leave shaded the overlap—the part that pertains to *both* inequalities:

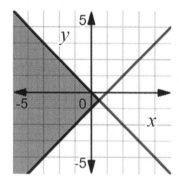

If instead the inequality had been "$y \geq x - 1$ or $y \leq -x$," our final graph would involve the *total* shaded area:

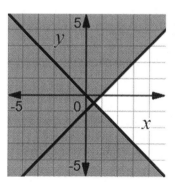

PRACTICE

P1. Analyze the following inequalities:

   (a) $2 - |x + 1| < 3$
   (b) $2(x - 1)^2 + 7 \leq 1$

P2. Graph the following on a number line:

   (a) $x \geq 3$

   (b) $-2 \leq x \leq 6$

   (c) $|x| < 2$

PRACTICE SOLUTIONS

P1. (a) Subtracting 2 from both sides yields $-|x + 1| < 1$; multiplying by -1 and flipping the inequality, since we're multiplying by a negative number, yields $|x + 1| > -1$. But since the absolute value cannot be negative, it's *always* greater than –1, so this inequality is true for all values of x.

   (b) Subtracting 7 from both sides yields $2(x - 1)^2 \leq -6$; dividing by 2 yields $(x - 1)^2 \leq -3$. But $(x - 1)^2$ must be nonnegative, and hence cannot be less than or equal to –3; this inequality has no solution.

P2. (a) We would graph the inequality $x \geq 3$ by putting a solid circle at 3 and filling in the part of the line to the right:

   (b) The inequality $-2 \leq x \leq 6$ is equivalent to "$x \geq -2$ and $x \leq 6$." To plot this compound inequality, we first put solid circles at –2 and 6, and then fill in the part of the line *between* these circles:

   (c) The inequality $|x| < 2$ can be rewritten as "$x > -2$ and $x < 2$." We place hollow circles at the points –2 and 2 and fill in the part of the line between them:

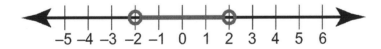

Measurement Principles

PRECISION, ACCURACY, AND ERROR

Precision: How reliable and repeatable a measurement is. The more consistent the data is with repeated testing, the more precise it is. For example, hitting a target consistently in the same spot, which may or may not be the center of the target, is precision.

Accuracy: How close the data is to the correct data. For example, hitting a target consistently in the center area of the target, whether or not the hits are all in the same spot, is accuracy.

Note: it is possible for data to be precise without being accurate. If a scale is off balance, the data will be precise, but will not be accurate. For data to have precision and accuracy, it must be repeatable and correct.

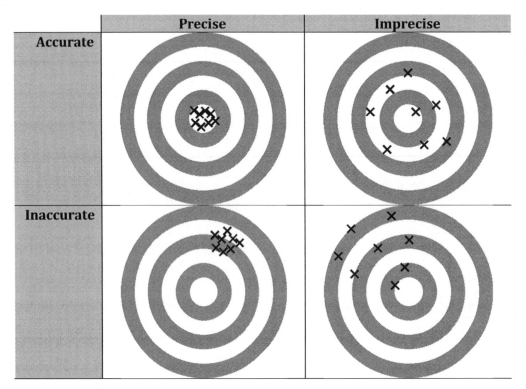

Approximate error: The amount of error in a physical measurement. Approximate error is often reported as the measurement, followed by the $\pm$ symbol and the amount of the approximate error.

Maximum possible error: Half the magnitude of the smallest unit used in the measurement. For example, if the unit of measurement is 1 centimeter, the maximum possible error is $\frac{1}{2}$ cm, written as ±0.5 cm following the measurement. It is important to apply significant figures in reporting maximum possible error. Do not make the answer appear more accurate than the least accurate of your measurements.

ROUNDING AND ESTIMATION

Rounding is reducing the digits in a number while still trying to keep the value similar. The result will be less accurate, but will be in a simpler form, and will be easier to use. Whole numbers can be rounded to the nearest ten, hundred or thousand.

When you are asked to estimate the solution to a problem, you will need to provide only an approximate figure or **estimation** for your answer. In this situation, you will need to round each number in the calculation to the level indicated (nearest hundred, nearest thousand, etc.) or to a level that makes sense for the numbers involved. When estimating a sum **all numbers must be rounded to the same level**. You cannot round one number to the nearest thousand while rounding another to the nearest hundred.

> **Review Video: Rounding and Estimation**
> Visit mometrix.com/academy and enter code: 126243

SCIENTIFIC NOTATION

Scientific notation is a way of writing large numbers in a shorter form. The form $a \times 10^n$ is used in scientific notation, where a is greater than or equal to 1 but less than 10, and n is the number of places the decimal must move to get from the original number to a. Example: The number 230,400,000 is cumbersome to write. To write the value in scientific notation, place a decimal point between the first and second numbers, and include all digits through the last non-zero digit ($a = 2.304$). To find the appropriate power of 10, count the number of places the decimal point had to move ($n = 8$). The number is positive if the decimal moved to the left, and negative if it moved to the right. We can then write 230,400,000 as 2.304×10^8. If we look instead at the number 0.00002304, we have the same value for a, but this time the decimal moved 5 places to the right ($n = -5$). Thus, 0.00002304 can be written as 2.304×10^{-5}. Using this notation makes it simple to compare very large or very small numbers. By comparing exponents, it is easy to see that 3.28×10^4 is smaller than 1.51×10^5, because 4 is less than 5.

> **Review Video: Scientific Notation**
> Visit mometrix.com/academy and enter code: 976454

PRACTICE

P1. Round each number to the indicated degree:

    (a) Round to the nearest ten: 11; 47; 118

    (b) Round to the nearest hundred: 78; 980; 248

    (c) Round each number to the nearest thousand: 302; 1,274; 3,756

P2. Estimate the solution to $345,932 + 96,369$ by rounding each number to the nearest ten thousand.

P3. A runner's heart beats 422 times over the course of six minutes. About how many times did the runner's heart beat during each minute?

PRACTICE SOLUTIONS

P1. (a) When rounding to the nearest ten, anything ending in 5 or greater rounds up. So, 11 rounds to 10, 47 rounds to 50, and 118 rounds to 120.

    (b) When rounding to the nearest hundred, anything ending in 50 or greater rounds up. So, 78 rounds to 100, 980 rounds to 1000, and 248 rounds to 200.

    (c) When rounding to the nearest thousand, anything ending in 500 or greater rounds up. So, 302 rounds to 0, 1,274 rounds to 1,000, and 3,756 rounds to 4,000.

P2. Start by rounding each number to the nearest ten thousand: 345,932 becomes 350,000, and 96,369 becomes 100,000. Then, add the rounded numbers: 350,000 + 100,000 = 450,000. So, the answer is approximately 450,000. The exact answer would be 345,932 + 96,369 = 442,301. So, the estimate of 450,000 is a similar value to the exact answer.

P3. "About how many" indicates that you need to estimate the solution. In this case, look at the numbers you are given. 422 can be rounded down to 420, which is easily divisible by 6. A good estimate is $420 \div 6 = 70$ beats per minute. More accurately, the patient's heart rate was just over 70 beats per minute since his heart actually beat a little more than 420 times in six minutes.

Units of Measurement

METRIC MEASUREMENT PREFIXES

Giga-	One billion	1 *giga*watt is one billion watts
Mega-	One million	1 *mega*hertz is one million hertz
Kilo-	One thousand	1 *kilo*gram is one thousand grams
Deci-	One-tenth	1 *deci*meter is one-tenth of a meter
Centi-	One-hundredth	1 *centi*meter is one-hundredth of a meter
Milli-	One-thousandth	1 *milli*liter is one-thousandth of a liter
Micro-	One-millionth	1 *micro*gram is one-millionth of a gram

MEASUREMENT CONVERSION

When converting between units, the goal is to maintain the same meaning but change the way it is displayed. In order to go from a larger unit to a smaller unit, multiply the number of the known amount by the equivalent amount. When going from a smaller unit to a larger unit, divide the number of the known amount by the equivalent amount.

For complicated conversions, it may be helpful to set up conversion fractions. In these fractions, one fraction is the **conversion factor**. The other fraction has the unknown amount in the numerator. So, the known value is placed in the denominator. Sometimes, the second fraction has the known value from the problem in the numerator and the unknown in the denominator. Multiply the two fractions to get the converted measurement. Note that since the numerator and the denominator of the factor are equivalent, the value of the fraction is 1. That is why we can say that the result in the new units is equal to the result in the old units even though they have different numbers.

It can often be necessary to chain known conversion factors together. As an example, consider converting 512 square inches to square meters. We know that there are 2.54 centimeters in an inch and 100 centimeters in a meter and that we will need to square each of these factors to achieve the conversion we are looking for.

$$\frac{512 \text{ in}^2}{1} \times \left(\frac{2.54 \text{ cm}}{1 \text{ in}}\right)^2 \times \left(\frac{1 \text{ m}}{100 \text{ cm}}\right)^2 = \frac{512 \text{ in}^2}{1} \times \left(\frac{6.4516 \text{ cm}^2}{1 \text{ in}^2}\right) \times \left(\frac{1 \text{ m}^2}{10,000 \text{ cm}^2}\right) = 0.330 \text{ m}^2$$

> **Review Video: Measurement Conversions**
> Visit mometrix.com/academy and enter code: 316703

COMMON UNITS AND EQUIVALENTS

METRIC EQUIVALENTS

1000 µg (microgram)	1 mg
1000 mg (milligram)	1 g
1000 g (gram)	1 kg
1000 kg (kilogram)	1 metric ton
1000 mL (milliliter)	1 L
1000 µm (micrometer)	1 mm
1000 mm (millimeter)	1 m
100 cm (centimeter)	1 m
1000 m (meter)	1 km

Review Video: Metric System Conversions
Visit mometrix.com/academy and enter code: 163709

DISTANCE AND AREA MEASUREMENT

Unit	Abbreviation	US equivalent	Metric equivalent
Inch	in	1 inch	2.54 centimeters
Foot	ft	12 inches	0.305 meters
Yard	yd	3 feet	0.914 meters
Mile	mi	5280 feet	1.609 kilometers
Acre	ac	4840 square yards	0.405 hectares
Square Mile	sq. mi. or mi.^{2}	640 acres	2.590 square kilometers

CAPACITY MEASUREMENTS

Unit	Abbreviation	US equivalent	Metric equivalent
Fluid Ounce	fl oz	8 fluid drams	29.573 milliliters
Cup	c	8 fluid ounces	0.237 liter
Pint	pt.	16 fluid ounces	0.473 liter
Quart	qt.	2 pints	0.946 liter
Gallon	gal.	4 quarts	3.785 liters
Teaspoon	t or tsp.	1 fluid dram	5 milliliters
Tablespoon	T or tbsp.	4 fluid drams	15 or 16 milliliters
Cubic Centimeter	cc or cm^3	0.271 drams	1 milliliter

WEIGHT MEASUREMENTS

Unit	Abbreviation	US equivalent	Metric equivalent
Ounce	oz	16 drams	28.35 grams
Pound	lb	16 ounces	453.6 grams
Ton	tn.	2,000 pounds	907.2 kilograms

VOLUME AND WEIGHT MEASUREMENT CLARIFICATIONS

Always be careful when using ounces and fluid ounces. They are not equivalent.

1 pint = 16 fluid ounces	1 fluid ounce ≠ 1 ounce
1 pound = 16 ounces	1 pint ≠ 1 pound

Having one pint of something does not mean you have one pound of it. In the same way, just because something weighs one pound does not mean that its volume is one pint.

In the United States, the word "ton" by itself refers to a short ton or a net ton. Do not confuse this with a long ton (also called a gross ton) or a metric ton (also spelled *tonne*), which have different measurement equivalents.

$$1 \text{ US ton} = 2000 \text{ pounds} \qquad \neq \qquad 1 \text{ metric ton} = 1000 \text{ kilograms}$$

PRACTICE

P1. Perform the following conversions:

(a) 1.4 meters to centimeters

(b) 218 centimeters to meters

(c) 42 inches to feet

(d) 15 kilograms to pounds

(e) 80 ounces to pounds

(f) 2 miles to kilometers

(g) 5 feet to centimeters

(h) 15.14 liters to gallons

(i) 8 quarts to liters

(j) 13.2 pounds to grams

PRACTICE SOLUTIONS

P1. (a) $\frac{100 \text{ cm}}{1 \text{ m}} = \frac{x \text{ cm}}{1.4 \text{ m}}$ Cross multiply to get $x = 140$

(b) $\frac{100 \text{ cm}}{1 \text{ m}} = \frac{218 \text{ cm}}{x \text{ m}}$ Cross multiply to get $100x = 218$, or $x = 2.18$

(c) $\frac{12 \text{ in}}{1 \text{ ft}} = \frac{42 \text{ in}}{x \text{ ft}}$ Cross multiply to get $12x = 42$, or $x = 3.5$

(d) $15 \text{ kilograms} \times \frac{2.2 \text{ pounds}}{1 \text{ kilogram}} = 33 \text{ pounds}$

(e) $80 \text{ ounces} \times \frac{1 \text{ pound}}{16 \text{ ounces}} = 5 \text{ pounds}$

(f) $2 \text{ miles} \times \frac{1.609 \text{ kilometers}}{1 \text{ mile}} = 3.218 \text{ kilometers}$

(g) $5 \text{ feet} \times \frac{12 \text{ inches}}{1 \text{ foot}} \times \frac{2.54 \text{ centimeters}}{1 \text{ inch}} = 152.4 \text{ centimeters}$

(h) $15.14 \text{ liters} \times \frac{1 \text{ gallon}}{3.785 \text{ liters}} = 4 \text{ gallons}$

(i) 8 quarts $\times \dfrac{1 \text{ gallon}}{4 \text{ quarts}} \times \dfrac{3.785 \text{ liters}}{1 \text{ gallon}} = 7.57$ liters

(j) 13.2 pounds $\times \dfrac{1 \text{ kilogram}}{2.2 \text{ pounds}} \times \dfrac{1{,}000 \text{ grams}}{1 \text{ kilogram}} = 6{,}000$ grams

Probability

PROBABILITY

Probability is the likelihood of a certain outcome occurring for a given event. An **event** is any situation that produces a result. It could be something as simple as flipping a coin or as complex as launching a rocket. Determining the probability of an outcome for an event can be equally simple or complex. As such, there are specific terms used in the study of probability that need to be understood:

- **Compound event** – event that involves two or more independent events (rolling a pair of dice and taking the sum)
- **Desired outcome** (or success) – an outcome that meets a particular set of criteria (a roll of 1 or 2 if we are looking for numbers less than 3)
- **Independent events** – two or more events whose outcomes do not affect one another (two coins tossed at the same time)
- **Dependent events** – two or more events whose outcomes affect one another (two cards drawn consecutively from the same deck)
- **Certain outcome** – probability of outcome is 100% or 1
- **Impossible outcome** – probability of outcome is 0% or 0
- **Mutually exclusive outcomes** – two or more outcomes whose criteria cannot all be satisfied in a single event (a coin coming up heads and tails on the same toss)
- **Random variable** – refers to all possible outcomes of a single event which may be discrete or continuous.

> **Review Video: Intro to Probability**
> Visit mometrix.com/academy and enter code: 212374

THEORETICAL AND EXPERIMENTAL PROBABILITY

Theoretical probability can usually be determined without actually performing the event. The likelihood of an outcome occurring, or the probability of an outcome occurring, is given by the formula:

$$P(A) = \frac{\text{Number of acceptable outcomes}}{\text{Number of possible outcomes}}$$

Note that $P(A)$ is the probability of an outcome A occurring, and each outcome is just as likely to occur as any other outcome. If each outcome has the same probability of occurring as every other possible outcome, the outcomes are said to be equally likely to occur. The total number of acceptable outcomes must be less than or equal to the total number of possible outcomes. If the two are equal, then the outcome is certain to occur and the probability is 1. If the number of acceptable outcomes is zero, then the outcome is impossible and the probability is 0. For example, if there are 20 marbles in a bag and 5 are red, then the theoretical probability of randomly selecting a red marble is 5 out of 20, $\left(\frac{5}{20} = \frac{1}{4}, 0.25, \text{ or } 25\%\right)$.

If the theoretical probability is unknown or too complicated to calculate, it can be estimated by an experimental probability. **Experimental probability**, also called empirical probability, is an estimate of the likelihood of a certain outcome based on repeated experiments or collected data. In other words, while theoretical probability is based on what *should* happen, experimental probability is based on what *has* happened. Experimental probability is calculated in the same way as theoretical, except that actual outcomes are used instead of possible outcomes. The more experiments performed or datapoints gathered, the better the estimate should be.

Theoretical and experimental probability do not always line up with one another. Theoretical probability says that out of 20 coin-tosses, 10 should be heads. However, if we were actually to toss 20 coins, we might record just 5 heads. This doesn't mean that our theoretical probability is incorrect; it just means that this particular experiment had results that were different from what was predicted. A practical application of empirical probability is the insurance industry. There are no set functions that define lifespan, health, or safety. Insurance companies look at factors from hundreds of thousands of individuals to find patterns that they then use to set the formulas for insurance premiums.

> **Review Video: Empirical Probability**
> Visit mometrix.com/academy and enter code: 513468

OBJECTIVE AND SUBJECTIVE PROBABILITY

Objective probability is based on mathematical formulas and documented evidence. Examples of objective probability include raffles or lottery drawings where there is a pre-determined number of possible outcomes and a predetermined number of outcomes that correspond to an event. Other cases of objective probability include probabilities of rolling dice, flipping coins, or drawing cards. Most gambling games are based on objective probability.

In contrast, **subjective probability** is based on personal or professional feelings and judgments. Often, there is a lot of guesswork following extensive research. Areas where subjective probability is applicable include sales trends and business expenses. Attractions set admission prices based on subjective probabilities of attendance based on varying admission rates in an effort to maximize their profit.

SAMPLE SPACE

The total set of all possible results of a test or experiment is called a **sample space**, or sometimes a universal sample space. The sample space, represented by one of the variables S, Ω, or U (for universal sample space) has individual elements called outcomes. Other terms for outcome that may be used interchangeably include elementary outcome, simple event, or sample point. The number of outcomes in a given sample space could be infinite or finite, and some tests may yield multiple unique sample sets. For example, tests conducted by drawing playing cards from a standard deck would have one sample space of the card values, another sample space of the card suits, and a third sample space of suit-denomination combinations. For most tests, the sample spaces considered will be finite.

An **event**, represented by the variable E, is a portion of a sample space. It may be one outcome or a group of outcomes from the same sample space. If an event occurs, then the test or experiment will generate an outcome that satisfies the requirement of that event. For example, given a standard deck of 52 playing cards as the sample space, and defining the event as the collection of face cards, then the event will occur if the card drawn is a J, Q, or K. If any other card is drawn, the event is said to have not occurred.

For every sample space, each possible outcome has a specific likelihood, or probability, that it will occur. The probability measure, also called the **distribution**, is a function that assigns a real number probability, from zero to one, to each outcome. For a probability measure to be accurate, every outcome must have a real number probability measure that is greater than or equal to zero and less than or equal to one. Also, the probability measure of the sample space must equal one, and

212

the probability measure of the union of multiple outcomes must equal the sum of the individual probability measures.

Probabilities of events are expressed as real numbers from zero to one. They give a numerical value to the chance that a particular event will occur. The probability of an event occurring is the sum of the probabilities of the individual elements of that event. For example, in a standard deck of 52 playing cards as the sample space and the collection of face cards as the event, the probability of drawing a specific face card is $\frac{1}{52} = 0.019$, but the probability of drawing any one of the twelve face cards is $12(0.019) = 0.228$. Note that rounding of numbers can generate different results. If you multiplied 12 by the fraction $\frac{1}{52}$ before converting to a decimal, you would get the answer $\frac{12}{52} = 0.231$.

TREE DIAGRAM

For a simple sample space, possible outcomes may be determined by using a **tree diagram** or an organized chart. In either case, you can easily draw or list out the possible outcomes. For example, to determine all the possible ways three objects can be ordered, you can draw a tree diagram:

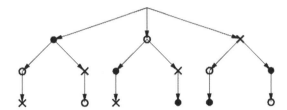

You can also make a chart to list all the possibilities:

First object	Second object	Third object
●	X	O
●	O	X
O	●	X
O	X	●
X	●	O
X	O	●

Either way, you can easily see there are six possible ways the three objects can be ordered.

If two events have no outcomes in common, they are said to be **mutually exclusive**. For example, in a standard deck of 52 playing cards, the event of all card suits is mutually exclusive to the event of all card values. If two events have no bearing on each other so that one event occurring has no influence on the probability of another event occurring, the two events are said to be independent. For example, rolling a standard six-sided die multiple times does not change that probability that a particular number will be rolled from one roll to the next. If the outcome of one event does affect the probability of the second event, the two events are said to be dependent. For example, if cards are drawn from a deck, the probability of drawing an ace after an ace has been drawn is different than the probability of drawing an ace if no ace (or no other card, for that matter) has been drawn.

In probability, the **odds in favor of an event** are the number of times the event will occur compared to the number of times the event will not occur. To calculate the odds in favor of an event, use the formula $\frac{P(A)}{1-P(A)}$, where $P(A)$ is the probability that the event will occur. Many times, odds in favor is given as a ratio in the form $\frac{a}{b}$ or $a{:}b$, where a is the probability of the event occurring and b is the complement of the event, the probability of the event not occurring. If the odds in favor are given as 2:5, that means that you can expect the event to occur two times for every 5 times that it does not occur. In other words, the probability that the event will occur is $\frac{2}{2+5}=\frac{2}{7}$.

In probability, the **odds against an event** are the number of times the event will not occur compared to the number of times the event will occur. To calculate the odds against an event, use the formula $\frac{1-P(A)}{P(A)}$, where $P(A)$ is the probability that the event will occur. Many times, odds against is given as a ratio in the form $\frac{b}{a}$ or $b{:}a$, where b is the probability the event will not occur (the complement of the event) and a is the probability the event will occur. If the odds against an event are given as 3:1, that means that you can expect the event to not occur 3 times for every one time it does occur. In other words, 3 out of every 4 trials will fail.

PERMUTATIONS AND COMBINATIONS

When trying to calculate the probability of an event using the $\frac{\text{desired outcomes}}{\text{total outcomes}}$ formula, you may frequently find that there are too many outcomes to individually count them. **Permutation** and **combination formulas** offer a shortcut to counting outcomes. A permutation is an arrangement of a specific number of a set of objects in a specific order. The number of **permutations** of r items given a set of n items can be calculated as $_nP_r=\frac{n!}{(n-r)!}$. Combinations are similar to permutations, except there are no restrictions regarding the order of the elements. While ABC is considered a different permutation than BCA, ABC and BCA are considered the same combination. The number of **combinations** of r items given a set of n items can be calculated as $_nC_r=\frac{n!}{r!(n-r)!}$ or $_nC_r=\frac{_nP_r}{r!}$.

Suppose you want to calculate how many different 5-card hands can be drawn from a deck of 52 cards. This is a combination since the order of the cards in a hand does not matter. There are 52 cards available, and 5 to be selected. Thus, the number of different hands is $_{52}C_5=\frac{52!}{5!\times47!}=$ 2,598,960.

Review Video: Probability - Permutation and Combination
Visit mometrix.com/academy and enter code: 907664

UNION AND INTERSECTION OF TWO SETS OF OUTCOMES

If A and B are each a set of elements or outcomes from an experiment, then the **union** (symbol ∪) of the two sets is the set of elements found in set A or set B. For example, if $A=\{2,3,4\}$ and $B=\{3,4,5\}$, $A\cup B=\{2,3,4,5\}$. Note that the outcomes 3 and 4 appear only once in the union. For statistical events, the union is equivalent to "or"; $P(A\cup B)$ is the same thing as $P(A\text{ or }B)$. The **intersection** (symbol ∩) of two sets is the set of outcomes common to both sets. For the above sets A and B, $A\cap B=\{3,4\}$. For statistical events, the intersection is equivalent to "and"; $P(A\cap B)$ is the same thing as $P(A\text{ and }B)$. It is important to note that union and intersection operations commute. That is:

$$A\cup B=B\cup A \text{ and } A\cap B=B\cap A$$

214

COMPLEMENT OF AN EVENT

Sometimes it may be easier to calculate the possibility of something not happening, or the **complement of an event**. Represented by the symbol $\bar{A}$, the complement of A is the probability that event A does not happen. When you know the probability of event A occurring, you can use the formula $P(\bar{A}) = 1 - P(A)$, where $P(\bar{A})$ is the probability of event A not occurring, and $P(A)$ is the probability of event A occurring.

ADDITION RULE

The **addition rule** for probability is used for finding the probability of a compound event. Use the formula $P(A \text{ or } B) = P(A) + P(B) - P(A \text{ and } B)$, where $P(A \text{ and } B)$ is the probability of both events occurring to find the probability of a compound event. The probability of both events occurring at the same time must be subtracted to eliminate any overlap in the first two probabilities.

CONDITIONAL PROBABILITY

Given two events A and B, the **conditional probability** $P(A|B)$ is the probability that event A will occur, given that event B has occurred. The conditional probability cannot be calculated simply from $P(A)$ and $P(B)$; these probabilities alone do not give sufficient information to determine the conditional probability. It can, however, be determined if you are also given the probability of the intersection of events A and B, $P(A \cap B)$, the probability that events A and B both occur. Specifically, $P(A|B) = \frac{P(A \cap B)}{P(B)}$. For instance, suppose you have a jar containing two red marbles and two blue marbles, and you draw two marbles at random. Consider event A being the event that the first marble drawn is red, and event B being the event that the second marble drawn is blue. $P(A)$ is $\frac{1}{2}$, and $P(A \cap B)$ is $\frac{1}{3}$. (The latter may not be obvious, but may be determined by finding the product of $\frac{1}{2}$ and $\frac{2}{3}$). Therefore $P(A|B) = \frac{1/3}{1/2} = \frac{2}{3}$.

CONDITIONAL PROBABILITY IN EVERYDAY SITUATIONS

Conditional probability often arises in everyday situations in, for example, estimating the risk or benefit of certain activities. The conditional probability of having a heart attack given that you exercise daily may be smaller than the overall probability of having a heart attack. The conditional probability of having lung cancer given that you are a smoker is larger than the overall probability of having lung cancer. Note that changing the order of the conditional probability changes the meaning: the conditional probability of having lung cancer given that you are a smoker is a very different thing from the probability of being a smoker given that you have lung cancer. In an extreme case, suppose that a certain rare disease is caused only by eating a certain food, but even then, it is unlikely. Then the conditional probability of having that disease given that you eat the dangerous food is nonzero but low, but the conditional probability of having eaten that food given that you have the disease is 100%!

> **Review Video: Conditional Probability**
> Visit mometrix.com/academy and enter code: 397924

INDEPENDENCE

The conditional probability $P(A|B)$ is the probability that event A will occur given that event B occurs. If the two events are independent, we do not expect that whether or not event B occurs should have any effect on whether or not event A occurs. In other words, we expect $P(A|B) = P(A)$.

This can be proven using the usual equations for conditional probability and the joint probability of independent events. The conditional probability $P(A|B) = \frac{P(A \cap B)}{P(B)}$. If A and B are independent, then $P(A \cap B) = P(A)P(B)$. So $P(A|B) = \frac{P(A)P(B)}{P(B)} = P(A)$. By similar reasoning, if A and B are independent then $P(B|A) = P(B)$.

TWO-WAY FREQUENCY TABLES

If we have a two-way frequency table, it is generally a straightforward matter to read off the probabilities of any two events A and B, as well as the joint probability of both events occurring, $P(A \cap B)$. We can then find the conditional probability $P(A|B)$ by calculating $P(A|B) = \frac{P(A \cap B)}{P(B)}$. We could also check whether or not events are independent by verifying whether $P(A)P(B) = P(A \cap B)$.

For example, a certain store's recent T-shirt sales:

Size \ Color	Small	Medium	Large	Total
Blue	25	40	35	100
White	27	25	22	74
Black	8	23	15	46
Total	60	88	72	220

Suppose we want to find the conditional probability that a customer buys a black shirt (event A), given that the shirt he buys is size small (event B). From the table, the probability $P(B)$ that a customer buys a small shirt is $\frac{60}{220} = \frac{3}{11}$. The probability $P(A \cap B)$ that he buys a small, black shirt is $\frac{8}{220} = \frac{2}{55}$. The conditional probability $P(A|B)$ that he buys a black shirt, given that he buys a small shirt, is therefore $P(A|B) = \frac{2/55}{3/11} = \frac{2}{15}$.

Similarly, if we want to check whether the event a customer buys a blue shirt, A, is independent of the event that a customer buys a medium shirt, B. From the table, $P(A) = \frac{100}{220} = \frac{5}{11}$ and $P(B) = \frac{88}{220} = \frac{4}{10}$. Also, $P(A \cap B) = \frac{40}{220} = \frac{2}{11}$. Since $\left(\frac{5}{11}\right)\left(\frac{4}{10}\right) = \frac{20}{220} = \frac{2}{11}$, $P(A)P(B) = P(A \cap B)$ and these two events are indeed independent.

MULTIPLICATION RULE

The **multiplication rule** can be used to find the probability of two independent events occurring using the formula $P(A \text{ and } B) = P(A) \times P(B)$, where $P(A \text{ and } B)$ is the probability of two independent events occurring, $P(A)$ is the probability of the first event occurring, and $P(B)$ is the probability of the second event occurring.

The multiplication rule can also be used to find the probability of two dependent events occurring using the formula $P(A \text{ and } B) = P(A) \times P(B|A)$, where $P(A \text{ and } B)$ is the probability of two dependent events occurring and $P(B|A)$ is the probability of the second event occurring after the first event has already occurred. Before using the multiplication rule, you MUST first determine whether the two events are *dependent* or *independent*.

Use a **combination of the multiplication** rule and the rule of complements to find the probability that at least one outcome of the element will occur. This is given by the general formula P(at least one event occurring) $= 1 - P$(no outcomes occurring). For example, to find the probability that at least one even number will show when a pair of dice is rolled, find the probability that two odd numbers will be rolled (no even numbers) and subtract from one. You can always use a tree diagram or make a chart to list the possible outcomes when the sample space is small, such as in the dice-rolling example, but in most cases it will be much faster to use the multiplication and complement formulas.

EXPECTED VALUE

Expected value is a method of determining expected outcome in a random situation. It is really a sum of the weighted probabilities of the possible outcomes. Multiply the probability of an event occurring by the weight assigned to that probability (such as the amount of money won or lost). A practical application of the expected value is to determine whether a game of chance is really fair. If the sum of the weighted probabilities is equal to zero, the game is generally considered fair because the player has a fair chance to at least break even. If the expected value is less than zero, then players lose more than they win. For example, a lottery drawing might allow the player to choose any three-digit number, 000–999. The probability of choosing the winning number is 1:1000. If it costs \$1 to play, and a winning number receives \$500, the expected value is $\left(-\$1 \times \frac{999}{1,000}\right) +$ $\left(\$499 \times \frac{1}{1,000}\right) = -\$0.50$. You can expect to lose on average 50 cents for every dollar you spend.

EXPECTED VALUE AND SIMULATORS

A die roll simulator will show the results of n rolls of a die. The result of each die roll may be recorded. For example, suppose a die is rolled 100 times. All results may be recorded. The numbers of 1s, 2s, 3s, 4s, 5s, and 6s, may be counted. The experimental probability of rolling each number will equal the ratio of the frequency of the rolled number to the total number of rolls. As the number of rolls increases, or approaches infinity, the experimental probability will approach the theoretical probability of $\frac{1}{6}$. Thus, the expected value for the roll of a die is shown to be $\left(1 \times \frac{1}{6}\right) +$ $\left(2 \times \frac{1}{6}\right) + \left(3 \times \frac{1}{6}\right) + \left(4 \times \frac{1}{6}\right) + \left(5 \times \frac{1}{6}\right) + \left(6 \times \frac{1}{6}\right)$, or 3.5.

PRACTICE

P1. Determine the theoretical probability of the following events:

(a) Rolling an even number on a regular 6-sided die.

(b) Not getting a red ball when selecting one from a bag of 3 red balls, 4 black balls, and 2 green balls.

(c) Rolling a standard die and then selecting a card from a standard deck that is less than the value rolled.

P2. There is a game of chance involving a standard deck of cards that has been shuffled and then laid on a table. The player wins $10 if they can turn over 2 cards of matching color (black or red), $50 for 2 cards with matching value (A-K), and $100 for 2 cards with both matching color and value. What is the expected value of playing this game?

P3. Today, there were two food options for lunch at a local college cafeteria. Given the following survey data, what is the probability that a junior selected at random from the sample had a sandwich?

	Freshman	Sophomore	Junior	Senior
Salad	15	12	27	36
Sandwich	24	40	43	35
Nothing	42	23	23	30

PRACTICE SOLUTIONS

P1. (a). The values on the faces of a regular die are 1, 2, 3, 4, 5, and 6. Since three of these are even numbers (2, 4, 6), The probability of rolling an even number is $\frac{3}{6} = \frac{1}{2} = 0.5 = 50\%$.

(b) The bag contains a total of 9 balls, 6 of which are not red, so the probability of selecting one non-red ball would be $\frac{6}{9} = \frac{2}{3} \cong 0.667 \cong 66.7\%$.

(c) In this scenario, we need to determine how many cards could satisfy the condition for each possible value of the die roll. If a one is rolled, there is no way to achieve the desired outcome, since no cards in a standard deck are less than 1. If a two is rolled, then any of the four aces would achieve the desired result. If a three is rolled, then either an ace or a two would satisfy the condition, and so on. Note that any value on the die is equally likely to occur, meaning that the probability of each roll is $\frac{1}{6}$. Putting all this in a table can help:

Roll	Cards < Roll	Probability of Card	Probability of Event
1	-	$\frac{0}{52} = 0$	$\frac{1}{6} \times 0 = 0$
2	1	$\frac{4}{52} = \frac{1}{13}$	$\frac{1}{6} \times \frac{1}{13} = \frac{1}{78}$
3	1,2	$\frac{8}{52} = \frac{2}{13}$	$\frac{1}{6} \times \frac{2}{13} = \frac{2}{78}$
4	1,2,3	$\frac{12}{52} = \frac{3}{13}$	$\frac{1}{6} \times \frac{3}{13} = \frac{3}{78}$
5	1,2,3,4	$\frac{16}{52} = \frac{4}{13}$	$\frac{1}{6} \times \frac{4}{13} = \frac{4}{78}$
6	1,2,3,4,5	$\frac{20}{52} = \frac{5}{13}$	$\frac{1}{6} \times \frac{5}{13} = \frac{5}{78}$

Assuming that each value of the die is equally likely, then the probability is the sum of the probabilities of each way to achieve the desired outcome: $\frac{0+1+2+3+4+5}{78} = \frac{15}{78} = \frac{5}{26} \cong 0.192 \cong$ 19.2%.

P2. First, determine the probability of each way of winning. In each case, the first card simply determines which of the remaining 51 cards in the deck correspond to a win. For the color of the cards to match, there are 25 cards remaining in the deck that match the color of the first, but one of the 25 also matches the value, so only 24 are left in this category. For the value of the cards to match, there are 3 cards remaining in the deck that match the value of the first, but one of the three also matches the color, so only 2 are left in this category. There is only one card in the deck that will match both the color and value. Finally, there are 24 cards left that don't match at all.

Now we can find the expected value of playing the game, where we multiply the value of each event by the probability it will occur and sum over all of them:

$$\$10 \times \frac{24}{51} = \$4.71$$

$$\$50 \times \frac{2}{51} = \$1.96$$

$$\$100 \times \frac{1}{51} = \$1.96$$

$$\$0 \times \frac{24}{51} = \$0$$

$$\$4.71 + \$1.96 + \$1.96 = \$8.63$$

This game therefore has an expected value of $8.63 each time you play, which means if the cost to play is less than $8.63 then you would, on average, *gain* money. However, if the cost to play is more than $8.63, then you would, on average, *lose* money.

P3. With two-way tables it is often most helpful to start by totaling the rows and columns:

	Freshman	Sophomore	Junior	Senior	Total
Salad	15	12	27	36	90
Sandwich	24	40	43	35	142
Nothing	42	23	23	30	118
Total	81	75	93	101	350

Since the question is focused on juniors, we can focus on that column. There was a total of 93 juniors surveyed and 43 of them had a sandwich for lunch. Thus, the probability that a junior selected at random had a sandwich would be $\frac{43}{93} \cong 0.462 \cong 46.2\%$.

Statistics

STATISTICS

Statistics is the branch of mathematics that deals with collecting, recording, interpreting, illustrating, and analyzing large amounts of **data**. The following terms are often used in the discussion of data and **statistics**:

- **Data** – the collective name for pieces of information (singular is datum)
- **Quantitative data** – measurements (such as length, mass, and speed) that provide information about quantities in numbers
- **Qualitative data** – information (such as colors, scents, tastes, and shapes) that cannot be measured using numbers
- **Discrete data** – information that can be expressed only by a specific value, such as whole or half numbers. (e.g., since people can be counted only in whole numbers, a population count would be discrete data.)
- **Continuous data** – information (such as time and temperature) that can be expressed by any value within a given range
- **Primary data** – information that has been collected directly from a survey, investigation, or experiment, such as a questionnaire or the recording of daily temperatures. (Primary data that has not yet been organized or analyzed is called **raw data**.)
- **Secondary data** – information that has been collected, sorted, and processed by the researcher
- **Ordinal data** – information that can be placed in numerical order, such as age or weight
- **Nominal data** – information that *cannot* be placed in numerical order, such as names or places

DATA COLLECTION

POPULATION

In statistics, the **population** is the entire collection of people, plants, etc., that data can be collected from. For example, a study to determine how well students in local schools perform on a standardized test would have a population of all the students enrolled in those schools, although a study may include just a small sample of students from each school. A **parameter** is a numerical value that gives information about the population, such as the mean, median, mode, or standard deviation. Remember that the symbol for the mean of a population is μ and the symbol for the standard deviation of a population is σ.

SAMPLE

A **sample** is a portion of the entire population. Whereas a parameter helped describe the population, a **statistic** is a numerical value that gives information about the sample, such as mean, median, mode, or standard deviation. Keep in mind that the symbols for mean and standard deviation are different when they are referring to a sample rather than the entire population. For a sample, the symbol for mean is $\bar{x}$ and the symbol for standard deviation is s. The mean and standard deviation of a sample may or may not be identical to that of the entire population due to a sample only being a subset of the population. However, if the sample is random and large enough, statistically significant values can be attained. Samples are generally used when the population is too large to justify including every element or when acquiring data for the entire population is impossible.

INFERENTIAL STATISTICS

Inferential statistics is the branch of statistics that uses samples to make predictions about an entire population. This type of statistic is often seen in political polls, where a sample of the population is questioned about a particular topic or politician to gain an understanding of the attitudes of the entire population of the country. Often, exit polls are conducted on election days using this method. Inferential statistics can have a large margin of error if you do not have a valid sample.

SAMPLING DISTRIBUTION

Statistical values calculated from various samples of the same size make up the **sampling distribution**. For example, if several samples of identical size are randomly selected from a large population and then the mean of each sample is calculated, the distribution of values of the means would be a sampling distribution.

The **sampling distribution of the mean** is the distribution of the sample mean, $\bar{x}$, derived from random samples of a given size. It has three important characteristics. First, the mean of the sampling distribution of the mean is equal to the mean of the population that was sampled. Second, assuming the standard deviation is non-zero, the standard deviation of the sampling distribution of the mean equals the standard deviation of the sampled population divided by the square root of the sample size. This is sometimes called the standard error. Finally, as the sample size gets larger, the sampling distribution of the mean gets closer to a normal distribution via the central limit theorem.

SURVEY STUDY

A **survey study** is a method of gathering information from a small group in an attempt to gain enough information to make accurate general assumptions about the population. Once a survey study is completed, the results are then put into a summary report.

Survey studies are generally in the format of surveys, interviews, or questionnaires as part of an effort to find opinions of a particular group or to find facts about a group.

It is important to note that the findings from a survey study are only as accurate as the sample chosen from the population.

CORRELATIONAL STUDIES

Correlational studies seek to determine how much one variable is affected by changes in a second variable. For example, correlational studies may look for a relationship between the amount of time a student spends studying for a test and the grade that student earned on the test or between student scores on college admissions tests and student grades in college.

It is important to note that correlational studies cannot show a cause and effect, but rather can show only that two variables are or are not potentially correlated.

EXPERIMENTAL STUDIES

Experimental studies take correlational studies one step farther, in that they attempt to prove or disprove a cause-and-effect relationship. These studies are performed by conducting a series of experiments to test the hypothesis. For a study to be scientifically accurate, it must have both an experimental group that receives the specified treatment and a control group that does not get the treatment. This is the type of study pharmaceutical companies do as part of drug trials for new medications. Experimental studies are only valid when the proper scientific method has been followed. In other words, the experiment must be well-planned and executed without bias in the testing process, all subjects must be selected at random, and the process of determining which subject is in which of the two groups must also be completely random.

OBSERVATIONAL STUDIES

Observational studies are the opposite of experimental studies. In observational studies, the tester cannot change or in any way control all of the variables in the test. For example, a study to determine which gender does better in math classes in school is strictly observational. You cannot change a person's gender, and you cannot change the subject being studied. The big downfall of observational studies is that you have no way of proving a cause-and-effect relationship because you cannot control outside influences. Events outside of school can influence a student's performance in school, and observational studies cannot take that into consideration.

RANDOM SAMPLES

For most studies, a **random sample** is necessary to produce valid results. Random samples should not have any particular influence to cause sampled subjects to behave one way or another. The goal is for the random sample to be a **representative sample**, or a sample whose characteristics give an accurate picture of the characteristics of the entire population. To accomplish this, you must make sure you have a proper **sample size**, or an appropriate number of elements in the sample.

BIASES

In statistical studies, biases must be avoided. **Bias** is an error that causes the study to favor one set of results over another. For example, if a survey to determine how the country views the president's job performance only speaks to registered voters in the president's party, the results will be skewed because a disproportionately large number of responders would tend to show approval, while a disproportionately large number of people in the opposite party would tend to express disapproval. **Extraneous variables** are, as the name implies, outside influences that can affect the outcome of a study. They are not always avoidable but could trigger bias in the result.

Statistical Analysis

MEASURES OF CENTRAL TENDENCY

A **measure of central tendency** is a statistical value that gives a reasonable estimate for the center of a group of data. There are several different ways of describing the measure of central tendency. Each one has a unique way it is calculated, and each one gives a slightly different perspective on the data set. Whenever you give a measure of central tendency, always make sure the units are the same. If the data has different units, such as hours, minutes, and seconds, convert all the data to the same unit, and use the same unit in the measure of central tendency. If no units are given in the data, do not give units for the measure of central tendency.

MEAN

The **statistical mean** of a group of data is the same as the arithmetic average of that group. To find the mean of a set of data, first convert each value to the same units, if necessary. Then find the sum of all the values, and count the total number of data values, making sure you take into consideration each individual value. If a value appears more than once, count it more than once. Divide the sum of the values by the total number of values and apply the units, if any. Note that the mean does not have to be one of the data values in the set, and may not divide evenly.

$$\text{mean} = \frac{\text{sum of the data values}}{\text{quantity of data values}}$$

For instance, the mean of the data set $\{88, 72, 61, 90, 97, 68, 88, 79, 86, 93, 97, 71, 80, 84, 89\}$ would be the sum of the fifteen numbers divided by 15:

$$\frac{88 + 72 + 61 + 90 + 97 + 68 + 88 + 79 + 86 + 93 + 97 + 71 + 80 + 84 + 88}{15} = \frac{1242}{15}$$
$$= 82.8$$

While the mean is relatively easy to calculate and averages are understood by most people, the mean can be very misleading if used as the sole measure of central tendency. If the data set has outliers (data values that are unusually high or unusually low compared to the rest of the data values), the mean can be very distorted, especially if the data set has a small number of values. If unusually high values are countered with unusually low values, the mean is not affected as much. For example, if five of twenty students in a class get a 100 on a test, but the other 15 students have an average of 60 on the same test, the class average would appear as 70. Whenever the mean is skewed by outliers, it is always a good idea to include the median as an alternate measure of central tendency.

A **weighted mean**, or weighted average, is a mean that uses "weighted" values. The formula is weighted mean $= \frac{w_1 x_1 + w_2 x_2 + w_3 x_3 \dots + w_n x_n}{w_1 + w_2 + w_3 + \dots + w_n}$. Weighted values, such as $w_1, w_2, w_3, \dots w_n$ are assigned to each member of the set $x_1, x_2, x_3, \dots x_n$. If calculating weighted mean, make sure a weight value for each member of the set is used.

MEDIAN

The **statistical median** is the value in the middle of the set of data. To find the median, list all data values in order from smallest to largest or from largest to smallest. Any value that is repeated in the set must be listed the number of times it appears. If there are an odd number of data values, the median is the value in the middle of the list. If there is an even number of data values, the median is the arithmetic mean of the two middle values.

223

For example, the median of the data set {88, 72, 61, 90, 97, 68, 88, 79, 86, 93, 97, 71, 80, 84, 88} is 86 since the ordered set is {61, 68, 71, 72, 79, 80, 84, **86**, 88, 88, 88, 90, 93, 97, 97}.

The big disadvantage of using the median as a measure of central tendency is that is relies solely on a value's relative size as compared to the other values in the set. When the individual values in a set of data are evenly dispersed, the median can be an accurate tool. However, if there is a group of rather large values or a group of rather small values that are not offset by a different group of values, the information that can be inferred from the median may not be accurate because the distribution of values is skewed.

> **Review Video: Mean, Median, and Mode**
> Visit mometrix.com/academy and enter code: 286207

MODE

The **statistical mode** is the data value that occurs the greatest number of times in the data set. It is possible to have exactly one mode, more than one mode, or no mode. To find the mode of a set of data, arrange the data like you do to find the median (all values in order, listing all multiples of data values). Count the number of times each value appears in the data set. If all values appear an equal number of times, there is no mode. If one value appears more than any other value, that value is the mode. If two or more values appear the same number of times, but there are other values that appear fewer times and no values that appear more times, all of those values are the modes.

For example, the mode of the data set {**88**, 72, 61, 90, 97, 68, **88**, 79, 86, 93, 97, 71, 80, 84, **88**} is 88.

The main disadvantage of the mode is that the values of the other data in the set have no bearing on the mode. The mode may be the largest value, the smallest value, or a value anywhere in between in the set. The mode only tells which value or values, if any, occurred the greatest number of times. It does not give any suggestions about the remaining values in the set.

> **Review Video: Mean, Median, and Mode**
> Visit mometrix.com/academy and enter code: 286207

DISPERSION

A **measure of dispersion** is a single value that helps to "interpret" the measure of central tendency by providing more information about how the data values in the set are distributed about the measure of central tendency. The measure of dispersion helps to eliminate or reduce the disadvantages of using the mean, median, or mode as a single measure of central tendency, and give a more accurate picture of the dataset as a whole. To have a measure of dispersion, you must know or calculate the range, standard deviation, or variance of the data set.

RANGE

The **range** of a set of data is the difference between the greatest and lowest values of the data in the set. To calculate the range, you must first make sure the units for all data values are the same, and then identify the greatest and lowest values. If there are multiple data values that are equal for the highest or lowest, just use one of the values in the formula. Write the answer with the same units as the data values you used to do the calculations.

> **Review Video: Statistical Range**
> Visit mometrix.com/academy and enter code: 778541

STANDARD DEVIATION

Standard deviation is a measure of dispersion that compares all the data values in the set to the mean of the set to give a more accurate picture. To find the standard deviation of a sample, use the formula

$$s = \sqrt{\frac{\sum_{i=1}^{n}(x_i - \bar{x})^2}{n-1}}$$

Note that s is the standard deviation of a sample, x represents the individual values in the data set, $\bar{x}$ is the mean of the data values in the set, and n is the number of data values in the set. The higher the value of the standard deviation is, the greater the variance of the data values from the mean. The units associated with the standard deviation are the same as the units of the data values.

> **Review Video: Standard Deviation**
> Visit mometrix.com/academy and enter code: 419469

VARIANCE

The **variance** of a sample, or just variance, is the square of the standard deviation of that sample. While the mean of a set of data gives the average of the set and gives information about where a specific data value lies in relation to the average, the variance of the sample gives information about the degree to which the data values are spread out and tells you how close an individual value is to the average compared to the other values. The units associated with variance are the same as the units of the data values squared.

PERCENTILE

Percentiles and quartiles are other methods of describing data within a set. **Percentiles** tell what percentage of the data in the set fall below a specific point. For example, achievement test scores are often given in percentiles. A score at the 80th percentile is one which is equal to or higher than 80 percent of the scores in the set. In other words, 80 percent of the scores were lower than that score.

Quartiles are percentile groups that make up quarter sections of the data set. The first quartile is the 25th percentile. The second quartile is the 50th percentile; this is also the median of the dataset. The third quartile is the 75th percentile.

SKEWNESS

Skewness is a way to describe the symmetry or asymmetry of the distribution of values in a dataset. If the distribution of values is symmetrical, there is no skew. In general the closer the mean of a data set is to the median of the data set, the less skew there is. Generally, if the mean is to the right of the median, the data set is *positively skewed*, or right-skewed, and if the mean is to the left of the median, the data set is *negatively skewed*, or left-skewed. However, this rule of thumb is not infallible. When the data values are graphed on a curve, a set with no skew will be a perfect bell curve.

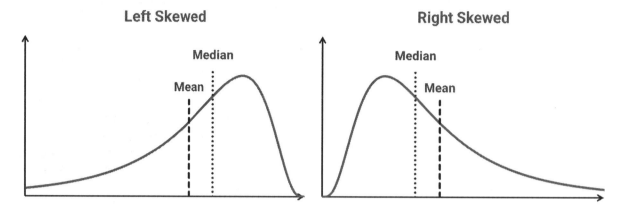

To estimate skew, use the formula:

$$\text{skew} = \frac{\sqrt{n(n-1)}}{n-2}\left(\frac{\frac{1}{n}\sum_{i=1}^{n}(x_i - \bar{x})^3}{\left(\frac{1}{n}\sum_{i=1}^{n}(x_i - \bar{x})^2\right)^{\frac{3}{2}}}\right)$$

Note that n is the datapoints in the set, x_i is the ith value in the set, and $\bar{x}$ is the mean of the set.

> **Review Video: Skew**
> Visit mometrix.com/academy and enter code: 661486

UNIMODAL VS. BIMODAL

If a distribution has a single peak, it would be considered **unimodal**. If it has two discernible peaks it would be considered **bimodal**. Bimodal distributions may be an indication that the set of data being considered is actually the combination of two sets of data with significant differences. A **uniform distribution** is a distribution in which there is *no distinct peak or variation* in the data. No values or ranges are particularly more common than any other values or ranges.

OUTLIER

An outlier is an extremely high or extremely low value in the data set. It may be the result of measurement error, in which case, the outlier is not a valid member of the data set. However, it may also be a valid member of the distribution. Unless a measurement error is identified, the experimenter cannot know for certain if an outlier is or is not a member of the distribution. There are arbitrary methods that can be employed to designate an extreme value as an outlier. One method designates an outlier (or possible outlier) to be any value less than $Q_1 - 1.5(IQR)$ or any value greater than $Q_3 + 1.5(IQR)$.

DATA ANALYSIS

SIMPLE REGRESSION

In statistics, **simple regression** is using an equation to represent a relation between independent and dependent variables. The independent variable is also referred to as the explanatory variable or the predictor and is generally represented by the variable x in the equation. The dependent variable, usually represented by the variable y, is also referred to as the response variable. The equation may be any type of function – linear, quadratic, exponential, etc. The best way to handle this task is to use the regression feature of your graphing calculator. This will easily give you the curve of best fit and provide you with the coefficients and other information you need to derive an equation.

LINE OF BEST FIT

In a scatter plot, the **line of best fit** is the line that best shows the trends of the data. The line of best fit is given by the equation $\hat{y} = ax + b$, where a and b are the regression coefficients. The regression coefficient a is also the slope of the line of best fit, and b is also the y-coordinate of the point at which the line of best fit crosses the y-axis. Not every point on the scatter plot will be on the line of best fit. The differences between the y-values of the points in the scatter plot and the corresponding y-values according to the equation of the line of best fit are the residuals. The line of best fit is also called the least-squares regression line because it is also the line that has the lowest sum of the squares of the residuals.

CORRELATION COEFFICIENT

The **correlation coefficient** is the numerical value that indicates how strong the relationship is between the two variables of a linear regression equation. A correlation coefficient of –1 is a perfect negative correlation. A correlation coefficient of +1 is a perfect positive correlation. Correlation coefficients close to –1 or +1 are very strong correlations. A correlation coefficient equal to zero indicates there is no correlation between the two variables. This test is a good indicator of whether or not the equation for the line of best fit is accurate. The formula for the correlation coefficient is

$$r = \frac{\sum_{i=1}^{n}(x_i - \bar{x})(y_i - \bar{y})}{\sqrt{\sum_{i=1}^{n}(x_i - \bar{x})^2}\sqrt{\sum_{i=1}^{n}(y_i - \bar{y})^2}}$$

where r is the correlation coefficient, n is the number of data values in the set, (x_i, y_i) is a point in the set, and $\bar{x}$ and $\bar{y}$ are the means.

Z-SCORE

A **z-score** is an indication of how many standard deviations a given value falls from the mean. To calculate a z-score, use the formula:

$$\frac{x - \mu}{\sigma}$$

x is the data value, μ is the mean of the data set, and σ is the standard deviation of the population. If the z-score is positive, the data value lies above the mean. If the z-score is negative, the data value falls below the mean. These scores are useful in interpreting data such as standardized test scores, where every piece of data in the set has been counted, rather than just a small random sample. In cases where standard deviations are calculated from a random sample of the set, the z-scores will not be as accurate.

CENTRAL LIMIT THEOREM

According to the **central limit theorem**, regardless of what the original distribution of a sample is, the distribution of the means tends to get closer and closer to a normal distribution as the sample size gets larger and larger (this is necessary because the sample is becoming more all-encompassing of the elements of the population). As the sample size gets larger, the distribution of the sample mean will approach a normal distribution with a mean of the population mean and a variance of the population variance divided by the sample size.

PRACTICE

P1. Suppose the class average on a final exam is 87, with a standard deviation of 2 points. Find the z-score of a student that got an 82.

P2. Given the following graph, determine the range of patient ages:

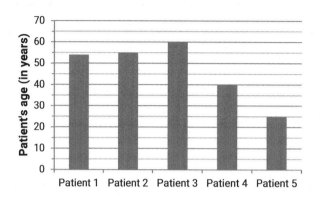

P3. Calculate the sample variance for the dataset $\{10, 13, 12, 5, 8, 18\}$

PRACTICE SOLUTIONS

P1. Using the formula for z-score: $z = \frac{82-87}{2} = -2.5$

P2. Patient 1 is 54 years old; Patient 2 is 55 years old; Patient 3 is 60 years old; Patient 4 is 40 years old; and Patient 5 is 25 years old. The range of patient ages is the age of the oldest patient minus the age of the youngest patient. In other words, $60 - 25 = 35$. The range of ages is 35 years.

P3. To find the variance, first find the mean:

$$\frac{10 + 13 + 12 + 5 + 8 + 18}{6} = \frac{66}{6} = 11$$

Now, apply the formula for sample variance:

$$
\begin{aligned}
s^2 &= \frac{\sum_{i=1}^{n}(x_i - \bar{x})^2}{n-1} = \frac{\sum_{i=1}^{6}(x_i - 11)^2}{6-1} \\
&= \frac{(10-11)^2 + (13-11)^2 + (12-11)^2 + (5-11)^2 + (8-11)^2 + (18-11)^2}{5} \\
&= \frac{(-1)^2 + 2^2 + 1^2 + (-6)^2 + (-3)^2 + 7^2}{5} \\
&= \frac{1 + 4 + 1 + 36 + 9 + 49}{5} \\
&= \frac{100}{5} = 20
\end{aligned}
$$

Displaying Information

FREQUENCY TABLES

Frequency tables show how frequently each unique value appears in a set. A **relative frequency table** is one that shows the proportions of each unique value compared to the entire set. Relative frequencies are given as percentages; however, the total percent for a relative frequency table will not necessarily equal 100 percent due to rounding. An example of a frequency table with relative frequencies is below.

Favorite Color	Frequency	Relative Frequency
Blue	4	13%
Red	7	22%
Green	3	9%
Purple	6	19%
Cyan	12	38%

Review Video: Data Interpretation of Graphs
Visit mometrix.com/academy and enter code: 200439

CIRCLE GRAPHS

Circle graphs, also known as *pie charts*, provide a visual depiction of the relationship of each type of data compared to the whole set of data. The circle graph is divided into sections by drawing radii to create central angles whose percentage of the circle is equal to the individual data's percentage of the whole set. Each 1% of data is equal to 3.6° in the circle graph. Therefore, data represented by a 90° section of the circle graph makes up 25% of the whole. When complete, a circle graph often looks like a pie cut into uneven wedges. The pie chart below shows the data from the frequency table referenced earlier where people were asked their favorite color.

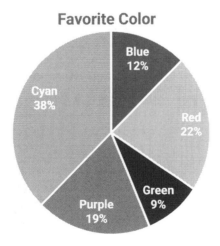

Favorite Color

PICTOGRAPHS

A **pictograph** is a graph, generally in the horizontal orientation, that uses pictures or symbols to represent the data. Each pictograph must have a key that defines the picture or symbol and gives the quantity each picture or symbol represents. Pictures or symbols on a pictograph are not always shown as whole elements. In this case, the fraction of the picture or symbol shown represents the same fraction of the quantity a whole picture or symbol stands for. For example, a row with $3\frac{1}{2}$ ears

229

of corn, where each ear of corn represents 100 stalks of corn in a field, would equal $3\frac{1}{2} \times 100 = 350$ stalks of corn in the field.

LINE GRAPHS

Line graphs have one or more lines of varying styles (solid or broken) to show the different values for a set of data. The individual data are represented as ordered pairs, much like on a Cartesian plane. In this case, the x- and y-axes are defined in terms of their units, such as dollars or time. The individual plotted points are joined by line segments to show whether the value of the data is increasing (line sloping upward), decreasing (line sloping downward), or staying the same (horizontal line). Multiple sets of data can be graphed on the same line graph to give an easy visual comparison. An example of this would be graphing achievement test scores for different groups of students over the same time period to see which group had the greatest increase or decrease in performance from year to year (as shown below).

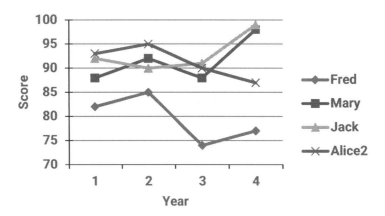

LINE PLOTS

A **line plot**, also known as a *dot plot*, has plotted points that are not connected by line segments. In this graph, the horizontal axis lists the different possible values for the data, and the vertical axis lists the number of times the individual value occurs. A single dot is graphed for each value to show the number of times it occurs. This graph is more closely related to a bar graph than a line graph. Do not connect the dots in a line plot or it will misrepresent the data.

STEM AND LEAF PLOTS

A **stem and leaf plot** is useful for depicting groups of data that fall into a range of values. Each piece of data is separated into two parts: the first, or left, part is called the stem; the second, or right, part is called the leaf. Each stem is listed in a column from smallest to largest. Each leaf that has the common stem is listed in that stem's row from smallest to largest. For example, in a set of two-digit numbers, the digit in the tens place is the stem, and the digit in the ones place is the leaf. With a stem and leaf plot, you can easily see which subset of numbers (10s, 20s, 30s, etc.) is the largest. This information is also readily available by looking at a histogram, but a stem and leaf plot also allows you to look closer and see exactly which values fall in that range. Using all of the test scores from above, we can assemble a stem and leaf plot like the one below.

Test Scores

7	4	8						
8	2	5	7	8	8			
9	0	0	1	2	2	3	5	8	9

BAR GRAPHS

A **bar graph** is one of the few graphs that can be drawn correctly in two different configurations – both horizontally and vertically. A bar graph is similar to a line plot in the way the data is organized on the graph. Both axes must have their categories defined for the graph to be useful. Rather than placing a single dot to mark the point of the data's value, a bar, or thick line, is drawn from zero to the exact value of the data, whether it is a number, percentage, or other numerical value. Longer bar lengths correspond to greater data values. To read a bar graph, read the labels for the axes to find the units being reported. Then, look where the bars end in relation to the scale given on the corresponding axis and determine the associated value.

The bar chart below represents the responses from our favorite-color survey.

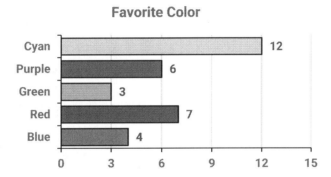

HISTOGRAMS

At first glance, a **histogram** looks like a vertical bar graph. The difference is that a bar graph has a separate bar for each piece of data and a histogram has one continuous bar for each *range* of data. For example, a histogram may have one bar for the range 0–9, one bar for 10–19, etc. While a bar graph has numerical values on one axis, a histogram has numerical values on both axes. Each range is of equal size, and they are ordered left to right from lowest to highest. The height of each column on a histogram represents the number of data values within that range. Like a stem and leaf plot, a histogram makes it easy to glance at the graph and quickly determine which range has the greatest quantity of values. A simple example of a histogram is below.

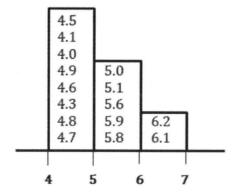

BIVARIATE DATA

Bivariate data is simply data from two different variables. (The prefix *bi-* means *two*.) In a *scatter plot*, each value in the set of data is plotted on a grid similar to a Cartesian plane, where each axis represents one of the two variables. By looking at the pattern formed by the points on the grid, you can often determine whether or not there is a relationship between the two variables, and what that relationship is, if it exists. The variables may be directly proportionate, inversely proportionate, or show no proportion at all. It may also be possible to determine if the data is linear, and if so, to find an equation to relate the two variables. The following scatter plot shows the relationship between preference for brand "A" and the age of the consumers surveyed.

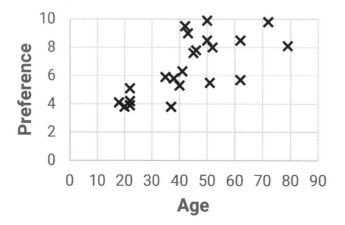

SCATTER PLOTS

Scatter plots are also useful in determining the type of function represented by the data and finding the simple regression. Linear scatter plots may be positive or negative. Nonlinear scatter plots are generally exponential or quadratic. Below are some common types of scatter plots:

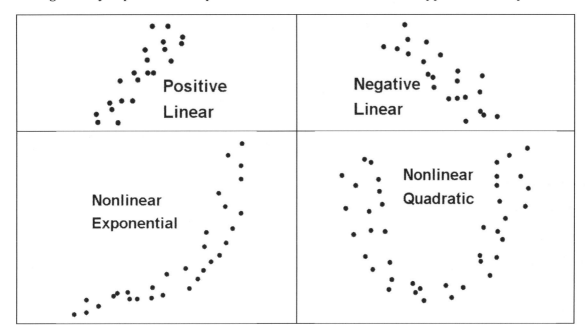

5-NUMBER SUMMARY

The **5-number summary** of a set of data gives a very informative picture of the set. The five numbers in the summary include the minimum value, maximum value, and the three quartiles. This information gives the reader the range and median of the set, as well as an indication of how the data is spread about the median.

BOX AND WHISKER PLOTS

A **box-and-whisker plot** is a graphical representation of the 5-number summary. To draw a box-and-whisker plot, plot the points of the 5-number summary on a number line. Draw a box whose ends are through the points for the first and third quartiles. Draw a vertical line in the box through the median to divide the box in half. Draw a line segment from the first quartile point to the minimum value and from the third quartile point to the maximum value.

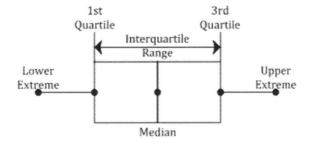

68-95-99.7 RULE

The **68–95–99.7 rule** describes how a normal distribution of data should appear when compared to the mean. This is also a description of a normal bell curve. According to this rule, 68 percent of the data values in a normally distributed set should fall within one standard deviation of the mean (34 percent above and 34 percent below the mean), 95 percent of the data values should fall within two standard deviations of the mean (47.5 percent above and 47.5 percent below the mean), and 99.7 percent of the data values should fall within three standard deviations of the mean, again, equally distributed on either side of the mean. This means that only 0.3 percent of all data values should fall more than three standard deviations from the mean. On the graph below, the normal curve is centered on the y-axis. The x-axis labels are how many standard deviations away from the center you are. Therefore, it is easy to see how the 68-95-99.7 rule can apply.

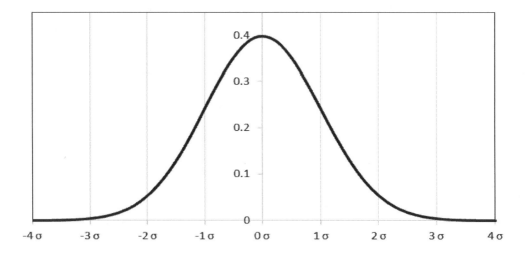

CBEST Practice Test

Want to take this practice test in an online interactive format?
Check out the bonus page, which includes interactive practice questions and much more: **http://www.mometrix.com/bonus948/cbest**

SCAN HERE

Mathematics

1. Which of the following would NOT satisfy $x \geq \frac{2}{5}$?

   a. $x = \frac{5}{11}$

   b. $x = \frac{3}{7}$

   c. $x = \frac{1}{2}$

   d. $x = \frac{1}{3}$

   e. $x = \frac{7}{15}$

2. Which of the following statements is true?

   a.   -6 is to the right of -5 on the number line.
   b.   -7 is to the left of -2 on the number line.
   c.   0 is to the right of 5 on the number line.
   d.   0 is to the left of -1 on the number line.
   e.   7 is to the left of -2 on the number line.

3. Consider the number set {-1, 19, -5, 0, 15.3, 15.05, -3}. Which of the following choices shows the number set in order from least to greatest?

   a.   -1, -3, -5, 0, 15.05, 15.3, 19
   b.   -1, -3, -5, 0, 15.3, 15.05, 19
   c.   -5, -3, -1, 0, 15.05, 15.3, 19
   d.   0, -1, -3, -5 15.05, 15.3, 19
   e.   0, -5, -3, -1, 15.05, 15.3, 19

4. Giselle is selling notebooks at the school store. She earns $45.00 for selling 30 notebooks. How much is Giselle charging for each notebook?

   a. $135.00
   b. $3.00
   c. $1.25
   d. $3.50
   e. $1.50

5. Krystal purchased a pair of sunglasses for $19.99 and a scarf for $27.50. She paid with a $50.00 bill. How much change did she receive?

    a. $47.49
    b. $17.49
    c. $3.61
    d. $2.99
    e. $2.51

6. The candy store charges $1.30 per pound. Artie's bag of candy weighs 2.1 pounds. How much will Artie have to pay for his candy?

    a. $2.73
    b. $3.40
    c. $27.30
    d. $5.40
    e. $0.80

7. Which of the following is equivalent to $5^3 + 18 \div 3$?

    a. 21
    b. 131
    c. $48\frac{2}{3}$
    d. 137
    e. 37

8. Find the value of $100 \div (9 + 1) \times 2$.

    a. 20
    b. 5
    c. 15
    d. 80
    e. 76

9. Simplify the expression $(10 + 4 \times 3) \div 2$.

    a. 22
    b. 21
    c. 6
    d. 20
    e. 11

10. A triangle has angles measuring 40°, 100°, and 40°. Its sides measure 15 inches, 19 inches, and 15 inches. Which of the following choices accurately describes the triangle?

    a. It is an acute equilateral triangle.
    b. It is an acute scalene triangle.
    c. It is an obtuse isosceles triangle.
    d. It is an acute scalene triangle.
    e. It is an acute isosceles triangle.

11. Which of the following choices best describes a three-dimensional figure comprised of only one square base and four triangular sides?

    a. Square prism
    b. Triangular prism
    c. Triangular pyramid
    d. Square pyramid
    e. Octahedron

12. A recipe calls for 2 cups of water for every 6 cups of flour. Josie wants to make a smaller batch using only two cups of flour. How much water should she use?

    a. $\frac{1}{2}$ cup
    b. 2 cups
    c. $\frac{2}{3}$ cup
    d. $2\frac{2}{3}$ cups
    e. 12 cups

13. A scaled drawing for a new building has walls measuring 4 inches in height. The key indicates that each inch on the drawing represents 2 feet in real life. Based on the scaled drawing, how tall will the actual walls measure?

    a. 8 feet
    b. 4 feet
    c. 32 feet
    d. 21 feet
    e. 12 feet

14. The ratio of boys to girls in a math class is 3 to 4. If there are 12 boys in the class, how many total students are in the class?

    a. 28 students
    b. 16 students
    c. 7 students
    d. 19 students
    e. 24 students

15. Justin wants to re-carpet his rectangular bedroom. The bedroom has a length of 12 feet and a width of 10 feet. Which of the following measures should Justin calculate to determine the amount of carpet he will need?

    a. Justin should calculate the perimeter of his bedroom.
    b. Justin should calculate the area of the floor of his bedroom.
    c. Justin should calculate the volume of his bedroom.
    d. Justin should calculate the circumference of his bedroom.
    e. Justin should calculate the surface area of his bedroom.

16. A Tyrannosaurus Rex is believed to have weighed 18,000 pounds. How can this weight be represented in scientific notation?

a. 18×10^4 lb
b. 1.8×10^{-4} lb
c. 1.8×10^4 lb
d. 1.8×10^3 lb
e. 18×10^{-4} lb

17. Andre is traveling at a speed of 65 miles per hour. At this rate, how long will it take Andre to travel 195 miles?

a. 585 minutes
b. 3.25 hours
c. 4.5 hours
d. 2 hours and 10 minutes
e. 3 hours

18. One inch is equivalent to 2.54 centimeters. How long, in centimeters, is a stick measuring 9.5 inches?

a. 241.3 centimeters
b. 24.13 centimeters
c. 12.70 centimeters
d. 18.55 centimeters
e. 3.7 centimeters

19. Hector's car holds 12 gallons of gasoline. He filled his tank for $22.44. Assuming Hector's tank was completely empty when he filled up, how much money did Hector pay per gallon for gasoline?

a. $1.87
b. $269.28
c. $18.70
d. $2.22
e. $2.05

20. Identify the property that has been applied to simplify the expression $4(5 + 8) = 20 + 32$.

a. The commutative property
b. The associative property
c. The distributive property
d. The multiplicative identity property
e. The multiplication property of zero

21. Which of the following expressions is equivalent to the expression $(17 + 18) + 2$ according to the associative property?

a. $35 + 2$
b. $(18 + 17) + 2$
c. $17 + 2(9 + 1)$
d. $17 + (18 + 2)$
e. $17 + 20$

22. Jackie and Jessie collect 12 seashells each. They decide to paint and sell their shells to earn some extra spending money. Jackie sells her shells for $1.00 each, while Jessie charges $1.25 per shell. Which of the following expressions can be used to determine the total amount of money the girls will earn, assuming they each sell all of their shells?

    a. $(12 \times \$1.25) \times 2$
    b. $(12 \times \$1.00) + (12 \times \$1.25)$
    c. $(12 \times \$1.00) \times (12 \times \$1.25)$
    d. $(24 \times \$2.25)$
    e. $(6 \times \$1.00) + (6 \times \$1.25)$

23. Connor and Pete have decided to split their tips equally. Connor earned $48.00 in tips, while Pete earned $62.00. Which of the following expressions can be used to find the amount of money each of them should receive if they are splitting their tips equally?

    a. $\$48.00 + \$62.00 \div 2$
    b. $(\$48.00 + \$62.00) \div 2$
    c. $(\$48.00 + \$62.00) \times 2$
    d. $(\$62.00 - \$48.00) \div 2$
    e. $\$62.00 - \$48.00 \div 2$

24. Solve for x if $5x + 12 = 72$.

    a. $x = 2.4$
    b. $x = 26.4$
    c. $x = 60$
    d. $x = 17$
    e. $x = 12$

25. Solve for y when $\frac{y}{2} - 8 = 0$.

    a. $y = 4$
    b. $y = 8$
    c. $y = 2$
    d. $y = 16$
    e. $y = 6$

26. Consider the inequality $6x + 8 \leq 56$. Which of the following choices is a solution for the inequality?

    a. $x \geq 8$
    b. $x = 8$
    c. $x \leq 48$
    d. $x \leq 8$
    e. $x \geq 48$

27. Joanie is four more than two times older than Robbie. If Joanie's age (j) is 56 years old, which of the following equations can be used to determine Robbie's age (r)?

    a. If $j = 4 + 2r$, then $r = 52$
    b. If $j = 4r$, then $r = 14$
    c. If $j = 4 + 2r$, then $r = 26$
    d. If $j = 4 + r$, then $r = 26$
    e. If $j = 4 + r$, then $r = 52$

28. Susie's class has three less than half the number of students enrolled in Ana's class. If Susie has 14 students in her class (s), which of the following equations best describes the number of students enrolled in Ana's class (a)?

    a. If $2a + 3 = s$, then $a = 22$
    b. If $\frac{a}{2} + 3 = s$, then $a = 7$
    c. If $\frac{a}{2} + 3 = s$, then $a = 31$
    d. If $2a - 3 = s$, then $a = 8$
    e. If $\frac{a}{2} - 3 = s$, then $a = 34$

29. Marlon pays \$45 for a jacket that has been marked down 25%. What was the original cost of the jacket?

    a. \$80
    b. \$75
    c. \$65
    d. \$70
    e. \$60

30. Which of the following statements is true?

    a. A number is divisible by 6 if the number is divisible by both 2 and 3.
    b. A number is divisible by 4 if the sum of all digits is divisible by 8.
    c. A number is divisible by 3 if the last digit is divisible by 3.
    d. A number is divisible by 9 if it is not even.
    e. A number is divisible by 7 if the sum of the last two digits is divisible by 7.

31. Which of the following is an irrational number?

    a. $4.\overline{2}$
    b. $\sqrt{2}$
    c. $\frac{4}{5}$
    d. 1.00000000007
    e. $\frac{21}{5}$

32. What is the constant of proportionality represented by the table below?

x	y
2	−8
5	−20
7	−28
10	−40
11	−44

    a. +12
    b. −8
    c. −6
    d. +8
    e. −4

33. What is the area of the shaded region in the figure shown below?

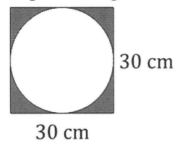

30 cm

30 cm

   a. 177 cm^2
   b. 181 cm^2
   c. 187 cm^2
   d. 190 cm^2
   e. 193 cm^2

34. Kendra uses the pie chart below to represent the allocation of her annual income. Her annual income is $40,000.

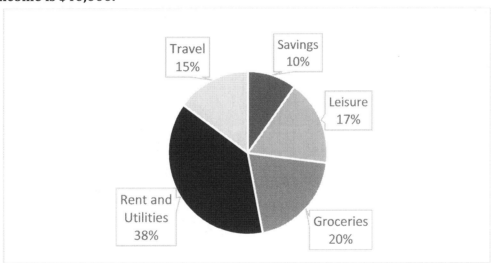

Which of the following statements is true?

   a.   The amount of money she spends on travel and savings is more than $11,000.
   b.   The amount of money she spends on rent and utilities is approximately $15,000.
   c.   The amount of money she spends on groceries and savings is more than $13,000.
   d.   The amount of money she spends on travel and leisure is more than $17,000.
   e.   The amount of money she spends on leisure is less than $5,000.

35. Based on the bar graph below, determine the number of students that were surveyed.

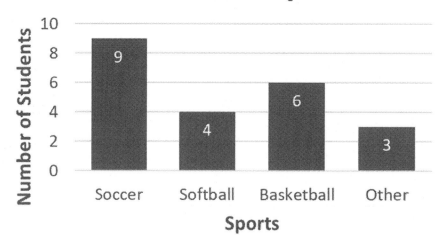

a. 9 students
b. 23 students
c. 19 students
d. 22 students
e. 15 students

36. A teacher asked her students how many hours of television they watched over the weekend. The results are displayed below. How many students watched more than 8 hours of television over the weekend?

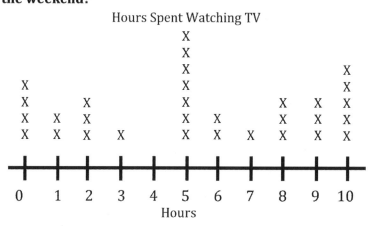

a. 3 students
b. 8 students
c. 11 students
d. 31 students
e. 20 students

37. Based on the histogram below, how many students scored 75 points or fewer on the math test?

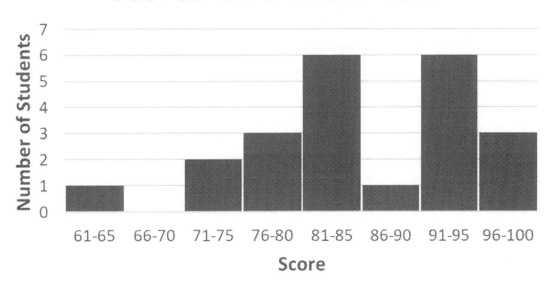

Scores on a Math Test

a. 3 students
b. 2 students
c. 0 students
d. 19 students
e. 6 students

38. Which of the following choices could display data in a misleading way?
    a. Starting the *y*-axis at zero, even when dealing with very large numbers
    b. Listing categorical data in alphabetical order along the *x*-axis
    c. Choosing very small intervals for the *y*-axis to exaggerate differences in data
    d. Letting the number of data points determine the number of bins for a histogram
    e. Including all data collected, even if it is not consistent with the outcome you were hoping for

39. Find the mean of the data set {76, 193, 83, 43, 105}.
    a. 500
    b. 100
    c. 83
    d. 80
    e. 150

40. Consider the data set {196, 832, 736, 271, and 573}. Which of the following best describes the range of the data set?
    a. 377
    b. 636
    c. 1,028
    d. 5
    e. 573

41. Identify the median for the data set {53, 81, 85, 82, 91, 72}.

    a. 81.5

    b. 81

    c. 77

    d. 38

    e. 83.5

42. Find the mode(s) of the data set {84, 29, 84, 93, 93, 84, 39, 84, 29, 93, 93, 29}.

    a. 84

    b. 93

    c. 29

    d. 84 and 93

    e. 29, 84, and 93

43. Kylie describes the mode of the data set {67, 29, 57, 27, 38, 91} as zero. Which option best explains Kylie's interpretation of the data?

    a. Kylie is correct because there is no value that occurs more than any other value so our mode is zero.

    b. Kylie is incorrect because 27 and 29 can be averaged to find a mode of 28.

    c. Kyle is correct because when we add all of our numbers and divide by 6 we get zero.

    d. Kylie is incorrect because zero is not a value in the data set, therefore it cannot be the mode.

    e. Kylie is incorrect because zero is never a valid mode for a data set.

44. Find and interpret the range for the data set {78, 29, 57, 10, 3, 84}.

    a. The range of the data set is 6, which means that the values differ by a maximum of 6.

    b. The range of the data set is 43.5, which means the average value in the set is 43.5.

    c. The range of the data set is 81, which means the values of the set differ by no more than 81 units.

    d. The range of the data set is 13.5, which means that the standard deviation is less than 13.5.

    e. The range of the data set is 43, which means the middle number is 43.

45. Marielle says the best descriptor of the data set {67, 2, 67, 73, 85, 60, 68} is the range. Choose the option that best describes Marielle's error.

    a. Marielle is incorrect because the range should never be used to describe a data set.

    b. Marielle is incorrect because this data set has an outlier.

    c. Marielle is incorrect because the mean is always the best choice for describing a data set.

    d. Marielle is incorrect because the median is best for a data set this small.

    e. Marielle is incorrect because the range for this data set is too small.

46. Joe plans to flip two coins. Which of the following choices demonstrates using the counting principle to determine the probability of both coins landing on tails?

    a. $\frac{1}{2}$

    b. TT, TH, HT, HH

    c. 2×2

    d. $2 + 2$

    e. $\frac{1}{2} \times \frac{1}{2}$

47. Aniyah has two pairs of jeans and three shirts. How many different outfits can she create, assuming each outfit consists of one pair of jeans and a shirt?

    a. 9 outfits
    b. 5 outfits
    c. 6 outfits
    d. 8 outfits
    e. 12 outfits

48. An ice-cream shop offers sundaes that include a choice of an ice cream flavor, a topping, and a sauce (either hot fudge or caramel). The different ice cream flavors are chocolate, vanilla, and strawberry. The choices of toppings are sprinkles and cherries. Which of the following tree diagrams correctly shows the total number of ice-cream sundaes that could be created using one flavor of ice cream, one topping, and either hot fudge or caramel?

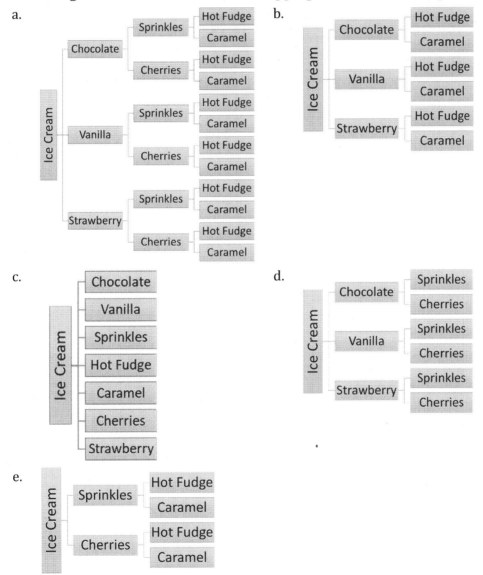

49. A bag contains 5 red marbles, 4 green marbles, and 3 yellow marbles. What is the probability that Fran pulls a red marble, keeps that marble in her possession, and then pulls a green marble?

a. $\dfrac{5}{36}$

b. $\dfrac{1}{6}$

c. $\dfrac{7}{132}$

d. $\dfrac{5}{33}$

e. $\dfrac{4}{11}$

50. Everyone in a class has blue, green, or brown eyes. 40% of the students have brown eyes and 90% of the other students have blue eyes. What can we infer from this information?

a. We can infer that there is a majority of students with brown eyes.
b. We can infer that there is a majority of students with blue eyes.
c. We can infer that there is a majority of students with green eyes.
d. We can infer that there is an equal number of students with each eye color.
e. We cannot infer anything from this information.

Reading

Directions: Use the following passage to answer questions 1-10.

"So that Nobody Has to Go to School if They Don't Want to"

An Excerpt by Roger Sipher

A decline in standardized test scores is but the most recent indicator that American education is in trouble. One reason for the crisis is that present mandatory-attendance laws force many to attend school that have no wish to be there. Such children have little desire to learn and are so antagonistic to school that neither they nor more highly motivated students receive the quality education that is the birthright of every American. The solution to this problem is simple: Abolish compulsory-attendance laws and allow only those who are committed to getting an education to attend.

Most parents want a high school education for their children. Unfortunately, compulsory attendance hampers the ability of public school officials to enforce legitimate educational and disciplinary policies and thereby make the education a good one. Private schools have no such problem. They can fail or dismiss students, knowing such students can attend public school. Without compulsory attendance, public schools would be freer to oust students whose academic or personal behavior undermines the educational mission of the institution.

Abolition of archaic attendance laws would produce enormous dividends:

- First, it would alert everyone that school is a serious place where one goes to learn. Schools are neither day-care centers nor indoor street corners. Young people who resist learning should stay away; indeed, an end to compulsory schooling would require them to stay away.
- Second, students opposed to learning would not be able to pollute the educational atmosphere for those who want to learn. Teachers could stop policing recalcitrant students and start educating.
- Third, grades would show what they are supposed to: how well a student is learning. Parents could again read report cards and know if their children were making progress.
- Fourth, public esteem for schools would increase. People would stop regarding them as way stations for adolescents and start thinking of them as institutions for educating America's youth.
- Fifth, elementary schools would change because students would find out early they had better learn something or risk flunking out later. Elementary teachers would no longer have to pass their failures on to junior high and high school.
- Sixth, the cost of enforcing compulsory education would be eliminated. Despite enforcement efforts, nearly 15 percent of the school-age children in our largest cities are almost permanently absent from school.

Communities could use these savings to support institutions to deal with young people not in school. If, in the long run, these institutions prove more costly, at least we would not confuse their mission with that of schools. Schools should be for education. At present, they are only tangentially so. They have attempted to serve an all-encompassing social function, trying to be all things to all people. In the process they have failed miserably at what they were originally formed to accomplish.

1. Which of the following statements supports the conclusion that abolishing mandatory attendance laws would prove economical for school districts?

    a. It would eliminate the misconception that schools are day-care centers or indoor street corners.

    b. Public esteem for schools would increase.

    c. The cost of enforcing compulsory education would be eliminated.

    d. Report cards would reflect how well a student is learning.

    e. Students who are motivated to learn would receive a more fulfilling education.

2. Which of the following statements would the author most likely agree with?

    a. The longer students attend school, the more productive the community will be.

    b. Schools should be responsible for providing students with extracurricular opportunities.

    c. Truancy officers should be doubled in districts with low attendance rates.

    d. Report cards should reflect the effort of a student, rather than the ability of that student.

    e. Students should not be forced or entitled to an education.

3. According to the author, abolishing attendance laws would allow school districts the freedom to _____.

    a. provide counseling to students with poor attendance

    b. fail or dismiss students who have attendance or discipline issues, which disrupt the education of others

    c. provide transportation to students unwilling to attend school

    d. move students from elementary to middle school without proof that learning has occurred

    e. provide scholarships for the highest performing students

4. Which of the following is an assumption made by the author?

    a. Private schools can choose to fail or dismiss students.

    b. Nearly 15 percent of the school-age children in our largest cities are almost permanently absent from school.

    c. If we can improve student attendance, we can improve standardized test scores.

    d. Most parents want a high school education for their children.

    e. Schools were originally formed to serve all adolescents.

5. Choose the option that best describes the central idea of the passage.

    a. Standardized test scores would increase if teachers could fail or dismiss students.

    b. Schools are intended to educate adolescents, not replace day-care centers or give adolescents a place to socialize.

    c. Report cards should communicate with parents how well a student is learning.

    d. Private schools have an easier time with absenteeism than public schools.

    e. Abolishing mandatory attendance laws would create better school environments for the students with a genuine desire to learn.

6. Which of the following best summarizes the first paragraph?

    a. American education is in trouble.

    b. Students with little desire to learn are often absent.

    c. Abolishing the mandatory attendance laws would improve the quality of education in schools.

    d. Standardized test scores are the best indicator of student success.

    e. Neither highly motivated students or highly unmotivated students are properly educated.

7. Which of the following statements LEAST supports the main idea of the passage?

   a. School is a serious place where one goes to learn.
   b. Students opposed to learning would not be able to pollute the educational atmosphere for those who want to learn.
   c. Grades would show what they are supposed to: how well a student is learning.
   d. Public esteem for schools would increase.
   e. Current truancy laws do not promote the original purpose of public education.

8. According to the text, what effect do mandatory attendance laws have on the esteem of schools?

   a. These laws prove that schools have the right to force education on all minors.
   b. These laws undermine the integrity of schools.
   c. These laws allow students to choose their own path of education.
   d. These laws provide teachers with freedom to grade and dismiss as they see fit.
   e. These laws allow promote every student's opportunity for quality education.

9. What can we infer from the text?

   a. The author believes that school districts should reexamine their procedures for standardized testing.
   b. The author believes that all students deserve an equal amount of attention from the teacher.
   c. The author believes that stricter attendance laws would improve classroom dynamics.
   d. The author believes that education is a privilege, not a right.
   e. The author believes that current truancy laws are effective and should not change.

10. Which of the following is a synonym of the word, "recalcitrant," as used in Paragraph 3?

   a. Absent
   b. Organized
   c. Disobedient
   d. Responsible
   e. Unintelligent

Directions: Use the following passage to answer questions 11-20.

> In 1603, Queen Elizabeth I of England died. She had never married and had no heir, so the throne passed to a distant relative: James Stuart, the son of Elizabeth's cousin and one-time rival for the throne, Mary, Queen of Scots. James was crowned King James I of England. At the time, he was also King James VI of Scotland, and the combination of roles would create a spirit of conflict that haunted the two nations for generations to come.

> The conflict developed as a result of rising tensions among the people within the nations, as well as between them. Scholars in the 21st century are far too hasty in dismissing the role of religion in political disputes, but religion undoubtedly played a role in the problems that faced England and Scotland. By the time of James Stuart's succession to the English throne, the English people had firmly embraced the teachings of Protestant theology. Similarly, the Scottish Lowlands were decisively Protestant. In the Scottish Highlands, however, the clans retained their Catholic faith. James acknowledged the Church of England and sanctioned the largely Protestant translation of the Bible that still bears his name.

James's son King Charles I proved himself to be less committed to the Protestant Church of England. Charles married the Catholic Princess Henrietta Maria of France, and there were suspicions among the English and the Lowland Scots that Charles was quietly a Catholic. Charles's own political troubles extended beyond religion in this case, and he was beheaded in 1649. Eventually, his son King Charles II would be crowned, and this Charles is believed to have converted secretly to the Catholic Church. Charles II died without a legitimate heir, and his brother James ascended to the throne as King James II.

James was recognized to be a practicing Catholic, and his commitment to Catholicism would prove to be his downfall. James's wife Mary Beatrice lost a number of children during their infancy, and when she became pregnant again in 1687, the public became concerned. If James had a son, that son would undoubtedly be raised a Catholic, and the English people would not stand for this. Mary gave birth to a son, but a story quickly circulated that the royal child had died, and the child named James's heir was a foundling smuggled in. James, his wife, and his infant son were forced to flee; and James's Protestant daughter Mary was crowned the queen.

In spite of a strong resemblance to the king, the young James was generally rejected among the English and the Lowland Scots, who referred to him as "the Pretender." But in the Highlands the Catholic princeling was welcomed. He inspired a group known as Jacobites, to reflect the Latin version of his name. His own son Charles, known affectionately as Bonnie Prince Charlie, would eventually raise an army and attempt to recapture what he believed to be his throne. The movement was soundly defeated at the Battle of Culloden in 1746, and England and Scotland have remained Protestant ever since.

11. According to the author, the tension between England and Scotland stemmed from what issue?
   a. Politics
   b. Rivalry within the royal families
   c. Religion
   d. Boundary disputes
   e. Economics

12. According to the text, who was the successor of Queen Elizabeth I?
   a. King Charles I
   b. James Stuart
   c. King James II
   d. Queen Mary
   e. King Charles II

13. Which of the following best summarizes paragraph 4?

    a.   The English were determined to convince the son of King James to bring Catholicism to England.

    b.   The son of King James died tragically as an infant, leaving no heir to the throne.

    c.   James and his wife had only one surviving child, a daughter named Mary.

    d.   The English feared that the son of King James would be raised Catholic, causing them to fabricate a story of his death and create a rumor of an illegitimate heir to the throne.

    e.   Mary became the queen because she was a Protestant, unlike her parents and siblings.

14. Which of the following best compares the religious beliefs of the Scottish Highlands and Lowlands?

    a.   Scotland was devoutly Protestant in both the Highlands and Lowlands.

    b.   The Highlands were devoutly Protestant, while the Lowlands embraced Catholicism.

    c.   The Highlands were devoutly Catholic, and the Lowlands were accepting of either religion.

    d.   Scotland embraced Catholicism in both the Highlands and the Lowlands.

    e.   The Highlands were accepting of Catholicism, while the Lowlands were devoutly Protestant.

15. Which of the following choices best describes the relationship between King James I of England and King James VI of Scotland?

    a.   They were cousins.

    b.   They were brothers.

    c.   King James VI was the successor of King James I.

    d.   King James I was the father of King James VI.

    e.   They were the same person.

16. Which of the following is a synonym for the term "foundling" as used in paragraph 4?

    a.   Orphan

    b.   Distant relative

    c.   Son

    d.   Foreigner

    e.   Impersonator

17. What can we infer from the text?

    a.   Queen Elizabeth I died at a young age.

    b.   King Charles I was not a devout Protestant.

    c.   King James II was committed to his family.

    d.   King James II was crowned after his brother, King Charles II, died.

    e.   James Stuart supported the Protestant faith in England.

18. According to the text, which statement best supports the author's claim that the downfall of King James II was due to his belief in Catholicism?

    a.   He was beheaded for forming the group known as the "Jacobites."

    b.   The fear of a Catholic king caused the English to create rumors of an illegitimate son, forcing James to flee England.

    c.   He was killed in the Battle of Culloden in 1746.

    d.   His wife lost a number of infants, causing a strain in their relationship.

    e.   He was the first in his family to embrace Catholicism, so he was forced to flee England.

19. Which of the following best describes the term "Jacobites"?
   a. A group of Catholics inspired by the young son of King James II
   b. A group of Protestants inspired by the young son of King James II
   c. A group of Protestants inspired by the young Bonnie Prince Charlie
   d. A group of Catholics inspired by the young son of King Charles II
   e. A group of Protestants inspired by the daughter of King James II

20. Choose the option that best describes the central idea of the passage.
   a. King James II tried to fool the English with an illegitimate son as heir to the throne.
   b. The troubles between England and Scotland were largely due to a clash in religious beliefs.
   c. Queen Elizabeth I was the head of a troubled royal family.
   d. James's wife, Mary Beatrice, suffered the loss of many infants.
   e. James II's daughter, Mary, facilitated a resurgence of the Protestant religion in England.

Directions: Refer to the following passage to answer questions 21–31.

Cultivation of Tomato Plants

Tomato plants should be started in window boxes or greenhouses in late March so that they will be ready for the garden after the last frost. Use a soil of equal parts of sand, peat moss, and manure, and plant the seeds about a quarter of an inch deep. After covering, water them through a cloth to protect the soil and cover the box with a pane of glass. Keep the box in a warm place for a few days, then place it in a sunny window. After the second leaf makes its appearance on the seedling, transplant the plant to another box, placing the seedlings two inches apart. Another alternative is to put the sprouted seedlings in four-inch pots, setting them deeper in the soil than they stood in the seed bed. To make the stem stronger, pinch out the top bud when the seedlings are four or five inches in height.

Finally, place the plants in their permanent positions after they have grown to be twelve or fifteen inches high. When transplanting, parts of some of the longest leaves should be removed. Large plants may be set five or six inches deep.

The soil should be fertilized the previous season. Fresh, stable manure, used as fertilizer, would delay the time of fruiting. To improve the condition of the soil, work in a spade full of old manure to a depth of at least a foot. Nitrate of soda, applied at about two hundred pounds per acre, may be used to give the plant a good start.

Plants grown on supports may be set two feet apart in the row, with the rows three or four feet apart depending upon the variety. Plants not supported by stakes or other methods should be set four feet apart.

Unsupported vines give a lighter yield and much of the fruit is likely to rot during the wet seasons. Use well-sharpened stakes about two inches in diameter and five feet long. Drive the stakes into the ground at least six inches from the plants so that the roots will not be injured. Tie the tomato vines to the stakes with strings made out of strips of cloth, as twine is likely to cut them. Care must be taken not to wrap the limbs so tightly as to interfere with their growth. The training should start before the plants begin to trail on the ground.

21. According to the text, why should tomato seedlings be watered through a cloth?

    a. To prevent over-watering
    b. To filter the water
    c. To water the seeds slowly
    d. To warm the water
    e. To protect the soil

22. Why does the author suggest pinching out the top bud of the tomato plant when the seedlings are four or five inches in height?

    a. To avoid over-crowding
    b. To allow for more air flow
    c. To avoid rotting
    d. To strengthen the stem
    e. To start a new tomato plant

23. Which of the following best describes the text structure of the passage?

    a. Sequence and order
    b. Compare and contrast
    c. Cause and effect
    d. Description
    e. Flashback

24. Identify the purpose of the author.

    a. To entertain
    b. To inform
    c. To persuade
    d. To compare
    e. To argue

25. According to the author, when should tomato plants be moved to their permanent positions?

    a. After the second leaf makes its appearance
    b. After the first fertilization
    c. When the seedling starts to sprout
    d. After they have grown to be 12 to 15 inches high
    e. After the last frost

26. Which of the following choices best defines "yield" as used in the last paragraph?

    a. A color or hue
    b. The amount produced
    c. The height of a plant
    d. An explosive force
    e. A delay in growth

27. Identify a synonym for the term "fruiting" as used in Paragraph 3.

    a. Ripening
    b. Decaying
    c. Watering
    d. Decomposing
    e. Wilting

28. Why does the author dissuade the use of twine?

    a. Because it gets too hot in the sun
    b. Because it is expensive
    c. Because it may wrap the tomato vines too tightly
    d. Because it is not porous
    e. Because it may cut the tomato vines

29. All of the following are recommended for starting new tomato plants EXCEPT _____.

    a. Using soil with peat moss, sand, and manure
    b. Starting the plants in late March
    c. Watering them through a cloth
    d. Planting the seeds about a quarter of an inch deep
    e. Replacing the soil daily

30. Choose the option that best describes the author's pattern of organization for Paragraphs 1 and 2.

    a. Cause and effect
    b. Problem and solution
    c. Sequential
    d. Persuasive
    e. Compare and contrast

31. The author would most likely agree with which of the following statements?

    a. Unsupported plants should be set farther apart than supported plants.
    b. Freshly fertilized soil should be used when planting tomatoes.
    c. Twine should be used to tie tomato vines to stakes.
    d. Tomato harvesting should begin in May.
    e. When transplanting, plants should remain intact with absolutely no parts removed.

Directions: Refer to the following passage to answer questions 32–41.

Stories have been a part of the world since the beginning of recorded time. For centuries before the invention of the printing press, stories of the world were passed down throughout the generations through oral tradition. With the invention of the printing press, which made written material available to a wide range of audiences, books were mass-produced and introduced into greater society. Before the printing press was invented, books had to be hand copied, which made books very difficult to make and very costly as a result.

For the last several centuries, books have been at the forefront of education and entertainment. With the invention of the Internet, reliance on books for information quickly changed. Soon, almost everything that anyone needed to know could be accessed through the Internet. Large printed volumes of encyclopedias became unnecessary, as all of the information was easily available on the Internet.

Despite the progression of the Internet, printed media was still very popular in the forms of both fiction and non-fiction books. Similarly, newspapers are a format of reading material that has been widespread in availability and use. While waiting for an appointment, enduring a several-hour flight, or relaxing before sleep, books, magazines, and newspapers have been a reliable and convenient source of entertainment, and one that society has not been willing to give up.

With the progression and extreme convenience of technology, printed books are soon going to become a thing of the past. Inventions such as the iPad from Apple and the Kindle have made the need for any kind of printed media unnecessary. With a rechargeable battery, a large screen, and the ability to have several books saved on file, electronic options will soon take over and society will no longer see printed books.

Some people still cling to the old format of printed books as they enjoy owning and reading from paper materials. Although some people may say that the act of reading is not complete without turning a page, sliding a finger across the screen or pressing a button to read more onto the next page is just as satisfying to the reader. The iPad and Kindle are devices that have qualities similar to a computer and can be used for so much more than just reading. These devices are therefore better than books because they have multiple uses.

In a cultural society that is part of the world and due to a longstanding tradition, stories will always be an important way to communicate ideas and provide information and entertainment. Centuries ago, stories could only be remembered and retold through speech. Printed media changed the way the world communicated and was connected, and now, as we move forward with technology, it is only a matter of time before we must say goodbye to the printed past and welcome the digital and electronic future.

32. Before the invention of the printing press, books were costly to make because _____.

    a. paper was scarce
    b. books were sold for less money than they cost to make
    c. people preferred spoken storytelling
    d. books were difficult to ship
    e. books had to be handwritten

33. How are the following two sentences related?

Sentence 1: While waiting for an appointment, enduring a several-hour flight, or relaxing before sleep, books, magazines, and newspapers have been a reliable and convenient source of entertainment, and one that society has not been willing to give up.

Sentence 2: With a rechargeable battery, a large screen, and the ability to have several books saved on file, electronic options will soon take over and society will no longer see printed books.

   a. Sentence 2 clarifies sentence 1.
   b. Sentence 1 supports the main idea of sentence 2.
   c. They are contradictory of one another.
   d. Sentence 2 offers a solution to a problem presented in sentence 1.
   e. Sentence 1 foreshadows the events described in sentence 2.

34. According to the text, why are printed encyclopedias no longer necessary?

   a. Because the information is outdated
   b. Because they have to be printed in separate volumes
   c. Because libraries could no longer store them
   d. Because they are too expensive to print
   e. Because all of the information can be found on the Internet

35. Why does the author feel that electronic devices are better than books?

   a. Because they have multiple uses
   b. Because they store more than one book at a time
   c. Because they make text easier to read
   d. Because they are rechargeable
   e. Because they are easier to transport

36. What act is the author describing in the phrase, "sliding a finger across the screen" in Paragraph 5?

   a. Cleaning and maintaining an electronic device
   b. Charging an electronic device
   c. Turning the page of an electronic book
   d. Turning the page of a newspaper
   e. Unlocking a touch-screen device

37. From the text we can infer that the author _____.

   a. believes books are more enjoyable than electronic devices
   b. would rather read a newspaper than a Kindle
   c. prefers informational text over fiction
   d. is ready to move forward with technological advances
   e. thinks everyone should get rid of their printed books

38. According to the text, stories provide all of the following, EXCEPT _____.

   a. communication of ideas
   b. news about current events
   c. support for the need for electronic devices
   d. entertainment
   e. a reliable and convenient pastime

39. Which of the following best defines "enduring," as used in Paragraph 3?

   a. Reading
   b. Traveling
   c. Avoiding
   d. Vacationing
   e. Tolerating

40. The sentence "With the invention of the printing press, which made written material available to wide ranges of audiences, books were mass-produced and introduced into greater society," is used to show _____.

   a. sequence
   b. description
   c. problem and solution
   d. compare and contrast
   e. cause and effect

41. According to the text, the first stories were told...

   a. through handwritten books.
   b. through printed material.
   c. through electronic devices.
   d. through speech.
   e. through cave illustrations.

Directions: Refer to the following passage to answer questions 42–50.

The process of making wine is one that is as old as history itself. For some wineries, the process has been the same for hundreds of years and is a highly valued and heavily guarded secret. Every winemaker has his or her own materials, ingredients, and processes that lend to the creation of a unique product. Modern research has taken place to look at the connection between the science behind winemaking and the resulting artwork.

Some wine aficionados prize the flavor of oak, usually imparted to the beverage through aging in wooden barrels. An alternative process, aging in metal casks with macerated wood chips, provides a stronger wood flavor in less time and therefore is less expensive. To test consumer preferences for wines processed in this manner, a survey of 618 people living in several East Coast cities was conducted early last year. Participants took a blind taste test of three samples of Oregon Pinot Noir. One sample was aged using macerated wood chips, one sample was aged under oak, and a third sample, the control, was aged in a metal tank. A questionnaire asked subjects to rate the wines and then asked a variety of other questions aimed at categorizing their consumption habits.

Although a variety of factors influenced wine preference, the test exposed a pattern concerning a preference for strongly wood-flavored wines. A large proportion of those persons interviewed (45%) did not care for the tannic wines. However, a sizable minority of 25% liked them very much, and preferred the tannic wines to the other samples. Younger consumers particularly fell into this category. Connoisseurs reported greater appreciation for wines aged "under oak," or in normal oak barrels.

Many high-quality wines are aged under oak today. Nonetheless, this process is time consuming; as a result, it makes wines more expensive. This survey demonstrated that price is very important in the buying decision, especially for people without extensive knowledge regarding wine. Many consumers are more concerned with price differences than with subtle differences in flavor. This trend defines a market segment that might be well served by wines aged with wood chips.

Although winemaking has been a generally unchanging tradition, modern research and practices may be able to change the standard methods of winemaking. In turn, these new methods make the process more efficient and will help to make unique and high-quality wine available for everyone at a much lower cost.

42. Which of the following winemaking processes produce the strongest flavor of oak in the least amount of time?
   a. Storing the wine in oak barrels
   b. Storing the wine with wood chips
   c. Storing the wine in metal containers
   d. Adding chemicals to the wine as it is mixed
   e. Adding oak tree sap to the wine as it is mixed

43. Modern research will affect the wine industry in each of the following ways EXCEPT _____.
   a. the process of making wine will be more efficient
   b. the cost of purchasing wine will decrease
   c. the shipping of wine will improve
   d. the quality of wine will improve
   e. the number of unique wines will increase

44. According to the survey, consumers are most interested in what aspect of purchasing wine?
   a. Price
   b. Taste
   c. Process
   d. Vintage year
   e. Brand

45. According to the text, wine that is aged under oak is expensive because _____.
   a. it is time-consuming
   b. wood barrels are expensive to make
   c. wood chips are in high demand
   d. tannic wine is becoming increasingly popular
   e. wood barrels are expensive to store

46. Choose the option that best defines the term "aficionados," as used in Paragraph 2.
   a. A person who participates in a taste-testing survey
   b. A type of wine
   c. A person who is very knowledgeable or enthusiastic about a topic
   d. A process for creating wine
   e. A person who mixes wine

47. Which of the following best describes the purpose of the text?

    a. To entertain
    b. To inform
    c. To persuade
    d. To solve a problem
    e. To compare

48. All of the following samples were part of the taste test EXCEPT _____.

    a. a sample that was aged under oak
    b. a sample with macerated wood chips
    c. a sample that contained pomegranate
    d. a sample that was aged in a metal tank
    e. a control sample

49. According to the survey, which group of people preferred the tannic wines?

    a. The younger population
    b. The wine aficionados
    c. The older population
    d. The East Coast population
    e. The population that regularly buys Oregon Pinot Noir

50. Based on the sentence, "A questionnaire asked subjects to rate the wines and then asked a variety of other questions aimed at categorizing their consumption habits," we can infer that...

    a. the surveyors were only interested in the favorite-tasting wine.
    b. the surveyors were interested in analyzing how people with various consumption habits preferred their wine.
    c. surveyors were interested in the amount of time it took taste-testers to complete the survey.
    d. surveyors were interested in the education level of taste-testers.
    e. the surveyors wanted to confuse the subjects and influence their answers.

Essay Questions

1. In peaceful protest of what they believe to be oppression in America, many athletes of the National Football League have decided to kneel rather than standing for our National Anthem. Some viewers see this as a platform for public figures to bring awareness and change, while others view it as a disrespectful action towards our country, our flag, and those who serve and protect. Do athletes have the right to protest during the National Anthem? Does it disrespect our country, flag, and military?

2. The American Academy of Pediatrics recently announced that children as young as 18 months old can benefit from high-value, academic screen time, when supervised by an adult. Others argue that introducing electronics to children at such a young age will limit their ability to interact in the real world as they grow and mature. Do the advantages of educational programs outweigh the disadvantages?

Answer Key and Explanations

Mathematics

1. D: To compare fractions with unlike denominators, we can rewrite each fraction with equivalent denominators. To do so, we must first identify the least common denominator, or LCD. The LCD is the least common multiple of the denominators. Here, the LCDs between $\frac{2}{5}$ and the answer choices are 55, 35, 15, and 10. Next, we must rewrite each fraction for comparison, while maintaining equivalence. Let's start with $\frac{5}{11}$. Our new denominator, 55, is five times greater than our original denominator, 11. To maintain equivalence, we must make our new numerator five times greater than our original numerator. To do so, we multiply our original numerator, 5, by 5, which equals 25. That makes our new fraction $\frac{5}{55}$. We do the same for $\frac{2}{5} = \frac{22}{55}$, and once our denominators are equivalent, we can simply compare our numerators to determine the greater value. Because 25 is greater than 22, we know that $\frac{25}{55}$ is greater than $\frac{22}{55}$, or $\frac{5}{11} > \frac{2}{5}$. We follow the same logic to evaluate each answer choice to find that $\frac{1}{3} < \frac{2}{5}$.

2. B: The number line orders numbers from least to greatest. When comparing any two numbers, the smaller value will always be to the left of the greater value. Because -7 is *less than* -2, -7 will always be to the *left* of -2 on the number line. All of the other options have greater values placed to the left of smaller values. This can never be true on any number line.

3. C: When ordering negative numbers, it helps to remember that the largest digit has the smallest value. That makes -5 our smallest value, followed by -3, and finally -1. Next comes 0 because 0 separates our negative numbers from our positive numbers. To compare decimals, we can insert zeros at the end of each number so that each value has the same number of digits. Here, that would look like 15.05 and 15.30. When we start comparing digits from left to right, we see that the first place value that differs is the tenths place. Because 3 is greater than 0, we know that 15.3 is greater than 15.05. Finally, our greatest number of the set is 19 because positive 19 is greater than all of the other numbers in the set. That makes our ordered list -5, -3, -1, 0, 15.05, 15.3, 19.

4. E: Each notebook costs $1.50. To find the cost of each notebook, we must divide the total amount of money earned, $45.00, by the number of notebooks sold, 30. When we divide 45 by 30, we know that 30 can "fit" into 45 one time, with a remainder of 15. We can turn our remainder into a fraction by making our remainder the numerator and our divisor the denominator, creating the fraction $\frac{15}{30}$, or $\frac{1}{2}$. When working with money, 1 whole and $\frac{1}{2}$ represents one and a half dollars, or $1.50. Giselle charged $1.50 for each notebook.

5. E: First, we must determine the total amount of money Krystal spent. To do so, we must add the cost of the sunglasses, $19.99, and the scarf, $27.50. To add decimals, we stack the numbers so that the decimal points are directly on top of one another. Then, we add using the traditional algorithm, bringing the decimal point straight down into our sum. This gives us a total cost of $47.49. To determine Krystal's change, we must subtract our total, $47.49, from $50.00. Again, we must be sure to stack our decimal points directly on top of one another. Then we subtract as normal, bringing our decimal point straight down into our answer. We need to be careful that we borrow when necessary. The difference of $50.00 and $47.49 is $2.51. Krystal will receive change in the amount of $2.51.

6. A: Artie will have to pay $2.73 for his candy. To find the answer, we must multiply the amount of candy Artie is purchasing, 2.1 pounds, by the price per pound, $1.30. When multiplying decimals, we can use the traditional algorithm, as if the decimal points weren't there. When we multiply 130 by 21, we get 2,730. To determine where to place the decimal point, we count the number of digits after each decimal point in each factor. Here, we have one digit after the decimal point in 2.1 and two digits after the decimal point in $1.30. That makes for a total of three digits after the decimal points in the factors. Because there are three digits to the right of the decimal points in the factors, we must have three digits after the decimal point in the product, turning 2,730 into 2.730, or $2.73.

7. B: Following the order of operations, we must start by finding the value of 5^3, which is equivalent to $5 \times 5 \times 5$, or 125. This simplifies our expression to $125 + 18 \div 3$. Next, we must solve the division of 18 and 3, which is 6, leaving us with a final expression of $125 + 6$. The sum of 125 and 6 is 131, making our solution 131.

8. A: Parentheses must be completed first. Here, $9 + 1 = 10$, so we can rewrite our expression as $100 \div 10 \times 2$. When dealing with multiplication and division, we must solve the operations in the order in which they appear, from left to right. Because division appears *before* multiplication, we must divide 100 by 10 before we multiply by 2. The quotient of 100 and 10 is 10, simplifying our expression to 10×2, or 20. Our final answer is 20.

9. E: When there are two operations within our parentheses, we must follow the order of operations *within* the parentheses as well. Because multiplication comes before addition, we must start by finding the product of 4 and 3, which is 12. Next, we add 10 and 12 to get 22. Finally, we can divide 22 by 2 to arrive at our final answer, 11.

10. C: Any triangle with an angle measuring over 90° is considered an obtuse triangle. Because this triangle has an angle measuring 100°, we must classify it as obtuse. To classify a triangle by its sides, we must determine how many of the sides are equivalent. Here, we have two sides measuring 15 inches. A triangle with two equivalent sides is described as an isosceles triangle. This triangle must be described as an obtuse isosceles triangle.

11. D: The three-dimensional shape being described must be a pyramid because it only has one base and all triangular sides. We can envision the sides meeting at the top, forming the point of the pyramid. Furthermore, a pyramid is named for the shape of its base. Here, the pyramid has a square base so we must classify it as a square pyramid.

12. C: To start, we can write our ratio in fractional form as $\frac{2}{6}$. We know Josie wants to lessen the flour to only 2 cups, making our proportion $\frac{2}{6} = \frac{x}{2}$. To find the value of x, we can cross multiply the two diagonal values we know (2 and 2), and divide their product by the remaining value (6). The product of 2 and 2 is 4, and 4 divided by 6 is simply $\frac{4}{6}$, or $\frac{2}{3}$. This means Josie should use $\frac{2}{3}$ cup of water for every 2 cups of flour.

13. A: The picture is scaled so that each inch on the drawing represents two feet in real life. We can multiply 4 inches by 2 to find the actual height of the wall. Because the product of 4 and 2 is 8, we know the real wall must measure 8 feet.

14. A: We know the ratio of boys to girls is 3 to 4, which means there are 3 boys for every 7 students (because $3 + 4 = 7$). We can write the ratio of boys to total students as $\frac{3}{7}$. We also know that there are 12 boys in the class, so we can create the proportion $\frac{3}{7} = \frac{12}{x}$. To solve for x, we must determine how many times greater 12 is than 3. Because 12 is four times greater than 3, we need to multiply 7 by 4 to complete our proportion. The product of 7 and 4 is 28, so we know there are 28 total students in the class.

15. B: Area is the measure we use to calculate the number of square units that will fit into a plane surface. To re-carpet his bedroom, Justin must calculate the total number of square feet that must be covered in order to fill the floor space. To find area, Justin should multiply the length of his bedroom, 12 feet, by the width, 10 feet. Because $12 \times 10 = 120$, Justin will need 120 square feet of carpet for his bedroom.

16. C: Scientific notation is a strategy for writing very large or very small numbers. To convert a number into scientific notation, we must first move the decimal point either left or right until we have a value that is between 1 and 10. For the number 18,000, we must move the decimal point four place values to the left, in order to create the value 1.8. Because we moved our decimal point four places to the left, our exponent will be positive 4. (Side note: If we had moved our decimal point 4 places to the right we would have expressed our exponent as -4.) Finally, we are able to write our value in scientific notation as 1.8×10^4.

17. E: We can express Andre's speed as the rate 65 miles to 1 hour, or $\frac{65}{1}$. Next, we can set up a proportion to determine how long it will take Andre to travel 195 miles. Our proportion should be $\frac{65}{1} = \frac{195}{x}$. To solve for x we must determine how much greater 195 is than 65. We can do this using division. The quotient of 195 and 65 is 3, which tells us that 195 is three times greater than 65. Now, we must multiply our denominator, 1, by 3 as well to keep our proportion balanced. The product of 1 and 3 is 3, making $x = 3$. It will take Andre 3 hours to travel 195 miles.

18. B: If one inch is equal to 2.54 centimeters, then we can multiply any measurement in inches by 2.54 to convert it to centimeters. To multiply decimals, we simply ignore the decimal points and multiply using the traditional algorithm. When finished, we count the total number of digits after the decimal point in each of the factors. The total number of digits after the decimal points in the factors should match the number of digits after the decimal point in the product. Here, $254 \times 95 = 24130$. There are two digits after the decimal point in 2.54 and one digit after the decimal point in 9.5, for a total of three digits after the decimal points in the factors. That means we must insert a decimal point in our product so that there are three digits after the decimal point, like this: 24.130. The final zero does not affect the value of our answer so we can drop it and conclude that 9.5 inches is equivalent to 24.13 centimeters.

19. A: To find Hector's price per gallon we must divide the total amount of money Hector paid, $22.44, by the number of gallons he received, 12. We start by recognizing that our divisor, 12, is a whole number. That allows us to bring our decimal point straight up into our quotient and then divide following the traditional algorithm for long division. The quotient of $22.44 and 12 is $1.87, so Hector paid $1.87 per gallon for gasoline.

20. C: The distributive property is used to "distribute" a value outside of the parentheses to each of the numbers *inside* the parentheses. Here, we can simplify $4(5 + 8)$ by first multiplying 4 times 5, which gives us a product of 20. Next, we must multiply 4 by 8, which equals 32. The distributive property allows us to rewrite the expression as the sum of our products, 20 and 32, or $20 + 32$.

21. D: The associative property states that moving the parentheses when adding or multiplying a string of numbers will not affect the sum or product. The associative property is often used to group compatible numbers in an effort to assist with mental math. By rewriting the problem as

17 + (18 + 2), we have grouped our compatible numbers, 18 and 2. These are considered compatible numbers because they have a sum of 20, which is an easy number to calculate mentally. Once we have the sum of 20 we can include our final addend, 17, to arrive at our total of 37.

22. B: Jackie and Jessie are both selling 12 seashells, but for different prices, so we need to keep their calculations separate until we have the total amount of money each girl has earned. Jackie is selling her shells for $1.00 each, while Jessie is selling hers for $1.25 each. We can express the amount of money each girl earns as $12 \times \$1.00$ and $12 \times \$1.25$. Once we have the total amount of money each girl sells, we can add those totals together to find the total amount of money earned. We can calculate the total amount of money the girls earned using the following expression: $(12 \times \$1.00) + (12 \times \$1.25)$.

23. B: If Connor and Pete want to split their tips equally, we must first combine their tips to find the amount of money they earned together. Because Connor earned $48.00 and Pete earned $62.00, we can add $48.00 + $62.00. Next, we must divide the total by 2 to determine how much money each of them should receive. It is important that we have our addition problem in parentheses so that the total amount of money earned is calculated before the total is divided by two. The expression $(\$48.00 + \$62.00) \div 2$ can be used to find the amount of money each person should receive.

24. E: When isolating the variable of a two-step equation, we must first apply the inverse operation for any addition or subtraction. Here, we must apply the inverse of addition, which is subtraction, to both sides of the equation. When we subtract 12 from both sides of the equation, we are left with $5x = 60$. Finally, we must apply the inverse operation of any multiplication or division. In this case, we must apply the inverse of multiplication, which is division. When we divide both sides of the equation by 5, we're left with $x = 12$. We can check our answer by inserting 12 into the original equation. Because $5(12) + 12 = 72$, we know that we have correctly solved for x.

25. D: To solve for y, we must first complete the inverse of any addition or subtraction. Here, we need to add 8 to both sides of the equation. This simplifies our equation to $\frac{y}{2} = 8$. Next, we need to complete the inverse of division, which is multiplication. When we multiply both sides of the equation by 2, we find that $y = 16$. To check our answer, we can insert 16 into our original equation. Because $\frac{16}{2} - 8 = 0$, we know we have the correct value for y.

26. D: To find solutions for any inequality, we must isolate the variable by applying the inverse operations of those included in the problem. To start, we apply the inverse operation for any addition or subtraction. In this case, we need to subtract 8 from both sides of the inequality, simplifying our inequality to $6x \leq 48$. Next, we need to apply the inverse operation for any multiplication or division. Here, we'll have to divide both sides of the inequality by 6, which leaves us with $x \leq 8$. This tells us that any number less than or equal to 8 can be written in place of x. We can check our answer by rewriting our inequality with a number that fits those parameters to check that our inequality remains true. For example, because 5 is less than 8, we can write $6(5) + 8 \leq 56$. This simplifies to $38 \leq 56$. Because 38 *is* less than 56, we know we've identified the correct solution set for the inequality.

27. C: The key operational words included in this scenario are "more than" and "twice." "Four more than" tells us to add 4, while "twice" tells us to multiply by two. The scenario describes Robbie's age in terms of Joanie's age. That means Joanie's age will represent one side of the equation. If Joanie is four more than twice Robbie's age, then we can take Robbie's age, multiply it by two and add four to determine Joanie's age. We can represent that as the equation $j = 4 + 2r$. We already know that Joanie is 56 years old so we can rewrite our equation as $56 = 4 + 2r$. To solve, we must isolate the variable by applying the inverse operations. To start, we subtract 4 from both sides of the equation, which simplifies to $52 = 2r$. Finally, we can divide both sides of the equation by 2, which determines that r must equal 26. If Joanie is 56 years old, then Robbie must be 26 years old.

28. E: To write our equation, we must start by looking for key operational words or phrases. In this situation we have "less than" and "half." "Less than" implies subtraction, while "half" can be represented by dividing a value by two or multiplying a value by $\frac{1}{2}$. The situation is describing the number of students enrolled in Ana's class by giving us the number of students enrolled in Susie's class. That makes Susie our "answer." If Susie represents one side of the equation, we need to determine the other side in terms of what we know about Susie's class size. We can express the "half" as $s = \frac{1}{2}a$ or $s = \frac{a}{2}$. When we include "three less than" we have two options for expressing the number of students enrolled in Ana's class. We can write $\frac{1}{2}a - 3 = s$, or $\frac{a}{2} - 3 = s$. Because $\frac{1}{2}a - 3 = s$ is not an answer choice, we must choose the latter. To solve, we must replace s with 14 because we know that Susie has 14 students in her class. That makes our equation $\frac{a}{2} - 3 = 14$. Then, we must work to isolate the variable. We can do this by first adding three to both sides of the equation, which simplifies to $\frac{a}{2} = 17$. Finally, we can multiply both sides of the equation by 2, which determines that a must represent 34. Ana has 34 students enrolled in her class.

29. E: The original cost may be represented by the equation $45 = x - 0.25x$ or $45 = 0.75x$. Dividing both sides of the equation by 0.75 gives $x = 60$.

30. A: If a number is divisible by 2 and 3, it is also divisible by the lowest common multiple of these two factors. The lowest common multiple of 2 and 3 is their product, 6.

31. B: The decimal expansion of an irrational number does not terminate or repeat. The decimal expansion of $\sqrt{2}$ does not terminate or repeat.

32. E: The constant of proportionality is equal to the slope. Using the points, (2, –8) and (5, –20), the slope may be written as $\frac{-20-(-8)}{5-2}$, which equals –4.

33. E: The area of the square is equal to $(30)^2$, or 900 square centimeters. The area of the circle is equal to $\pi(15)^2$, or approximately 707 square centimeters. The area of the shaded region is equal to the difference of the area of the square and the area of the circle, or $900 \text{ cm}^2 - 707 \text{ cm}^2$, which equals 193 cm². So, the area of the shaded region is about 193 cm².

34. B: The amount she spends on rent and utilities is equal to 0.38(40,000), or $15,200, which is approximately $15,000.

35. D: To determine the number of students surveyed, we must find the sum of the bar heights. When we look at the height of each bar, we can see that 9 students chose soccer, 4 students chose softball, 6 chose basketball, and 3 replied "other." The sum of $9 + 4 + 6 + 3 = 22$, so we can conclude that 22 students were surveyed.

36. B: On a dot plot, each dot (or "x"), represents one response. Here, we're trying to determine how many students watched more than 8 hours of television over the weekend. "More than 8" tells us to only include students who responded with 9 or 10 hours because 9 and 10 are the only numbers on the graph that are greater than 8. We can't include the students who responded exactly 8 hours because 8 is not greater than 8 (8 is equal to 8). We can see that 3 students reported watching 9 hours of television, while 5 say they watched 10 hours of television. The sum of 3 and 5 is 8, which means 8 students watched more than 8 hours of television this weekend.

37. A: The question asks us how many students scored "75 points or fewer" on the math test. This means we are looking for all of the data contained in the intervals 61-65, 66-70, and 71-75. From the histogram we may not know the exact scores of these students, but we do know that all of the scores contained in these intervals must be 75 points or less. Only one student scored between 61 and 65 points, zero students scored between 66 and 70 points, and two students scored between 71 and 75 points. Because $1 + 0 + 2 = 3$, we can conclude that 3 students scored 75 points or fewer on the math test.

38. C: When displaying data collected in a survey, we must always choose intervals appropriate for the data collected. This includes starting our y-axis at zero, and choosing intervals that are appropriate for the data being collected. For example, imagine we are comparing the purchase prices of homes in an area. If the homes sold for $280,000, $282,000, and $284,000, most people would consider the homes to have sold for very similar prices, given that $2,000 increments are only marginally different when describing the cost of a house. If these prices were graphed with y-axis intervals of $10.00, the bar representing the $284,000 house would be much higher than the bar representing the house that sold for $282,000, even though the difference in price is only $2,000. That graph would mislead people into thinking the houses sold for prices that were considerably different from each other, which was not the case.

39. B: The mean of a data set is considered a measure of center. To calculate the mean (sometimes known as the "average"), we must first find the sum of all numbers included in the data set. Here, the sum of 76, 193, 83, 43, and 105 is 500. Next, we need to divide the sum of our data set by the number of values included in the set. This data set contains five values, so we'll divide our sum, 500, by 5. The quotient of 500 and 5 is 100, making our mean 100.

40. B: To calculate the range of any data set, we must find the difference between the largest value (known as the maximum) and the smallest value (known as the minimum). In this data set, our maximum is 832, while our minimum is 196. The difference of 832 and 196 is 636, so the range of the data set is also 636.

41. A: The median is the middle number of a data set when the set is listed from least to greatest. To find the median, we must first rewrite our set from least to greatest as: 53, 72, 81, 82, 85, 91. Because there are six data values, we have two numbers, 81 and 82, that can be described as the "middle numbers." To find the median of the set, we must find the mean of the two middle numbers. The mean of 81 and 82 is 81.5, so the median of our entire data set is also 81.5.

42. D: The mode of any data set is the value(s) that appears most often. Here, we have two values, 84 and 93, that both occur four times. No other value occurs more than four times so we can say that we have two modes: 84 and 93.

43. D: In the data set {67, 29, 57, 27, 38, 91} there is no value that occurs more than any other value. However, we cannot describe the mode as "zero" because that would imply that the value "0" is part of the data set and appears more than any other value. When we have a data set without any repeating numbers, we must describe that set as having "no mode," rather than "zero."

44. C: We calculate the range of any data set by subtracting the smallest value from the largest value, or the maximum – the minimum. Here, our maximum is 84, while our minimum is 3. Because $84 - 3 = 81$, our range is 81. The range tells us how "spread out" our data is. Having a range of 81 means that our data is spread out by no more than 81 units.

45. B: The data set {67, 2, 67, 73, 85, 60, 68} contains seven numbers, six of which are within 15 units of each other. The seventh piece of data, 2, is an outlier, meaning it is much greater or smaller than the rest of the data. Using the range of this data set, 83 (because $85 - 2 = 83$), would give the impression that the entire data set greatly varies, which is not the case. For this type of data set, the median would be a better representation of the set because the outlier does not have as great an effect.

46. B: The counting principle is the strategy in which we list out all of the possible combinations that *could* occur in order to determine the probability of a specific event occurring. Here, Joe is flipping two coins and trying to find the probability of both coins landing on tails. When we write out all of the possible flip combinations we get: TT, TH, HT, HH. Using this strategy, we would then circle the outcomes that meet our designated outcome (both coins landing on tails) and determine that the probability is 1 out of 4, or $\frac{1}{4}$. Although $\frac{1}{2} \times \frac{1}{2}$ would lead us to this answer, it is not an example of the counting principle being applied.

47. C: To find the number of options Aniyah can create, we can start by making an ordered list of the different options. To start, we can assign each piece of clothing an abbreviation, such as J1 for the first pair of jeans or S1 for shirt number 1. When we list all of the different options in an organized way, we find the following combinations: J1/S1, J1/S2, J1/S3, J2/S1, J2/S2, J2/S3. We can count the numbers of combinations created to conclude that Aniyah is able to create six different outfits from two pairs of jeans and three shirts. Another way to solve this problem is to simply multiply the number of options within each category. There are two options for jeans and three options for shirts. The product of 3 and 2 is 6, again confirming that Aniyah has six possible outfit combinations.

48. A: A tree diagram shows the different combinations possible by listing each option as a sort of hierarchy. To start, we list all possibilities for the first category. Here, our first category is ice cream flavor, so we need three branches to represent the three different flavors. Next, we must decide between three different toppings. Because each topping can be paired with any flavor, we need two branches coming from each flavor, to show all the flavor/topping combinations. Finally, we must decide on hot fudge or caramel. Again, each choice can be added to any of our already existing combinations, so we'll need two more branches coming from each topping choice. When finished, we can follow the branches from top to bottom to see every possible combination of ice cream sundae that can be created. So, the correct option shows every possible branch.

49. D: To find the probability of Fran pulling two different marbles from the bag, we must find the probability of each event occurring individually, then multiply those probabilities together. To start, we can determine that Fran's chance of pulling a red marble is $\frac{5}{12}$ because there are 5 red marbles out of a total 12 marbles. Next, we must determine that Fran has a $\frac{4}{11}$ chance of pulling a green marble because there are 4 green marbles out of a new total 11 marbles. Notice, our total must now be reduced to 11 because Fran has one marble already in her possession. When we multiply our two events, $\frac{5}{12} \times \frac{4}{11}$, we get $\frac{20}{132}$, or $\frac{5}{33}$. The chance of Fran pulling a red marble followed by a green marble is $\frac{5}{33}$.

50. B: Regardless of the exact number of students, we can determine the relative percentages of each eye color. We are given that 40% of the total have brown eyes, which means that $100\% - 40\%$ or 60% of the students have either blue or green eyes. Since 90% of those have blue eyes, we know that 10% have green eyes. Now, 90% of 60% can be found by converting both percentages to decimals and multiplying them: $(0.9) \times (0.6) = 0.54$ or 54%. So, in total, 40% have brown eyes,

54% have blue eyes, and 6% have green eyes and we can definitively say that blue eyed students are the majority.

Reading

1. C: Although all five options are arguably benefits to eliminating mandatory attendance laws, the term "economical" tells us we're looking for a cost-effective advantage. According to the author, the cost of enforcing compulsory education is money ill-spent and could be better spent on students who *want* to be there.

2. E: According to the author, many problems that arise in schools are a direct result of students who are forced to be there. The author believes that attendance laws should be abolished in order to make education more valuable to students with a desire to learn.

3. B: The author believes that education is failing because teachers and schools spend far too much time disciplining behavior issues and mandating attendance. Teachers could better serve conscientious students if given the opportunity to fail or dismiss those who are disrupting the education of others.

4. D: An assumption is something we believe to be true because it is something we have been taught to believe and do not question. Here, the author is assuming that most parents want a high school education for their children. There is no evidence in the text supporting that claim, but the author believes it to be true based on his own experiences and beliefs.

5. E: Although all five options reflect the author's beliefs, only one of them describes the central idea, or main idea, of the writing. The author is trying to prove that abolishing mandatory attendance laws would create better school environments for the students with a genuine desire to learn. The other answer choices are used as supporting evidence to reinforce that claim.

6. C: A summary is a brief statement used to describe the main idea of writing, or a portion of that writing. The first paragraph of this article mentions all five choices, but the main idea is that abolishing mandatory attendance laws would improve the quality of education in schools. The other answer choices list ways in which the abolition of these laws could improve the climate of education or reasons why this abolition is necessary.

7. C: The author's main idea is that abolishing mandatory attendance laws would allow teachers the ability to dismiss disruptive students, preserving the sanctity of schools as a place for students to receive an esteemed education. Bullet three does not support that specific claim, but instead describes an issue with the grading of such students.

8. B: According to the text, mandatory attendance laws undermine the integrity of schools because teachers have no choice but to provide all students, regardless of behavior or attendance, the same educational opportunities. When there is no recourse for disrupting the learning environment, schools can be perceived as day cares or, as the author described, "indoor street corners."

9. D: An inference is defined as a conclusion reached on the basis of evidence and reasoning. Throughout the passage, the author has provided several reasons why students with behavior or attendance concerns should not be afforded the opportunity to disrupt the education of others. From these claims, we can infer that the author believes education is a privilege to those who want to put in the effort and not a birthright of every juvenile in a community.

10. C: Context clues are hints we can use within an author's writing to determine the meaning of an unknown word. The author writes, "Teachers could stop policing recalcitrant students and start educating." We can use context clues to determine that the term "recalcitrant" most similarly describes students who are disobedient, if they require the policing of teachers.

11. C: According to the author, the major clash between England and Scotland stemmed from religious differences. The countries clashed over Catholic and Protestant beliefs, causing tension among the citizens as well as members of the royal families.

12. B: According to the text, Queen Elizabeth I died in 1603. With no heir to her throne, the son of her cousin, James Stuart, was crowned king.

13. D: Paragraph 4 states that James and his wife lost many children during infancy. His son survived infancy, but the English feared that he would be raised Catholic and eventually become king, influencing Catholicism throughout England. To avoid this, they fabricated a story of his death and created a rumor that the king had replaced the young prince with an imposter, forcing James, his wife, and their young son to flee.

14. E: While England and the Scottish Lowlands were Protestant, the Highlands were accepting of Catholicism and even formed a group of Catholic followers known as "Jacobites."

15. E: When Queen Elizabeth I of England died, she had no heir. Therefore, her cousin's son, James, became King of England. He was named King James I of England, while already crowned King James VI of Scotland.

16. A: In paragraph 4, the author writes, "Mary gave birth to a son, but the story quickly circulated that the royal child had died, and the child named James's heir was a foundling smuggled in." We can use context clues to determine that the rumored child was illegitimate, and therefore most likely an orphan with no lawful rights to the throne.

17. C: An inference is a conclusion we make based on evidence and reasoning without the text explicitly giving us the information. The text states that King James II was being accused of having an illegitimate son as heir to the throne. The text also states that, rather than risk the safety of his family, James chose to flee with his wife and son, relinquishing his rightful seat as the King of England. From this, we can infer that King James II was committed to his family.

18. B: King James II was believed to be raising his son as a Catholic. The English were so fearful at the thought of a Catholic king that they created rumors of an illegitimate son, forcing James to flee England and abdicate his throne.

19. A: The term "Jacobites" refers to a group of Catholics inspired by the young son of King James II. The group was named to reflect the Latin version of James' name and gathered to practice Catholicism in the Highlands.

20. B: Although it is true that true that Mary Beatrice suffered the loss of many infants and Queen Elizabeth I was part of a troubled royal family, neither of these statements summarize the central idea of the passage. The author's main assertion is that the troubles between England and Scotland were largely due to a clash in religious beliefs.

21. E: As stated in the first paragraph, watering tomato plants through a cloth helps to protect the soil.

269

22. D: The author states, "to make the stem stronger, pinch out the top bud when the seedlings are four or five inches in height." Therefore, the purpose of pinching out the top bud is to strengthen the stem.

23. A: A nonfiction passage that is written to reflect the sequence and order text structure gives readers a chronological list of events or a list of steps in a procedure. Here, the text is describing the process for growing tomatoes as a step-by-step procedure, making it a sequence and order text structure.

24. B: The author is trying to convey the best way to grow tomatoes. The article is not persuasive, nor is it attempting to entertain the reader. The purpose of the text is strictly to inform the reader.

25. D: According to the text, tomato plants should be moved to their permanent position after they have grown to be 12 to 15 inches high. The author recommends removing parts of the larger leaves at this time as well.

26. B: The term "yield" refers to the amount of tomatoes produced by unsupported vines. Here, the text is stating that unsupported vines will produce fewer tomatoes than supported vines.

27. A: The author is giving advice in an effort to "avoid a delay in fruiting." Using context clues, we can determine that fruiting is something that we *want* to occur in a timely manner. The only answer choice that describes a desired part of the harvesting process is "ripening," therefore we can conclude that ripening is a synonym for fruiting.

28. E: The author warns that wrapping tomato vines in twine may cut them. Instead, the author suggests using strips of cloth to tie the vines.

29. E: According to the text, tomato plants should be started in late March, watered through a cloth, and planted about a quarter of an inch deep into soil made of sand, peat moss, and manure. The passage does not discuss replacing the soil for new tomato plants.

30. C: The information is organized in a way that describes the step-by-step process for harvesting tomatoes. This type of text is described as sequential writing.

31. A: In Paragraph 4, the author states "Plants grown on supports may be set two feet apart in the row, with the rows three or four feet apart depending upon the variety. Plants not supported by stakes or other methods should be set four feet apart." We can summarize this information to conclude that unsupported vines should be set farther apart than supported vines.

32. E: Before the invention of the printing press, books had to be handwritten, making them difficult to create and costly to produce.

33. C: Sentence 1 states that printed materials are still valued and cherished in our society. Sentence 2 asserts that printed materials are a thing of the past. The points contradict one another, making the sentences contradictory.

34. E: Volumes of encyclopedias are large and cumbersome. They are no longer necessary to store and refer to because all of the information in them can easily be found on the Internet. To clarify further, although the information on the Internet is more current, encyclopedias being outdated is not a reason stated in the text, so choice A cannot be our answer.

35. A: The author states that electronic devices can store more than one book at a time, as well as serve many other purposes. Because these devices have multiple uses, the author believes they are better than books.

36. C: In order to read the next page of an electronic book, most devices require the reader to swipe his or her finger across the screen. The term "sliding a finger across the screen" refers to turning the page of an electronic book.

37. D: The author concludes his passage with the sentence, "Printed media changed the way the world communicated and was connected, and now, as we move forward with technology, it is only a matter of time before we must say goodbye to the printed past and welcome the digital and electronic future." From this, we can infer that the author is ready to move forward with advances in the world of technology.

38. C: Since the beginning of time, stories have been a reliable pastime and a way for people to share ideas, information, and entertain one another. It wasn't until recent technology that devices have proved their worth in the world of storytelling.

39. E: The phrase "enduring a long flight" refers to tolerating a lengthy plane ride. Here, the referral of an unpleasant travel experience is used to provide an example of when people enjoy printed material to pass the time.

40. E: The sentence cites the invention of the printing press as the reason for books being produced at a faster rate, thus giving them the opportunity to be dispersed to larger audiences. This shows cause and effect, where the cause is the invention of the printing press, and the effect is the widespread distribution of books.

41. D: According to the text, the first stories were told from generation to generation through speech. Stories needed to be remembered and retold in order to keep their legacy alive. The invention of the printing press changed all of that.

42. B: According to the text, storing wine in metal casks with macerated wood chips provides a stronger wood flavor in less time and therefore is less expensive.

43. C: The author states, "these new methods make the process more efficient and will help to make unique and high-quality wine available for everyone at a much lower cost." The article does not discuss how the shipping of wine will be affected.

44. A: Results from the survey concluded, "Many consumers are more concerned with price differences than with subtle differences in flavor."

45. A: Wine that is aged under oak tends to cost more money because the process is time-consuming.

46. C: A wine aficionado refers to a person who is very knowledgeable and interested in the production and consumption of wine. The phrase "wine aficionados," in this context, describes someone who values the wine's flavor. Later in the passage, the results of the survey show that a large portion of wine consumers value the price of wine over other factors, like flavor. This shows a difference between the aficionados and the less-knowledgeable consumer and suggests that an aficionado has a greater appreciation for wine and how it is produced.

47. B: The article is written to inform the reader of different processes for making wine, as well as to describe the preferences of wine drinkers by providing feedback from a blind taste test. The text does not try to persuade the reader to feel a certain way, nor is it written to entertain, compare, or solve a problem.

48. C: The text states that one of the wines involved in the taste test included macerated wood chips, one sample was aged under oak, and the control sample was aged in a metal tank. There is no mention of pomegranate being a part of the taste test.

49. A: According to the text, 25% of those surveyed preferred tannic wines. The younger population represented the majority of that 25%.

50. B: The text states, "A questionnaire asked subjects to rate the wines and then asked a variety of other questions aimed at categorizing their consumption habits." Because surveyors took the time to collect information about consumption habits, we can infer that they were interested in analyzing how people with various consumption habits preferred the tastes of different wines.

Essay Sample Response #1

Many athletes of the National Football League have decided to kneel rather than standing for our national anthem. Most of these athletes are kneeling during the anthem in an effort to peacefully protest the unfair treatment and oppression of certain groups within our borders. While I agree with the need for change in America, I believe that kneeling during the national anthem is a disrespectful action toward our country, our flag, and those who serve and protect.

Historically, the national anthem is played as a sign of respect and gratitude for our Armed Forces. It is a way for America to stand at attention and show their appreciation for the men and women who have fought and continue to fight for our country. The anthem also shows the greatest respect toward those who have lost their lives protecting our freedoms. Kneeling during this time minimizes the sacrifices that these brave soldiers have made and continue to make for the citizens of the United States of America.

The athletes protesting the anthem have a right to show their discontent with oppression in America; however, they should do so using a different platform and in a way that does not disrespect those who have selflessly fought to protect our freedoms. Perhaps these athletes can volunteer their time in educating people on the unfair treatment of certain subgroups, or donate money to fund programs that are already making great strides towards equality in America. There are many avenues athletes can take in an effort to shine a light on these issues, but it seems that kneeling is their only action.

In conclusion, I support the athletes' right to bring awareness to causes that they feel strongly about and urge them to use their fame to improve cohesiveness and unite the citizens of our great country. However, during the national anthem is not the time or place to make a political statement. Kneeling does not solve the problem; it only adds more of a divide in a country that is already fractured.

Essay Sample Response #2

The American Academy of Pediatrics recently announced that children as young as 18 months old can benefit from high-value, academic screen time, when supervised by an adult. Though screen time may prove advantageous for curious minds, it also has the power to negatively affect the social development of very young children. In an ever-evolving world, parents often find themselves caught between wanting their children to succeed in a technology-rich environment without losing the ability to interact face-to-face. When used responsibly, the advantages of screen time definitely outweigh the disadvantages.

The biggest factor of the screen time debate lies in what people consider to be "screen time." Many critics depict screen time as non-educational videos or mindless games. These critics suggest the image of a child placed on a chair and given a tablet, for the sole purpose of keeping that child entertained and/or quiet for long periods of time. If this were the case, then screen time would absolutely be disadvantageous for developing minds. This depiction, however, is certainly not the type of activity that The American Academy of Pediatrics is endorsing.

For many parents, screen time consists of educational programs, most of which are interactive and involve young learners in a host of activities. In addition to videos, there are countless applications that are geared towards young learners that actually teach and practice concepts such as shape recognition, counting, phonics, and even reading. When used with parental supervision, these videos and applications can aid parents in creating educational environments at home, even if the parent has no experience "teaching" these skills.

Each year, the world depends on technology more and more. Young children should absolutely be exposed to this technology at a young age so that they are comfortable using the devices that they will eventually rely on for everyday tasks. In addition, educational screen time can provide parents and caretakers with endless opportunities to teach and engage in ways that might not be possible without the assistance of technology. When used appropriately, the advantages of electronic devices most certainly outweigh the disadvantages.

How to Overcome Test Anxiety

Just the thought of taking a test is enough to make most people a little nervous. A test is an important event that can have a long-term impact on your future, so it's important to take it seriously and it's natural to feel anxious about performing well. But just because anxiety is normal, that doesn't mean that it's helpful in test taking, or that you should simply accept it as part of your life. Anxiety can have a variety of effects. These effects can be mild, like making you feel slightly nervous, or severe, like blocking your ability to focus or remember even a simple detail.

If you experience test anxiety—whether severe or mild—it's important to know how to beat it. To discover this, first you need to understand what causes test anxiety.

Causes of Test Anxiety

While we often think of anxiety as an uncontrollable emotional state, it can actually be caused by simple, practical things. One of the most common causes of test anxiety is that a person does not feel adequately prepared for their test. This feeling can be the result of many different issues such as poor study habits or lack of organization, but the most common culprit is time management. Starting to study too late, failing to organize your study time to cover all of the material, or being distracted while you study will mean that you're not well prepared for the test. This may lead to cramming the night before, which will cause you to be physically and mentally exhausted for the test. Poor time management also contributes to feelings of stress, fear, and hopelessness as you realize you are not well prepared but don't know what to do about it.

Other times, test anxiety is not related to your preparation for the test but comes from unresolved fear. This may be a past failure on a test, or poor performance on tests in general. It may come from comparing yourself to others who seem to be performing better or from the stress of living up to expectations. Anxiety may be driven by fears of the future—how failure on this test would affect your educational and career goals. These fears are often completely irrational, but they can still negatively impact your test performance.

> **Review Video: <u>3 Reasons You Have Test Anxiety</u>**
> Visit mometrix.com/academy and enter code: 428468

274

Elements of Test Anxiety

As mentioned earlier, test anxiety is considered to be an emotional state, but it has physical and mental components as well. Sometimes you may not even realize that you are suffering from test anxiety until you notice the physical symptoms. These can include trembling hands, rapid heartbeat, sweating, nausea, and tense muscles. Extreme anxiety may lead to fainting or vomiting. Obviously, any of these symptoms can have a negative impact on testing. It is important to recognize them as soon as they begin to occur so that you can address the problem before it damages your performance.

> **Review Video: 3 Ways to Tell You Have Test Anxiety**
> Visit mometrix.com/academy and enter code: 927847

The mental components of test anxiety include trouble focusing and inability to remember learned information. During a test, your mind is on high alert, which can help you recall information and stay focused for an extended period of time. However, anxiety interferes with your mind's natural processes, causing you to blank out, even on the questions you know well. The strain of testing during anxiety makes it difficult to stay focused, especially on a test that may take several hours. Extreme anxiety can take a huge mental toll, making it difficult not only to recall test information but even to understand the test questions or pull your thoughts together.

> **Review Video: How Test Anxiety Affects Memory**
> Visit mometrix.com/academy and enter code: 609003

Effects of Test Anxiety

Test anxiety is like a disease—if left untreated, it will get progressively worse. Anxiety leads to poor performance, and this reinforces the feelings of fear and failure, which in turn lead to poor performances on subsequent tests. It can grow from a mild nervousness to a crippling condition. If allowed to progress, test anxiety can have a big impact on your schooling, and consequently on your future.

Test anxiety can spread to other parts of your life. Anxiety on tests can become anxiety in any stressful situation, and blanking on a test can turn into panicking in a job situation. But fortunately, you don't have to let anxiety rule your testing and determine your grades. There are a number of relatively simple steps you can take to move past anxiety and function normally on a test and in the rest of life.

> **Review Video: How Test Anxiety Impacts Your Grades**
> Visit mometrix.com/academy and enter code: 939819

Physical Steps for Beating Test Anxiety

While test anxiety is a serious problem, the good news is that it can be overcome. It doesn't have to control your ability to think and remember information. While it may take time, you can begin taking steps today to beat anxiety.

Just as your first hint that you may be struggling with anxiety comes from the physical symptoms, the first step to treating it is also physical. Rest is crucial for having a clear, strong mind. If you are tired, it is much easier to give in to anxiety. But if you establish good sleep habits, your body and mind will be ready to perform optimally, without the strain of exhaustion. Additionally, sleeping well helps you to retain information better, so you're more likely to recall the answers when you see the test questions.

Getting good sleep means more than going to bed on time. It's important to allow your brain time to relax. Take study breaks from time to time so it doesn't get overworked, and don't study right before bed. Take time to rest your mind before trying to rest your body, or you may find it difficult to fall asleep.

> **Review Video: <u>The Importance of Sleep for Your Brain</u>**
> Visit mometrix.com/academy and enter code: 319338

Along with sleep, other aspects of physical health are important in preparing for a test. Good nutrition is vital for good brain function. Sugary foods and drinks may give a burst of energy but this burst is followed by a crash, both physically and emotionally. Instead, fuel your body with protein and vitamin-rich foods.

Also, drink plenty of water. Dehydration can lead to headaches and exhaustion, especially if your brain is already under stress from the rigors of the test. Particularly if your test is a long one, drink water during the breaks. And if possible, take an energy-boosting snack to eat between sections.

> **Review Video: <u>How Diet Can Affect your Mood</u>**
> Visit mometrix.com/academy and enter code: 624317

Along with sleep and diet, a third important part of physical health is exercise. Maintaining a steady workout schedule is helpful, but even taking 5-minute study breaks to walk can help get your blood pumping faster and clear your head. Exercise also releases endorphins, which contribute to a positive feeling and can help combat test anxiety.

When you nurture your physical health, you are also contributing to your mental health. If your body is healthy, your mind is much more likely to be healthy as well. So take time to rest, nourish your body with healthy food and water, and get moving as much as possible. Taking these physical steps will make you stronger and more able to take the mental steps necessary to overcome test anxiety.

Mental Steps for Beating Test Anxiety

Working on the mental side of test anxiety can be more challenging, but as with the physical side, there are clear steps you can take to overcome it. As mentioned earlier, test anxiety often stems from lack of preparation, so the obvious solution is to prepare for the test. Effective studying may be the most important weapon you have for beating test anxiety, but you can and should employ several other mental tools to combat fear.

First, boost your confidence by reminding yourself of past success—tests or projects that you aced. If you're putting as much effort into preparing for this test as you did for those, there's no reason you should expect to fail here. Work hard to prepare; then trust your preparation.

Second, surround yourself with encouraging people. It can be helpful to find a study group, but be sure that the people you're around will encourage a positive attitude. If you spend time with others who are anxious or cynical, this will only contribute to your own anxiety. Look for others who are motivated to study hard from a desire to succeed, not from a fear of failure.

Third, reward yourself. A test is physically and mentally tiring, even without anxiety, and it can be helpful to have something to look forward to. Plan an activity following the test, regardless of the outcome, such as going to a movie or getting ice cream.

When you are taking the test, if you find yourself beginning to feel anxious, remind yourself that you know the material. Visualize successfully completing the test. Then take a few deep, relaxing breaths and return to it. Work through the questions carefully but with confidence, knowing that you are capable of succeeding.

Developing a healthy mental approach to test taking will also aid in other areas of life. Test anxiety affects more than just the actual test—it can be damaging to your mental health and even contribute to depression. It's important to beat test anxiety before it becomes a problem for more than testing.

> **Review Video: <u>Test Anxiety and Depression</u>**
> Visit mometrix.com/academy and enter code: 904704

Study Strategy

Being prepared for the test is necessary to combat anxiety, but what does being prepared look like? You may study for hours on end and still not feel prepared. What you need is a strategy for test prep. The next few pages outline our recommended steps to help you plan out and conquer the challenge of preparation.

STEP 1: SCOPE OUT THE TEST

Learn everything you can about the format (multiple choice, essay, etc.) and what will be on the test. Gather any study materials, course outlines, or sample exams that may be available. Not only will this help you to prepare, but knowing what to expect can help to alleviate test anxiety.

STEP 2: MAP OUT THE MATERIAL

Look through the textbook or study guide and make note of how many chapters or sections it has. Then divide these over the time you have. For example, if a book has 15 chapters and you have five days to study, you need to cover three chapters each day. Even better, if you have the time, leave an extra day at the end for overall review after you have gone through the material in depth.

If time is limited, you may need to prioritize the material. Look through it and make note of which sections you think you already have a good grasp on, and which need review. While you are studying, skim quickly through the familiar sections and take more time on the challenging parts. Write out your plan so you don't get lost as you go. Having a written plan also helps you feel more in control of the study, so anxiety is less likely to arise from feeling overwhelmed at the amount to cover. A sample plan may look like this:

- Day 1: Skim chapters 1–4, study chapter 5 (especially pages 31–33)
- Day 2: Study chapters 6–7, skim chapters 8–9
- Day 3: Skim chapter 10, study chapters 11–12 (especially pages 87–90)
- Day 4: Study chapters 13–15
- Day 5: Overall review (focus most on chapters 5, 6, and 12), take practice test

STEP 3: GATHER YOUR TOOLS

Decide what study method works best for you. Do you prefer to highlight in the book as you study and then go back over the highlighted portions? Or do you type out notes of the important information? Or is it helpful to make flashcards that you can carry with you? Assemble the pens, index cards, highlighters, post-it notes, and any other materials you may need so you won't be distracted by getting up to find things while you study.

If you're having a hard time retaining the information or organizing your notes, experiment with different methods. For example, try color-coding by subject with colored pens, highlighters, or post-it notes. If you learn better by hearing, try recording yourself reading your notes so you can listen while in the car, working out, or simply sitting at your desk. Ask a friend to quiz you from your flashcards, or try teaching someone the material to solidify it in your mind.

STEP 4: CREATE YOUR ENVIRONMENT

It's important to avoid distractions while you study. This includes both the obvious distractions like visitors and the subtle distractions like an uncomfortable chair (or a too-comfortable couch that makes you want to fall asleep). Set up the best study environment possible: good lighting and a comfortable work area. If background music helps you focus, you may want to turn it on, but otherwise keep the room quiet. If you are using a computer to take notes, be sure you don't have any other windows open, especially applications like social media, games, or anything else that could distract you. Silence your phone and turn off notifications. Be sure to keep water close by so you stay hydrated while you study (but avoid unhealthy drinks and snacks).

Also, take into account the best time of day to study. Are you freshest first thing in the morning? Try to set aside some time then to work through the material. Is your mind clearer in the afternoon or evening? Schedule your study session then. Another method is to study at the same time of day that you will take the test, so that your brain gets used to working on the material at that time and will be ready to focus at test time.

STEP 5: STUDY!

Once you have done all the study preparation, it's time to settle into the actual studying. Sit down, take a few moments to settle your mind so you can focus, and begin to follow your study plan. Don't give in to distractions or let yourself procrastinate. This is your time to prepare so you'll be ready to fearlessly approach the test. Make the most of the time and stay focused.

Of course, you don't want to burn out. If you study too long you may find that you're not retaining the information very well. Take regular study breaks. For example, taking five minutes out of every hour to walk briskly, breathing deeply and swinging your arms, can help your mind stay fresh.

As you get to the end of each chapter or section, it's a good idea to do a quick review. Remind yourself of what you learned and work on any difficult parts. When you feel that you've mastered the material, move on to the next part. At the end of your study session, briefly skim through your notes again.

But while review is helpful, cramming last minute is NOT. If at all possible, work ahead so that you won't need to fit all your study into the last day. Cramming overloads your brain with more information than it can process and retain, and your tired mind may struggle to recall even previously learned information when it is overwhelmed with last-minute study. Also, the urgent nature of cramming and the stress placed on your brain contribute to anxiety. You'll be more likely to go to the test feeling unprepared and having trouble thinking clearly.

So don't cram, and don't stay up late before the test, even just to review your notes at a leisurely pace. Your brain needs rest more than it needs to go over the information again. In fact, plan to finish your studies by noon or early afternoon the day before the test. Give your brain the rest of the day to relax or focus on other things, and get a good night's sleep. Then you will be fresh for the test and better able to recall what you've studied.

STEP 6: TAKE A PRACTICE TEST

Many courses offer sample tests, either online or in the study materials. This is an excellent resource to check whether you have mastered the material, as well as to prepare for the test format and environment.

Check the test format ahead of time: the number of questions, the type (multiple choice, free response, etc.), and the time limit. Then create a plan for working through them. For example, if you have 30 minutes to take a 60-question test, your limit is 30 seconds per question. Spend less time on the questions you know well so that you can take more time on the difficult ones.

If you have time to take several practice tests, take the first one open book, with no time limit. Work through the questions at your own pace and make sure you fully understand them. Gradually work up to taking a test under test conditions: sit at a desk with all study materials put away and set a timer. Pace yourself to make sure you finish the test with time to spare and go back to check your answers if you have time.

After each test, check your answers. On the questions you missed, be sure you understand why you missed them. Did you misread the question (tests can use tricky wording)? Did you forget the information? Or was it something you hadn't learned? Go back and study any shaky areas that the practice tests reveal.

Taking these tests not only helps with your grade, but also aids in combating test anxiety. If you're already used to the test conditions, you're less likely to worry about it, and working through tests until you're scoring well gives you a confidence boost. Go through the practice tests until you feel comfortable, and then you can go into the test knowing that you're ready for it.

Test Tips

On test day, you should be confident, knowing that you've prepared well and are ready to answer the questions. But aside from preparation, there are several test day strategies you can employ to maximize your performance.

First, as stated before, get a good night's sleep the night before the test (and for several nights before that, if possible). Go into the test with a fresh, alert mind rather than staying up late to study.

Try not to change too much about your normal routine on the day of the test. It's important to eat a nutritious breakfast, but if you normally don't eat breakfast at all, consider eating just a protein bar. If you're a coffee drinker, go ahead and have your normal coffee. Just make sure you time it so that the caffeine doesn't wear off right in the middle of your test. Avoid sugary beverages, and drink enough water to stay hydrated but not so much that you need a restroom break 10 minutes into the test. If your test isn't first thing in the morning, consider going for a walk or doing a light workout before the test to get your blood flowing.

Allow yourself enough time to get ready, and leave for the test with plenty of time to spare so you won't have the anxiety of scrambling to arrive in time. Another reason to be early is to select a good seat. It's helpful to sit away from doors and windows, which can be distracting. Find a good seat, get out your supplies, and settle your mind before the test begins.

When the test begins, start by going over the instructions carefully, even if you already know what to expect. Make sure you avoid any careless mistakes by following the directions.

Then begin working through the questions, pacing yourself as you've practiced. If you're not sure on an answer, don't spend too much time on it, and don't let it shake your confidence. Either skip it and come back later, or eliminate as many wrong answers as possible and guess among the remaining ones. Don't dwell on these questions as you continue—put them out of your mind and focus on what lies ahead.

Be sure to read all of the answer choices, even if you're sure the first one is the right answer. Sometimes you'll find a better one if you keep reading. But don't second-guess yourself if you do immediately know the answer. Your gut instinct is usually right. Don't let test anxiety rob you of the information you know.

If you have time at the end of the test (and if the test format allows), go back and review your answers. Be cautious about changing any, since your first instinct tends to be correct, but make sure you didn't misread any of the questions or accidentally mark the wrong answer choice. Look over any you skipped and make an educated guess.

At the end, leave the test feeling confident. You've done your best, so don't waste time worrying about your performance or wishing you could change anything. Instead, celebrate the successful completion of this test. And finally, use this test to learn how to deal with anxiety even better next time.

> **Review Video: 5 Tips to Beat Test Anxiety**
> Visit mometrix.com/academy and enter code: 570656

Important Qualification

Not all anxiety is created equal. If your test anxiety is causing major issues in your life beyond the classroom or testing center, or if you are experiencing troubling physical symptoms related to your anxiety, it may be a sign of a serious physiological or psychological condition. If this sounds like your situation, we strongly encourage you to seek professional help.

How to Overcome Your Fear of Math

Not again. You're sitting in math class, look down at your test, and immediately start to panic. Your stomach is in knots, your heart is racing, and you break out in a cold sweat. You're staring at the paper, but everything looks like it's written in a foreign language. Even though you studied, you're blanking out on how to begin solving these problems.

Does this sound familiar? If so, then you're not alone! You may be like millions of other people who experience math anxiety. Anxiety about performing well in math is a common experience for students of all ages. In this article, we'll discuss what math anxiety is, common misconceptions about learning math, and tips and strategies for overcoming math anxiety.

What Is Math Anxiety?

Psychologist Mark H. Ashcraft explains math anxiety as a feeling of tension, apprehension, or fear that interferes with math performance. Having math anxiety negatively impacts people's beliefs about themselves and what they can achieve. It hinders achievement within the math classroom and affects the successful application of mathematics in the real world.

SYMPTOMS AND SIGNS OF MATH ANXIETY

To overcome math anxiety, you must recognize its symptoms. Becoming aware of the signs of math anxiety is the first step in addressing and resolving these fears.

NEGATIVE SELF-TALK

If you have math anxiety, you've most likely said at least one of these statements to yourself:

- "I hate math."
- "I'm not good at math."
- "I'm not a math person."

The way we speak to ourselves and think about ourselves matters. Our thoughts become our words, our words become our actions, and our actions become our habits. Thinking negatively about math creates a self-fulfilling prophecy. In other words, if you take an idea as a fact, then it will come true because your behaviors will align to match it.

AVOIDANCE

Some people who are fearful or anxious about math will tend to avoid it altogether. Avoidance can manifest in the following ways:

- Lack of engagement with math content
- Not completing homework and other assignments
- Not asking for help when needed
- Skipping class
- Avoiding math-related courses and activities

Avoidance is one of the most harmful impacts of math anxiety. If you steer clear of math at all costs, then you can't set yourself up for the success you deserve.

LACK OF MOTIVATION

Students with math anxiety may experience a lack of motivation. They may struggle to find the incentive to get engaged with what they view as a frightening subject. These students are often overwhelmed, making it difficult for them to complete or even start math assignments.

PROCRASTINATION

Another symptom of math anxiety is procrastination. Students may voluntarily delay or postpone their classwork and assignments, even if they know there will be a negative consequence for doing so. Additionally, they may choose to wait until the last minute to start projects and homework, even when they know they need more time to put forth their best effort.

PHYSIOLOGICAL REACTIONS

Many people with a fear of math experience physiological side effects. These may include an increase in heart rate, sweatiness, shakiness, nausea, and irregular breathing. These symptoms make it difficult to focus on the math content, causing the student even more stress and fear.

STRONG EMOTIONAL RESPONSES

Math anxiety also affects people on an emotional level. Responding to math content with strong emotions such as panic, anger, or despair can be a sign of math anxiety.

LOW TEST SCORES AND PERFORMANCE

Low achievement can be both a symptom and a cause of math anxiety. When someone does not take the steps needed to perform well on tests and assessments, they are less likely to pass. The more they perform poorly, the more they accept this poor performance as a fact that can't be changed.

FEELING ALONE

People who experience math anxiety feel like they are the only ones struggling, even if the math they are working on is challenging to many people. Feeling isolated in what they perceive as failure can trigger tension or nervousness.

FEELING OF PERMANENCY

Math anxiety can feel very permanent. You may assume that you are naturally bad at math and always will be. Viewing math as a natural ability rather than a skill that can be learned causes people to believe that nothing will help them improve. They take their current math abilities as fact and assume that they can't be changed. As a result, they give up, stop trying to improve, and avoid engaging with math altogether.

LACK OF CONFIDENCE

People with low self-confidence in math tend to feel awkward and incompetent when asked to solve a math problem. They don't feel comfortable taking chances or risks when problem-solving because they second-guess themselves and assume they are incorrect. They don't trust in their ability to learn the content and solve problems correctly.

PANIC

A general sense of unexplained panic is also a sign of math anxiety. You may feel a sudden sense of fear that triggers physical reactions, even when there is no apparent reason for such a response.

CAUSES OF MATH ANXIETY

Math anxiety can start at a young age and may have one or more underlying causes. Common causes of math anxiety include the following:

THE ATTITUDE OF PARENTS OR GUARDIANS

Parents often put pressure on their children to perform well in school. Although their intentions are usually good, this pressure can lead to anxiety, especially if the student is struggling with a subject or class.

Perhaps your parents or others in your life hold negative predispositions about math based on their own experiences. For instance, if your mother once claimed she was not good at math, then you might have incorrectly interpreted this as a predisposed trait that was passed down to you.

TEACHER INFLUENCE

Students often pick up on their teachers' attitudes about the content being taught. If a teacher is happy and excited about math, students are more likely to mirror these emotions. However, if a teacher lacks enthusiasm or genuine interest, then students are more inclined to disengage.

Teachers have a responsibility to cultivate a welcoming classroom culture that is accepting of mistakes. When teachers blame students for not understanding a concept, they create a hostile classroom environment where mistakes are not tolerated. This tension increases student stress and anxiety, creating conditions that are not conducive to inquiry and learning. Instead, when teachers normalize mistakes as a natural part of the problem-solving process, they give their students the freedom to explore and grapple with the math content. In such an environment, students feel comfortable taking chances because they are not afraid of being wrong.

Students need teachers that can help when they're having problems understanding difficult concepts. In doing so, educators may need to change how they teach the content. Since different people have unique learning styles, it's the job of the teacher to adapt to the needs of each student. Additionally, teachers should encourage students to explore alternate problem-solving strategies, even if it's not the preferred method of the educator.

FEAR OF BEING WRONG

Embarrassing situations can be traumatic, especially for young children and adolescents. These experiences can stay with people through their adult lives. Those with math anxiety may experience a fear of being wrong, especially in front of a group of peers. This fear can be paralyzing, interfering with the student's concentration and ability to focus on the problem at hand.

TIMED ASSESSMENTS

Timed assessments can help improve math fluency, but they often create unnecessary pressure for students to complete an unrealistic number of problems within a specified timeframe. Many studies have shown that timed assessments often result in increased levels of anxiety, reducing a student's overall competence and ability to problem-solve.

Debunking Math Myths

There are lots of myths about math that are related to the causes and development of math-related anxiety. Although these myths have been proven to be false, many people take them as fact. Let's go over a few of the most common myths about learning math.

MYTH: MEN ARE BETTER AT MATH THAN WOMEN

Math has a reputation for being a male-dominant subject, but this doesn't mean that men are inherently better at math than women. Many famous mathematical discoveries have been made by women. Katherine Johnson, Dame Mary Lucy Cartwright, and Marjorie Lee Brown are just a few of the many famous women mathematicians. Expecting to be good or bad at math because of your gender sets you up for stress and confusion. Math is a skill that can be learned, just like cooking or riding a bike.

MYTH: THERE IS ONLY ONE GOOD WAY TO SOLVE MATH PROBLEMS

There are many ways to get the correct answer when it comes to math. No two people have the same brain, so everyone takes a slightly different approach to problem-solving. Moreover, there isn't one way of problem-solving that's superior to another. Your way of working through a problem might differ from someone else's, and that is okay. Math can be a highly individualized process, so the best method for you should be the one that makes you feel the most comfortable and makes the most sense to you.

MYTH: MATH REQUIRES A GOOD MEMORY

For many years, mathematics was taught through memorization. However, learning in such a way hinders the development of critical thinking and conceptual understanding. These skill sets are much more valuable than basic memorization. For instance, you might be great at memorizing mathematical formulas, but if you don't understand what they mean, then you can't apply them to different scenarios in the real world. When a student is working from memory, they are limited in the strategies available to them to problem-solve. In other words, they assume there is only one correct way to do the math, which is the method they memorized. Having a variety of problem-solving options can help students figure out which method works best for them. Additionally, it provides students with a better understanding of how and why certain mathematical strategies work. While memorization can be helpful in some instances, it is not an absolute requirement for mathematicians.

MYTH: MATH IS NOT CREATIVE

Math requires imagination and intuition. Contrary to popular belief, it is a highly creative field. Mathematical creativity can help in developing new ways to think about and solve problems. Many people incorrectly assume that all things are either creative or analytical. However, this black-and-white view is limiting because the field of mathematics involves both creativity and logic.

MYTH: MATH ISN'T SUPPOSED TO BE FUN

Whoever told you that math isn't supposed to be fun is a liar. There are tons of math-based activities and games that foster friendly competition and engagement. Math is often best learned through play, and lots of mobile apps and computer games exemplify this.

Additionally, math can be an exceptionally collaborative and social experience. Studying or working through problems with a friend often makes the process a lot more fun. The excitement and satisfaction of solving a difficult problem with others is quite rewarding. Math can be fun if you look for ways to make it more collaborative and enjoyable.

MYTH: NOT EVERYONE IS CAPABLE OF LEARNING MATH

There's no such thing as a "math person." Although many people think that you're either good at math or you're not, this is simply not true. Everyone is capable of learning and applying mathematics. However, not everyone learns the same way. Since each person has a different learning style, the trick is to find the strategies and learning tools that work best for you. Some people learn best through hands-on experiences, and others find success through the use of visual aids. Others are auditory learners and learn best by hearing and listening. When people are overwhelmed or feel that math is too hard, it's often because they haven't found the learning strategy that works best for them.

MYTH: GOOD MATHEMATICIANS WORK QUICKLY AND NEVER MAKE MISTAKES

There is no prize for finishing first in math. It's not a race, and speed isn't a measure of your ability. Good mathematicians take their time to ensure their work is accurate. As you gain more experience and practice, you will naturally become faster and more confident.

Additionally, everyone makes mistakes, including good mathematicians. Mistakes are a normal part of the problem-solving process, and they're not a bad thing. The important thing is that we take the time to learn from our mistakes, understand where our misconceptions are, and move forward.

MYTH: YOU DON'T NEED MATH IN THE REAL WORLD

Our day-to-day lives are so infused with mathematical concepts that we often don't even realize when we're using math in the real world. In fact, most people tend to underestimate how much we do math in our everyday lives. It's involved in an enormous variety of daily activities such as shopping, baking, finances, and gardening, as well as in many careers, including architecture, nursing, design, and sales.

Tips and Strategies for Overcoming Math Anxiety

If your anxiety is getting in the way of your level of mathematical engagement, then there are lots of steps you can take. Check out the strategies below to start building confidence in math today.

FOCUS ON UNDERSTANDING, NOT MEMORIZATION

Don't drive yourself crazy trying to memorize every single formula or mathematical process. Instead, shift your attention to understanding concepts. Those who prioritize memorization over conceptual understanding tend to have lower achievement levels in math. Students who memorize may be able to complete some math, but they don't understand the process well enough to apply it to different situations. Memorization comes with time and practice, but it won't help alleviate math anxiety. On the other hand, conceptual understanding will give you the building blocks of knowledge you need to build up your confidence.

REPLACE NEGATIVE SELF-TALK WITH POSITIVE SELF-TALK

Start to notice how you think about yourself. Whenever you catch yourself thinking something negative, try replacing that thought with a positive affirmation. Instead of continuing the negative thought, pause to reframe the situation. For ideas on how to get started, take a look at the table below:

Instead of thinking...	Try thinking...
"I can't do this math." "I'm not a math person."	"I'm up for the challenge, and I'm training my brain in math."
"This problem is too hard."	"This problem is hard, so this might take some time and effort. I know I can do this."
"I give up."	"What strategies can help me solve this problem?"
"I made a mistake, so I'm not good at this."	"Everyone makes mistakes. Mistakes help me to grow and understand."
"I'll never be smart enough."	"I can figure this out, and I am smart enough."

PRACTICE MINDFULNESS

Practicing mindfulness and focusing on your breathing can help alleviate some of the physical symptoms of math anxiety. By taking deep breaths, you can remind your nervous system that you are not in immediate danger. Doing so will reduce your heart rate and help with any irregular breathing or shakiness. Taking the edge off of the physiological effects of anxiety will clear your mind, allowing your brain to focus its energy on problem-solving.

DO SOME MATH EVERY DAY

Think about learning math as if you were learning a foreign language. If you don't use it, you lose it. If you don't practice your math skills regularly, you'll have a harder time achieving comprehension and fluency. Set some amount of time aside each day, even if it's just for a few minutes, to practice. It might take some discipline to build a habit around this, but doing so will help increase your mathematical self-assurance.

USE ALL OF YOUR RESOURCES

Everyone has a different learning style, and there are plenty of resources out there to support all learners. When you get stuck on a math problem, think about the tools you have access to, and use them when applicable. Such resources may include flashcards, graphic organizers, study guides, interactive notebooks, and peer study groups. All of these are great tools to accommodate your individual learning style. Finding the tools and resources that work for your learning style will give you the confidence you need to succeed.

REALIZE THAT YOU AREN'T ALONE

Remind yourself that lots of other people struggle with math anxiety, including teachers, nurses, and even successful mathematicians. You aren't the only one who panics when faced with a new or challenging problem. It's probably much more common than you think. Realizing that you aren't alone in your experience can help put some distance between yourself and the emotions you feel about math. It also helps to normalize the anxiety and shift your perspective.

ASK QUESTIONS

If there's a concept you don't understand and you've tried everything you can, then it's okay to ask for help! You can always ask your teacher or professor for help. If you're not learning math in a traditional classroom, you may want to join a study group, work with a tutor, or talk to your friends. More often than not, you aren't the only one of your peers who needs clarity on a mathematical concept. Seeking understanding is a great way to increase self-confidence in math.

REMEMBER THAT THERE'S MORE THAN ONE WAY TO SOLVE A PROBLEM

Since everyone learns differently, it's best to focus on understanding a math problem with an approach that makes sense to you. If the way it's being taught is confusing to you, don't give up. Instead, work to understand the problem using a different technique. There's almost always more than one problem-solving method when it comes to math. Don't get stressed if one of them doesn't make sense to you. Instead, shift your focus to what does make sense. Chances are high that you know more than you think you do.

VISUALIZATION

Visualization is the process of creating images in your mind's eye. Picture yourself as a successful, confident mathematician. Think about how you would feel and how you would behave. What would your work area look like? How would you organize your belongings? The more you focus on something, the more likely you are to achieve it. Visualizing teaches your brain that you can achieve whatever it is that you want. Thinking about success in mathematics will lead to acting like a successful mathematician. This, in turn, leads to actual success.

FOCUS ON THE EASIEST PROBLEMS FIRST

To increase your confidence when working on a math test or assignment, try solving the easiest problems first. Doing so will remind you that you are successful in math and that you do have what it takes. This process will increase your belief in yourself, giving you the confidence you need to tackle more complex problems.

FIND A SUPPORT GROUP

A study buddy, tutor, or peer group can go a long way in decreasing math-related anxiety. Such support systems offer lots of benefits, including a safe place to ask questions, additional practice with mathematical concepts, and an understanding of other problem-solving explanations that may work better for you. Equipping yourself with a support group is one of the fastest ways to eliminate math anxiety.

REWARD YOURSELF FOR WORKING HARD

Recognize the amount of effort you're putting in to overcome your math anxiety. It's not an easy task, so you deserve acknowledgement. Surround yourself with people who will provide you with the positive reinforcement you deserve.

Remember, You Can Do This!

Conquering a fear of math can be challenging, but there are lots of strategies that can help you out. Your own beliefs about your mathematical capabilities can limit your potential. Working toward a growth mindset can have a tremendous impact on decreasing math-related anxiety and building confidence. By knowing the symptoms of math anxiety and recognizing common misconceptions about learning math, you can develop a plan to address your fear of math. Utilizing the strategies discussed can help you overcome this anxiety and build the confidence you need to succeed.

Tell Us Your Story

We at Mometrix would like to extend our heartfelt thanks to you for letting us be a part of your journey. It is an honor to serve people from all walks of life, people like you, who are committed to building the best future they can for themselves.

We know that each person's situation is unique. But we also know that, whether you are a young student or a mother of four, you care about working to make your own life and the lives of those around you better.

That's why we want to hear your story.

We want to know why you're taking this test. We want to know about the trials you've gone through to get here. And we want to know about the successes you've experienced after taking and passing your test.

In addition to your story, which can be an inspiration both to us and to others, we value your feedback. We want to know both what you loved about our book and what you think we can improve on.

The team at Mometrix would be absolutely thrilled to hear from you! So please, send us an email at tellusyourstory@mometrix.com or visit us at mometrix.com/tellusyourstory.php and let's stay in touch.

Additional Bonus Material

Due to our efforts to try to keep this book to a manageable length, we've created a link that will give you access to all of your additional bonus material.

Please visit http://www.mometrix.com/bonus948/cbest to access the information.

Made in the USA
Las Vegas, NV
04 March 2022

45019903R10164